Affordable Housing Governance and Finance

There is a large shortage of affordable housing across Europe. In high-demand urban areas housing shortages lead to unaffordable prices for many target groups. This book explores innovations to support a sufficient supply of affordable and sustainable rental housing.

Affordable housing is increasingly developed, financed and managed by a mix of market, state, third sector and community actors. Recent decades in large parts of the Western world have consecutively shown state-dominated, non-profit housing sectors, an increased role for market forces and the private sector, and the rise of initiatives by citizens and local communities. The variety of hybrid governance and finance arrangements is predicted to increase further, leading to new affordable housing delivery and management models. This book explores these innovations, with a focus on developments across Europe, and comparative chapters from the USA and Australia. The book presents new thinking in collaborative housing, co-production and accompanying finance mechanisms in order to support the quantity and the quality of affordable rental housing.

Combining academic robustness with practical relevance, chapters are written by renowned housing researchers in collaboration with practitioners from the housing sector. The book not only presents, compares and contrasts affordable housing solutions, but also explores the transferability of innovations to other countries. The book is essential reading for researchers and professionals in housing, social policy, urban planning and finance.

Gerard van Bortel is Assistant Professor of Housing Management at Delft University of Technology, the Netherlands.

Vincent Gruis is Professor of Housing Management at Delft University of Technology, the Netherlands.

Joost Nieuwenhuijzen is managing director of the European Federation for Living (EFL) network. He worked for social housing providers in the Netherlands and has an extensive network in the affordable housing industry across Europe.

Ben Pluijmers is chairman of the board of the European Federation for Living (EFL). He worked in various executive management positions in the social housing industry.

Affordable Housing Governance and Finance

Innovations, Partnerships and Comparative Perspectives

Edited by Gerard van Bortel, Vincent Gruis, Joost Nieuwenhuijzen and Ben Pluijmers

Routledge
Taylor & Francis Group
LONDON AND NEW YORK

First published 2019
by Routledge
2 Park Square, Milton Park, Abingdon, Oxon OX14 4RN

and by Routledge
52 Vanderbilt Avenue, New York, NY 10017, USA

First issued in paperback 2020

Routledge is an imprint of the Taylor & Francis Group, an informa business

British Library Cataloguing-in-Publication Data
A catalogue record for this book is available from the British Library

Library of Congress Cataloging-in-Publication Data
Names: Bortel, Gerard van, editor.
Title: Affordable housing governance and finance : innovations, partnerships and comparative perspectives / edited by Gerard van Borte [and three others].
Description: Abingdon, Oxon ; New York, NY : Routledge, 2019. | Includes index.
Identifiers: LCCN 2018021452 | ISBN 9781138082786 (hardback : alk. paper) | ISBN 9781315112350 (ebook)
Subjects: LCSH: Housing–Europe. | Housing. | Housing policy–Europe. | Housing policy. | Housing–Europe–Finance | Housing–Finance.
Classification: LCC HD7332.A3 A44 2019 | DDC 363.5/83–dc23
LC record available at https://lccn.loc.gov/2018021452

ISBN 13: 978-0-367-58680-5 (pbk)
ISBN 13: 978-1-138-08278-6 (hbk)

Typeset in Goudy
by Wearset Ltd, Boldon, Tyne and Wear

Contents

Figures

Tables

Contributors

David Adamson, OBE, is Knowledge Manager at Compass Housing Australia. He is also Emeritus Professor at University of Wales, UK where he worked for 30 years, from 2009 as Chair of Community and Social Policy. He was the founding CEO of the Centre for Regeneration Excellence Wales. He continues to work for Compass Housing on tenant empowerment, poverty alleviation and social housing policy and delivery.

Wolfgang Amann, as director of IIBW, the Institute of Real Estate, Construction and Housing Ltd, Vienna/Austria, has executed some 300 research and consulting projects on housing finance, housing policy and housing legislation in Austria, the EU and many CEE and transition countries. He is a consultant to the UN and World Bank and teaches real estate economics at several graduate programmes in Austria.

Anita Blessing originally trained as an urban planner in Australia and then worked in public housing development, community renewal and social housing policy reforms. She later completed a University of Amsterdam PhD (2014) that explored market-oriented reforms of social housing systems and organisational hybridity within not-for-profit social housing associations. She is currently doing a Marie Curie Fellowship on affordable housing finance at the University of Birmingham that explores drivers for institutional investment. Since 2012, she has been a joint coordinator of the ENHR Working Group: *Social Housing: Institutions, Organisations and Governance*.

Rachel G. Bratt, Professor Emerita, Tufts University (Massachusetts, USA) works on issues related to affordable housing and community development, with a focus on the role of non-profit housing organisations. She is the author or co-editor of three books, and has written or co-authored dozens of academic and popular articles and book chapters. She is currently a Senior Research Fellow at the Joint Center for Housing Studies, Harvard University. During 2017, she was a Visiting Scholar at the Federal Reserve Bank of Boston.

Gala Cano is a sociologist in Murcia, Spain. She works in research at the University of Murcia as a member of the project research team, with national funding, *Entornos sociales de cambio* (Social Settings for Change). She has taught sociology at the University of Murcia. Her research interests are housing, family, social innovation and urban policy. She has published nationally and internationally in academic magazines.

Maurice Coen is a visiting fellow at Nyenrode Business Universiteit. His research focuses on the influence of the energy transition in the built environment on (project) organisations. He is also involved in educational projects. He studied management consultancy at the RSM Erasmus University Rotterdam. He combines this position with his work as an independent senior consultant. He was closely involved in the Energiesprong, a national programme concerning sustainability in the built environment and he works for its successor, the Stroomversnelling.

Kees Dol is a researcher at the Faculty of Architecture and the Built Environment, Delft University of Technology. His key interests are home ownership, housing markets and housing finance. He has authored several peer reviewed publications. He is working on a PhD thesis which includes a selection of these publications.

Aitziber Etxezarreta is a professor at the Faculty of Economy and Business at the University of the Basque Country, UPV/EHU, in Spain, and member of the University Institute of Social Economy and Cooperative Law GEZKI (UPV/EHU). She was recently appointed director of the *Revista Vasca de Economía Social* (Basque Magazine of Social Economy). Her research interests are housing policy, housing cooperatives, social innovation and social economy. She has published in national and international academic journals.

Giordana Ferri is in charge of developing new concept plans for social and affordable housing as architect for Politecnico di Milano and Executive Director at the Fondazione Housing Sociale in Milan. Co-director of the Master's course *Social and Collaborative Housing* at the Politecnico di Milano, she has also taught Service Design. Recently, she has focused on Service Design for residential projects, on co-housing, and on experimental programmes where residents actively participate in planning and managing the communal spaces. Her books and articles are published both at national and international level.

Charles Glover-Short is Head of Public Affairs and Corporate Research for Optivo, one of the UK's leading housing associations. He coordinates Optivo's research programme, conducting and commissioning research to improve service delivery, influence housing policy and boost Optivo's reputation for thought-leadership. In 2015 he worked alongside Dr Tony Manzi from the University of Westminster on "Success, Satisfaction and Scrutiny", a first of its kind study into the business benefits for housing associations brought about by involving residents in scrutiny and decision-making.

Ernst Gruber works as an architect in Vienna. He has been head of the Austrian Co-Housing umbrella association "Initiative for Collective Building and Living" (*Initiative für gemeinschaftliches Bauen und Wohnen*). He is presently part of the multidisciplinary team wohnbund:consult which engages in designing and implementing social and participatory processes, mainly in the field of housing and city planning. He also teaches at the department of urban planning at the Technical University Vienna and publishes on a regular basis.

Vincent Gruis is Professor of Housing Management at Delft University of Technology. His chair focuses on organisational strategies for the management and redevelopment of the housing stock in order to contribute to increasing the socioeconomic and environmental sustainability of housing provision. Key themes include circular asset management strategies for housing organisations, collaborative housing and improvement of the quality of private (home-ownership) housing.

Joris Hoekstra is Assistant Professor at the Faculty of Architecture and the Built Environment, Delft University of Technology, the Netherlands. He also holds a position as visiting professor at the University of the Free State in Bloemfontein, South Africa. His research interests are international comparative research, housing policy, social innovation and asset-based welfare. He has published widely in international academic journals and served as managing editor of the *Journal of Housing and the Built Environment* between 2010 and 2017.

Susanne Juranek, MSc, is coordinator of the European Network for Housing and Urban Development (ENH), providing information on EU funding and other European topics for the German housing sector at EBZ (European Education Centre for Housing and Real Estate) since 2015. EBZ and its affiliated EBZ Business School–University of Applied Sciences are among the leading education providers for housing in Germany. The question of affordable housing is one of the key issues that she is dealing with in a European perspective.

Janina Kleist, MA, graduated in social sciences and European studies. She is experienced in the development and management of local and international projects. Her main topics are social policy and structural change. Her fields of work are digitisation, housing, health and employment. She has worked for non-profit organisations, legislative and administrative entities, e.g. the Regional State Parliament of North-Rhine Westphalia.

Richard Lang, PhD, is Assistant Professor at the Institute for Innovation Management (IFI) at Johannes Kepler University Linz (JKU), Austria. He was Marie Curie Senior Research Fellow at the University of Birmingham, UK, and APART-Fellow of the Austrian Academy of Sciences. His research interests include collaborative housing, social innovation and social enterprises in urban and regional development. He has published in *European Planning Studies*, *International Journal of Housing Policy*, *International Small Business Journal*, *Technological Forecasting and Social Change* and *Voluntas*.

Tony Manzi is a Reader in Housing at the University of Westminster. He completed his PhD – on housing associations and the management of change – in 2006. He has published extensively, most recently on resident involvement, the nature of housing professionalism, localism and the politics of housing. He is a committee member of the Housing Studies Association and a Fellow of the Royal Society of Arts, the Chartered Institute of Housing and the Higher Education Agency.

Santiago Merino has been a member of the High Council of Cooperatives of the Basque Country since 1991. He has conducted all his professional activity in the Basque public sector, oriented towards the cooperative field. Additionally, he has been a member and professor at the Institute of Social Economy and Cooperative Law GEZKI (UPV/EHU) since 1994, and director of the *Revista Vasca de Economía Social* (Basque Magazine of Social Economy) (from 2004 through 2010, and from 2017 to present). His research interests are housing cooperatives, social economy, housing policy and sports law.

Nicky Morrison is the Director of the Not for Profit Housing Research Programme in the Department of Land Economy at the University of Cambridge, with over 25 years of experience in examining how changes in government policy and market conditions impact on affordable housing delivery. She is the Co-Chair of the *Social Housing: Institutions, governance and organisations* working group of the European Network for Housing Researchers. She has acted as Coordinator and Principle Investigator on comparative housing projects funded by the European Commission, Nordic-Baltic, German and UK governments.

Alexis Mundt, economist and historian by education, is research associate at the Vienna-based IIBW (Institute for Real Estate, Construction and Housing Ltd). His areas of research include social policy, housing economics, comparative housing policy and social housing. He has worked on a number of projects that have investigated and evaluated housing policy in Austria and Europe.

Michael Neitzel, Dipl.-Ökonom, is an economist and has been working as a researcher at InWIS (Institute for the Housing and Real Estate Sector), Urban and Regional Development since 1996 in various functions. Since 2008, he has been part of the executive management. His key fields of work are economic aspects of energy efficiency and energy efficient refurbishment, market and location analysis, housing market analysis, compilation of rent indexes and consultancy for the housing sector, e.g. impact analysis of recent changes in tenant law for housing federations.

Joost Nieuwenhuijzen is Master in Urban Planning and Social Housing and in Real Estate (MSRE). He worked in different positions at Dutch housing associations in the Amsterdam region and ended as regional director of Rochdale Housing Association. Soon after finalising his second Master's degree in 2005, he started working for an international network of social housing providers which evolved into the European Federation for Living (EFL). He is now managing director at EFL.

Ben Pluijmers holds a Master's degree in Engineering from Delft University of Technology and complemented his education with business studies at Nyenrode Business University and the University of Michigan Business School. Currently he is Chairman of the Board of the European Federation for Living (EFL) and member of the board of Lhedco (holding Groupe Polylogis in France). Furthermore, he holds several positions on supervisory and advisory boards. He has a vast board level experience in the affordable housing industry.

Laura Pogliani is Associate Professor, PhD in Urban and Territorial Planning, MSc Architecture, Dipartimento di Architettura e Studi Urbani DAStU (Architecture and Urban Studies Department), Politecnico di Milano. Her research field concentrates on land use planning, spatial design and regulation tools. She participates in the Editorial Board of *Urbanistica* journal and publishes in national and international scientific journals. She is also vice president of the regional board and coordinator of the national working group on "Policies for Inclusive Housing" of the National Institute of Urbanism (INU).

Chiara Rizzica, PhD, architect and Project Manager at Fondazione Housing Sociale in Milan, is also responsible for coordinating International Partnerships projects. She taught Architectural Design at Architecture School in Syracuse, Italy, from 2007 to 2013. Housing design has always been a key interest of hers since her Master's degree on Urbino's University Campus (by Giancarlo De Carlo, a pioneer of "participatory design"), which began her work through social and collaborative housing. In 2014, she completed a Master's at Politecnico di Milano in Social and Collaborative Housing.

Larry A. Rosenthal is Senior Lecturer with UC Berkeley's Goldman School of Public Policy. He also directs the School's online pedagogy initiatives and provides programmatic support to its Center on Civility and Democratic Engagement. His current research focuses on municipal fiscal distress, urban policy-making, housing affordability, civic engagement and the ethics of public discourse. He is a member of the California State Bar. He holds advanced degrees from Berkeley and University of Wisconsin (Madison), and an AB from Oberlin College.

Jean-Pierre Schaefer, is a graduate engineer of Ecole Centrale Lille, and holds Master's degrees in Economic Science (Lille) and Urban Planning (IUP-PARIS). He has a wide expertise on housing markets and housing economics. Member of the board of housing companies (social and private housing), he worked on housing finance at Caisse des Dépôts and as an expert for Conseil

National de l'Habitat. He has published articles in various French and international journals (*HFI*, *CHA*) and a book *Aides et financements des projets de logements* (2015).

Eefje Stutvoet studied Architecture, Urbanism and Building Sciences. After her graduation, she started with her PhD research about the transition towards an energy neutral existing housing stock in the Netherlands. The research is carried out in close cooperation with the national innovation and transition programme Energy Leap. She combined her PhD research and project leader at this Energy Leap programme for three years. In September 2014, she started as a researcher for the chair of Sustainable Housing Transformation at Delft University of Technology.

Lionel Toutain Rosec, is managing partner at CitéCréation. He holds more than 15 years of experience on public stakes linked with territory design and urban planning. As project manager in CitéCréation, he drives monumental mural design programmes in both urban and rural areas. He is especially in charge of the co-conception approaches and projects narrative design definitions. He graduated from EM Lyon, holds a Master of Science in Finance and followed executive education in design thinking at the ESSEC.

Gerard van Bortel, PhD, is Assistant Professor of Housing Management at Delft University of Technology. He coordinates the Housing team within the Faculty of Architecture's Management in the Built Environment department. He specialises in organisational strategies, cross-sector partnerships and governance of social and affordable housing providers, and has published widely on these topics. He is supervisory board member of a large Dutch housing association and works as a social housing performance auditor in the Netherlands and Belgium (Flanders).

Anke van Hal, PhD, MSc is Professor of Sustainable Building and Development at the Centre for Entrepreneurship and Stewardship at Nyenrode Business University (since January 2008). She was also professor of Sustainable Housing Transformation at the Faculty of Architecture of the Delft University of Technology (from November 2007 till November 2017). Before her professorship she was active for 20 years as a sustainable building specialist, including her own consultancy firm. She was also editor in chief of two sustainable building magazines.

Stig Westerdahl is Associate Professor at Malmö University, Department of Urban Studies. His research is based on an interest in organisational issues and accounting, where Stig prefers to work with participatory observation and qualitative interviews. Recent studies have targeted the role of Municipal Housing Companies and their position in domestic housing policies. The impact of accounting practices in these companies in, view of social responsibility, has been studied along with the consequences of these practices for affordable housing.

Robert J. Wiener, PhD, has been Director of the California Coalition for Rural Housing since 1981. In addition, he is a Lecturer at the University of California, Davis, where he teaches courses on Housing and Social Policy in the US and Barcelona. He has published works in four books. His honours include: "Distinguished Educator" (2004), "Inspirational Nonprofit Housing Leader of the Year" (2006), "Housing Hero" (2006), "Lecturer of the Year" (2011, 2013) and "Rural Organization of the Year" (2013).

Acknowledgements

It takes a village to raise a child, the saying goes, but it also takes a small village to craft an edited book. This publication is the work of many hands and took several years to complete. We want to thank everybody that contributed to letting this book see the light of day. Especially the over 30 authors and co-authors that contributed their chapters to this tome. But many more hands were involved. We would like to thank Daniëlle Veenhof, Alix Goldstein and Adam Ruprecht for their meticulous proofreading and correcting of the chapters. Sally Quinn for her thorough copy editing and the comprehensive way she addressed author queries. A special thanks to our editor Catherine Holdsworth at Routledge Taylor & Francis for her unwavering support and patience.

This book is a collaborative project of Delft University of technology and the European Federation for Living (EFL). We would especially like to thank the following EFL members for providing valuable feedback on readability and relevance of draft chapters:

- Marcus Eilers, Deutsche Wohnen, Germany
- Elke Heidrich, housing association Eigen Haard, the Netherlands
- Ad Hereijgers, EFL Expertise, the Netherlands
- Johannes Noske, Gewobag Wohnungsbau-Aktiengesellschaft, Germany
- Petra Saudi, GloBLD International B.V., the Netherlands
- Mike Ward, Mojo Advisory Services Ltd, UK
- David Williams, Campbell Tickell, UK

The editorial team,
Gerard van Bortel
Vincent Gruis
Joost Nieuwenhuijzen
Ben Pluijmers

Supporting partners:

TU Delft
Delft University of Technology

EFL
EUROPEAN FEDERATION FOR LIVING

1 Introduction

Gerard van Bortel, Vincent Gruis, Joost Nieuwenhuijzen and Ben Pluijmers

Introduction

Affordable housing is increasingly developed, financed and managed by a mix of state, third sector, market and community actors, leading to a variety of hybrid governance and finance arrangements. If seen as a logical response to a more or less general long-term neoliberal trend in policies, sociocultural changes and more recent economic developments, it is likely that the hybridity and variety of governance and finance of affordable housing will continue to grow.

Taking into account the already diverse models for provision of affordable housing across Europe, there will be many opportunities for international exchange of experiences in this domain. Therefore, a group of researchers and practitioners started a collaborative project to explore, collate and compare innovations in affordable housing governance and finance across Europe and beyond. This book is the result of that endeavour.

This chapter describes the aims, contexts and concepts applied in the project. Building on a short overview of international developments in affordable housing governance and finance, we subsequently define and discuss the key concepts that are pivotal to the project, such as affordable housing, governance, finance and hybridity. The chapter continues with a short introduction of the three core themes of the book, namely collaborative housing, co-production, and housing finance models. The themes are further developed in subsequent chapters. We employ these concepts in a discussion of trends in, and the potential for, innovations in affordable housing, distinguishing increased market and community involvement in affordable housing, focusing on initiatives, often in collaboration with, or channelled through, traditional state and third sector providers. These concepts are then applied to analyse some of the examples that are included in the project.

Hybridity in housing provision: impact on housing governance and finance

Social or public housing has always been provided through a variety of actors, such as public agencies (state and local authorities), third sector organisations (housing associations and foundations) and cooperatives or private investors (supported with state grants). The dominant type of provider and tenure (rent, ownership, cooperative) varies from country to country, but, traditionally, there has been a more or less singular relationship between the providing entity and the tenant. In recent decades, however, more hybrid shapes of provision have emerged, in which housing is provided through cooperation between different types of actors, including a growing collaboration between tenants and professional housing providers, as well as an increasing mix of public and private finance.

The trend towards more hybrid forms of housing provision can be explained by various developments. In general, it can be seen as a response to, or part of, a long-term neoliberal trend and an associated retrenchment of the state in direct support and provision of social housing. This, for example, forces third sector housing providers to rely more and more on private finance (Haffner, Hoekstra, Oxley, & Van der Heijden, 2009). In the UK, this is visible in housing associations' interest in attracting finance through bonds from institutional investors (Haffner, Hoekstra, Tang, & Oxley, 2015). In France, tax incentives have led to increased activity of private developers in affordable housing (Hoekstra, 2013). The abolishment of the public status of social housing providers in the 1980s and the subsequent acquisitions of social housing portfolios by institutional investors in Germany can be seen as a 'radical' front-runner in this respect. Thus, reduced state support, combined with the recent stagnating economy and often long waiting lists for the existing social housing stock has also stimulated citizens' interest in becoming more active in providing their own housing, often in collaborative arrangements of groups of citizens supported by public, third sector and/or private actors (Czischke, 2017). The latter can also be seen as part of a wider trend of citizens wanting to organise collective services by themselves for various reasons, which does not only take place in the housing sector, but in various other services, such as energy, child-care, and education (e.g. Krokfors, 2012; Tummers, 2015). In the rental sector, this hybrid form of housing provision is mainly found in the segment between low-rent social housing and free market housing, because of the higher financial resources needed and fewer legal and regulatory restraints.

The increased involvement of citizens taking matters into their own hands is also embraced in state policies, with the Big Society agenda in the UK and the Participation Society in the Netherlands as notable examples (Verhoeven & Tonkens, 2013). Additionally, the social housing challenge has also been broadened to 'affordable' housing in the policy discourse. Fuelled by the financial crisis and increasing shortage of housing that is affordable not only to low-income households but also middle-income groups, 'affordable housing' is increasingly used as a concept to indicate the housing challenge instead of social or public housing. Combined with the currently substantial available finance among institutional investors, this has also increased interest among private investors to gear more of their investments to affordable housing. In the Netherlands, for example, institutional investments in affordable housing have increased for the first time in decades, mainly by acquisition of stock from housing associations and, to a lesser extent, by investing in newly built housing.

The abovementioned recent developments have led to a number of questions related to the governance and finance of affordable housing. To mention a few:

- How are the rights and responsibilities divided between the actors in these hybrid shapes of housing provision?
- How do these new arrangements fit into existing institutional frameworks? Are they stimulated, enabled or hampered by current legislative and administrative arrangements?
- Which of these hybrid arrangements is more likely to grow and which will remain a marginal phenomenon?
- What impact can be expected on the currently dominant providers of affordable housing? Will they lose a significant part of their market share? (How) can or should they adapt to these trends to remain future proof and keep, or increase, their added value to and associated legitimacy in society?
- What can be expected from the long-term effects of these new arrangements? Will they prove to be sustainable in terms of availability, quality and affordability? What is the impact of increased private finance on long-term performance according to these universal criteria of social housing?

To contribute to answering these questions, a group of researchers and practitioners started a collaborative project to describe innovations in the governance and finance of affordable housing in Europe and beyond. Researchers from the European Network of Housing Researchers (ENHR) linked up with practitioners from the European Federation for Living (EFL) to describe thematic developments in various (mainly North-Western European) countries, illustrated with examples from contemporary practice. In this introductory chapter, we describe the aims and context of the project. Further, we discuss and define the key concepts that will be used in the project, such as affordable housing, governance, finance and hybridity. We employ these concepts in a discussion of trends, potential for (mass) innovation in affordable housing provision and possible concerns, focusing on the increased involvement of community and market actors. The chapter ends with an explanation of the structure of the book and an overview of the contributions by the various authors.

Defining the key concepts

In this section, we define the key concepts that will be used to frame the various thematic contributions in the collaborative research project, building on definitions of affordable housing, governance, finance and hybridity derived from literature on housing studies.

Affordable housing

The lack of affordable rental housing is mainly an urban issue and is increasingly recognised as one of the major challenges facing European cities (European Union, 2011). Many cities lack an adequate supply of affordable rental housing for low- and middle-income households, including key urban professionals. This may lead to soaring rents, high levels of commuting, congestion, poor tenure mobility and, ultimately, to cities where people work, play and shop, but do not live. In the current context of reduced job security and tougher lending conditions, the need for affordable housing is growing. The economic significance of well-developed affordable housing sectors is paramount. Only with sufficient and affordable housing supply may urban areas attract a qualified workforce at competitive personnel costs. Guaranteeing affordable housing is therefore one of the basic requirements for the development of opportunities and talent (Large European Cities, 2013).

Before we can define affordable housing, we first need to provide a description of 'social housing'. Social housing in Europe is characterised by a wide variety of national situations, conceptions and policies across different countries. There is no common definition of 'social housing' at the European level. Overall, the terms 'social', 'housing' and other related concepts are used in varying combinations in different Member States to refer to housing that is provided at below-market price for selected categories of the population. The latter are defined nationally, regionally or even locally, based on specific (housing) needs and eligibility criteria set by the competent authority.[1]

'Affordable housing' is often seen as a form of tenure that is complementary to social housing; however, for this concept, a clear cross-national definition is lacking (Czischke &Van Bortel, 2018; EU Urban Agenda Housing Partnership, 2017). Housing markets are nationally and locally specific. While definitions of affordability vary, it may be understood as housing that is adequate in standard and location for low- to middle-income households at fees that enable them to meet other basic needs on a sustainable basis (see, for example, Haffner & Boumeester, 2010). Thus, the concept of affordable housing refers to housing for a broader range of household incomes than social housing. The affordable segment includes the gap between the traditional social and public housing segments and the level of expenditure that is still affordable for moderate-income households (based on housing expenses/income ratios or residual income) or that are not able to buy a home and cannot afford to pay full market rents (see Figure 1.1). The size of the affordable housing segment can vary as a result of local market conditions. Rents in social (provided by not-for-profit organisations) and public housing (delivered by government entities) are mostly determined related to costs, and allocated based on needs. Affordable housing rents are derived from, but lower than, market fees. This segment borders the full market housing segment and can be provided by various actors, profit, non-profit and public actors. In Figure 1.1 we have included two definitions of affordable housing, the first (narrow) definition refers to housing for low- to

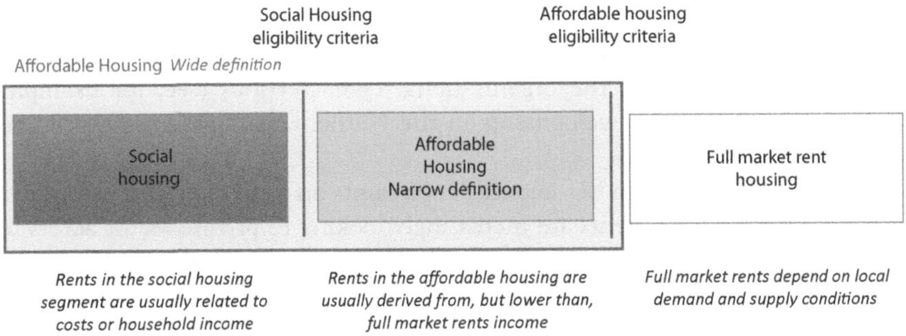

Figure 1.1 Rental housing segments.

Source: Czischke and Van Bortel (2018), adapted by authors.

moderate-income households not eligible for social housing, but also not able to pay full market prices. The wider definition of affordable housing is often used as a concept to indicate the housing challenge in general rather than specific rental housing segments.

Governance

Governance refers to the processes of governing, whether undertaken by a government, market or network, whether over a family, tribe, formal or informal organisation or territory and whether through laws, norms, power or language (Bevir, 2013). For the purpose of this chapter, we focus on governing processes between public, private and not-for-profit organisations. These processes take place within the context of national policies, economies and welfare regimes. Recent developments across Europe suggest a move towards more modern-corporatist welfare regimes with an indirect style of governance (Hoekstra, 2010). These new policy frameworks allow local authorities and non-state providers of welfare services, such as profit and not-for-profit actors, to operate with a certain degree of freedom in the delivery of public services.

There is a broad consensus that decision-making between actors has become more interdependent. There is, however, very little common ground among scholars and practitioners about the distribution of power and influence. These shifts in governance do not necessarily lead to a reduction of state power, but could indicate a shift from formal to informal techniques of government steering (De Bruijn & Ten Heuvelhof, 1991), such as steering in the 'shadow of hierarchy' (Scharpf, 1993, pp. 145–147; Koffijberg, 2005; Van Bortel & Elsinga, 2007). Rhodes (1997) claims that interdependent networks of state and non-state actors weaken the hierarchical powers of the state. Davies, on the other hand, insists that the state is still dominant and power relations are asymmetrical and still favour the state (2002, 2011). Similarly, Jones and Evans contend that many fail to see the state-centredness in many network arrangements (2006). In several European countries there is a clear movement of governments strengthening their influence on (social) housing providers by restricting activities and regulating the organisational characteristics (see, for example, Van Bortel (2017) on developments in the Netherlands, Sweden, France and Belgium [Flanders]).

Facing budget cuts and EU-imposed constraints on state support of affordable rental housing, governments are increasingly looking to private sector actors to expand housing supply (Oxley, Brown, Richardson, & Lishman, 2014). At the same time, existing social landlords, forced to work without subsidies, are becoming more commercially oriented, and increasingly adopt private sector management strategies (Czischke, 2009; Rhodes & Mullins, 2009; Gruis & Nieboer, 2004; Elsinga & Lind, 2012). The inherent contradictions between affordability and the profit-maximizing nature of some actors generate new governance challenges. It is within this complex landscape that we want to find innovative governance frameworks that combine formal and informal, hierarchical, network and market-based instruments (Osborne, 2010b) needed to support decision-making processes in the affordable housing sector.

Finance

Basically, finance can be defined as the way in which cash is provided to develop and maintain affordable housing. Social housing is traditionally financed by mixing various resources. Most dominant combinations in North-Western Europe are:

- state guarantees, grants and/or loans combined with bank loans, attracted by the social housing provider and paid from rental income, in the case of social rent (public or third sector);
- state grants and institutional investments, in the case of market actors providing social housing;
- state grants combined with mortgages, attracted by the household, in the case of home-ownership;
- state grants combined with cooperative funding mechanisms, in which households buy shares in a cooperative (funded by specific mortgage schemes and/or own resources) and/or paying a rent to the cooperative;
- bond finance (corporate bonds; national, regional or local bonds).

In recent decades, direct funding through state grants has decreased significantly. Social housing providers have become increasingly dependent on income from rent and sales to finance the development and management of their housing stock. This has also increased interest in attracting funding from institutional investors, as can be seen in the examples from France, the Netherlands and the UK, discussed in the introduction to this chapter. Moreover, the share of household finance has increased, most notably visible in the rise of initiatives from and/or with households to develop and manage their housing. The decreased state finance and associated alternative finance sources lead to less straightforward public governance arrangements of housing and contribute to the hybridity in housing provision and governance (see also Haffner et al. 2009).

Hybridity

Mullins, Czischke and Van Bortel (2012) have explored hybridity in the context of social housing organisations. They refer to Anheier's (2011) view that a necessary condition of hybridity is the presence of relatively persistent multiple stakeholder configurations and to Billis' (2010) view that hybrid organisations possess 'significant' characteristics of more than one sector (public, private and third). Furthermore, they include hybrid financial dependencies (mixing state and market funding), hybrid governance structures (reflecting stakeholder mix or separating charitable and commercial activities) and hybrid products and services (combining housing with social and neighbourhood support services). A key characteristic, according to Blessing (2012, p. 190), is

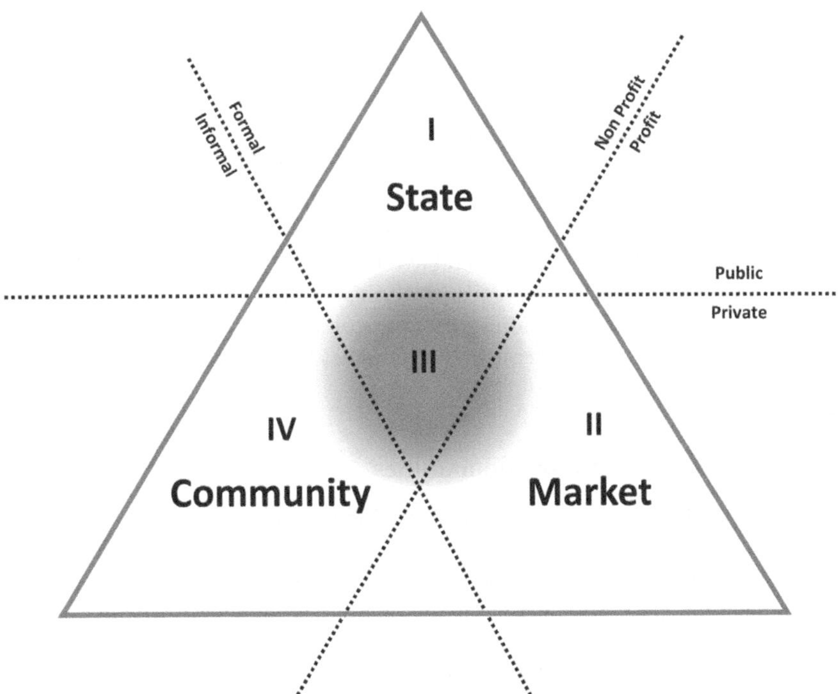

Figure 1.2 Classification of state, market, community and third sector organisations.

Source: Brandsen et al. (2005), based on Zijderveld (1999) and Pestoff (1992). Adapted by Van Bortel (2016, p. 50).

that hybridity implies 'spanning state and market, combining public and private action logics, and [being] subject to multiple sets of institutional conditions'. Therefore, Mullins et al. (2012, p. 411) stress that 'one of the most compelling reasons for considering change in housing organisations through the lens of hybridity and social enterprise is to capture the underlying tensions associated with competing institutional logics (Mullins, 2006; Scott, 2001; Thornton, 2004)'. While Mullins et al. (2012) focus mainly on hybridity in one organisation, this project takes a slightly different approach, focusing on collaborative structures between different types of actors (with varying degrees of 'dominance' of one of the actors), and with the housing provision as outcome or product of these collaborative structures. In order to classify these hybrid structures, we also need to classify the individual actors. In doing so, following Czischke, Gruis and Mullins (2012), we employ the model developed by Brandsen, Van den Donk and Putters (2005), based on Pestoff (1992) and Zijderveld (1999), to classify organisations. They distinguish four types of organisations, including state, market, community and third sector organisations. As Czischke et al. (2012) point out, 'one limitation of this model may be that the third sector is not seen as a domain in its own right but rather as a tension field between the state, market and community (Buckingham, 2010)'. Following Billis (2010), we view third sector organisations as an organisational form in its own right, acknowledging they are subject to state, market and community drivers or values. However, they still have their own characteristics, which distinguish them from 'pure' state, market or community organisations, perhaps most clearly seen in the absence of (direct) governance through members, shareholders or public administration.

In the following sections, we employ these concepts in a discussion of the trends in and the potential for innovation in affordable housing and possible concerns for affordability, quality and availability in the longer term. We focus on recent developments and trends involving community and market actors in the provision of affordable housing, often in collaboration with third sector and/ or state actors, thereby increasing the hybridity in the provision of affordable housing.

Increased involvement of communities

The increased role of citizens in the provision of public services and the development of joint solutions to social problems is often referred to as 'co-production' or 'co-creation' (Voorberg, Bekkers, & Tummers, 2015); or as an umbrella term, including a broad array of housing solutions oriented towards active involvement of users and collaboration between residents (Boyle & Harris, 2009). Various scholars point at the (re)emergence of resident-led initiatives in the provision of (formerly public) services, including affordable housing (see, for example, Krokfors, 2012; Tummers, 2015, Czischke, 2017), employing concepts such as co-housing and collaborative housing, which have varying meanings attached to them. As, for example, Krokfors (2012, p. 309) points out, co-housing 'holds many meanings, with a wide array of interpretations among academics as well as laymen'. The same goes for collaborative housing, which is sometimes used to refer to an aspect of co-housing (e.g. Vestbro, 2010; Fromm, 2012). Krokfors (2012, p. 309) states, 'co-housing seems to be very much in the making from a bottom-up basis, but it is in fact, at least in the European context (e.g. Germany and Scandinavia), increasingly being helped along by the authorities in a top-down fashion' (see, for example, Czischke, 2017) and, thus, hinting at hybridity and collaboration with traditional providers in its provision. In this book, in which we look at such hybrid structures of housing provision, we follow Fromm's wider definition of 'collaborative housing' as an umbrella term that encompasses the large variety of (inter)national variations of collective self-organised housing forms. More specifically, we focus on collaborative housing forms where a group of residents takes the lead in the development and management of housing and is often supported by 'traditional' state or third sector providers.

While there is recognition that collaborative housing forms are still a marginal phenomenon in terms of numbers (see, for example, Krokfors, 2012, p. 311), these types of housing are gradually attracting the attention of city authorities and middle-class people wanting to affect their housing solutions. These initiatives are also increasingly supported by local authorities by providing lots, developing support services and giving financial backing (Krokfors, 2012). As stated in the introduction, there are several reasons that can explain the growing interest in collaborative housing. Nevertheless, it is questionable if it can become a mainstream shape of housing provision within a few decades. Although collaborative housing initiatives are increasingly applied in urban renewal processes (e.g. Krokfors, 2012; Fromm, 2012; Droste, 2015), they may be easiest to apply to new housing developments in locations where it can be matched with groups with similar interests. In existing neighbourhoods, the chance of having sufficient residents interested in moving into collaborative housing, already living together in the same estate, is probably low. For a larger take-up, however, increased community involvement in the existing stock is crucial, if only because of the low share of new developments in housing provision, as compared to the existing stock. Furthermore, Ache and Fedrowitz (2012) point out that it is still quite an effort to initiate and set-up a co-housing project, including organising the group formation, finding the right building and/or plot, defining the design, arranging the finance, finding the appropriate legal form and managing the building during use. This also points to the need for support from, among others, the traditional housing providers. However, as Fromm (2012) points out, the non-profit developer's ability to patch together many different types of assistance and the collaborative group's ability to leverage their resources hampers duplication. Moreover, many authors point at institutional barriers in current housing systems, (spatial) planning, public administration, construction industry and finance structure, which will require time and effort to adapt to facilitate a massive scale-up of community-driven provision of housing (Lang & Stoeger, 2018; Scanlon & Arrigoitia, 2015).

Many potential positive effects are accredited to increased community involvement in housing provision. It can, for example, lead to higher housing satisfaction, increase social capital and cohesion, as well as generate housing opportunities that do not exist within the mainstream housing provision in terms of affordability, sustainability and lifestyle. As Ache and Fedrowitz (2012) argue, it can also be beneficial for the housing providers who

> know at the start how many units and which size and lay out are required. In the case of rental projects, future tenants are 'secured' and fluctuation is kept to a minimum and is partly organized through the project groups. Conflict mechanisms are usually in place as part of the self-organizing capacity of the tenants and/or owners. Also, maintenance and appearance of those projects is usually less of a problem, as the groups take 'ownership' of their projects (MBV, 2008).

Nevertheless, there can also be longer-term concerns. It can, for example, lead to social exclusion (e.g. Droste, 2015) through screenings and perhaps even discrimination of aspirant households. Also, there is the risk of neglecting management when there are no 'best persons' around anymore. International research on co-production processes and outcomes is, however, still limited and inconclusive. Some research results suggest that the involvement of citizens can increase the efficiency and effectiveness of public service delivery, as well as increase the affective connection between citizens and government (Clark, Brudney, & Jang, 2013; Dunston, Lee, Boud, Brodie, & Chiarella, 2009; Osborne, 2010a, 2010b; Thomas, 2012). Other findings suggest that third sector organisations are better able to develop higher and more sustainable levels of citizen participation in the provision of public services compared to public and for-profit providers, insofar as they have a strong focus on local communities (Pestoff, 2006, 2008, 2014). In contrast, based on an extensive literature review, Voorberg et al. (2015) concluded that little is known about the actual benefits and the effects of co-production with citizens.

Increased involvement of market actors

Market actors are increasingly involved in the provision of affordable rental housing. These actors can be regarded as part of the private rented sector (PRS), but multiple drivers lead them to provide rental housing below full market rents (see Figure 1.2). Sometimes market actors are subsidised – or otherwise incentivised – to provide housing below market rents. Consequently, not all privately rented dwellings are allocated or priced according to market forces (Oxley et al., 2014; Crook & Kemp, 2014).

Private sector investments in affordable housing are often combined with co-investments by national or supra-national government agencies. A very recent loan-finance example is the GBP one billion loan from the European Investment Bank (EIB), which was provided for new social housing investments across the UK. This programme is delivered in partnership with the Housing Finance Corporation (THFC) and represents the largest support for social housing by the EIB in Europe to date. THFC will further allocate loan-finance to registered providers of social housing in the UK. The 30-year long-term EIB loan needs to be matched by 50 per cent co-investments by private sector actors, and will benefit from a guarantee by the UK government.[2] In total, this programme will support GBP two billion of overall investment in new, affordable housing across the UK. It remains to be seen if the EIB will remain committed to this agreement now that the UK has decided to leave the EU.

Bonds constitute another form of private sector investment in affordable housing. Especially in the UK, bond finance helps a growing number of housing associations to invest in affordable housing and balance the opportunities and risks in combining social and economic goals (Tang, Oxley, & Mekic, 2017). Also, in other European countries, there is a considerable appetite among market actors to invest in social and affordable housing. For example, institutional investments in affordable housing facilitated through tax incentives in France (Hoekstra, 2013) and the acquisition by German (Patrizia) and UK (Roundhill) actors of portfolios owned by housing associations in the Netherlands.

The combination of readily available funding among investors, increasing need for affordable rental housing for moderate-income households and neoliberal government policies indicate that the involvement of market actors in the affordable rental market is likely to increase. However, there are also barriers, such as the competition of the ownership market as an alternative investment category (often generating a higher return on investments), the dominance of traditional housing providers in many national rental markets, and the risk averse attitude of institutional investors.

What are the potential benefits and risks of increased involvement of market actors? Potential benefits are the financial leverage that can be attained by combining public/third sector and institutional finance that lead to increased investment capabilities (see EIB example above) and perhaps increased business efficiency resulting from more business-like behaviour from the traditional social and public housing providers. This development is further enforced as a result of closer scrutiny by (commercial) lenders on business models, financial viability, management capabilities and transparency. Potential risks could be related to the question of how long-term market actors are committed to the affordable rental market, as well as how quality and sustainability of housing will be safeguarded in the context of the increasingly financial return-driven behaviour of the actors involved.

The chapters introduced

The increased involvement of residents and market actors lead to new hybrid shapes of housing provision, management and finance, which are discussed by the contributing authors employing various examples from different countries. In this book, we have structured the chapters into three interrelated themes:

1 *Collaborative housing*, focusing on initiatives in which residents have a relatively leading role in partnerships with each other and other actors for affordable housing provision and management.
2 *Co-production*, focusing on initiatives in which social and/or public housing providers have a relatively leading role in the formation of partnerships with tenants and/or market actors.
3 *Housing finance models*, focusing on innovative financial arrangements that often encompass an increased role of private (market) and/or resident finance, leading to more hybrid finance structures.

Now, we will briefly introduce the themes and the chapters.

Part I Collaborative housing

Collaborative housing models, often emerging from small resident-led initiatives, suggest alternative approaches to design, financing, management and community life in affordable housing. The collaborative housing initiatives presented in this publication emerge from increasing affordability problems due to rising housing prices, but, also, from an insufficient supply of adequate housing and increasing numbers of evictions in some countries. Collaborative housing is strongly connected to the increased involvement of community actors, as discussed earlier in this chapter.

The segment on collaborative housing starts with a contribution on emerging co-housing cooperatives in Spain (Chapter 2). The contribution by Etxezarreta, Cano, Merino, Dol and Hoekstra highlight the lack of adequate affordable housing for vulnerable households in Spain as an important driver for collaborative housing initiatives. Traditional government support in the form of *subsidized home-ownership housing in Spain is not affordable for these households*. The chapter explores how initiatives in other European countries inspire and inform these grass roots cooperatives in Spain. *The authors adopt a social innovations perspective to explore emerging cohousing cooperatives* in a context where market and government actors fail to provide affordable housing solutions and, thus, social movements take matters into their own hands. Social innovation often comes at a time when unmet social needs increase, when the market and authorities fail to provide good alternatives. In such circumstances, social movements can mobilise and engage residents to address their social needs, and transform existing social relations by improving residents' access to power and resources (see Moulaert, MacCallum, Mehmood, & Hamdouch, 2013).

The second contribution to this part is provided by Lang and Gruber (Chapter 3). The authors explore collaborative housing models in Vienna and, similar to the previous chapter on Spain, adopt a social innovations perspective. In contrast to the Spanish case, the Austrian housing system, supported by housing policies developed by the Viennese government actors, is generally successful at providing affordable housing. However, demand for apartments in Vienna is rising rapidly, putting more pressure than ever on the affordable housing sector, which traditionally relies heavily on subsidies (see also Chapter 10 by Mundt and Amann on new housing finance models in Vienna). Lang and Gruber explore various collaborative housing initiatives, ranging from small-scale resident-led initiatives ('braugruppen') towards more large-scale and top-down organised participatory social housing projects.

The chapters by Etxezarreta et al. and Lang and Gruber share a social innovations perspective as a theoretical framework, focusing on possibilities to improving residents' access to power and resources and developing housing solutions that seek to secure long-term affordability for residents and safeguard these schemes from market dynamics. However, both chapters do so from very divergent housing systems. Collaborative housing in Spain emerges in the context of a largely absent government, while, in Austria, the collaborative housing initiatives often benefit from government support in a mature social housing system.

Rizzica, Pogliani and Ferri (Chapter 4) present an emerging form of social and affordable housing that is new in the Italian context. The innovation consists of two elements: the financial model underpinning this new housing offer and the collaborative character of the housing development and management. An integrated system of national and local social housing investment funds has created possibilities for hybrid housing partnerships containing public, private, third-sector and community actors. The system of the housing fund employs management and financing procedures that have proven their robustness in the private real estate market, but which had never previously been applied in affordable housing. The second element of the innovation is the mix of bottom-up and top-down approaches to involve residents. The development and management strategies resemble the top-down governance approaches of cooperatives (found in Italy and elsewhere). The shared use of facilities and mutual support services and activities are more similar to those often found in co-housing estates.

Table 1.1 Part I: collaborative housing

Chapter	*Authors*	*Country*	*Summary*
2	Etxezarreta, Merino, Cano, Dol and Hoekstra	Spain	Collaborative housing as social innovation in a context of failing markets and absent government
3	Gruber and Lang	Austria	Collaborative housing as social innovation in a context of high demand markets and a supportive government
4	Ferri, Pogliani and Rizzica	Italy	Innovative system of housing investment funds together with a combination of cooperative and co-housing modes of resident involvement

Part II Co-production

The second part of this book focuses on the co-production of housing and housing services. Pestoff, Brandsen and Verschuere (2012) define co-production as 'the mix of activities that both public service agents and citizens contribute to the provision of public services' (p. 18). In contrast to collaborative housing, where mutual collaboration between the residents is central, co-production focuses more on the collaboration between residents and public agencies. While collaborative housing has a bottom-up character, in co-production actors collaborate on a more equal footing, although some innovations in this book also present more top-down, institution-led approaches aimed at activating and empowering residents.

Manzi and Glover-Short's contribution (Chapter 5) focuses on the profound impact of increased resident involvement on the quality of landlord services but, also, on the direct positive impact on the residents themselves. The chapter explores the case of a large London-based housing association and demonstrates how resident participation can result in value for money, management innovation and a changed organisational culture. Manzi and Glover-Short's investigation suggests that much of the value of participation can be gauged by the social benefits to residents (such as greater trust, self-confidence and sense of belonging), and not only organisational benefits, but a contribution to deliberative democracy through tenant participation. Residents can benefit from participation in a way that is revelatory and transformative. However, the innovation presented in this chapter seems to take place most often in England and towards a managerial model of participation, which limits discussions of power and could result in the loss of much of the wider potential impact of resident involvement.

Westerdahl's contribution to the book (Chapter 6) explores the role of a small private sector housing provider in the Swedish City of Malmö in housing refurbishment and new housing construction. The case presented by Westerdahl focuses on the collaboration of this young and agile private sector company with the Malmö local authority. This co-production partnership appears to generate affordable housing solutions better and quicker than interactions between the local authority and established housing cooperatives and the municipal housing company. Affordable housing was delivered by reducing costs through industrialisation and standardisation, and by stripping away non-essential housing features. Further, Westerdahl critically reflects on the downsides of this form of public–private co-production, as the price paid by the local authority is a lack of political influence on the private sector actor, such as housing allocation. The actor delivered affordable housing, but also applied strict income criteria for potential tenants, making the properties affordable in theory, but, in practice, restricting access to this housing for households with a low or unstable income.

The chapter contributed by Bratt, Rozenthal and Wiener (Chapter 7) focuses on the organisational adaptations of non-profit housing organisations in the United States. The chapter connects to all three themes of this book, as the authors address the challenges that are caused by dwindling government recourses in competitive and high-demand housing markets (areas where affordable housing is most in need). Moreover, the chapter focuses on organisational adaptation and the factors that increase the robustness of the non-profit housing sector. There is a strong connection with co-production (and to a lesser extent, with collaborative housing) through the focus of many of the non-profit housing providers on using housing as a platform for residents' social progress by facilitating resident involvement and empowerment, by inviting resident feedback to identify investment needs, and to determine the amenities and services that add the most value for residents (co-production with residents). Resource scarcity and competitive housing markets in the USA trigger inter-organisational collaboration and network formation and collective action (co-production between organisations) and the need to use the equity built into the housing portfolio to attract investment funding and develop partnerships with financial actors (related to Housing Finance Models). Increasingly, sophisticated and hybrid networks are emerging. Initiatives – regulation, but also financial instruments – developed by government actors on various levels (local, state, federal) provide important incentives for affordable housing.

Adamson (Chapter 8) provides an international comparative contribution to the book by exploring the evolution of co-production in the social housing systems of the United Kingdom and Australia. These systems share many key characteristics, but also demonstrate critical differences, which have led to contrasting involvement of tenants in the co-production of housing services. Adamson identifies two distinct modes of co-production: 'service co-production' and 'tenancy co-production'. The first mode, 'service co-production', involves communal engagement of tenants in managerial and governance processes of the organisation itself. The emphasis is on a relationship between the tenant collective and the housing provider. The second mode can be termed 'tenancy co-production' and is a model in which tenants are primarily supported at a personal level to maintain the behaviour required to sustain a tenancy. The emphasis is on the relationship between individual tenants and the housing provider. Adamson found that service co-production needs a higher level of social capital, which can be found in the less residualised social housing system in the United Kingdom. In Australia, a housing cohort with severe social and wellbeing challenges is less likely to participate in the governance structures of the housing organisation. Hence, in Australia, tenants tend to be co-producers of their personal tenancy rather than co-producers of the housing service itself.

Instead of focusing on the co-production of housing or housing services, Toutain Rosec and Schaefer (Chapter 9) discuss the co-production of a shared history and identity by crafting monumental mural designs, especially for the side facades of multi-family apartment blocks. The chapter analyses the activities of CitéCreation, an enterprise specialising in facilitating resident participation processes, and the technical execution and management of mural design projects. Often part of the regeneration of social housing neighbourhoods, the participative monumental mural designs aim to mitigate the impact of growing urban uniformity and the loss of identity and heritage of places and people.

Table 1.2 Part II: co-production

Chapter	*Authors*	*Country*	*Summary*
5	Manzi and Glover-Short	UK	Co-production between residents and housing association to improve housing services
6	Westerdahl	Sweden	Co-production between local authority and young private sector actors
7	Bratt, Rosenthal and Wiener	USA	Organisational adaptations of non-profit housing organisations, and co-production of housing and housing services in high demand markets
8	Adamson	Australia/UK	Synergies between communal housing services co-production and personal tenancy co-production
9	Toutain Rosec and Schaefer	France	Facilitated co-production of shared identity and history

Residents are involved from the start of the development of the narrative that the murals need to convey, and often have a role in showing the murals to visitors in the neighbourhood.

Part III Housing finance models

The increased involvement of market actors and communities has implications for the instruments used to finance affordable housing. This part of the book explores these instruments. The contributions to the book highlight that – parallel to market involvement – there is still a strong role needed for government interventions; for example, in the form of regulation, subsidies, guaranties and other incentives.

Mundt and Amann (Chapter 10) explore innovative developments in the already internationally acclaimed social rental housing sector of Vienna, Austria. Austria has a long tradition of supply-side housing subsidies, such as the Limited-Profit Housing Associations (LPHAs), which construct and manage rental housing targeted at low- and middle-income households. In Vienna, this traditional subsidy scheme was recently supplemented by a new initiative, the so-called 'Wohnbauinitiaitive' (WBI) (Housing Construction Initiative), to additionally encourage multi-apartment housing construction and address high housing demand in the city. Mundt and Amann's contribution explores new elements within subsidy arrangements, including (1) the orientation of both commercial and LPHA housing providers, (2) the inclusion of capital from institutional investors, municipal building plots and municipal medium-term loans, and (3) the limited-term nature of maximum rents for new contracts.

Blessing (Chapter 11) explores two key institutional structures that have acted as important enablers in the delivery of millions of affordable homes in the USA. First, the Low-Income Housing Tax Credit (LIHTC) Program acted as the 'carrots' to attract private sector capital with tax deductions stimulating a wide range of organisations and institutions to invest in affordable housing. Second, the Community Reinvestment Act (CRA) functioned as the 'sticks' to compel banks to reinvest the savings of their customers back into the areas where they lived. These federal policies and legal structures have been credited with creating a cross-sectoral 'organisational field' that helps connect local opportunities for investment in affordable rental housing with investors' organisational goals. Thus, Blessing examines these two key institutional structures and considers how they are used by key actors in affordable housing provision and community development.

However, governments in many countries have retreated from direct involvement in the delivery of affordable housing. Also in England, council housing has long been a dormant legacy form of social housing, gradually declining in numbers due to the 'right to buy' and housing stock transfers to housing associations. That situation has recently changed considerably, as explored by Morrison (Chapter 12).

Increasingly and across England, local authorities are looking for innovative new models where they can take the lead again in delivering affordable homes. Moreover, the national government acknowledges that local authorities should be part of the solution to help fix the 'broken' English housing market. As such, it has begun to loosen regulatory restrictions in order to allow entrepreneurial local authorities to innovate and explore these different delivery models. There has been a recent surge in the interest of local authorities to set up joint ventures with not-for-profit housing associations, particularly as they are able to access sources of private funding that are not available to local authorities. Morrison explores how the UK's government regulatory framework has changed and investigates how these innovative joint ventures between a local authority and a housing association works.

Van Hal, Coen and Stutvoet (Chapter 13) present a new financial model to make highly ambitious investments in sustainable housing economically feasible for housing providers. The classic problem with these investments is the split incentive, as the investments by the housing provider lead to savings for the residents. By introduction an Energy Performance Fee (EPF), both incentives can be combined. Thus, the model can be applied in new housing construction and housing refurbishment. Also here, the government played an important role by introducing changes in the rent regulation framework to enable this innovation.

Neitzel, Juranek and Kleist (Chapter 14) discuss the disparity in the German housing market, where population growth is concentrated in large cities and metropolitan areas, while, in rural areas, the trend of a shrinking population continues. Due to housing shortages, rents have been on the rise in high-demand areas, raising questions about the affordability of housing

Table 1.3 Part III: housing finance models

Chapter	*Authors*	*Country*	*Summary*
10	Mundt and Amann	Austria	Combining capital from institutional investors, municipal building plots and municipal medium-term loans for affordable housing construction
11	Blessing	USA	'Carrots and sticks' to incentivise private actors to invest in affordable housing
12	Morrison	UK	Joint ventures between local authorities and housing associations to access private sector funding
13	Van Hal, Coen and Stutvoet	The Netherlands	New financial instrument, the Energy Performance Fee, to create a viable business model for ambitious investments in housing
14	Neitzel, Juranek and Kleist	Germany	Government initiatives to support affordable housing: (1) housing benefit system with a 'climate component' supplement, (2) subsidy programmes for elderly, students and refugees, and (3) 'concept procurement' methods that include the quality of housing solutions and urban concepts

even for households with average incomes. Neitzel et al. investigate new approaches to support and regulate affordable housing in Germany. The chapter explores how the housing benefit system can be supplemented with a 'climate component' that could incentivise tenants to rent an apartment with higher energy efficiency standards. Another innovation discussed in the chapter is the special subsidy programmes for specific target groups, such as elderly, students and refugees. The third innovation concerns the system of 'concept procurement', a land allocation method that includes the quality of the housing solutions and urban concepts. The approach allows municipalities to develop building areas faster, and to use the planning-related increase in land value to cover public costs and to ensure construction of subsidised or affordable housing.

Conclusion

This chapter introduced the aims, contexts and concepts applied in the book project on innovations in affordable housing and governance. The main driver behind the project is the increasing hybridity and variety of actors involved in affordable housing governance, development, management and finance. This book especially focuses on the increased market and community involvement in affordable housing, often in collaboration with, or channelled through, traditional state and third sector providers.

Building on a short overview of international developments, the chapter defined and discussed the key concepts that are pivotal to the project, such as affordable housing, governance, finance and hybridity. The chapter continued with a short introduction of the three core themes of the book, including collaborative housing, co-production and housing finance models. We will employ these concepts in a discussion of trends in, and the potential for, innovations in affordable housing governance and finance in the concluding chapter.

Notes

1 See the overview 'Social Housing in Europe' on the Housing Europe website (www.housingeurope.eu) for more information on how social housing is organised in various European countries.

2 Press-release European Investment Bank 'GBP 1 billion EIB backing for UK social housing', 25 April 2016.

References

Ache P., & Fedrowitz, M. (2012). The development of co-housing initiatives in Germany. *Built Environment*, *38*(3), 395–412.

Anheier, H. (2011). *Governance and leadership in hybrid organisations: Comparative and interdisciplinary perspectives* (Background paper). Heidelberg: Centre for Social Investment, University of Heidelberg.

Bevir, M. (2013). *Governance: A very short introduction*. Oxford: Oxford University Press.

Billis, D. (Ed.). (2010). *Hybrid organizations and the third sector: Challenges for practice, theory and policy*. Basingstoke: Palgrave Macmillan.

Blessing, A. (2012). Magical or monstrous? Hybridity in social housing governance. *Housing Studies*, *27*(2), 189–207.

Boyle, D., & Harris, M. (2009). *The challenges of co-production: How equal partnerships between professionals and the public are crucial to improving public service*. Discussion paper. New Economics Foundation (NEF) and the National Endowment for Science, Technology and the Arts (NESTA).

Brandsen, T., Van den Donk, W., & Putters, K. (2005). Griffins or chameleons? Hybridity as a permanent and inevitable characteristic of the third sector. *International Journal of Public Administration*, *28*(9/10), 749–765.

Buckingham, H. (2010). *Capturing diversity: A typology of third sector organisations' responses to contracting based on empirical evidence from homelessness services* (TSRC Working Paper 41). Birmingham.

Clark, B. Y., Brudney, J. L., & Jang, S. G. (2013). Coproduction of government services and the new information technology: Investigating the distributional biases. *Public Administration Review*, *73*(5), 687–701.

Crook, T., & Kemp, P. (2014). *Private rental housing: Comparative perspectives*. Cheltenham: Edward Elgar.

Czischke, D. (2009). Managing social rental housing in the EU: A comparative study. *International Journal of Housing Policy*, 9(2), 121–151.

Czischke, D. (2017). Collaborative housing and housing providers: Towards an analytical framework of multistakeholder collaboration in housing coproduction. *International Journal of Housing Policy* (published online). http://dx.doi.org/10.1080/19491247.2017.1331593.

Czischke, D., & Van Bortel, G. (2018). An exploration of concepts and polices on 'affordable housing' in England, Italy, Poland and the Netherlands. *Journal of Housing and the Built Environment*. https://doi.org/10.1007/s10901-018-9598-1.

Czischke, D., Gruis, V., & Mullins, D. (2012). Conceptualising social enterprise in housing organisations. *Housing Studies*, *27*(4), 418–437.

Davies, J. (2002). The governance of urban regeneration: A critique of the 'governing without government' thesis. *Public Administration*, *80*(2), 301–322.

Davies, J. (2011). *Challenging governance theory*. Bristol: Policy Press.

De Bruijn, J. A., & Ten Heuvelhof, E. F. (1991). *Sturingsinstrumenten voor de overhead: over complexe netwerken en een tweede generatie sturingsinstrumenten* [Steering instruments for the state, on complex networks and second generation steering instruments]. Leiden: Stenfert Kroeze.

Droste, C. (2015). German co-housing: An opportunity for municipalities to foster socially inclusive urban development? *Urban Research and Practice*, 8(1), 79–92.

Dunston, R., Lee, A., Boud, D., Brodie, P., & Chiarella, M. (2009). Co-production and health system reform: Re-imagining to re-making. *Australian Journal of Public* Administration, 68, 39–52.

Elsinga, M., & Lind, H. (2012). The effect of EU-legislation on rental systems in Sweden and the Netherlands. *Housing Studies*, *28*(7), 1–13.

EU Urban Agenda Housing Partnership. (2017). *Guidance paper on EU regulation & public support for housing*. Brussels: Author.

European Union. (2011). *Cities of tomorrow*. Brussels: Author.

Fromm, D. (2012). Seeding community: Collaborative housing as a strategy for social and neighbourhood repair. *Built Environment*, *38*(3), 364–394.

Gruis, V., & Nieboer, N. (Eds.). (2004). *Asset management in the social rental sector: Policy and practice in Europe and Australia in Europe and Australia*. Dordrecht: Springer/Kluwer Academic Publishers.

Haffner, M., & Boumeester, H. (2010). The affordability of housing in the Netherlands: An increasing income gap between renting and owning? *Housing Studies*, *25*(6), 799–820.

Haffner, M., Hoekstra, J., Oxley, M., & Van der Heijden, H. (2009). *Bridging the gap between social and market rented housing in six European countries?* Amsterdam: IOS Press under the imprint of Delft University Press.

Haffner, M., Hoekstra, J., Tang, C., & Oxley, M. (2015). *Institutional investment in social rental housing: France, the Netherlands and the United Kingdom explored*. Paper presented at ENHR 2015 Conference 'Housing and Cities in a time of change: are we focusing on People?' Lisbon.

Hoekstra, J. (2010). *Divergence in European welfare and housing systems* (PhD thesis). Delft: Delft University Press.

Hoekstra, J. (2013). *Affordable rental housing produced by private rental landlords: The case of France*. Paper written as part of the project on 'Boosting the supply of affordable rented housing: Learning from other countries'. Centre for Comparative Housing Research, De Montfort University, Leicester, UK and Places for People, London, UK.

Jones, P., & Evans, J. (2006). Urban renewal, governance and the state: Exploring notions of distance and proximity. *Urban Studies*, 43(9), 1491–1509.

Koffijberg, J. (2005). *Getijden van beleid: omslagpunt in volkshuisvesting. Over de rol van hiërarchie en netwerken bij grote veranderingen* [Tides of policy: turning points in public housing. On the role of hierarchy and networks in the management of change]. Delft: Delft University Press.

Krokfors, K. (2012). Co-housing in the making. *Built Environment*, 38(3), 309–314.

Large European Cities. (2013). *Resolution for Social Housing in Europe*. Retrieved from www.eesc.europa.eu/resources/docs/resolution-for-social-housing-in-europe.pdf.

Lang, R., & Stoeger, H. (2018). The role of the local institutional context in understanding collaborative housing models: Empirical evidence from Austria. *International Journal of Housing Policy*, *18*(1), 35–54.

MBV (Ministerium für Bauen und Verkehr des Landes Nordrhein-Westfalen). (2008). *Neues Wohnen mit Nachbarschaft: Wohnprojekte von Baugruppen, Genossenschaft en und Investoren*. Düsseldorf: MBV NRW.

Moulaert, F., MacCallum, D., Mehmood, A., & Hamdouch, A. (2013). *The international handbook on social innovation*. Cheltenham: Edward Elgar Publishing.

Mullins, D. (2006). Exploring change in the housing association sector in England using the Delphi method. *Housing Studies*, *21*(2), 227–251.

Mullins, D., Czischke, D., & Van Bortel, G. (2012). Exploring the meaning of hybridity and social enterprise in housing organisations. *Housing Studies*, *27*(4), 405–417.

Osborne, S. (2010a). Delivering public services: Time for a new theory? *Public Management Review*, *12*(1), 1–10.

Osborne, S. (Ed.). (2010b). *The new public governance: Emerging perspectives on the theory and practice of public governance*. New York: Routledge.

Oxley, M., Brown, T., Richardson, J., & Lishman, R. (2014). Boosting the supply of affordable rented housing: Learning from other countries. Leicester: De Montfort University and Places for People.

Pestoff, V. (1992). Third sector and co-operative services: An alternative to privatisation. *Journal of Consumer Policy*, *15*, 21–45.

Pestoff, V. (2008). *A democratic architecture for the welfare state: Promoting citizen participation, the third sector and co-production*. New York: Routledge.

Pestoff, V. (2006). Citizens as co-producers of welfare services: Preschool services in eight European countries. *Public Management Review*, 8(4), 503–520; reprinted in V. Pestoff and T. Brandsen (Eds.). (2013). *Co-production: The third sector and the delivery of public services*. New York: Routledge.

Pestoff, V. (2014). Collective action and the sustainability of co-production. *Public Management Review*, *16*(3), 383–401.

Pestoff, V., Brandsen, T., & Verschuere, B. (Eds.). (2012). *New public governance, the third sector and co-production*. Oxford: Routledge.

Rhodes, M. L., & Mullins, D. (2009). Market concepts, coordination mechanisms and new actors in social housing. *European Journal of Housing Policy*, 9(2), 107–119.

Rhodes, R. (1997). *Understanding governance, policy networks, governance, reflexivity and accountability*. Milton Keynes: Open University Press.

Scanlon, K., & Arrigoitia, M. F. (2015). Development of new cohousing: Lessons from a London scheme for the over-50s. *Urban Research and Practice*, 8(1), 106–121.

Scharpf, F. W. (1993). Coordination in hierarchies and networks. In F. W. Scharpf (Ed.), *Games in hierarchies and networks: Analytical and empirical approaches to the study of governance institution* (pp. 125–165). Boulder, CO: Westview Press.

Scott, W. R. (2001). *Institutions and organisations* (2nd ed.). London: Sage.

Tang, C., Oxley, M., & Mekic, D. (2017). Meeting commercial and social goals: Institutional investment in the housing association sector. *Housing Studies*, *32*(4), 411–427.

Thomas, J. (2012). *Citizen, customer, partner: Engaging the public in public management*. Armonk, NY: M.E. Sharp.

Thornton, P. H. (2004). *Markets from culture: Institutional logics and organisational decisions in higher education publishing*. Stanford, CA: Stanford University Press.

Tummers, L. (2015). Introduction to the special issue: Towards a long-term perspective of self-managed collaborative housing initiatives. *Urban Research and Practice*, 8(1), 1–4.

Van Bortel, G. (2016). *Networks and fault lines: A network perspective on the role of housing associations in neighbourhood renewal*. PhD thesis. Delft: AB+E Press.

Van Bortel, G. (2017). Sociale Huisvesting en de invloed van de EU-Staatssteunregels [Social housing and the impact of EU State Aid regulation]. In B. Hubeau & T. Vandromme (Eds.), *Twintig jaar Vlaamse Wooncode* (Twenty years Flemish Housing Code] (pp. 241–256). Brugge: De Keure.

Van Bortel, G., & Elsinga, M. (2007). A network perspective on the organization of social housing in the Netherlands: The case of urban renewal in The Hague. *Housing and the Built Environment*, *24*(2), 93–101.

Verhoeven, I., & Tonkens, E. (2013). Talking active citizenship: Framing welfare state reform in England and the Netherlands. *Social Policy and Society*, *12*(3), 415–426.

Vestbro, D. U. (2010). *Living together: Co-housing ideas and realities around the world*. Proceedings from the international collaborative housing conference in Stockholm, 5–9 May 2010.

Voorberg, W., Bekkers, V., & Tummers, L. (2014). A systematic review of co-creation and co-production: Embarking on the social innovation journey. *Public Management Review*, *17*(9), 1333–1357.

Zijderveld, A. C. (1999). *The waning of the welfare state: The end of comprehensive state succor*. New Brunswick, NJ: Transaction Publishers.

Part I

Collaborative housing

2 The emergence of housing cooperatives in Spain

Aitziber Etxezarreta,[1] *Santiago Merino, Gala Cano,*[2] *Kees Dol and Joris Hoekstra*

Introduction

This chapter analyses the shortage of affordable housing in Spain (see Etxezarreta, 2008; Ararteko, 2007) and bottom-up, collaborative initiatives to address this problem. In Spain, social and public rental housing amounts to less than 5 per cent of the entire housing stock. Traditionally, most public support for housing has been targeted at subsidized owner-occupied housing. However, this is not an option for the most vulnerable households, as it is too expensive (Hoekstra, Heras, & Etxezarreta, 2010). Economic trends have also contributed to the housing scarcity. Between 2000 and 2008, affordable housing was scarce because of a land boom. After 2008, the economic crisis has given rise to new housing-related problems, such as increases in evictions and foreclosures (Cano, Etxezarreta, Dol, & Hoekstra, 2013; Human Rights Watch, 2014). It has become clear that secure affordable housing is much in need by economically vulnerable households. Experts and stakeholders have repeatedly stressed the need to enlarge such an affordable housing sector, for example through a larger supply of affordable dwellings and specific subsidy schemes targeted at vulnerable households (Pareja Eastaway and Sánchez Martínez, 2015). Regional authorities, who act as autonomous communities, are also seeking ways to cushion the effects of the eviction crisis. However, it remains to be seen whether these initiatives will materialize into tangible projects, as authorities have limited financial means at their disposal. Moreover, their policy proposals are sometimes at odds with the national legal framework, which may make it impossible to implement them (see Dol, Cruz, Lambea, Hoekstra, Etxezarreta, & Cano, 2016).

The above situation offers a window of opportunity for social innovation. Social innovation often comes at a time when unmet social needs increase, when the market and authorities fail to provide good alternatives. In such circumstances, social movements may drive initiatives (see Jessop, Moulaert, Hulgard, & Hamdouch, 2013 on social innovation and Garcia and Vicari-Haddock, 2016 for social innovation with regard to housing). Experts in the field have observed a strong increase in so-called co-housing projects in Spain, which are a result of unmet housing needs and an increasing interest in collective, bottom-up solutions. Pareja-Eastaway and Sánchez Martínez state:

> When rethinking social housing provision in Spain, alternatives such as cooperatives and self-build models, which are so common in other European countries, are considered innovative instruments and are being explored and developed to provide affordable housing. Most of these initiatives are bottom-up or community-led instruments. Among them, housing cooperatives represent the most established alternative.
>
> (2017, p. 128)

Housing cooperatives imply that a group of people organize themselves in order to build and/or manage housing for the group as a whole. Housing affordability is usually a main driver of such initiatives. By omitting the traditional developers and intermediaries and avoiding marketing costs and profit margins, they make housing access more affordable (Pareja Eastaway and Sánchez Martínez, 2017). Moreover, municipalities may decide to provide the building land at a lower price because they have sympathy for the objectives of the cooperative. However, cost considerations are generally not the only motives for setting up a housing cooperative. Other motives, such as the wish of living together with people of similar orientations or the desire to build ecological housing (see Tummers, 2015) also play a role. The first literature on the topic uncovers how Spanish co-housing often uses a specific cooperative form (*cesión de uso*) (Etxezarreta, Hoekstra, Cano, Cruz, & Dol, 2015).

Although there are now a few notable publications on senior co-housing in the Basque Country (Emakunde, 2016) and a one-case study on cooperative housing in Catalonia (Cabré & Andrés, 2017),[3] literature on the emerging housing cooperatives in Spain is still scarce. Therefore, the aim of this chapter is to examine these housing innovations in Spain in more detail and to learn about their organization and management. Against this background, the following research questions have been formulated:

1. What are the main characteristics of co-housing cooperatives in Spain?
2. How do they organize themselves? Is there a hybrid structure in which existing actors/institutions actively support the initiators of Spanish co-housing cooperatives?
3. Which projects are regarded as the best examples over the past years? Which lessons can be drawn from these references?
4. Is it possible to assess whether these co-housing cooperatives will become a significant contributor to housing provision in Spain?

Research approach

This research is based on a qualitative analysis of two emerging Spanish housing cooperatives. We think that our two cases are illustrative for the emerging housing cooperatives in Spain. However, it is always dangerous to draw too firm conclusions on the basis of two cases and nine interviews only.

Structure of the chapter

The following section commences with the general institutional and historical background of the housing cooperatives in Spain. The connections between these new initiatives and the existing institutions (hybridity) are then explored in the third section. The chapter then outlines the research methods, followed by explanations of the emergence of housing co-operatives in Spain in general terms. The two case studies are then presented and, finally, we discuss the empirical results and draw overall conclusions.

Housing cooperatives in Spain

Historical evolution of cooperative housing in Spain

Cooperatives have been a well-known institution in the construction of new dwellings in Spain. In the past, they acted as so-called building cooperatives with the aim of providing owner occupancy dwellings at a lower price to their members. Once the construction was completed, the cooperative allocated the dwellings to the members and was then abolished. In the case of cooperative apartment complexes, it would be divided into individual apartment rights and a home-owner's association would take over the maintenance of the complex. In this way, there would be no cooperative ownership of the building after the construction was completed.

Historically, building cooperatives in Spain have built houses for lower and middle income groups whose income was too low to enter the non-subsidized, owner occupied sector (Etxezarreta & Merino, 2013). Consequently, the building cooperatives could use the subsidy and allocation system, Vivienda de Protección Oficial (VPO), which was similarly used by the subsidized owner occupancy sector.

In recent years, new developments of housing cooperatives have emerged in Spain (Etxezarreta et al., 2015). Within these models, the housing cooperative remains the owner of the building and grants, so-called, usage rights (*cesión de uso*) to the residents. Although such models have a long history in other European countries, they were virtually non-existent in Spain until recently.

Definition and characteristics of housing cooperatives based on usage rights

Cooperative housing models based on a distinction between ownership rights and usage rights appear in different forms and by various names depending on the country. What they all have in common, however, is cooperative ownership that remains after the construction of a property. The residents are all members of the cooperative. They can buy a share within this cooperative, which grants them the right to use their dwelling for an indefinite period. This type of cooperative is common in countries like Sweden and Denmark. It is related to the so-called *Andel model*, deeply rooted for decades in Scandinavian countries but with practically no presence in Spain. However, this is about to change in the future. Recently the Basque government introduced the concept of the Andel model into the Basque Housing Law of 2015[4] (Observatorio Vasco de la Vivienda, 2015). This was a result of various initiatives undertaken to discover new formulas that might serve to cover the housing needs in the Basque Country.[5]

Housing cooperatives are non-commercial organizations and are thus by definition non-profits. They do not need to cover more than the costs of the maintenance of the building and the shared facilities. Furthermore, cooperatives are often based on cooperative principles, such as the ones mentioned by the Cooperative Housing Federation of Canada (CHF, 2011):

- voluntary and open membership,
- democratic member control,
- economic participation of members,
- autonomy and independence,
- cooperative provides education, training and information,
- cooperation among cooperatives,
- concern for community.

Institutional background: hybridity in housing provision by cooperatives?

The core theme of this book revolves around an increase of affordable housing production by a mix of state, market, non-profits and community actors, which precipitates into hybrid arrangements. The underlying cause for this development is the gradual government retrenchment from direct social housing provision and/or subsidization of non-profit, social housing providers under the influence of neo-liberalization. One result of this shift is the direct action by community actors to initiate co-housing cooperative projects. Traditional social housing provision and housing provision by co-operatives are not two completely separate worlds. For example, Krokfors (2012) claims that new collaborative housing initiatives are "increasingly helped along in a top-down fashion" and suggests that traditional, social housing providers still have a role to play. She indicates that bottom-up initiatives are increasingly institutionalized by existing actors, such as the government or housing associations. In order to frame this research on housing co-operatives in Spain within the international literature, it is highly pertinent to identify the institutional context in which these cooperatives emerge. Despite government retrenchment in direct social housing provision, the authorities can still play key roles in assisting cooperative housing and/or co-housing (see Czischke, 2017; Krokfors, 2012). They may (still) have subsidies available for affordable housing, which can be used by co-housing and/or cooperative housing projects. Government involvement at the local level is often regarded as crucial because new housing cooperatives may need assistance from municipalities in getting access to (affordable) land.

Czischke (2017) draws attention to the role of existing providers of social housing such as housing associations. They may be inclined to assist co-housing initiatives and/or housing cooperatives with expertise or even by providing access to land and finance. In this way, affordable housing becomes a practice where resident groups have more control over what is provided, but still operate within the institutional framework related to existing affordable housing providers. Furthermore, established umbrella organizations might play a role. For instance, in the Nordic countries, umbrella organizations for housing cooperatives are important for establishing, building and financing new cooperative housing projects.

An often-mentioned institutional problem concerns the inexperience of the financial sector with financing housing cooperatives. For instance, Fenster (1999) mentioned that the cooperative legal form is little known in the financial sector which may make banks reluctant to finance cooperatives. This is related to the fact that the cooperative and not the individual is the legal entity that takes out a mortgaged loan. Banks have little experience in handling defaults from individual members of a cooperative. In many cases, they prefer co-housing projects, which are split into clearly defined condominium rights. Especially during the genesis of cooperative housing projects, "friendly" banks from the cooperative sector or guarantees from government and/or housing associations may be helpful.

Research methods

A first step in the research was to collect some general information on the emerging housing cooperatives in Spain. In a second step, the aim was to find more detailed and practical information on these housing cooperatives so that we could illustrate the new developments with the help of some case studies. During the first research phase, a number of housing co-operative experts and residents were approached. Due to the wide variety of backgrounds of the people who were to be interviewed, including academics, practitioners and residents, it was decided to use a methodology of unstructured interviews. Such interviews tend to have an open and flexible character (Del Rincón, Arnal, Latorre, & Sans, 1995). This enabled the formation of common questions for the experts and residents, while, at the same time, left room to ask specific questions depending on their specialization.

A total of nine interviews were held. The interviewees were recruited through our own networks and by making use of the "snowball" method (interviewees suggesting other interviewees). The interviews took place in person or online using Skype. Appendix Table 2.a.1 provides an overview of the characteristics of the interviewees.

Based on the results of the interviews, two iconic cooperative housing projects were selected for deeper examination. The first initiative is the Trabensol cooperative housing project for senior citizens in the Madrid region. According to the interviewed experts, this project serves as an example for the increasing number of cooperative housing initiatives in Spain, particularly those aimed at the older generations. The second case study is the Entrepatios project, which is also located in the Madrid region. This is an intergenerational cooperative housing project, where several generations live together.

The emergence of housing cooperatives in Spain: senior and intergenerational initiatives

This section presents the findings of research Phase 1 and gives an outline of recent developments in the genesis of the cooperative housing projects in Spain. All experts mention an increase of senior cooperative or co-housing projects in Spain, while some also mention new initiatives for intergenerational co-housing (E1, E7, E8).[6]

Motivations for housing cooperatives

Senior co-housing is conducted by people aged 50 and above, who prepare a joint co-habitation project for their third age, taking into account the social and care needs they might have when they are older). Intergenerational cooperative housing projects include people of different ages living together in a, more or less, communal fashion. An important motive to begin housing cooperatives is often a lack of affordable housing, but there are certainly other motives as well. In many cases, senior cooperative housing initiatives seem to stem from the lack of specific affordable housing arrangements where older individuals can live together (E5). The Spanish welfare system provides minimal housing dedicated to seniors, and, as a result, older people launch their own initiatives. This also appears to connect to changing societal structures in Spain, where intergenerational living of senior citizens with their adult children is traditionally quite common (Allen, Barlow, Leal, Maloutas, & Padovani, 2004). However, as a result of individualization and migration, such intergenerational family living may not always be appreciated or feasible. This not only results in cooperative housing initiatives for seniors, where seniors live together and help each other, but also in intergenerational co-housing projects. In the latter projects, the main aim is letting different generations benefit from one another. Contrary to the traditional, intergenerational living arrangement with older parents and adult children (and often grandchildren), participants in intergenerational co-housing projects do not need to be biologically related. Reciprocal help is very important in these projects. For instance, younger generations may help older individuals with strenuous tasks, while older individuals might look after the children of the younger generation. Both arrangements of senior co-housing and intergenerational co-housing are not uncommon in other European countries (see Tummers, 2015).

Spanish experts regard the emergence of cooperative housing projects as an alternative to housing provision by capitalist, profit maximizing companies that give residents little influence on price levels and design. Under the influence of the price boom of the early 2000s and the withdrawal of many commercial developers from the market during the subsequent crisis, it appears that many people wish to develop their own initiatives. This is related to a general distrust in the commercial sector. The experts and residents also indicated that the Spanish cooperative housing projects are not solely focused on affordability. There may definitely be some price benefits, but co-housing nevertheless does not always lead to cheap housing for lower incomes. Furthermore, the Andel model, as used in Spain, may require individuals to buy a share in order to be able to use the dwelling. This may mean that prospective residents have to invest a significant amount of money into their housing. Monthly payments for maintenance and services may also be significant. Tummer's (2015) overview of the European co-housing literature comes to similar conclusions and indicates that cooperative and co-housing projects often accommodate middle class households. Only a minority of the projects involves low-income housing. Lastly, ecological considerations play an important part in many initiatives. Bio-climatic architecture and sustainable buildings occupy a prominent position in many of the projects (E2, E5, E6, E7, E8).

Organization

Experts indicate that the Spanish housing cooperatives are very much a bottom-up practice where the members have to learn by doing or find some guidance in practices from peers. However, in recent years, there has been an increase in small organizations and consultancies that assist these initiatives, usually on a commercial basis. For instance, the Entrepatios project, a case study presented in this chapter, started developing with the assistance of Logica'eco-Cohousing Verde (E7, E2). Other consultants have carried out similar projects, including Sostre Civic, Jubilee Association, Sustraiak and Habitat Design (E1, E6, E8).

The governance scheme of a housing cooperative includes a President or Director of the cooperative and a Governing Council (E2 and E5). For each step of the project, a working group is formed. In this sense, there are specific groups for each purpose, such as a germ group, community construction, land searching, open design, conflict resolution or co-habitation norms.

Within the housing cooperatives, decisions tend to be made by unanimity and consensus. Some users and experts comment that consensus can be difficult to reach in the short term, but it provides a good basis for the long-term success of the communal living project (E7, E8, E2).

Senior co-housing

Various experts agree that senior housing cooperatives have been more successful than intergenerational cooperatives (E1 and E9). The first senior co-housing initiatives were realized with little or no assistance of any kind (E5, E8). The Jubilee Association recently translated Charles Durrett's Manual on Senior

Cohousing from American English into Spanish. The goal was to help new projects getting off the ground and becoming successful.

In Spain over the last few years, numerous projects have been successfully built up in the field of cooperative housing for seniors. The most important ones are displayed in the map in Figure 2.1: Trabensol, Convivir, Profuturo, La Muralleta, Servi-mayor, Cooperativa 60/70, Vitápolis, Centro de convivencia colaborativo, Santa Clara, Brisa del Cantábrico, and Egunsentia.

Intergenerational co-housing

In an intergenerational context, the cooperative housing formula is experiencing more problems. There are several reasons for this, although two stand out specifically: the financial and the cultural issues (E1, E3, E6, E7, E8). The financial dimension is probably the most limiting factor. The situation of precarious employment that many young people are facing can be an incentive in the search for innovative and affordable housing solutions. However, precarious employment can also be an insurmountable obstacle, as young people may not meet the minimum requirements set by funding entities, such as monthly payments not exceeding more than 30–35 per cent of the family income (E1, E7, E8).

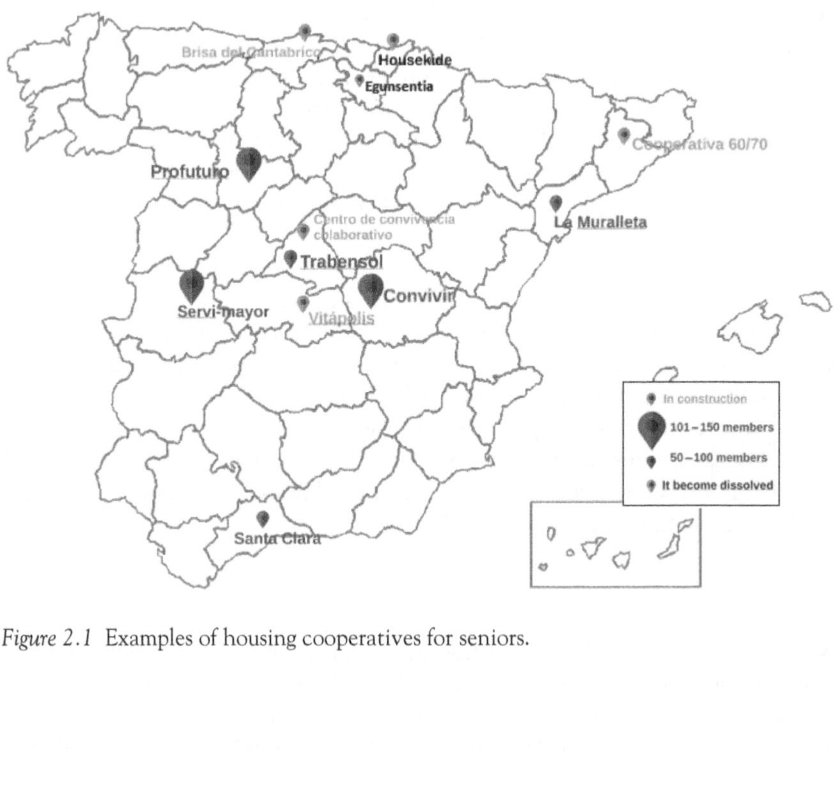

Figure 2.1 Examples of housing cooperatives for seniors.

Two case studies

Trabensol (senior co-housing)

Trabensol is one of the best-known senior housing cooperatives in Spain. It was opened in Torremocha del Jarama, a borough of Madrid in 2013. The preparations for the project started before 2000 and the project was entirely self-organized, without using references or external professional guidance. This initiative was taken by neighbourhood associations from Vallecas and Moratalaz, traditionally active social neighbourhoods of Madrid.

In the interview, Jaime Moreno (E5) emphasized that they did not receive any public help and that the cooperative answered to new care needs. He insisted that Trabensol was not a pastime or "an adventure of a snob group". The founders of the project had already been involved in the care of their parents and knew that they did not want their children to repeat this experience. They looked for a way to satisfy their old age needs in an independent way. They claim that the current result even surpasses their own expectations.

The cooperative found a proper location after a long period of searching. One of the cooperative members knew the mayor of the town of Torremocha, and this town was interested in the initiative. Once they bought the land, around 22,000 square metres, the town council gave them permission to build. After they had transferred the legal percentage of land necessary to develop public facilities to the town council, they still had 16,000 square metres left. There were 6,000 square metres built, consisting of apartments with a surface area of around 50 square metres. The rest of the surface is covered by plant and vegetable gardens. Once the cooperative and the bases of the organization were created, it was important to establish the management and governance arrangements in accordance with the agreements reached among the members. The scheme of management revolves around the general assembly, which is the expression of the social will. General Assembly agreements bind all partners, including absentees and dissidents. The Board of the Assembly is formed by at least a President and Secretary, the same as those of the Governing Council, unless there is a conflict of interest.

The Governing Council is the governing body of the cooperative and it is responsible for general management and legal representation. The Governing Council is composed of nine titular members, elected by the General Assembly from among the members of the Cooperative, according to the electoral procedure regulated in the cooperative's statutes. The elected positions include President, Vice President, Secretary, Treasurer and five additional members. The ordinary term of office for the members of the Governing Council is four years, after which re-election is possible.

Trabensol has a mediator team that is coordinated by a cooperative member who works as a sociology professor at the University Complutense of Madrid. Other working groups involve gardening, activities or healthy living.

Figure 2.2 Hall of the property, social interactions park. Trabensol cooperative, Torremocha de Jarama, Madrid.

Regarding financial aspects, the cooperative did not need a loan to buy the land because members sold their previous houses and used the proceedings from the sale. At the beginning, all 54 cooperative members paid €145,000 each. The monthly fee includes cleaning services once a week, catering for lunch, laundry that is collected, washed and ironed, paperwork and management services, and few hours of receptionist services. During the week and on Saturday mornings one of the collective tasks is providing voluntary receptionist services. Another collective task is setting up the lunch table where the members of the cooperative can have lunch together. The lists for these particular tasks have always been full since they opened.

The building revolves around the central fountain patio with a south orientation of the apartments, in order to better conserve energy. The building is completely wheelchair accessible.

All the inhabitants are registered as citizens of Torremocha del Jarama since the inauguration of the project in 2013. The project now has 54 member-shareholders (one for each apartment) with a total of 85 inhabitants. One of the common gardens is open for use by other residents of the municipality in order to stimulate social interactions. The activities that are organized by the cooperative, such as yoga, pilates or a summer cinema, are also open for the residents of the town.

Figure 2.3 Vegetable gardens. Trabensol cooperative, Torremocha de Jarama, Madrid.

The Entrepatios Cooperative (intergenerational co-housing)

Entrepatios is an iconic and exemplary project of intergenerational cooperative housing in Spain. There are more projects that are recently being built, such as the La Borda project in Catalonia (Cabré & Andrés, 2017), but Entrepatios is still regarded as the predominant representative of intergenerational co-housing. The general aim of the cooperative is to provide collective housing for their group under a non-commercial regime. On top of that, ecological considerations play a role. This will be visible in aspects such as solar panels, rainwater collection and a green rooftop garden. The (envisioned) project consists of 17 apartments, varying in size from about 60 to 80 square metres, within a dense urban setting. It does not have much outdoor space but it includes a ground floor patio and a rooftop garden. There are also two collective meeting rooms at the ground floor and the second floor (74 and 60 square metres).

In 2012, an embryonic group of families named COBIJO cooperative came up with the idea for this co-housing project. The group grew from six families to 30 during a process of participatory workshops called the dream phase, where it was agreed upon to set up a housing cooperative. After that, the search for building land began. They ultimately found some land at Las Carolinas (Usera, city of Madrid). In total 17 households entered the Las Carolinas housing cooperative which is now in the phase of design and project implementation. The cooperative approached the regional government for support but finally did not receive any. The group used the cooperative Andel model as a reference, but also found some inspiration in Uruguay which has a strong cooperative housing tradition. In senior co-housing projects, thanks to the property assets usually acquired by elderly people, it is relatively easy to find enough funds to start initiatives. This is in contrast to intergenerational cooperatives where finance tends to be a problem. With regard to this Project, the interview with resident Nacho García (E2) conveys how the mortgage was negotiated for the cooperative as a whole. It also is the cooperative itself that is responsible for making the payments. TRIODOS bank advanced a loan to the collective for the construction. Furthermore, the members of the collective pay a 20 per cent fee of the construction costs. This fee will be returned when a member leaves the collective. In addition to this, the members of the cooperative pay €600 monthly rent, which will be used for interest payments, the loan repayment and maintenance during the first years. In case of non-payment, there is a reserve fund that allows the cooperative to face total non-payment for three months. This allows the cooperative to be able to calmly deal with individual defaults, understand why they occurred and to find a solution.

Discussion and conclusions

This chapter shows that the start-up of housing cooperatives in Spain was complicated and hard work. They are decidedly bottom-up initiatives and have received little institutional support from the start. The Trabensol senior project did not receive any support from professionals. The Entrepatios project had hired support from a professional bureau (Lógica'eco, E7) but it met little goodwill from the municipality with regard to planning permits and finding a suitable location turned out to be difficult.

Overall, in the two case studies, there was no hybrid network with established actors from the housing field, as suggested in the international literature on this topic (see above). The most obvious explanation seems to be that such literature appears to relate to the context of the Northern European countries, which traditionally operate large, but declining, social and non-profit housing sectors (see Krokfors, 2012). However, Spain has a very small and fragmented affordable social rental sector of no more than 5 per cent of the entire stock. What is more, some of the larger municipalities are under severe financial pressure and have actually sold several thousands of their public rental stock in order to repay mounting debts (Lambea Llop, 2016). This is also the case in Madrid and possibly one of the reasons why its own municipal housing company does not actively involve itself in supporting housing cooperatives. Looking beyond the two selected Madrilenian cases, the emerging literature indicates that some regional and municipal governments have a more positive stance. This is illustrated by the proposed Basque Housing Law (Act 3/2015).

Interestingly, it seems that a well-organized local community group can be quite crucial, as they may be able to push for more support from governmental institutions. This is also shown in the case of Barcelona (Cabré & Andrés, 2017). In time, more successful initiatives may set up a base for dissemination of practical knowledge.

A fundamental question is whether the Spanish housing cooperatives have prospects of becoming more widely used. Because only two case studies have been analysed, it is necessary to be careful drawing general conclusions. However, evidence suggests that apart from political support, finance is a crucial point here. The international literature indicated that inexperience in the regular banking sector hampers the provision of loans. The senior co-housing initiatives certainly have an advantage in this respect because most Spanish senior households are outright home owners, which allows them to finance an entire cooperative, co-housing project up front. Because of this, one cannot really speak of affordable housing and it is more a middle class affair. This also implies that relatively little impact can be expected on the currently dominant providers of affordable housing: the social rental landlords. There is another dimension which may make senior co-housing cooperatives more likely to grow than intergenerational housing cooperatives, namely the severe lack of senior housing in Spain. As the traditional family care provision structures (mainly by female relatives) for older households are gradually losing support in the changing Spanish society, there seems to be a growing market for senior cooperative housing projects. A wide scope of administrative levels in the Spanish context could potentially be interested in supporting these initiatives. There is some recent research[7] on this topic, which offers evidence of a strong relation between senior housing cooperatives and innovative ways to address care needs and gender issues in Spanish society. New cooperative senior housing arrangements could become a real alternative for private and state provision of old age housing and residential care. Care services are already handled by cooperatives (Etxezarreta & Bakaikoa, 2012) and cooperation with senior cooperative projects may be relatively easy. In cases where the senior cooperative housing initiatives in Spain reveal that they are a good alternative for the contemporary lack of old age housing provision, commercial providers, possibly assisted with state welfare, may also enter the market. Since Spain is one of the most ageing countries in the world, it may be a real front runner in this respect and it may serve as a source of inspiration for other ageing countries.

Intergenerational initiatives acquiring sufficient funding seems to be the most important obstacle, although the Entrepatios example shows that there are ways to overcome this problem. Cooperative housing is essentially a project that arises from the wish of groups of people to live with peers in a cooperative, non-profit housing environment. It may not be the preferred option for young persons that carry the Spanish tradition of owner occupied housing as a private investment. Therefore, the conclusion is that senior co-housing has more potential in Spain than intergenerational co-housing. The future will learn whether this assumption is correct.

Appendix

Table 2.a.1 Overview of the interviewees and their main characteristics

Ref.	*Name*	*Category*	*Field*	*Association/group*
E1	Miguel Ángel Mira	Expert	Senior co-housing	Jubilee Association
E2	Nacho García	Resident	Intergenerational co-housing	Entrepatios Cooperative
E3	Mario Yoldi	Expert	Intergenerational co-housing	Basque Government
E4	Ana Lambea	Expert	Intergenerational co-housing	Complutense University of Madrid
E5	Jaime Moreno	Resident	Senior co-housing	Trabensol Cooperative
E6	Raúl Robert	Expert	Intergenerational co-housing	Sostre Civic
E7	Leo Bensadón	Expert	Intergenerational co-housing	Lógica'eco, Cohousing Verde
E8	Borja Izaola	Expert and resident	Intergenerational co-housing	Sustraiak, hábitat design
As he was mentioned by the previous interviewees, this interview was added to the list:				
E9	Daniel López	Expert	Senior co-housing	Universitat Oberta de Catalunya

Notes

1 Aitziber Etxezarreta is a member of the research Group "Gizarte Ekonomia eta bere Zuzenbidea", GIU 17/052, attached to the GEZKI Institute, University of the Basque Country (UPV/EHU).

2 Gala Cano is a member of the research project HAR2017-84226-C6-1-P, "A new story of social change: Hierarchies and kinship (XVI–XX centuries)", funded by the Ministry of Economy and Competitiveness of the Government of Spain.

3 The topic has sparked much interest and in time more publications are expected, for instance from the large MOVICOMA research project. This project focuses on a number of senior co-housing initiatives, their structure, organization, services, etc.

4 Due to a conflict between the Basque Country and the central government about some specific issues (not over housing cooperatives) this law has been suspended by the Constitutional Court until a decision is reached. www.tribunalconstitucional.es/es/jurisprudencia/Paginas/Auto.aspx?cod=24571.

5 The Basque government organized several study tours in Europe and eventually considered the successful Andel model of Sweden a good method to adapt.

6 The letters and numbers refer to the list of interviewees presented in Table 2.a.1.

7 The project MOVICOMA and the project of Emakunde – the Basque Institute of Women (Emakunde, 2016).

References

Allen, J., Barlow, J., Leal, J., Maloutas, T., & Padovani, L. (2004). *Housing and welfare in Southern Europe*. Oxford: Blackwell Publishing.

Ararteko. (2007). *Las políticas públicas de vivienda dirigidas a la población joven en la CAPV* [Public housing policies for the young population in the autonomous region of Basque Country]. Informe extraordinario del Ararteko al Gobierno Vasco, Vitoria-Gasteiz.

Cabré, E., & Andrés, A. (2017). La Borda: A case on the implementation of cooperative housing in Catalonia. *International Journal of Housing Policy*. http://dx.doi.org/10.1080/19491247.2017.1331591 (published ahead of print).

Cano, G., Etxezarreta, A., Dol, K., & Hoekstra, J. (2013). From housing bubble to repossessions: Spain compared to other West European countries. *Housing Studies*, *28*(8), 1197–1217.

Cooperative Housing Federation. (2011). *Getting our co-op principles right*. Ottawa: Cooperative Housing Federation of Canada.

Czischke, D. (2017). Collaborative housing and housing providers: Towards an analytical framework of multi-stakeholder collaboration in housing co-production. *International Journal of Housing Policy*, *18*(1), 55–81.

Del Rincón, D., Arnal, J., Latorre, A., & Sans, A. (1995). *Técnicas de Investigación en Ciencias Sociales* [Research methods in social science]. Madrid: Dykinson.

Dol, K., Cruz Mazo, E., Lambea Llop, N., Hoekstra, J., Etxezarreta, A., & Cano Fuentes, G. (2017). Regionalization of housing policies? An exploratory study of Andalusia, Catalonia and the Basque Country. *Journal of Housing and the Built Environment*, *32*(3), 581–598.

Durrett, C. (2015). *El Manual del Senior Cohousing* [Senior co-housing manual] (Asociacion Jubilares, Trans.). Madrid: Dykinson.

Emakunde. (2016). *Arquitecturas del Cuidado* [City architecture]. Vitoria-Gasteiz: Instituto Vasco de la mujer.

Etxezarreta, A. (2008). *Avances en el derecho ciudadano a una vivienda digna: Reflexiones sobre el anteproyecto de ley de la CAPV* [Civil Housing rights: Reflections on the proposed new law in the autonomous region of Basque Country]. Conference contribution, XL Jornadas de Economía Crítica de 27–29 de marzo 2008, Bilbao.

Etxezarreta, E., & Bakaikoa, B. (2012). Changes in the welfare state and their impact on the social economy: Contributions to the theoretical debate from a systemic and comparative approach. *Annals of Public and Cooperative Economics*, *83*(3), 259–280.

Etxezarreta, A., & Merino, S. (2013). Las cooperativas de vivienda como alternativa al problema de la vivienda en la actual crisis económica [Housing cooperatives as alternative solution for the housing problems in the current economic crisis]. *REVESCO, Revista de Estudios Cooperativos*, (113), 92–119.

Etxezarreta, A., Hoekstra, J., Cano Fuentes, G., Cruz Mazo, E., & Dol, K. (2015). *Social innovation and social economy: A new framework in the Spanish housing context*. ENHR conference, Lisbon.

Fenster, M. (1999). Community by covenant, process, and design: Cohousing and the contemporary common interest community. *Journal of Land Use and Environmental Law*, *15*(3), 3–54.

Garcia, M., & Vicari-Haddock, S. (2016). Special issue: Housing and community needs and social innovation responses in times of crisis. *Journal of Housing and the Built Environment*, *31*(3), 393–407.

Hoekstra, J., Heras, I., & Etxezarreta, A. (2010). Recent changes in Spanish housing policies: Subsidized owner-occupancy dwellings as a new tenure sector? *Journal of Housing and the Built Environment*, *25*(1), 125–138.

Human Rights Watch. (2014). Shattered dreams: Impact of Spain's housing crisis on vulnerable groups. Washington, DC: Author.

Jessop, B., Moulaert, F., Hulgard, L., & Hamdouch, A. (2013). Social innovation research: A new stage innovation analysis? In F. Moulaert, D. MacCallum, A. Mehmood, & A. Hamdouch (Eds.), *The international handbook on social innovation, collective action, social learning and transdisciplinary research* (pp.110–130). Cheltenham: Edward Elgar Publishing.

Krokfors, K. (2012). Co-housing in the making. *Built Environment*, *38*(3), 309–314.

Lambea Llop, N. (2016). Social housing management models in Spain. *Revista Catalana de dret public*, *52*, 116–128.

Moulaert, F., MacCallum, D., Mehmood, A., & Hamdouch, A. (2013). *The international handbook on social innovation*. Cheltenham: Edward Elgar Publishing.

Observatorio Vasco de la Vivienda. (2015). *Informe sobre las cooperativas y la promoción de VPP* [Research on cooperatives and publicly provided affordable Housing]. Vitoria-Gasteiz: Author.

Pareja Eastaway, M., & Sánchez Martinez, M. T. (2015). El retorno del alquiler en España. *Temas para el debate*, *252*, 44–46.

Pareja Eastaway, M., & Sánchez Martínez, M. T. (2017). More social housing? A critical analysis of social housing provision in Spain. *Critical Housing Analysis*, *4*(1), 124–131.

Tummers, L. (2015). The re-emergence of self-managed co-housing in Europe: A critical review of co-housing research. *Urban Studies*, *53*(10), 2023–2040.

3 Collaborative housing models in Vienna through the lens of social innovation

Austria

Ernst Gruber and Richard Lang[1]

Introduction

The quantitative demand for flats in Vienna is rising rapidly, putting more pressure than ever on the affordable housing sector which traditionally relies heavily on subsidies. However, an increase in demand in housing has not always had such a dramatic impact on affordability. Sinking interest rates since the early 1990s have contributed to relative affordability until around 2004. In the 1990s, the local authority was able to increase the yearly output of new social housing development from about 4,000 new flats in 1989 to around 10,000 between 1994 and 1996 (Tockner, 2015). Recently, housing speculation has become a major part of the city's life and discourse, and the financial crisis has added to the growing demand for low-risk assessment opportunities of real estate. According to a study by the Austrian National Bank, the relation between the fundamental factors and market prices has increased significantly in the past ten years resulting in an overvaluation of real estate properties in Vienna of about 20 per cent. This makes it almost impossible for individuals or groups to find an existing flat, house or even a building plot on the free market. In combination with a growing demand in alternative forms of living through demographic changes, this favours alternative models such as the collaborative ones described in this chapter.

Collaborative housing models (e.g. small resident-led cooperatives such as *Baugruppen*) suggest alternative and radical approaches to both financing affordable housing in the city and increasing the diversity of urban living. We use collaborative housing in this chapter as an umbrella term which stretches across different forms of housing oriented towards active involvement of users and collaboration of residents among each other (Fromm, 2012; Vestbro, 2010). Collaborative housing initiatives emphasise self-organisation which can reduce maintenance costs and also increase quality of decision making and pluralism in housing governance. Moreover, collaborative models often seek to secure long-term affordability for residents and aim at the exclusion of their schemes from market speculation. Nevertheless, in contrast to social housing, only a limited amount of theory-informed academic research has been published on collaborative housing in Austria (e.g. Wankiewicz, 2015), especially on its relation to social housing provision (e.g. Lang & Stoeger, 2018).

Based on a review of academic and practitioner literature and using additional empirical data, this chapter critically investigates the potential of driving social innovations through new collaborative models within the affordable housing sector. We understand social innovation as a process which mobilises and engages residents to address their social needs in a way that is new to the local housing context. Social innovations further aim to transform existing social relations by improving residents' access to power and resources (Moulaert, MacCallum, & Hillier, 2013; TEPSIE, 2014). The analysis in this chapter focuses on the following collaborative models in the local housing spectrum of Vienna: *Baugruppen*, the "Syndicate model" and large-scale participatory social housing projects. The next section presents the theoretical framework which is based on a social innovation and a housing systems approach. Based on this framework, the third section provides an analysis of the institutional context of housing in Vienna before the fourth section introduces the case studies of particular collaborative housing models presented thereafter. The final section discusses key findings of this study and provides conclusions.

Theoretical framework

This chapter draws on the concept of social innovation as developed in the fields of spatial planning and development as well as in the third sector literature. Social innovation dynamics broadly refer to three interrelated dimensions (Moulaert et al., 2013; TEPSIE, 2014):

1 *Satisfaction of social needs*. Social innovations address essential needs of residents that are inadequately met within the local housing context. Such needs can refer to affordability and good quality housing.
2 *Engagement and mobilisation of beneficiaries*. Residents and members of the wider community need to be given the opportunity to actively participate in the governance of their housing. Thus, their actual needs can be identified and they can actively shape the respective housing solution.
3 *Transformation of social relations and empowerment*. Social innovations should encompass long-term changes in the relations between residents and key stakeholders in the local housing context, such as social housing providers or local authorities. This ensures sustainable resident empowerment through combining organisational governance innovation (dimension 2) with innovative need satisfaction (dimension 1).

The above outlined dimensions of social innovation suggest an overlap with the concept of collaborative housing which also aims to combine fundamental housing needs (dimension 1) such as affordability, with an emphasis on democratic and participatory governance (dimension 2) (Fromm, 2012).

Dimension 3 additionally highlights that an analysis of social innovation cannot be limited to the organisational level and needs to include the institutional and policy context which shapes the scope of action for collaborative housing models. According to the housing systems literature, the institutional context primarily relates to housing policy interventions in the form of regulations and subsidies (van der Heijden, Dol, & Oxley, 2011). Specific elements of the institutional context can either enable social innovation by establishing favourable rules and standards or have a constraining effect, if they discourage innovative housing developments. Direct producer subsidies, for instance, are crucial for collaborative forms of housing by way of reducing the costs of housing production and by leveraging additional private market financing as well as resident contributions.

Furthermore, this chapter focuses its analysis on the local institutional level which has recently attracted considerable attention in housing research. It is supposed to provide a locus for social innovation focusing on new forms of direct resident involvement and accompanying policy experiments (Brenner & Theodore, 2002; Obinger, Leibfried, & Castles, 2005). Austria represents a case of substantial devolution in the housing system with a powerful role of provinces (*Bundesländer*) and cities in designing housing policy and subsidy schemes, and thus also policies to promote social innovation.

In the light of this, the following questions correspond to the three dimensions of the analytical framework and will guide the subsequent empirical analysis of the socially innovative potential of collaborative housing models in Vienna:

1 Satisfaction of social needs

- How does the collaborative housing model address residents' needs in terms of affordability?

2 Engagement and mobilisation of beneficiaries

- To what extent are residents involved in the governance of the collaborative housing model?

The above questions deal with dimensions 1 and 2 of social innovation and will structure the case analysis for each collaborative model later in the chapter.

3 Transformation of social relations and empowerment

- How does housing policy create the conditions for social innovations through collaborative models?
- What is the scope of influence of collaborative housing models on the institutional environment of social housing?

These final two questions deal with dimension 3 of social innovation, i.e. the relationship between collaborative models and housing institutions in Vienna (local authority, housing associations). The following section addresses the policy conditions for collaborative housing and the final section explores how collaborative models can shape the institutional housing environment in Vienna.

Vienna's housing policy context

This section addresses the question *how housing policy creates the conditions for social innovations through collaborative models*.

Viennese social housing has been subject to gradual commodification in line with an international trend since the 1990s. In 1993, a right to buy was introduced for subsidised flats in Vienna which exceed a certain limit of equity capital. In 2013, two-thirds of all 15,200 subsidised flats built by the limited-profit housing associations in Austria were subject to this right. In the same year through this law, 3,000 of these flats were transferred into private property, losing rent caps and thus transforming them into speculative property (Putschögl, 2014a, 2014b).

Today, the local authority generally no longer acts as a housing provider itself but has a steering role. It has transferred the responsibility of construction on to large limited-profit housing associations who engage in developer competitions (*Bauträgerwettbewerbe*) for cheap land and public funding, which in recent years, focused on inner-city locations, such as the area south of the new *Hauptbahnhof* (Central Station).

The possibility for collaboration among future tenants relies heavily on the possibility to allocate flats within a house among like-minded future residents. However, building within the subsidised framework grants the municipality at least a third of all flats constructed to be allocated directly through their housing services. The other two-thirds are allocated by the housing associations. For collaborative housing models, this practice of dividing the responsibility of flat allocation is problematic as dwellings are possibly allocated to tenants who do not belong to the same community of interest (Temel, Lorbek, Ptaszyńska, & Wittinger, 2009). Similarly, it is not possible for groups of individuals to apply collectively in either of those two ways of allocation. Therefore, groups interested in collaborative models need to find more complicated ways to meet their goal within the system of public subsidies and affordable housing.

The internationally outstanding policy goal of a broad target group also puts high standards on to the quality of social housing. At present, the income for a single person must not exceed around 44,000 euro per year after tax at the time of moving in – more than double the average yearly income after tax for employed people. In order to successfully target such a broad mix of income strata, an exceptional practice across Europe (Lang & Stoeger, 2018), it has to meet the requirements of a wide range of people from the growing segment of elderly, to single parents looking to combine working and living as well as to collective demands in housing. The consequence is an unarticulated assumption that communities and collaboration can be designed by specific architectural elements which often leads to frictions within the practice of community design in housing. One of the key social design elements has become the so-called "social sustainability", an additional assessment criterion within the housing developer competitions introduced in 2009 (Gutmann & Huber, 2014; Wohnfonds Wien, 2015). Designed to respond to specific needs of different resident groups, it has led to the introduction of "hardware" and "software" approaches to foster socially innovative elements in housing.

On the level of physical infrastructure ("hardware"), shared facilities or various aspects of flexibility have been introduced, such as coupleable units or flats with multiple accesses. This allows for changing requirements of accommodation and needs of specific user groups. The non-physical organisational factor ("software") in developer competitions puts a strong emphasis on community-building and tenant self-organisation programmes to secure use of shared spaces. This results in initiatives ranging from afternoon learning clubs for children to tenant catered communal kitchens. These amenities – vital to any form of community – come at a relatively low price: an analysis of 18 subsidised housing projects concluded that for those parameters affiliated with "social sustainability", none could be regarded as extraordinary cost drivers (ArchiMedia ZT GmbH, 2012). The introduction of social sustainability criteria in housing developer competitions in Vienna has put pressure on large limited-profit developers to consider participatory approaches and community building in subsidised housing schemes. It has further created noticeable public awareness and new opportunities for collaborative housing models. Thus, developer competitions increasingly encourage cooperation between collaborative initiatives, such as *Baugruppen*, and limited-profit providers who are better positioned to access public funding and to secure plots in competitions. Furthermore, they can bring their professional expertise in the planning and development process from which the groups can benefit. Developer competitions in Vienna generally promote a culture of cooperation and knowledge transfer between different stakeholder groups in social housing (e.g. architects, developers, planners, residents) which is favourable for inducing social innovations (Temel et al., 2009).

Case studies of collaborative housing models

The following sections complement developments on the level of housing policy in Vienna with short case studies of collaborative housing models relevant to the same local context. For the case studies, additional expert interviews and semi-structured, qualitative interviews with initiators and members of selected collaborative housing initiatives were carried out between 2014 and 2016, complemented by field observations of housing sites.

Most of the criticism about the human scale in Vienna's social housing policy centres on its pronounced top-down approach and the inherent hypothesis that communities can be created by specific means of architectural and social design. The core of this problem is closely tied to the way flats are allocated in the housing provisional framework of the subsidised housing system discussed earlier. The underlying logic is social mixing which the city proclaims as one of its key elements in securing social stability throughout the city.

Collaborative housing models postulate an alternative to this top-down approach. A core group of future residents develop "their" ideas and goals of a housing project within a given financial, ecological and architectural

Figure 3.1 Players involved in the production of collaborative housing models.
Source: Ernst Gruber.

framework. In the given housing market, affordable collaborative housing models can hardly be initiated without cooperation with either the municipality or with professional limited-profited housing associations, mainly because of their general lack of financial capacities to compete on the free market against investors (see Figure 3.1). Currently there are three main ways of realising a collaborative housing project within the realm of subsidised housing and one on the private housing market. These models and their socially innovative potential will be discussed in more detail in the following paragraphs.

Participatory project (Model A)

The contemporary case project "so.vie.so"[2] (an acronym for "Sonnwendviertel Solidarity" and colloquial for "without a doubt") represents an emerging type of resident participation in the limited-profit housing sector. The scheme is located close to the new *Hauptbahnhof* (Central Station) in Vienna and was realised between March 2012 and December 2013. It was one of the first projects to be finalised within the creation of an entirely new neighbourhood, mainly consisting of subsidised housing schemes (5,000 homes for about 13,000 residents). "So.vie.so" consists of 111 subsidised rented apartments, communal facilities of different sizes and shared greenspace with the neighbouring housing schemes.

- To what extent are residents involved in the governance of the model?

In contrast to resident-led *Baugruppen*, this model represents a top-down approach to collaborative housing where tenants can participate in a predesigned structure, offered by architects and facilitating consultants cooperating with large limited-profit developers – in this case a large housing cooperative (see Figure 3.2). The facilitated participation process kicks off two to three years before the actual completion of the scheme and sharpens residents' awareness

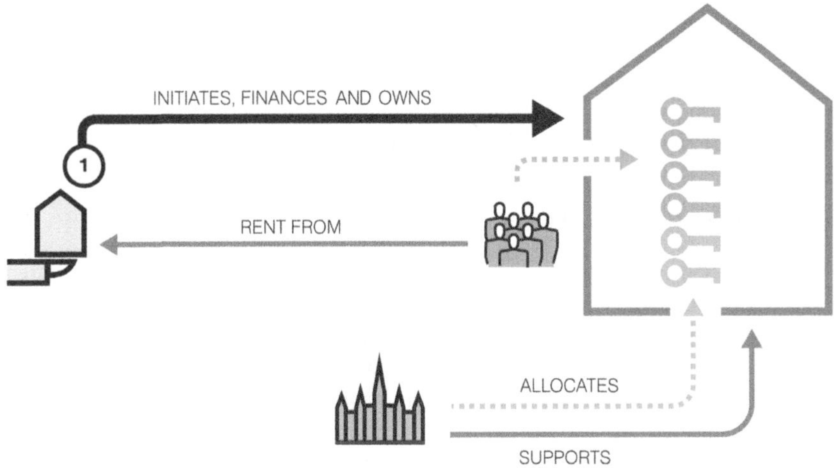

Figure 3.2 "Participatory projects": a housing association kicks off a participatory project within a subsidised housing scheme, usually together with experienced planners. A group is found and initially moderated through specialised consulting offices.

Source: Ernst Gruber.

for their immediate social environment through regular meetings. Participation within the planning process by the future tenants is regarded as a key to a democratic planning approach, such as elements of the floor plan, the equipment and organisation of use of communal spaces such as the rooftop, a workshop or fitness classes. As consultants gradually move away, residents are encouraged to take over responsibility for managing communal spaces and resident groups. In contrast to mainstream social housing schemes in Vienna, residents are also organised within a tenant's advisory board as well as increased opportunities for tenant consultation in the governance of the scheme.

- How does the model address residents' needs in terms of affordability?

Financing for this collaborative model mainly comes from direct housing subsidies which are secured by a large housing cooperative in a developer competition for the specific site. In return the provider guarantees affordable rents meeting the requirements of subsidised housing and high design quality. Residents pay an initial one-off contribution to the building costs which is usually between 15,000 and 30,000 euro for a medium sized to large flat. Higher initial contributions lower the monthly rents. At the end of the tenancy, this financial contribution is paid back (including 1 per cent write off). Residents also have to buy cooperative shares and have a buy-out option. The cooperative has the right to nominate residents for the scheme from their own housing waiting list.

Rents are fixed for ten years and existing rent contracts can be extended beyond ten years. The resident structure in the scheme can be considered as middle-class, without a pronounced social and ethnic mixing which is probably representative for social housing in Vienna. The costs for the communal facilities and basic equipment are covered through the overall construction sum, their maintenance through service charges and donations.

Baugruppen (Models B1 and B2)

Baugruppen can broadly be defined as housing projects that are (co-)initiated, (co-)planned and (co-)constructed by future residents. Additionally, they can aim at the creation of an intentional community (Temel et al., 2009). Inspired by examples from Germany, in Vienna, two sub-models of *Baugruppen* have emerged within the subsidised housing framework. In the following, we discern these two sub-models of *Baugruppen* with different grades of dependence from a limited-profit housing association and different grades of financial risk.

Model B1 "Baugruppe *in Partnership": lower initial cost for the individual*

Typical case studies for this model would be the project "Pegasus"[3] in the recently developed Viennese neighbourhood Aspern Seestadt or the projects of the "Frauenwohnprojekt [ro*sa]".[4] Pegasus, for instance, consists of 25 housing units of different sizes with a shared rooftop and basement communal areas and a children's playing area.

- To what extent are residents involved in the governance of the model?

Essentially, this model is based on the mainstream provision of social housing in Vienna mostly carried out by large limited-profit housing associations. The significant difference is that in this collaborative model, a constituted resident group organises as an independent association and teams up with a limited-profit housing association. The housing association builds and finances the house for the group who enjoys possibilities of participation in the planning process (see Figure 3.3). In the initial stage of such projects, architects play a leading role too. The residents of the group individually rent two-thirds of the flats from the limited-profit housing association and can, as a group, decide on their re-allocation. The rest of the flats are allocated by the municipality. Thus, the resident group has less say in the allocation of flats and questions of maintenance. This can be regarded as a potential for conflicts in the governance of this collaborative model.

- How does the model address residents' needs in terms of affordability?

Making use of standard procedures within social housing in Vienna enables the use of direct housing subsidies for this collaborative model. This leads to a cap

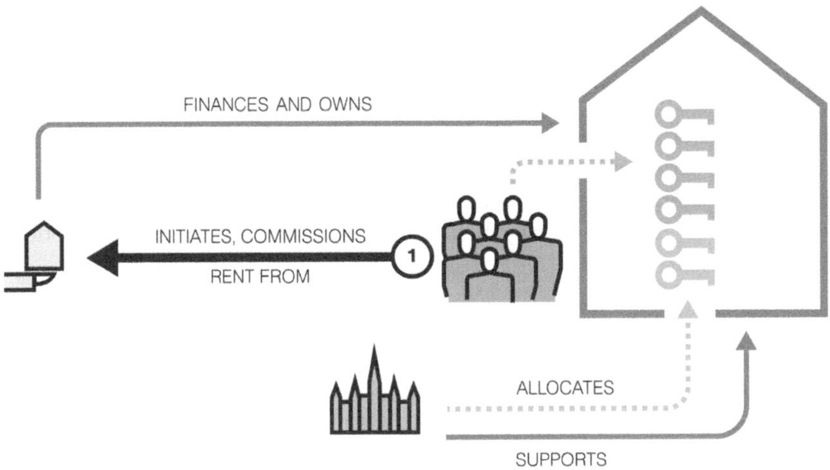

Figure 3.3 "*Baugruppe* in Partnership": a group finds a housing developer and builds by using housing subsidies.

Source: Ernst Gruber.

in maximum rents according to the limits set by the municipality for social housing as well as ensuring the entitlement of housing allowances for the lowest-income segment of the population. Initial individual costs are reduced, which results in a greater financial accessibility of this model. In the case of "Pegasus", for instance, cooperation between the initiator group of residents and those residents allocated through the local authority seems to work well, and the latter tenants also support the tenant association with a small monthly financial contribution. A coherent group with a strong identity can lead to more frictions with tenants allocated through the municipality. Such cases have been experienced within the "Frauenwohnprojekt".

Model B2 The "Autonomous **Baugruppe: Wohnheim"**

The case project for the Autonomous *Baugruppe* model is the "Sargfabrik"[5] in Vienna's 14th district. It represents Austria's largest collaborative housing project finalised in 1996 after more than ten years of participatory planning. The project consists of 112 units for around 160 adults and 50 children and teenagers. It has also become a cultural centre well known beyond the neighbourhood, organising concerts, hosting seminars and offering a membership swimming pool.

- To what extent are residents involved in the governance of the model?

Given the lack of a suitable legal body manageable for small, limited-profit (*gemeinnützige*) cooperatives (such as in Germany or Switzerland), the key was an interpretation of a model for temporary accommodation within the building code and the Austrian act of tenancy: the *Wohnheim*. Initially designed for student accommodation or homes for elderly, this model has been adopted for the purpose of living collectively and turned into a sort of mini-cooperative within the framework of Viennese housing provision. It offers independent management of a whole house by an association, which in these cases is composed of the actual residents. This personal union of tenants and owners secures collective ownership with the association owning the house, guaranteeing a personal union of use and management (responsibility), corresponding to one of the key elements of a cooperative (see Figure 3.4).

- How does the model address residents' needs in terms of affordability?

In contrast to Model B1, this collaborative housing model makes use of a specific organisational legal form (the *Wohnheim*) which provides a resident group access to housing subsidies, yet only for the construction and not for housing allowances. Moreover, the *Wohnheim* offers a number of exclusions from the general building regulations, most notably heavily reduced requirements to create car parking by almost 90 per cent to the conventional model or more flexible regulations for ceiling heights or flat sizes. These exceptions from several building codes accidentally and unwantedly for the administration to standard housing contribute to lower building costs that could be re-invested into the social infrastructure of the project.[6] In the example of the case project "Sargfabrik", these amount for a café and restaurant as well as child-care facilities. In combination with self-imposed solidarity goals such as practical diversity within the housing project or the creation and preservation of the economic security of

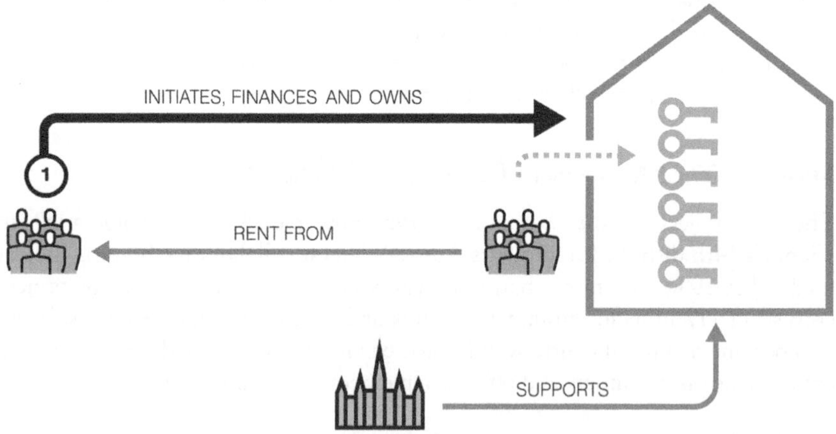

Figure 3.4 The "Autonomous *Baugruppe*": a group finances, plans, builds and allocates the flats by itself, possibly by using housing subsidies.

Source: Ernst Gruber.

the project's tenants, the "Sargfabrik" contributes to the life within the neighbourhood. This is done by social and cultural activities which go beyond the project through a swimming pool for the community as well as for the general public and the implementation of cultural programmes in an in-house event space for cultural activities. A fixed fee of 27 cents per square metre useable living area is levied for a solidarity pool. Ten per cent of this money is used to cover loss-making in the project's cultural activities (Verein Initiative, 2015).

By such means, the "Sargfabrik" thrives to make solidarity perceptible to the public. These activities would have been economically extremely difficult within an "ordinary" housing project. With regards to the organisational and social impact they would have been virtually impossible which is why the *Wohnheim* has become a role model for future projects and emblematic for the implementation of intentional communities within the collaborative housing movement.

"Syndicate model" (Model C)

This model originated in Germany under the name "Mietshäuser Syndikat" ("Tenant Syndicate") and reflects the traditional cooperative principles of self-help, solidarity and self-management. While it is already well developed in Germany, it has just recently managed to establish its first housing project called "Willy*Fred"[7] in Linz,[8] Austria, with an existing house consisting of 14 flats of different size and semi-public communal spaces. More "Syndicate" projects are currently under way in Austria, three in Vienna, one in Salzburg and one in Innsbruck. The projects are developed within the Austrian umbrella association "Dachverband habiTAT".

- To what extent are residents involved in the governance of the model?

This model consists of a form of secondary cooperative which in the German context already supports about 100 individual community-led housing projects for low-income groups across the country, based on solidarity values and self-help contributions by its tenants. Each individual project is organised as a "Hausbesitz-GmbH" (limited house-owning company) with two shareholders (*Gesellschafter*). One shareholder represents the interests of the tenants of the respective project who are organised as an association ("Hausverein"). The second shareholder is the "Mietshäuser Syndikat-GmbH" (secondary level limited company) with the "Mietshäuser-Syndikat Verein" (secondary level tenant association) – in Austria called "Dachverband habiTAT" – as its only shareholder that can veto any privatisation of individual housing projects and guarantees its non-profit status (Gruber, 2015). The "Willy*Fred Hausverein" (individual project, its tenant association), for instance, operates as a grass-roots democratic model and represents 20 tenants who also form volunteer groups which manage and maintain the building. Besides its distinct cooperative nature, the "Syndicate model" also shows similarities to the English community land trust movement with its broader aims of turning building land into community ownership with an asset lock on resale, thus counteracting increasing private land speculation (Moore & McKee, 2012).

- How does the model address residents' needs in terms of affordability?

To secure long-term affordable rent spaces, the "Willy*Fred" group had to buy the house from the former owner. In order to secure the required bank loan, a third of the overall sum needed to be constituted through a direct crowdfunding loan and 20 per cent was contributed by the German "Mietshäuser Syndikat". About half of the crowd-investors are in fact friends or relatives of the future tenants. The group attracted sympathisers of the general Syndicate idea, adding another 25 per cent of the overall sum to the asset pool. This money – in the case of "Willy*Fred" about one million euros – is used to finance the loan thus reducing interest rates. The investors may take out their share after a brief announcement time and are granted self-chosen interest rates (on average less than 1 per cent). This leaves the group constantly seeking new investors to keep the model running and popular. These loans are treated as subordinate loans.

The money put into this loan is invested into a "Hausbesitz-GmbH" (limited house-owning company). This is the economic core to keep the rents down as there are very low interest rates paid for the money invested. Each tenant also pays a solidarity contribution additional to the monthly rent which should jump start new housing projects within the "Dachverband habiTAT". There has been an intense exchange of knowledge with representatives of the German "Mietshäuser Syndikat" when designing the case project in Linz.

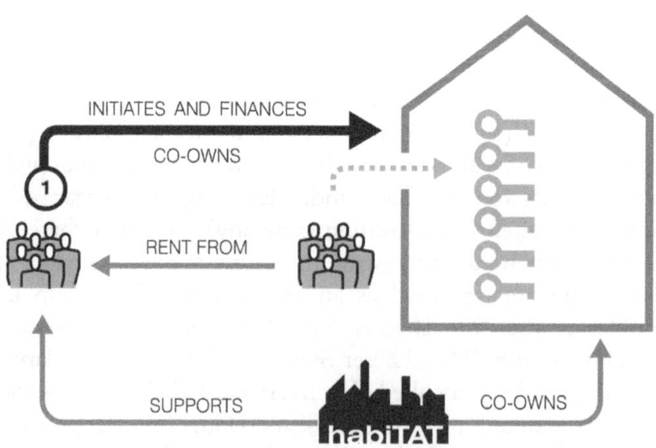

Figure 3.5 The "Syndicate model": a group co-finances, plans, builds and allocates the flats by itself, the house is co-financed and co-owned by the "Dachverband habiTAT".

Source: Ernst Gruber.

Discussion of results and conclusions

This chapter has examined collaborative housing models in the local context of Vienna as social innovations by applying an analytical framework of social innovation and drawing on a review of academic and practitioner literature as well as some empirical data. The presented framework represents a context-sensitive approach that takes into account organisational innovations as well as the configuration of the local institutional environment in which collaborative models are embedded and which can have supportive or constraining effects on social innovations.

On the *organisational level* of social innovations, the chapter has identified three main models: participatory projects (Model A), *Baugruppen* (Model B) and the "Syndicate model" (Model C). The first two models focus on the realisation of collaborative housing within the subsidised framework whereas the third model offers an alternative approach on the free housing market. All models represent different approaches to social innovation in how they combine the need for affordable housing in the city with participatory governance innovations (see Figure 3.6).

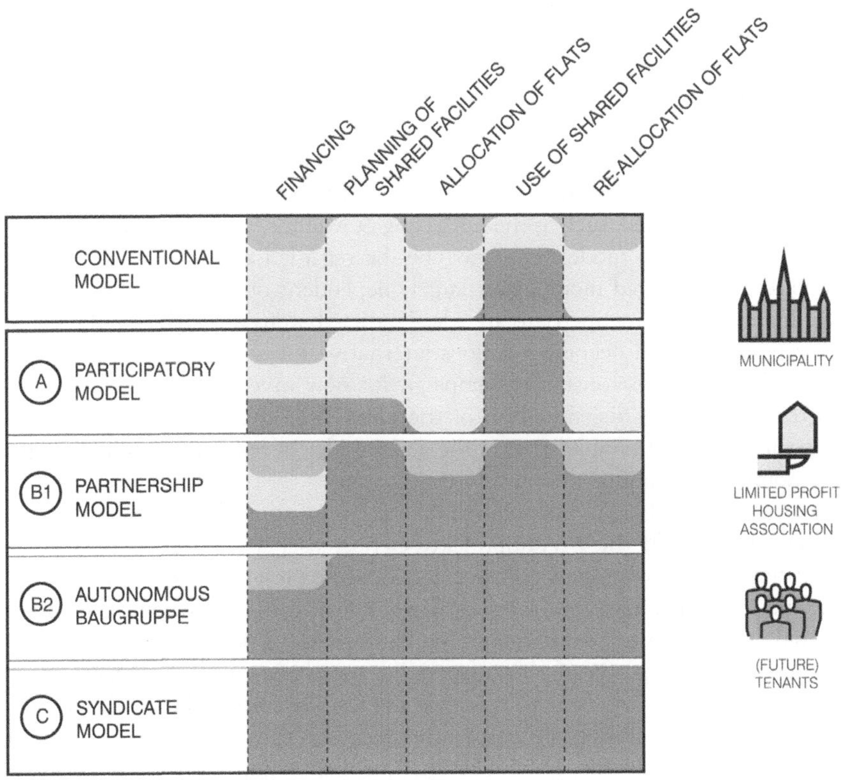

Figure 3.6 Levels of stakes and self-determination between the discussed models.

Source: Ernst Gruber.

Returning to the third aspect of social innovation in the theoretical model (see the second section), we now briefly explore the remaining question: *What is the scope of influence of collaborative housing models on the institutional environment of social housing?*

The analysis suggests that, so far, all models appear to be limited in their ability to reconfigure the pronounced top-down governance in social housing in Vienna represented by dominant large limited-profit providers and the local authority in its steering role. Although they target the exclusion of their housing schemes from market speculation, neither the *Baugruppen* (Model 1), nor the "Syndicate model" (Model 3) are going to solve fundamental financial issues of urban housing production. These problems need to be solved where they are created: at the roots of housing politics and its (de-)regulatory restraints on the free housing market economy. What these models can do is provide socially innovative elements within the given individually financed as well as the subsidised framework. However, longitudinal case studies need to deliver more insights on the effects of these models.

Mainstream social housing in Vienna already addresses many basic social needs of residents to a high degree, such as affordability of homes due to fairly generous income ceilings; ensuring high quality of new housing development as well as considerable investments in refurbishing existing stock (Förster, 2002). This local welfare state environment leaves little room for collaborative housing projects in Vienna to qualify as radical social innovations which – according to the theory – would solve more fundamental social problems of residents, as is the case in very market-driven European contexts where social housing has been substantially dismantled, such as the UK (Lang & Mullins, 2015; Ronald, 2014).

The "Syndicate model" can probably be regarded as the most radical and ideologically charged model, thus largely dependent on house-owners who are willing to sell their property to an "idea" rather than to the highest bidder. This in return may well become a serious alternative for the current generation of heirs. The need to constantly campaign for new investors of this model will further add to the dissemination of the idea. The "Syndicate model" has the capacity to attract sympathisers of the general idea of redistribution in its purest economic sense applied to housing.

One of the first "real" cooperative housing associations for decades in Vienna emerged in 2015, the "Wohnprojekte-Genossenschaft (WoGen)",[9] primarily targeted at developing new collaborative housing projects. It acts similarly to a secondary cooperative and services new projects with legal advice, organisational development and community building expertise as well as property management. The deposits of the cooperative members can help support initial financing thus contributing to reducing interest on borrowed capital. New and existing projects can become cooperative members thus adding to the idea of it as an umbrella network. This in return can help to put more pressure on the well-established housing associations, of which many still use the label "cooperative" although they have long lost touch with their members (Lang & Novy, 2014).

Without direct subsidies from the local authority and conceptual competitions for building plots at fixed land prices, the affordability of both – the *Baugruppen* model as well as the participatory model – could not be secured. In this respect, the latter model, including its external facilitation process, appears to be less resource-intensive than providing support for smaller scale *Baugruppen* projects, which require much closer cooperation between residents, architects, planners and consultants. Thus, participatory projects might have more long-term potential to be scaled-up in Vienna's social housing sector. With case projects like "so.vie.so", it is possible to provide social benefits for more residents and maybe also to reconfigure social relations on a larger scale by reaching out to them with key values of collaborative housing, such as solidarity, self-responsibility and democracy. Nevertheless, *Baugruppen* projects should be considered as test-beds for social innovations in urban housing with elements to be eventually mainstreamed. The "Sargfabrik", for example, has ambitiously shown how a swimming pool can be self-catered by a community, open to the public and at the same time economically sustainable. This example has been picked up recently by a large-scale subsidised housing project close to the central station. Another example is the introduction of single-space units inserted between regular flats to be rented temporarily compensating for extra demand of space within a household. Demonstrated in another "*Baugruppe* as *Wohnheim*" project called "Seestern Aspern" it has been repeated numerously since. However, within the scope of subsidised housing, *Baugruppen* still play a minor role with regards to their quantitative impact. In 2015, for example, a peak of about 180 flats has been realised through *Baugruppen* which makes for about 2.5 per cent of all subsidised flats handed over in that year in Vienna. About 120 of these were realised as *Wohnheim*. Before and after that year, the percentage has to be estimated lower.[10]

In short, collaborative housing projects, and especially *Baugruppen*, contribute to diversification in social housing, opening it up to ideas regarded as alien so far. The socially innovative potential of collaborative models in Vienna can be seen in addressing needs of residents who are interested in combining affordable living with self-determination and community which are insufficiently covered by mainstream social housing. However, to fulfil their innovative potential, the analysis in this chapter has highlighted the crucial role of the local authority in Vienna as an external enabler of collaborative housing through its developer competitions and especially the criteria on social sustainability. Both, participatory projects (Model A) as well as *Baugruppen* projects (Model B) are carried out within the direct subsidy framework of social housing, facilitating resident groups' direct access to affordable land in central urban locations. Our analysis suggests that these *Baugruppen* in Vienna can only exist because there is a political will to support them. The provision of land has been the crucial question for the settlers' cooperatives in the 1920s (Novy & Förster, 1991) and still is today. Developer competitions for collaborative projects on plots reserved for them have emerged as a successful path in recent years. The international transferability of collaborative housing models discussed in this chapter is limited, and depends on similarities of institutional conditions, such as the availability of comparable legal forms. However, the "Syndicate model" and *Baugruppen* models show that ideas and elements can indeed be transferred between countries, as is the case between Austria and Germany. In principle, the developer competition model of Vienna can also be applied anywhere, regardless of financial scope of a local authority. It has potential for application to any country characterised by a certain degree of federalism or devolution in housing.

Notes

1 Richard Lang's contribution was supported by an APART-fellowship of the Austrian Academy of Sciences [Project number 11696] and by a Marie Curie Intra-European Fellowship (IEF) [Project number 622728].
2 See also www.gat.st/en/news/wohnbau-sovieso-mitbestimmt.
3 See also www.baugruppe-pegasus.at/joomla/index.php.
4 See also www.frauenwohnprojekt.info and Hendrich (2012).
5 See also www.sargfabrik.at/Home/Die-Sargfabrik/Wohnen.
6 It has to be stated here that these exceptions are being heavily challenged by the authorities within the planning processes. The model of the *Wohnheim* is thus confronted with additional regulative standards such as fire regulations, effectively cancelling the economic benefits.
7 See also https://habitat.servus.at/willy-fred/.
8 In contrast to Vienna, the Austrian regional capitals, such as Linz, cannot design their own housing policies but have to negotiate the subsidy framework with the respective provincial government. The Conservative party (*ÖVP*) has traditionally been strong in the Upper Austrian provincial government promotes private market housing and is making sure that new subsidised housing development has to contain a substantial share of owner-occupied houses or flats. In contrast, the city of Linz is a traditional stronghold of Social Democrats (*SPÖ*) who have a preference for subsidised rental flats in their housing policy approach.
9 See also https://diewogen.at.
10 Calculations by the authors based on Geschäftsgruppe Wohnen, Wohnbau und Stadterneuerung (2016, p. 10).

References

ArchiMedia ZT GmbH. (2012). *Entwurfs- und Planungsparameter für Kostengünstigen Wohnbau in Wien* [Design and planning parameters for affordable housing in Vienna]. Vienna, Austria: Department for Housing Research, Municipality of Vienna.

Brenner, N., & Theodore, N. (2002). Preface: From the "new localism" to the spaces of neoliberalism. *Antipode*, *34*(3), 341–347.

Förster, W. (2002). *80 years of social housing in Vienna*. Vienna, Austria: Housing Subsidies Department, Municipality of Vienna. Retrieved from www.wien.gv.at/english/housing/promotion/pdf/socialhous.pdf.

Fromm, D. (2012). Seeding community: Collaborative housing as a strategy for social and neighbourhood repair. *Built Environment*, *38*(3), 364–394.

Geschäftsgruppe Wohnen, Wohnbau und Stadterneuerung (Ed.). (2016). *Wiener Wohnbau Jahresbericht 2015* [Vienna housing annual report 2015]. Retrieved from www.wohnbauforschung.at/index.php?inc=download&id=5805.

Gruber, E. (2015). Nutzen statt Besitzen [Using instead of owning]. *RaumPlanung, 179*(3), 41–46.

Gutmann, R., & Huber, M. (2014). *Die Sicherung der "Sozialen Nachhaltigkeit" im zweistufigen Bauträgerwettbewerb: Evaluierung der soziologischen Aspekte – Eine Zwischenbilanz* [Ensuring social sustainability in the two-stage housing developers competition: An evaluation of sociological aspects. An interim result]. Vienna: wohnbund:consult. Retrieved from www.wohnbauforschung.at/index.php?id=432.

Hendrich, P. (2012). [ro*sa]. In id22: Institute for Creative Sustainability: experimentcity (Ed.), *CoHousing cultures: Handbook for self-organized, community-oriented and sustainable housing* (pp. 132–147). Berlin, Germany: Jovis.

Lang, R., & Mullins, D. (2015). *Bringing real localism into practice through co-operative housing governance: The role and prospects for community-led housing in England.* Housing and Communities Research Group WP1–2015, University of Birmingham. Retrieved from www.birmingham.ac.uk/Documents/college-social-sciences/social-policy/IASS/housing/2015/working-paper-series/HCR-WP-1-2015.pdf.

Lang, R., & Novy, A. (2014). Cooperative housing and social cohesion: The role of linking social capital. *European Planning Studies, 22*(8), 1744–1764.

Lang, R., & Stoeger, H. (2018). The role of the local institutional context in understanding collaborative housing models: Empirical evidence from Austria. *International Journal of Housing Policy, 18*(1), 35–54.

Moore, T., & McKee, K. (2012). Empowering local communities: An international review of community land trusts. *Housing Studies, 27*(1), 280–290.

Moulaert, F., MacCallum, D., & Hillier, J. (2013). Social innovation: Intuition, precept, concept, theory and practice. In F. Moulaert, D. MacCallum, A. Mehmood, & A. Hamdouch (Eds.), *The international handbook on social innovation: Collective action, social learning and transdisciplinary* (pp. 13–24). Cheltenham, UK: Edward Elgar.

Novy, K., & Förster, W. (1991). *Einfach bauen: Genossenschaftliche Selbsthilfe nach der Jahrhundertwende. Zur Rekonstruktion der Wiener Siedlerbewegung* [Building simple: Co-operative self-help after the turn of the century. Reconstructing the Viennese settlers' movement]. Vienna, Austria: Picus.

Obinger, H., Leibfried S., & Castles, F. G. (Eds.). (2005). *Federalism and the welfare state: New world and European experiences.* Cambridge: Cambridge University Press.

Putschögl, M. (2014a, March 25). Mehr geförderte Wohnungen, Lücke bleibt [More subsidised flats, gap remains]. *Der Standard.* Retrieved from http://derstandard.at/1395363147481/Mehr-gefoerderte-Wohnungen-doch-Luecke-bleibt.

Putschögl, M. (2014b, October 26). Kaufoption auf dem Prüfstand [Buying option on the test bench]. *Der Standard.* Retrieved from http://derstandard.at/2000007263684/Kaufoption-auf-dem-Pruefstand.

Ronald, R. (2014). Housing and welfare in Western Europe: Transformations and challenges for the social rented sector. *LHI Journal, 4*(1), 1–13.

Temel, R., Lorbek, M., Ptaszyńska, A., & Wittinger, D. (2009). *Baugemeinschaften in Wien: Endbericht 1, Potenzialabschätzung und Rahmenbedingungen* [Building groups in Vienna: Final report I, assessment of potential and conditions]. Vienna, Austria: Housing Subsidies Department, Municipality of Vienna. Retrieved from www.wohnbauforschung.at/index.php?id=340.

TEPSIE. (2014). *Social innovation theory and research: A summary of the findings from TEPSIE.* Brussels: European Commission, DG Research. Retrieved from https://iupe.files.wordpress.com/2015/11/tepsie-research_report_final_web.pdf.

Tockner, L. (2015). Wohnungsangebot und Wohnungsnachfrage in Wien seit dem Fall des Eisernen Vorhangs [Housing provision and housing demand in Vienna since the fall of the Iron Curtain]. In P. Prenner (Ed.), *Wien wächst – Wien wohnt: Gutes Wohnen in einer wachsenden Stadt* [Vienna grows – Vienna lives: Good housing in a growing city] (pp. 80–89). Vienna, Austria: Vienna Chamber of Labour. Retrieved from https://media.arbeiterkammer.at/wien/PDF/studien/Stadtpunkte14.pdf.

van der Heijden, H., Dol, C., & Oxley, M. J. (2011). Western European housing systems and the impact of the international financial crisis. *Journal of Housing and the Built Environment*, *26*(3), 295–313.

Verein Initiative für gemeinschaftliches Bauen und Wohnen. (Ed.). (2015). *Gemeinsam Bauen Wohnen in der Praxis: Workshopreihe 2014 über, für und mit Baugruppen in Wien* [Collaborative building housing in practice: Workshop series 2014 about, for and with building groups in Vienna]. Retrieved from http://issuu.com/asperndieseestadtwiens/docs/gemeinsam_bauen_wohnen_in_der_praxi?e=0/31425281.

Vestbro, D. (Ed.). (2010). *Living together: Co-housing ideas and realities around the world.* Stockholm, Sweden: Royal Institute of Technology Division of Urban Studies in collaboration with Kollektivhus NU.

Wankiewicz, H. (2015). The potential of cohousing for rural Austria. *Urban Research and Practice*, 8(1), 46–63.

Wohnfonds Wien (Ed.). (2015). *Beurteilungsblatt 4-Säulen Modell* [Assessment form 4-pillar model]. Retrieved from www.wohnfonds.wien.at/media/file/Neubau/4-Saulen-Modell.pdf.

4 Towards a collaborative way of living

Innovating social and affordable housing in Italy

Giordana Ferri, Laura Pogliani and Chiara Rizzica

Introduction

In Italy, homeownership represents 67.2 per cent of the total housing stock, private rentals account for 16.3 per cent and social rentals comprise 5.5 per cent, the majority of which are homes owned by local or regional government entities and managed by public agencies (CITTALIA, 2010; Pittini, Ghekiere, Kijol, & Kiss, 2015).

Built between the beginning of the last century and the 1970s, the public housing stock is now outdated and insufficient, and requires substantial investment. However, due to the lack of available public funding, the role of the national government is heavily constrained. The private rental market has decreased substantially – from 44.2 per cent in 1971 to 16 per cent in 2015 (ISTAT, 2012; Pittini et al., 2015) – because private developers have built housing that is almost entirely for sale. Moreover, the absence of significant incentives for rental housing provision, as well as increasingly easy access to mortgages and tax concessions for buying a "first home" (Del Gatto, 2013), have produced a residential model that is predominantly based on homeownership.

Since 2008, the economic crisis has caused a collapse in the housing market and impacted the income of a large percentage of the population, while at the same time banks have also tightened their lending practices. Furthermore, housing demand has grown and become more complex (Torri, 2006). This makes access to housing very difficult for a vast share of the population; the current housing requirement is estimated to be more than 2.5 million households. This includes an increasing demand from middle- and low-income households that are unable to find affordable homes, as well as from very vulnerable groups (Pittini et al., 2015).

Scarce national funding and fluctuating national policies have recently led to the creation of a testing ground for "new" Social and Affordable Housing (SAH) practices on a local scale (Calavita & Caudo, 2010). In these initiatives, new development and management strategies are shaping innovative approaches to respond to a growing demand for more inclusive and sustainable – that is, more collaborative – way of urban living (Mullins, Czischke, & Van Bortel, 2012; Ferri, 2017).

With this is mind, our chapter will discuss to what extent the development of the institutional framework, financing tools and local housing policies in the Italian system since the late 2000s is designed to satisfy the demand for new SAH models. Furthermore, our research question focuses on the consequences of this innovation for the Italian housing system and planning approach. In particular, the chapter examines those processes where housing policy mingles with urban and social policy, as complementary elements in the local welfare system.

In the first section, we investigate the current formal and informal rules for providing SAH and their enforcement mechanisms, analyse the incentives and tools (at different levels of government) to provide SAH, discuss arising planning problems and consider the changing nature of the current dominant SAH providers.

In the second section, we explore the evolution of SAH provision since the early 2000s, in order to clarify how recent changes fit into the Italian institutional background. We outline a brief history of SAH legislation, discussing the present focus of national, regional and local housing policies and practices. This background picture is needed to understand the resurfacing of a "new" housing question and the emergence of a hybrid and decentralised SAH model. This model originated from pioneering experiences in the Lombardy Region, specifically in Milan. It is based on a new funding platform called "SIF" (System of Integrated Funds) which, although being developed into a prototype already implemented nationwide, has been hardly studied so far (Poggio & Boreiko, 2017).

In the third section, we present two case studies from the portfolio of *Fondazione Housing Sociale* (FHS)[1] – a key stakeholder within SIF – and describe the respective roles of key players in relation to the framework of the new culture of collaborative housing. The two selected projects were implemented in Milan between 2012 and 2015 and are symbolic, not only because of their experimental character in relation to hybrid financial and governance models, but also because of the interaction between "diffuse design" and "expert design" (Manzini, 2015), which characterised both their planning and management. In this framework the process of Community Start Up, through which residents collaborate with each other to plan and manage shared services and common spaces, represents a principal element of what can be defined as a relational chain of system innovation in the local welfare (Polizzi & Vitale, 2017).

Finally, we conclude with some remarks on the new Italian SAH regime that contribute to the understanding of long-term effects in terms of quality and affordability of the housing offer. Taking into account that, while innovative, the SIF programme represents only a partial solution to SAH demand, as it mainly targets mid-income households, we present a set of reflections and paths for future research.

Multifaceted innovation and future challenges: policies, providers and institutional design

To understand the current innovation underlying the Italian SAH system as well as the political and institutional responses to the strong housing demand, it is necessary to outline some key aspects of the situation. Considering the variety of the demand, the impracticality of single solutions and the inefficiency of a single (public) provider, SAH policies are making efforts to harness a range of measures and consider different stakeholders and funding methods that can cooperate successfully (Bronzini, 2014). Beyond this, trust in social innovation principles (Minora, Mullins, & Jones, 2013; Czischke, Mullins, & Van Bortel, 2014) is growing notably in Italy, and encourages different perspectives of implementation and management of the housing stock.

In the first subsection, we note the changes in the nature and role of providers, as well as the variations in institutional design. In following subsections, we will outline opportunities and future challenges to enlarge the supply of SAH and other good practices.

Traditional and new actors emerging in a revised regulatory framework

In examining the parties involved in the provision and implementation of SAH, a significant shift can be seen in recent years that strongly influences not only the increasing variety of actors, but also their different attitudes and expectations (Plebani, 2010).

Traditionally, state and regional representatives were the key stakeholders. However, since the state government continues to decentralise its responsibilities, regional authorities have assumed greater responsibility. They are in charge of promoting the development of projects by providing regulations and financial means (guarantee funds, contributions) and by defining an accreditation system for those operating in the SAH sector.

Municipalities act as the main public planning authority. They decide on strategies and interventions through regulations, incentives and actions in order to promote the supply of affordable housing. For example, local authorities can reduce construction costs, fees and planning charges, as well as manage both builders and tenants. In addition, through careful planning, municipalities can make areas available for SAH projects by reducing the cost of land. This represents a key issue for all housing policies.

Housing cooperatives have historically implemented, financed and managed SAH projects. Their financial tools include member shares, capital raised through indivisible reserves, member loans, tax exemptions and mutual funds. They mainly provide access to homeownership at cost, and despite being more affordable compared to market prices (10–30 per cent lower costs, on average), this sector has also been affected by the economic crisis.

Housing cooperatives exist mainly as one of two types: social and conventional. Social cooperatives aim to ensure that their properties are affordable in the long term. They have a long history in building and managing rental dwellings, often working with people with special needs or low income. This often includes the elderly, young couples and the disabled (Zangheri, Galasso, & Castronovo, 1987). On the other hand, with conventional cooperatives homes belong to individual members who buy them at a price slightly below market value, taking advantage of special government subsidies in the process.

Following the National Housing Plan of 2008 (Decree 112/2008, "Piano Casa"), new providers have emerged to complement traditional stakeholders: banking foundations, real estate investment firms, insurance companies and a public development bank (*Cassa Depositi e Prestiti*[2] – Deposits and Loans Fund) appointed by the state to manage the system of integrated public and private funds. Among the new actors, bank foundations are the most innovative private players in the market. For example, they offer investment opportunities through new instruments, such as ethical funds. These investments have a low return, but offer a low-risk profit. However, profits cannot be withdrawn until the end of the investment. It should also be noted that the target group for ethical real estate funds is not the same as the target group for subsidised housing. Homes are sold or rented not to low-income or vulnerable families, but to those who can afford to purchase or rent a house at a fixed, yet discounted price.

Bank foundations often play both the role of intermediaries and organisers in initiatives involving joint public–private participation. Originally operating in Milano and northern Italy, these initiatives are spreading to other regions (Cassa Depositi e Prestiti, 2014; Caruso, 2017). Two of the most notable bank foundations are *Fondazione Cariplo* (FC)[3] and *Compagnia San Paolo* (CSP). The role and commitment of FHS among the key actors within the social housing programme started in 2000 and is discussed in the following two sections.

In addition to the number of players (institutional, public and private), the strengthening of the autonomous bodies and of the non-profit sector (named "Third Sector") in Italy has led to increased cooperation in attempts to remedy the home accessibility crisis through local initiatives. The explicit goal of these few but high quality initiatives is to bring residents together to foster community (Ferri & Rizzica, 2016; Pogliani, 2016), creating an innovative organisation to improve social inclusion. Furthermore, they aim to reduce social risks as well as the risk of insolvency and depreciation of properties.

Obviously, multilevel governance is required to guarantee transparency and accountability for all public, private and Third Sector interventions. Cooperation between state, regional and local representatives as well as non-profit and private developers is in its early stages, but it is a crucial concern.

Drivers of change

The brief presentation of how the mechanisms for providing, managing, and financing SAH have evolved warrants a deeper reflection of the factors that encourage it. Three key opportunities are widely discussed in literature (Pogliani, 2014; Cognetti & Delera, 2017): (1) land provision, (2) regeneration of existing public housing stock and (3) rental of abandoned private stock. The regulatory system has so far been unable to sufficiently harness these opportunities. Recently, however, a few, mostly locally designed pioneering practices have come to the forefront, as the following subsections will briefly illustrate.

Land provision for SAH

Land provision is considered a fundamental component in the supply of affordable housing (Barrett & Healey, 1985; Needham & De Kam, 2000; Monk, Whitehead, & Tang, 2013). If land is publicly owned, the municipality can more easily promote affordable housing (Alterman, 2009; Muñoz Gielen & Burón Cuadrado, 2014). New conditions can be arranged to give land either to public housing actors, social housing providers or even market developers, as well as to communities. Rental fees can be regulated and measures can be introduced to prevent speculation of property values. If local governments do not actively manage land purchase and assembly (land banking) for these purposes (van der Krabben & Jacobs, 2013), town planning tools can regulate the housing market and make it more attractive for lower income groups. In combination with private property owners, new local plans can be developed to assess land use in order to allocate a certain percentage of the land to SAH. Furthermore, inclusionary housing policies that have recently been introduced in Europe and the United States (De Kam, Needham, & Buitelaar, 2014) can also help increase the supply of affordable housing. Planning regulations require that a percentage of housing in private schemes be sold at a discounted price or rented at a reduced rate: market developers can build houses and then transfer them to a registered social landlord, or they can share building rights upstream. This goes beyond traditional zoning enforcing extensive supply of social housing and promoting urban *mixitè*, a notion referring to a mix of urban uses, income groups, generations and lifestyles (ENHR, 2011).

An interesting example of effective land provision in Italy is the recent urban masterplan for Milan that represents a decisive move towards inclusiveness and integration of uses, public facilities and innovative activities, such as co-housing and co-working, start-ups and so on. A breakthrough occurred with traditional planning approaches. Indeed, in the recent past, new social housing ensembles were built in suburbs because the land was already publicly owned (including the cases illustrated in the next section). The municipality decided to sell the land to developers at a symbolic price, to reduce significantly the costs of social projects. On the contrary, the new plan, through inclusionary planning, combines the increase in value of private sector property with the construction of social housing units. A mix of affordable housing (for purchase and for rent) is mandatory in all urban projects on private land to be evenly distributed in the different parts of the city (Pogliani, 2014). This requirement is compulsory for all redevelopments larger than 10,000 m^2, and is optional for smaller projects.

In addition, all private proposals that include social housing give 30 per cent of the total land free of charge to accommodate the social buildings.

Several alternatives are possible within this approach, making it more flexible and easier to implement. For example, one option enables private developers (in agreement with cooperatives) to build social housing in parallel with market houses, in order to ensure an effective housing mix and greater financial sustainability for the development. Another alternative consists of a fee that developers are allowed to pay instead of building social housing, so to finance a special "municipal purpose fund" for public housing.

To sum up, the plan includes different measures to increase opportunities to build SAH, encompassing land grants provided by private developments, and funds collected from the market developers who opt to pay cash in exchange for building.

Reusing, refurbishing and innovating public housing

A second opportunity is the reuse, refurbishment (improvement) and innovation (redevelopment) of the vast supply of obsolete public housing. The renovation of these structures (at times of significant architectural and historical value) is a major challenge, due to the sheer quantity of homes available. In the Lombardy Region, 22 per cent of the rental housing stock consists of traditional public estates, while only 4 per cent is social housing, and the remaining part (74 per cent) is private (Regione Lombardia 2015, Regional Observatory on the State of Housing based on Census Data *Istat*). The public estates are mainly located in large cities where demand is strong. They include only residential uses and are managed centrally (and often inefficiently). Due to the low level of public funding available for redevelopment of these areas, various efforts have been made to include social stakeholders to encourage better management. Hopefully current policies for the partial sale or transfer of public homes will integrate effective commercial and social services to make such estates more liveable, as has happened in new social housing projects (see the next section). Some of these pilot projects have facilitated innovative processes and products, especially in resident engagement and collective learning in urban regeneration projects (Drewe, Klein, & Hulsbergen, 2008). This is particularly the case in settings of poor quality with low average income. The most recent approaches focus on novel types of employment (start-ups, co-working spaces, Fab Labs) and the new generation of workers as a catalyst to trigger the rejuvenation of abandoned assets and the revitalisation of the social fabric (Vinci, 2017).

The ongoing redevelopment of the public district of Lorenteggio is a good example to learn from (Figure 4.1). The once modern style project from the 1940s, located in southwest Milan, close to a railway station, a metro station and to the historic *Naviglio* canal, now struggles with considerable social issues. Many homes are vacant, many are illegally occupied and many are below standard. Several demolition projects had been initiated, but due to strong opposition from residents, the local and regional authorities who own and

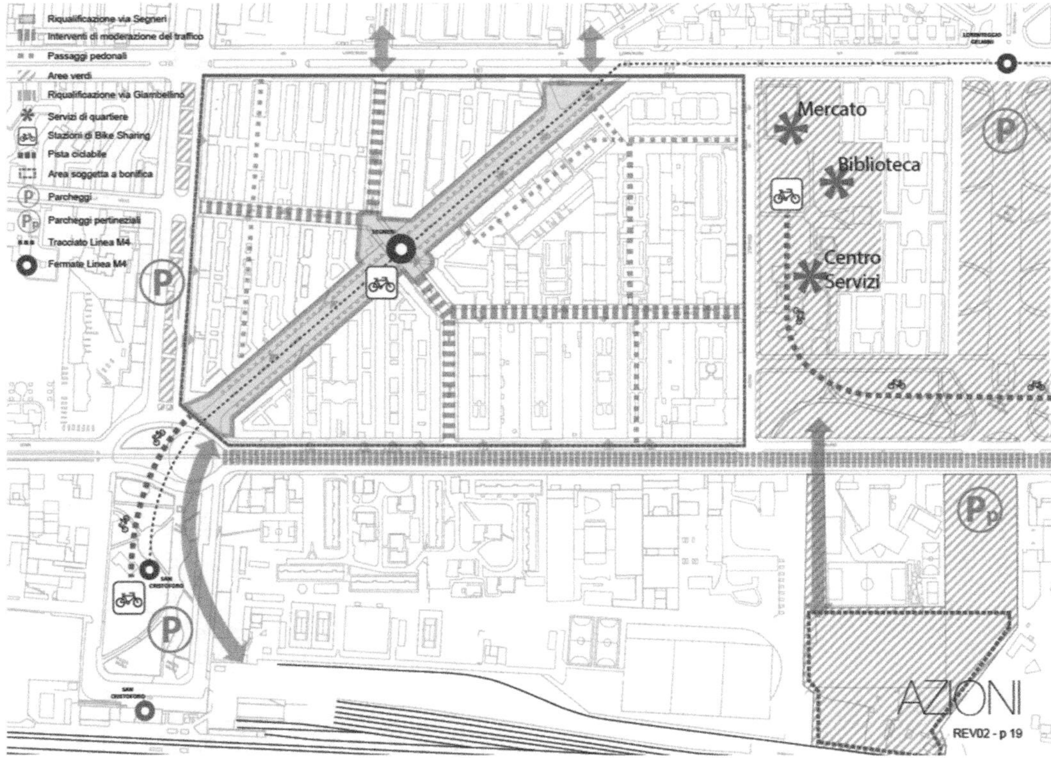

Figure 4.1 Milano. The regeneration of the Lorenteggio public district – masterplan.

Source: Regione Lombardia, Comune di Milano, Aler Milano.

manage the housing blocks were forced to change their plans. The rehabilitation programme – launched in 2015 under the EU Structural and Investment Funds 2014–2020 with a cost of €73 million – affects 1,500 households and attempts to combine the physical restoration of buildings and open spaces with a social programme to foster inclusiveness. The municipality has provided additional funding for the renovation of public spaces and the construction of more urban facilities, in order to enhance a sense of community and support economic activities. It is currently the most important redevelopment project in the city in decades, and represents a sound step towards the rebirth of a deteriorated district whose low-income inhabitants are passionate to reinvigorate (Ostanel, 2017).

Repurposing private sector housing for affordable renting

A third opportunity to encourage SAH is the repurposing of abandoned private stock for affordable renting (Cucca & Gaeta, 2016), which require more efficient tools and fiscal constraints. To this end, national and local initiatives are experimenting with different arrangements. A recent measure focused on the consequences of the real estate crisis and the ensuing bankruptcy of private building companies, which caused a large number of units to be repossessed by the banks as well as the creation of large distressed assets. Recently, Parliament has considered creating a special fund against arrears for private rental housing, provided that homeowners agree to rent one-fifth of their stock at affordable prices. A fitting comment is that social housing offers opportunities for new investment, especially following an economic crisis or in less desirable areas (Pawson, Lawson, & Milligan, 2011).

On a local level, it is worth mentioning that Milan's "Regolamento Edilizio" (building code) was approved in 2014. At that time, Milan had 80,000 vacant units (out of almost 400,000 total units), in addition to more than 120,000 m^2 of estimated vacant office space. Owners have been warned that buildings that have been abandoned, contaminated or underused for at least five years must take appropriate action to upgrade the property (art. 15, Milan building code). If no such action is taken, the municipality can designate those buildings and areas for public use, and deny any new development projects until the original neglected properties have been taken care of. Although this mandatory regulation is controversial, it attempts to bring together political strategies and administrative concerns in repurposing existing private-sector stock to improve urban welfare.

Recent innovations in SAH legislation in Italy

The availability of a living space that is appropriate to individual development constitutes a specific application of the principle of equality and equal dignity as laid out in the documents that form the basis of current institutional and functional order in Italy: the Constitution of the Italian Republic, as well as the UN

Universal Declaration of Human Rights and International Covenant on Economic, Social and Cultural Rights.[4]

With regard to universal rights in Italy, the right to housing is intended as a collective duty which the State "cannot abdicate under any circumstances". This is a central pillar in the architecture of the welfare state, in which the home is recognised to be a fundamental right (Constitutional Court of Italy, judgements No. 217/1988, No. 49/1988 and No. 404/1988). This approach helps explain how the policies relating to the right to housing in Italy have – up until very recently – traditionally been public policies. That is to say that they have been exclusively promoted, governed and financed by the state.

If for Western Europe the "history" of social housing policies begins after the end of the Second World War and covers the period up until the end of the 1990s (Boelhouwer & Van der Heijden, 1992), in the Italian context, on the other hand, the phenomenon has older origins and extends up to the first decade of the 2000s (Ferri & Rizzica, 2016; Poggio & Boreiko, 2017). In fact in 2008, legislative tools were radically modified with the introduction of "alloggio sociale" (social home): a rent-controlled home for those who "are unable to access rental accommodation on the free market" (Ministerial Decree, D.M. Infrastructure, 22 April 2008).

Recent innovations of Italian SAH have their roots in a number of legislative and governmental initiatives that date back to early 2000s.

From 2001 onwards: the resurfacing of the "new" housing question

In 2001, a legislative provision was introduced that relates specifically to "edilizia privata convenzionata" (private affordable housing) – housing created by private operators (i.e. housing cooperatives) on the basis of agreements stipulated with municipalities on sale and rental prices – and this has a significant effect on the start-up of a new wave of policies regarding SAH in Italy. It is, in fact, determined that the Regional Councils are the legal entities of reference and that the cost of the areas, rental costs and sale prices must be fixed in collaboration with local councils in accordance with indications given to the regional authorities (DPR, Presidential Decree 370/2001 – arts 17 and 18). However, it is from 2007 onwards (Act No. 244/2007; art. 11 of Decree 112/2008, "Piano Casa") that it becomes necessary to include private players or provide forms of public–private collaboration aimed at promoting social rental housing. This leaves behind once and for all the traditional model which saw public financing as being the only possible method for social housing, as well as the central administration of the state having a leading role in the definition and realisation of such interventions.

Along these lines, the 2008 definition of "alloggio sociale" introduces a series of fundamental innovations. "Alloggi sociali" are homes for permanent rent and are intended for "individuals and disadvantaged households". They have a task of general interest and are essential elements in the SAH system that consists of not only the dwellings themselves, but also a set of residential services. This therefore represents a hybrid service offer, acting as an intermediary between economic activities, which are managed according to standards of efficiency and within a competitive context, and non-economic activities, which are managed according to general interest and are oriented towards social cohesion and the redistribution of equality. These services may be provided by either public or private operators without coming up against the rigid regulations of the European Commission regarding state aid (Ministerial Decree, D.M. Infrastructure, 22 April 2008).

This is a major breakthrough: "alloggio sociale" definition extends the boundaries of the social rental market, allowing private developers to build social rental housing on private land, unlike former public housing plans which were only allowed on public land. This supports investments in the private social housing sector even through government incentives, such as tax exemptions and land-use concessions.

In 2009, there was a structured response on a national scale to the affordable housing question. The "Piano Nazionale di Edilizia abitativa" (National Social and Affordable Housing Plan, DPCM 16 July 2009) was approved along with setting up of the "Sistema Integrato dei Fondi per l'Housing Sociale" (SIF, Integrated System of Funds for Social Housing). This is a real estate ethical funds system designed to support lease to rent at discounted prices, using capital with a capped return and a medium- to long-term investment horizon. SIF has raised a total of €3 billion and currently consists of a national "fund of funds", the "Fondo Investimenti per l'Abitare" (FIA, Housing Investment National Fund) to the value of €2.028 billion, into which flow resources from the Cassa Depositi e Prestiti (€1 billion), the Ministry of Infrastructure and Transport (€140 Million) and other private investors (banking and insurance groups: €888 million).

The FIA is managed by CDP Investimenti Sgr, an asset management company, and invests its own resources in local, ethical real estate funds managed by other asset management companies through shareholdings between 40 and 80 per cent. Investors in the relevant territory, such as banking foundations, local councils, housing cooperatives and providers, private operators and social enterprises provide the remaining portion of the resources of the local funds.

This represents a series of ethical real estate funds, each of which is managed by a local and qualified real estate asset management company and which are dedicated to SAH initiatives being promoted by stakeholders who are active on a local basis and which meet the conditions of public interest (Rizzica, 2015). As of August 2017, there are 31 approved local funds spread throughout Italy with nine different local fund managers. This means that more than 275 projects may be implemented by 2020, creating over 20,000 "alloggi sociali" and 8,500 beds for temporary and student housing, in addition to neighbourhood services. According to a 2017 CDP report, there are currently 168 of such projects ongoing across Italy, which include 12,310 homes and 4,145 beds (CDP Investimenti SGR, 2017).

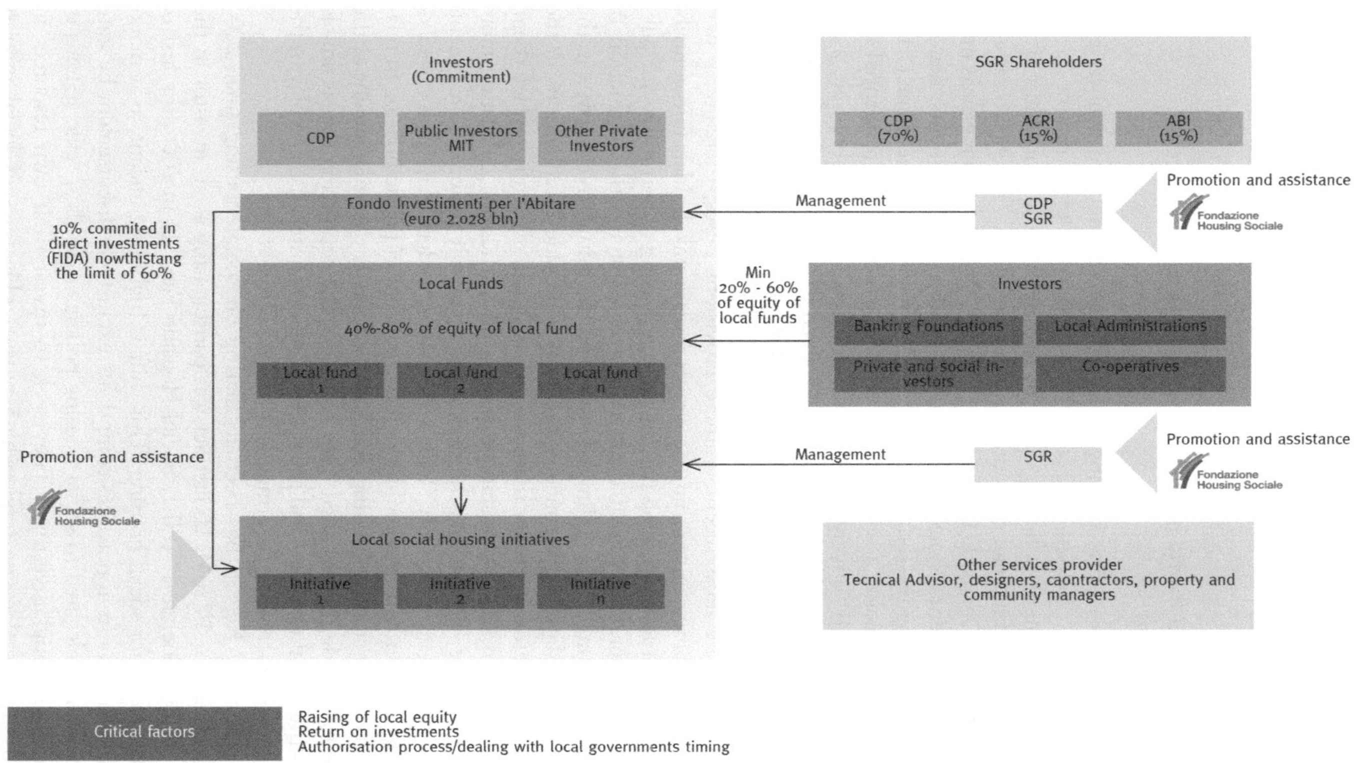

Figure 4.2 SIF funding system map.

Source: FHS.

After 2008, the introduction of "alloggi sociali", the birth of FIA and the implementation of SIF led to the formal startup of private SAH in Italy. This was an innovative method of developing programmes aimed at expanding the supply of SAH units, using resources and means of implementation that had previously only been a prerogative of the private real estate market.

Decentralisation and hybrid models in the pioneering experience of the Lombardy Region

The old idea of considering housing policy as an instrument to counter economic downturn by "helping" the construction sector rapidly returns to the forefront of government policy in 2015, in response to the worsening of the effects of the global financial crisis on the Italian economy. Through a series of "urgent measures" (Decree D.l. No. 47, 28 March 2014), an attempt was made to boost the social rental housing sector using traditional instruments: new tax deductions, extending the rental period, potential to purchase the home ("right to buy") and introducing a series of elements on which urban, residential and social policies start to converge: (1) priority is given to financial resources directed towards SAH projects that can be achieved without the consumption of new land (e.g. brownfield locations); (2) SAH is identified as a key element in urban regeneration to provide incentives for constructors.

A picture of the most recent of these provisions raises, therefore, a new concept of ethical investment that encourages private stakeholders into contributing to SAH initiatives, taking part in ever-increasing opportunities for public–private collaboration. But if these initiatives – having the distinction of being "self-sustaining" through limited returns on the initial investment – in the vision of the legislator were conceived to work alongside interventions in the public housing sector, in reality there is a risk they will gradually replace them. In this scenario in which the state incrementally withdraws, delegating more and spending little, we also find the case of the Lombardy regional government. Acting as a pioneer, Lombardy Region has acknowledged ten years ahead of national legislation both the evolution of the concept of public housing in relation to new dimensions of housing discomfort – namely the enlargement of the user base to include the so-called "grey sector" of the population that is unable to access the rental market – and the role that private enterprise can play in the sector in accordance with the principles of subsidiarity.

The Lombardy Region has been legislating on social housing since 2004 (Regional Act No. 5/2204). Its first act was participating as an investor in the "Fondo Abitare Sociale 1" (FIL1, Social Housing Fund 1) in 2006, the first of the Italian funds for social housing. This shift is highly significant, as it marks the transition away from practices comprising exclusively disbursement by state administrations delegated to social housing policies towards specific systems of "ethical institutional investors". They seek to invest their own resources in a capped-return real estate fund, which pursues objectives of social interest (Decision of the Regional Government DGR No. 1981, 22 February 2006).

An additional legislative step in 2009 (Regional Council Law No. 27/2009) concerned capped rental housing within SAH, giving the private sector the opportunity to build social rental housing provided that they enlarged the offer of long-term tenancy contracts. Finally, in 2012, the Lombardy regional government launched the "Piano casa regionale" (Regional Housing Plan – Regional Council Law No. 4/2012) to assign grants and awards for the construction of SAH, even waiving zoning, land-use and development regulations. In particular, the plan allows SAH projects to be implemented by requesting extra building floor area and land-use exceptions for new and existing structures.

The proliferation of new legislative and financial instruments that has characterised Lombardy development efforts since 2004 also inspired the organisation of international architectural competitions in 2009 and 2010 (*Abitare a Milano*). They were promoted by FHS and FC for projects to be undertaken in a variety of areas in Milan. These competitions inspired the construction of the two residential complexes: *Cenni di Cambiamento* ("hints of change") in 2013 and *Borgo Sostenibile* ("sustainable village") in 2015 (Ferri, Pacucci, & Pero, 2011). Taking into account the evolution in the aforementioned legislative and financial arenas, the experience gained in Lombardy, and more specifically in Milan as part of FIL1, can be seen as the local prototype of a model which was to be relaunched at national level through the setting up of the FIA in 2009.

Collaborative ways of living and innovative housing models in Italy

In addition to innovations in the economic and legislative framework, it is necessary to consider certain aspects of SAH projects in Italy which are linked to recent research on social innovation. In particular, in the area of studies about new hybrid enterprises of the Third Sector (Venturi & Zandonai, 2016) and, more specifically, in the field of collaborative living (Manzini, 2017). A new culture of living is emerging in both private and public spaces, a collection of spaces in which people seek to improve their own living conditions by putting into practice collaborative and sustainable solutions. The result of this interaction is to make day-to-day living more efficient and pleasant by meeting the challenges of daily life reducing waste, optimising the use of available time and available resources. This trend, by now widespread, encourages people to actively construct their own living situation in a broad sense, such as: the social street, ethical purchasing groups, community gardens and carpooling (Ferri & Rizzica, 2016).

This is, in brief, the scenario in which the most recent SAH programme come into being and in which the FHS operates as social and technical adviser. Among the examples that FHS has studied, both Italian and foreign, there are two which have had the greatest influence: cohousing and the Italian cooperatives experience. While they are quite different, they both cast inhabitants as a leading role. Cohousing is a bottom-up endeavour – it is entirely guided by its residents and mostly undertaken in the real estate market and especially for sale, even if recent opportunities have also emerged in rental properties. The indivisible-ownership cooperatives have also always adopted a model based on sharing, but with top-down governance. The proposal, which for reasons of convention we shall call the "FHS model", is certainly similar to cohousing in its outcomes, but is dissimilar in the development and management strategies it employs (Ferri, 2017).

This model gained traction in Italy through the SIF programme through certain projects in which real estate aspects are not considered as an end in themselves, but rather as an element to be taken advantage of, inside an integrated approach that puts particular emphasis on social matters. In such a strategy, the architectural design becomes part of an articulated process that is different from a traditional housing project, which is only partly focused on the buildings themselves. The process, in fact, extends to cover the management of homes as well as strengthening the community and its services. Accompanying activities for the community are planned by FHS to become an integral part of the investment activity.

Social and collaborative housing in Italy within the SIF

In projects promoted and "accompanied" by FHS under SIF, residents are offered the opportunity to share spaces and services with their neighbours in order to perform all the activities of daily life without necessarily possessing everything they need themselves. Thus, on one hand, making spaces and tools available to perform common activities offers people a certain quality of life which, given the economic crisis, seemed unimaginable. On the other, people express a new level of commitment, they demonstrate a desire for greater contact with their own territory to be able to have a bigger impact on decisions made, and this is not only stimulated by fewer economic resources, but also expresses a willingness to enliven one's social environment, simply because doing so makes life easier.

To spread and facilitate these initiatives in the residential sphere, it is necessary to empower individuals and groups to create their own neighbourhood by making several resources available to them: tools and platforms to facilitate organisation and communication, physical spaces (other than those that are strictly residential), a structured pathway to plan common activities, and the know-how to accelerate community development and initiate social services. In practice, the project is structured along the lines of a Community Start Up Process (Figure 4.3) that starts around six months before the first residents move in and finishes when all residents have been living in their homes for one year. It aims to empower residents to design the use of the common spaces available to them and to define the rules that will govern them.

Social aims also influence the conception of living spaces inside and outside the home. The relationship between the form of an urban space and its "social success" depends largely on its capacity to accommodate and encourage

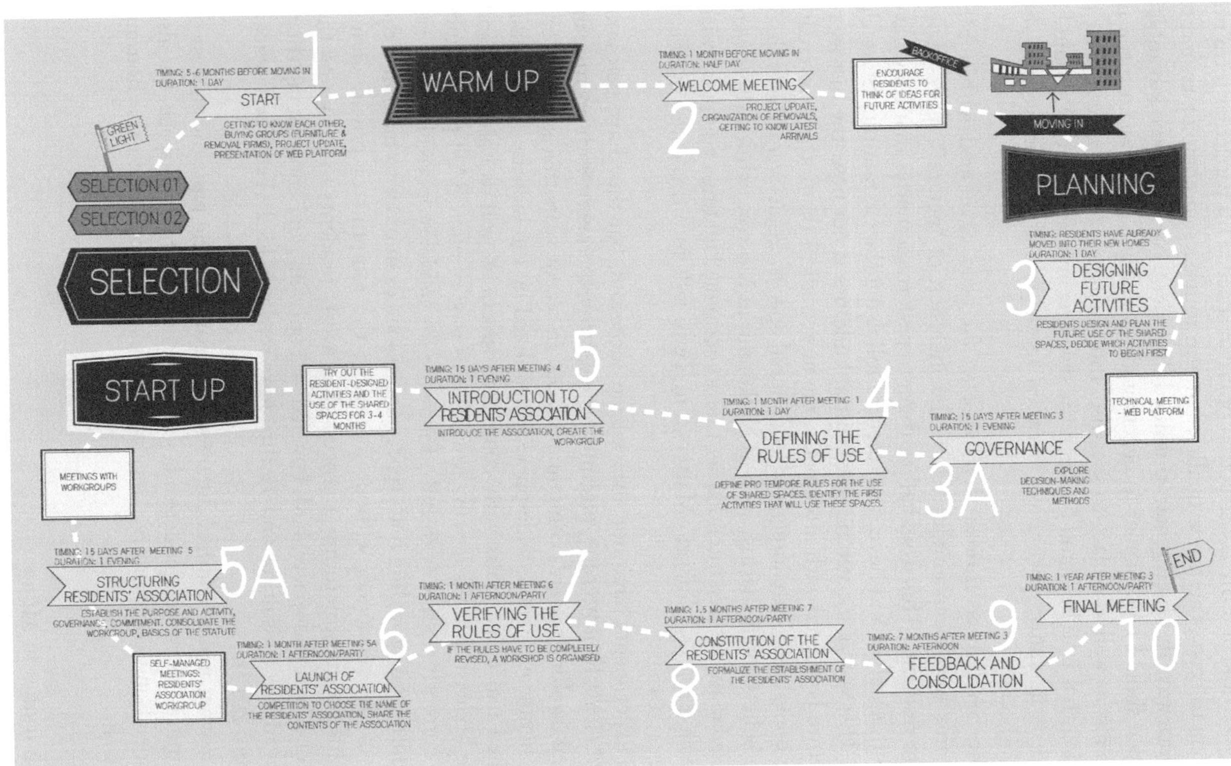

Figure 4.3 Concept scheme: the Community Start Up process map.

Source: FHS.

activities from its position as a crossroads where paths and goals come together. It can be argued that the form of a physical space may strongly influence its use and appreciation, the distinction between various levels of perception of what belongs to whom and the construction of urban space. This particular form not only refers to space's aesthetic quality, but also to its design complexity and to the various ways in which it can be utilised. In order to be best taken advantage of, a space should be designed to accommodate multiple functions: a place to cross, to rest as well as a place to socialise. Intermediate external spaces (that is everything that is to be found between the dwelling and public areas) should be designed to maximise encounters between residents and thus enlivening the neighbourhood.

In the SAH interventions that have so far been developed within SIF, experiments have been conducted on the inclusion of "neutral" spaces to be loaned to residents. This would allow them to perform activities that they have selected themselves and have structured by following the Community Start Up process. This way of interpreting residential buildings is not new: the history of architecture is littered with attempts, some more radical than others, to create housing complexes with integrated communal spaces. Some were the fruit of extreme beliefs about sharing, such as Narkomfin in Moscow, while others were more secular in nature, intended as multifunctional buildings equipped with self-managed spaces. Villaggio Matteotti in Terni falls into this category (Ferri & Pacucci, 2015).

Such experiments have not always been successful, but they have certainly catalysed ideas about housing, pushing designers to experiment with opening up individual dwelling towards communal spaces. In recent years this approach has become significantly more widespread, exemplified by the increase of individually owned real estate units with communal spaces as well as cohousing and even the luxury market is moving towards this type of offer. SAH programmes that are currently underway in Italy, following the model proposed by FHS, are concentrating on providing both spaces and resources in order to maximise the comfort of the residence, without increasing the footprint of private living space. This means structuring a process that assists residents in designing the purpose of communal spaces, both covered and open-air, and encouraging them to use available consulting and facility resources provided (Ferri & Pacucci, 2015; Ferri, 2017).

This is what makes the real difference compared to the past: the success of housing initiatives no longer depends solely on the availability of space, but also on the social and collaborative development plans connected to the housing project itself.

Two case studies in Milan

The recognition of two projects in Milan – "Cenni di Cambiamento" and "Borgo Sostenibile" – can be considered a first step towards a collection of case studies of SAH in Italy that outline the different strategies and directions recently adopted. This allowed us to share research and innovation products, such as funding system models, prototypes, tools and collaborative platforms (Ferri & Pedercini, 2016).

These projects are emblematic of the experimentation in the design and realisation of SAH in Lombardy, which has given rise to a number of affordable residential quarters. The two areas, owned by the Municipality of Milan, have been those in which this experimentation has marked the most fundamental stages: the partnership with the Municipality of Milan, FC and FHS; the selection of design projects through International Architecture Competitions; the development of projects by FIL1; the implementation of innovative ways to manage the dwelling units and the resident community. In addition, FC has provided contributions that were specifically aimed at supporting energy efficiency, residential services for vulnerable people (which are assigned to operators in the Third Sector), and projects for temporary affordable housing.

"Cenni di Cambiamento" (Figures 4.4 and 4.5.) is one of the largest residential complexes ever built in Europe that features wooden support structures. It is located in a district to the west of central Milan and comprises four blocks of 122 homes. They are rated energy class A and are offered either for affordable rent or on a rent-to-buy agreement. The target beneficiaries for priority assignment of dwelling units were mainly younger families and single individuals leaving their family home.

In addition, the complex offers common services as well as recreational and cultural spaces. They are mainly managed by Third Sector operators, who have been drawn into the project seeking to create the best possible conditions for a network of supportive neighbourly relationships.

The opening up of the community to the local neighbourhood is further aided by the restoration of the *Cascina Torrette di Trenno* (a traditional farmstead). It is located within the area covered by the "Cenni di Cambiamento" project and houses a cultural centre for the performing arts. In the last two years, it has become an attractive new hub for both the local neighbourhood and the entire city of Milan.

The project also includes numerous spaces designated to the use of residents, including a collective lounge with a kitchen, four communal spaces – each with a terrace – situated on the top floors of the towers and other smaller areas for storage. These spaces that are part and parcel of the residence are free for residents to use, and represent the basis on which the Community Start Up process was built. "Cenni di Cambiamento" in this sense is an exception: it offers a generous amount of communal space (250 m^2 for residents and 1,800 m^2 for the neighbourhood) and if it does not represent a new standard itself, it certainly has contributed towards raising the expectations for other projects.

The Community Start Up programme is preceded by several meetings organised before the opening of the construction site, during the resident selection stage. Afterward, social exchanges between residents are concentrated on the activation of special interest groups which each have a specific focus, such as

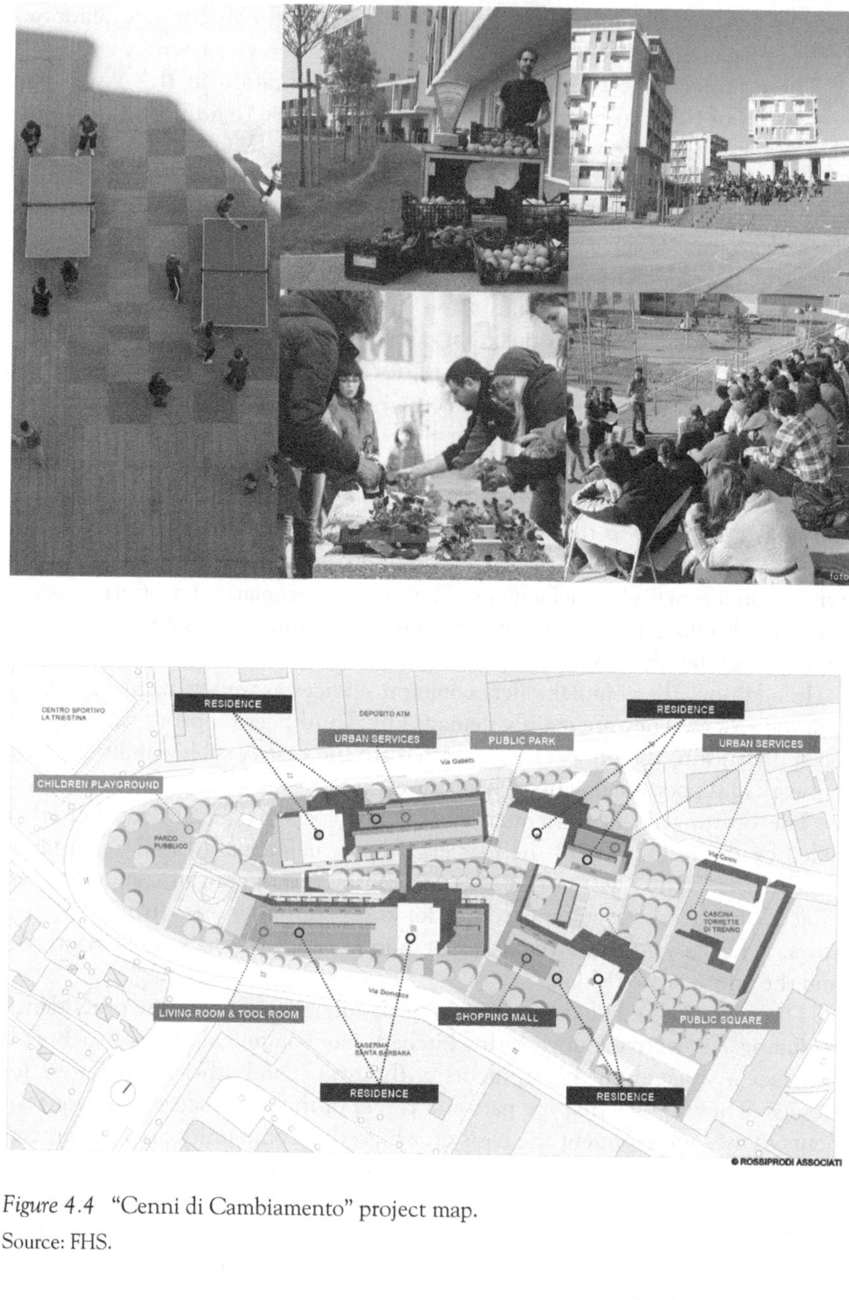

Figure 4.4 “Cenni di Cambiamento” project map.

Source: FHS.

CENNI DI CAMBIAMENTO

122 homes, including:

- 44 affordable rent homes
- 46 rent-to-buy homes
- 14 controlled rent* homes
- 16 residential services (for example, for people with physical or mental disabilities, for single mothers with children etc.)
- 5 units rented under the Foyer project (which provides temporary accommodation for young people who have just left their family home)
-

9 shared spaces, including:

- Social Manager's Office
- Living Room (100 sq.m.)
- Children's Play Room (70 sq.m.)
- space for the Ethical Buying Group (GAS) (60 sq.m.)
- Storage room (14 sq.m.)
- 4 shared spaces on the top floors of each block (100 sq.m. plus roof terrace)

3 services open to the local neighbourhood, including:

- Cascina Torrette di Trenno, managed by "Mareculturaleurbano" – a space where projects and artistic residences combine with commercial services, training courses and entertainment
- Headquarters of "Azione Solidale", where the social cooperative provides services for disabled people and others (450 sq.m.)
- "Ludoteca Stregatto", a children's play area and the headquarters of the social cooperative "Il Grafo" (250 sq.m.)

6 commercial spaces of various dimensions:

- a social dairy managed by the "Saman" organization
- an ice-cream parlour and pastry shop that also supplies Ethical Buying Groups
- an organic produce shop for fruit and vegetables

Community Profile

- 20% young single people
- 20% young couples
- 25% young families with children
- 15% elderly people
- Irrespective of the categories, around 30% of the dwellings is for assignment to single parent families (either father or mother, with one or more children)

Start of works: March 2012
Commencement of Community Start-up Process: November 2013
First occupancy: October 2013

* these dwellings are designated to those who have the right to Council Housing under the regulations of Milan Council. The tenants assigned these dwellings are selected by the Council and pay a rental price that is equivalent to that which the Council would apply to dwellings in its own properties. However, these dwellings are not public property, neither are they transferable: they remain the property of the FIL, the Ethical Read-Estate Fund for Social Housing in Lombardy which, under the public-private partnership that it has with Milan Council, applies this type of "controlled rent". This type of rental price, as it is the result of a specific partnership between the FIL and Milan Council, is at present only applicable to the projects located in Milan.

Figure 4.5 "Cenni di Cambiamento" fact sheet.

Source: FHS.

the moving-in process or the purchase of furniture. These groups encourage residents to take an active interest in managing initial collaborative activities. Such activities include taking care of green spaces, managing communal spaces and organising ethical purchasing groups.

After the residents move in, a Community Start Up process is created to bring out shared values and interests, which will subsequently be translated into concrete initiatives to start up in the available communal spaces. Today the project is well on its way to reaching maturity, assisted by the Cooperative Dar=Casa, the Social Manager of this project, as well as numerous non-profit organisations who have found affordable rent spaces to be suitable to their needs. In 2014, "Officina Gabetti 15", the residents association, was set up to manage the collaborative activities and services proposed by the residents themselves.

In 2017, acknowledging its role of forerunner project, "Cenni di Cambiamento" was awarded the European Collaborative Housing Award by Un-Habitat, specifically for "its bottom-up approach and the ample provision of shared and public spaces" (UrbaMonde, 2017).

"Borgo Sostenibile" (Figures 4.6. and 4.7) is a SAH complex in Figino, a peri-urban district west of Milan. The project consists of 321, energy class A, homes, again offered either for affordable rent or on a rent-to-buy agreement. The units were intended for young couples and families with young children, as well as elderly people. There are communal spaces available for residents, a linear park, a promenade and a public square with shops and services. The project also includes cohousing for the elderly, managed by a cooperative and the "Borgo Assistito", a services system which includes a day care facility for the elderly and those in special need. It is open to the whole neighbourhood and hosts both accommodation for the elderly who are self-sufficient and a family centre to provide support and services to promote wellbeing. In addition, there are the "Case Bottega" (Atelier Houses) – a specific residential service dedicated to support the self-employed, artisans, craftsmen or anyone who could work from home – with accommodation that combines the domestic living space with a home office or studio.

The objective of the project is to spread sustainable and collaborative living, paying particular attention to the social dimension of the "Borgo" and actively encourage environmentally aware lifestyles.

The new complex has been incorporated into the historic village of Figino, whose character still reflects its agricultural past. This can be seen in several urban and architectural aspects, as well as in the persisting relationships between its inhabitants. The 321 new homes in Figino have doubled the number of residents of the existing village. To face this critical condition, a Community Start Up process began in 2015 as the resident selection phase was already in progress. Here, too, the goal was to assist the future inhabitants in joining the project and to establish a primary core of active residents around which the new community will grow.

The neighbourhood of Figino is characterised by a high level of civic participation. Its inhabitants discovered a major reason for cohesion as they

Figure 4.6 "Borgo Sostenibile" project map.

Source: FHS.

BORGO SOSTENIBILE

312 homes, including:

- 172 affordable rent homes
- 112 rent-to-buy homes
- 37 controlled rent* homes
- 20 residential services (community for teenagers/young people, mother and baby facilities etc.)
- 9 Atelier Houses for people who can work at home
- 10 units designated towards cohousing for elderly people

8 shared spaces, including:

- Social Manager's Office
- Living Room (150 sq.m.)
- Laundry Room (45 sq.m.)
- the "Thirteenth Floor" (25 sq.m.)
- 4 store rooms and storage spaces of various dimensions

3 services open to the local neighbourhood, including:

- Headquarters of the Cooperativa CBM (240 sq.m.) which promotes child protection through the activities in the following areas: promotion of well-being, clinics and treatment and training and education)
- "Borgo Assistito" (2,900 sq.m.) – a system of support services for the neighbourhood which includes a Day Care facility for the elderly and people with special needs, accommodation for self-sufficient elderly people and a family centre.

11 commercial spaces of various dimensions

Community Profile

50% families

23% elderly people

Priority category: family units who are already resident in the Figino neighbourhood, relatives of Figino residents, people who work in the local area.

Start of works:

December 2012

Commencement of Community Start-up Process:

January 2015

First occupancy:

June 2015

* these dwellings are designated to those who have the right to Council Housing under the regulations of Milan Council. The tenants assigned these dwellings are selected by the Council and pay a rental price that is equivalent to that which the Council would apply to dwellings in its own properties. However, these dwellings are not public property, neither are they transferable: they remain the property of the FIL, the Ethical Read-Estate Fund for Social Housing in Lombardy which, under the public-private partnership that it has with Milan Council, applies this type of "controlled rent". This type of rental price, as it is the result of a specific partnership between the FIL and Milan Council, is at present only applicable to the projects located in Milan.

Figure 4.7 "Borgo Sostenibile" fact sheet.

Source: FHS.

protested the construction of a nearby waste-to-energy plant. Therefore, it was vital to the development of the community project to build trust with the "historic residents". This was achieved by prioritising clear communication from the onset of the project, ensuring that the new SAH neighbourhood could not be perceived as a threat but, rather, as an opportunity to attract services and activities that Figino still lacked. The Community Start Up process thus started with a series of meetings open to all the neighbouring residents during the planning phase. It was essential at this stage that those in charge of the construction site were empathetic to the concerns of the residents regarding the disturbance that would be caused by the building work.

These Community Start Up meetings mainly seek to build community, create the resident association and open up the design process to residents so they can participate in organising activities of their interest and in taking charge of the communal areas on free loan from the owner. In the case of Figino, taking into consideration the concerns and requests of the existing neighbourhood led to additional decisions, such as: selecting a Social Manager – QLS, a cooperatives consortium – who was already active in the district and providing priority accommodation to individuals who were connected to the Figino area through family or work. The residents' association of "Borgo Sostenibile" was formalised in 2016.

Conclusions

The objective of this chapter was to describe the recent evolution in Italian SAH provision by looking at the processes/dimensions in which housing policy intersects with urban and social policy, redefining the boundaries of the local welfare system. We demonstrated how this junction comes about through the synergy of three innovative elements: (1) the ethical real estate fund, (2) public–private partnerships and (3) the collaborative governance model.

We reviewed how, since the economic crisis of 2008, the demand for housing has grown and diversified. New divisions of responsibilities between state, regional and local government, together with this diversification of demand, the vertical reduction of public funding, and the cancellation of public policies in the sector, have pushed governments – first regional and then national – into supporting innovation in SAH practices. We also described how the new measures and instruments to expand housing affordability have had their roots principally in "alloggio sociale" (social home) since 2008. Among these arrangements, SIF in particular has made synergy possible between financing methods and the formation of public–private partnerships. This has enabled new SAH, notably housing for rent, whose main features are to be: (1) integrated with local urban planning, and (2) strongly connected to tenants' mutual commitment to collaborative living. The latter seems to be the most relevant innovation in regard to the quality of the housing offered in the long term, considering the congruence between living spaces and living practices is crucial to the dynamics of change that are shaping the contemporary residential environment in Europe (Zanfi, 2015).

Against the "renaissance of collective housing" that some observers have started to point out (Müller, Niggli, Ruby, & Ruby, 2017), we were particularly interested in setting up the basis for exploring the evolutions of SAH projects in the mid to long term; if and how these new arrangements could support further institutionalisation, and the potential to be scaled-up and transferred to other countries. By the expiry date of the fund – 2040 for SIF – a number of questions will have arisen regarding the impact and implications of the innovations produced.

From a technical point of view, SIF is itself innovative as it set up a structured system of procedures and financing borrowed from the private real estate market, but which had never previously been implemented in affordable housing. From a different perspective, the experience of the SIF projects is by its very nature connected to the local region, as the dedicated ethical real estate funds have a predominantly regional dimension. All of this raises clear problems of local governance, where both authorities and operators of SAH find themselves facing non-standardised processes with uncertain results. However, it also provides opportunities for experimentation and an intensive collective learning experience for everyone involved. The most serious limits seem to be posed by the rather unequal distribution of these practices – while they are widespread in northern and central Italy, they have only been pursued in limited numbers in the south.

If a complete reform of the affordable housing system on a national scale is still a long way off, it is nevertheless true that local administrations can incorporate insights gained from the SIF projects to transfer new issues and new procedures – in terms of affordability and quality of the housing offer – into new measures that also relate to public housing. For example, a new law by the Lombardy Region, "Disciplina regionale dei servizi abitativi" ("Regional regulation of accommodation services", l.r.16/2016), has embraced the concept of social mix and extended its own housing initiative to include both residential and communal spaces dedicated to self-managed community services. Moreover, in the SIF projects in Milan, both affordable and "social tenure" (a controlled rent equivalent to that which the municipality would apply to homes in its own properties) were combined in the same SAH settlements thanks to the partnership between the Milan Municipality and SIF developers. This indicates an effective method to develop public and private affordable housing in combination, overcoming one of the "older vices" in the Italian social housing system that scholars have documented so far (Poggio & Boreiko, 2017).

Alongside these developments, some innovative elements are now being scaled up to the national level. This includes strengthening the design of integrated projects, as well as the initiation of collaborative governance models that are in line with European collaborative practices in housing co-production (Czischke, 2018). As described in the two case studies, residents in SIF projects express heightened levels of engagement due to their willingness to adopt greater responsibility in designing their communities and, consequently, in the decision-making process.

The extended resident participation through the Community Start Up process is one of the most easily transferable results to other countries. It is made possible through the contributions of key new actors, most notably non-profit organisations and Social Managers. However, the resilience and timing of this increased involvement, in light of the likely changes in ownership at the end of the SIF, present an ongoing challenge that should be closely monitored in the long term.

We outlined how several key new actors have begun to operate within the SIF environment, such as non-profit organisations and cooperatives. The presence of these operators in SAH complements, but evidently cannot substitute, the involvement of the public authorities. Experiences with SIF, as well as the onset of regeneration of public housing neighbourhoods through public–private partnerships, both seem to require public agencies to gradually adopt a more pronounced management role. These agencies should improve their initiative by creating the conditions for the implementation of the projects, modifying the legislative and regulatory provisions, improving urban infrastructure, devising new strategies to provide land at a greatly reduced cost and revising urban planning instruments.

Finally, from a short-term perspective, we can also draw attention to what extent SIF projects would revamp the current model of housing provision in Italy. According to the vision of SIF planners, the programme targets individuals whose income exceeds levels that are entitled to public housing, yet who are still unable to afford market costs. Therefore, although SIF cannot offer a solution to meet the primary housing demand, it still presents an interesting approach to extend access to the housing ladder and could respond to changing housing needs beyond those traditionally related to families.

Acknowledgements

The general structure of the chapter and the conclusions are the result of collaboration between the three authors. Laura Pogliani was responsible for the first section: Multifaceted innovation and future challenges: policies, providers and institutional design, Chiara Rizzica for the introduction and the second section: Recent innovations in SAH legislation in Italy, and Giordana Ferri for the third section: Collaborative ways of living and innovative housing models in Italy.

The authors would like to thank Roberta Conditi and Luciana Pacucci (FHS) for data and figures relating to the case studies.

Notes

1 FHS is a private, non-profit entity, which works to promote public interest. FHS's mission is to experiment with innovative solutions for economically sustainable social housing initiatives that are not based on free grants. FHS was created by FC in 2004, to develop its Social Housing Programme and carry out real estate projects dedicated to vulnerable segments of the population. Among the founders were Regione Lombardia (Lombardy regional government) and ANCI Lombardia (Association of Lombardy

Municipalities), who make up the public–private partnership that characterises the project. In 2008, with the establishment of SIF, the operations of FHS scaled up to the national level, as FHS was already acting as the social and technical adviser of the FIA.

2 CDP is a major Italian financial institution and a leading provider of funds for social housing. The Italian Ministry of Finance controls it for around 80 per cent. The CDP Group operates as an investment bank and among its main operations is the participation in the share capital of medium and large domestic enterprises, which are considered strategic for national development.

3 FC is one of the world's main philanthropic organisations and manages the assets of *Cassa di Risparmio delle Provincie Lombarde*, a leading Italian banking institution. Its mission is to act as a resource to help social and civil organisations to better serve their community.

4 Constitution of the Italian Republic (arts 2 and 3), Constituent Assembly 1947; Universal Declaration of Human Rights (art. 25), UN General Assembly 1948; International Covenant on Economic, Social and Cultural Rights (art. 11), UN General Assembly 1966.

References

Alterman, R. (2009). *Can the "unearned increment" in land values be harnessed to supply affordable housing?* Paper presented at UN Habitat Conference, Warsaw.

Baldini, M., & Poggio, T. (2013). The Italian housing system and the global financial crisis. *Journal of Housing and the Built Environment*, *29*(2), 317–334.

Barrett, S., & Healey, P. (Eds.). (1985). *Land policy: Problems and alternatives*. Aldershot: Glover.

Boelhouwer, P., & Van der Heijden, H. (1992). *Housing systems in Europe*. Part 1. The Hague: Delft University Press.

Bronzini, M. (2014). *Nuove forme dell'abitare: L'housing sociale in Italia* [New forms of housing: social housing in Italy]. Rome: Carocci.

Calavita, N., & Caudo, G. (2010). Italy: Variety and creativity in approaching inclusionary housing. In N. Calavita & A. Mallach, *Inclusionary Housing in International Perspective* (pp. 275–321). Cambridge, MA: Lincoln Institute of Land Policy.

Caruso, N. (2017). *Policies and practices in Italian welfare housing*. Milano: Springer Brief.

Cassa Depositi e Prestiti. (2014). *Social housing: il mercato immobiliare in Italia: focus sull'edilizia sociale. Report monografico 03* [Social housing: real estate market in Italy: focus on social housing. Monographic report 03]. Rome: Cassa Depositi e Prestiti.

CDP Investimenti SGR. (2017). *Housing Sociale: Stato attuale in Italia e nei principali paesi europei* [Social housing: Current state in Italy and in major EU countries]. Working paper, UrbanPromo Social Housing, Turin, 5–6 October.

CITTALIA. (2010). *I comuni e la questione abitativa* [Municipalities and the housing question]. Rome: Anci.

Cognetti, F., & Delera, A. (2017). *For rent: Politiche e progetti per la casa accessibile*. [For rent: Policy and projects for affordable housing]. Milan – Udine: Mimesis.

Cucca, R., & Gaeta, L. (2016). *Ritornare all'affitto: evidenze analitiche e politiche pubbliche* [Back to rent: analytical evidence and public policy]. Paper presented at For Rent Seminar, Politecnico di Milano, May.

Czischke, D. (2018). Collaborative housing and housing providers: Towards an analytical framework of multi-stakeholder collaboration in housing co-production. *International Journal of Housing Policy*, *18*(1), 55–81.

Czischke, D., Mullins, D., & Van Bortel, G. (2014). *Hybridising housing organizations: Meanings, concepts and processes of social enterprise*. London: Routledge.

De Kam, G., Needham, B., & Buitelaar, E. (Eds.). (2014). The embeddedness of inclusionary housing in planning and housing systems: Insights from an international comparison. *Journal of Housing and the Built Environment, 29*(3), 389–520.

Del Gatto, M. L. (2013). *Social housing: oltre il progetto* [Social housing: beyond the project]. Milan: Ed. Il Sole XXIV Ore.

Di Biagi, P. (Ed.). (2001). La "città pubblica" e l'Ina-Casa [The "public city" and Ina-Casa]. In *La grande ricostruzione: il piano Ina-Casa e l'Italia degli anni cinquanta* (pp. 3–30). Roma: Donzelli.

Drewe, P., Klein, J. L., & Hulsbergen, E. (2008). *The challenge of social innovation in urban revitalization*. Amsterdam: Techne Pr.

ENHR – European Network for Housing Research. (2011). *Mixitè: An urban and housing issue?* Proceedings of the XXIII Conference, Toulouse, July.

Ferri, G. (Ed.). (2017). *Starting up communities: A design kit for collaborative housing.* Milan-Turin: Bruno Mondadori-Pearson.

Ferri, G., & Pacucci, L. (2015). *Social housing. A handbook for designers*. Milan-Turin: Bruno Mondadori-Pearson.

Ferri, G., & Pedercini, C. (2016). *Il valore sociale degli interventi di housing sociale: il caso del Borgo Sostenibile di Figino* [The social value of social housing initiatives: The Figino Borgo Sostenibile case study]. Working paper, X edizione del Colloquio Scientifico sull'impresa sociale – Iris Network, Naples, 10–11 June.

Ferri, G., & Rizzica, C. (2016). *Social housing in Italy: New models in organizing a sociable way of living.* Working paper, ENHR 2016 conference, Belfast, 28 June to 1 July.

Ferri, G., Pacucci, L., & Pero, E. (2011). *Nuove forme dell'abitare sociale* [New forms of social housing]. Milan: Altreconomia.

ISTAT. (2012). *Censimento Popolazioni Abitazioni* [Population and housing census]. Rome: Author.

Manzini, E. (2015). *Design, when everybody designs: An introduction to design for social innovation.* London, Cambridge, MA: MIT Press.

Manzini, E. (2016). Collaborative housing comes of age: A manual to make the exception the norm. In G. Ferri (Ed.), *Starting up communities: A design kit for collaborative housing* (pp. 5–10). Milan-Turin: Bruno Mondadori-Pearson.

Minora, F., Mullins, D., & Jones, P. (2013). Governing for habitability: Self-organized communities in England and Italy. *International Journal of Cooperative Management*, 6(2), 33–45.

Monk, S., Whitehead, C., & Tang, C. (2013). *International review of land supply and planning systems*. York: Joseph Rowntree Foundation.

Müller, M., Niggli, D., Ruby, A., & Ruby, I. (Eds.). (2017). Together! On the renaissance of the collective in contemporary urban architecture. In *Together! The new architecture of collective* (pp. 37–42). Berlin: Ruby Press.

Mullins, D., Czischke, D., & Van Bortel, G. (2012). Exploring the meaning of hybridity and social enterprise in Housing organizations. *Housing Studies, 27*(4), 405–417.

Muñoz Gielen, D., & Burón Cuadrado, J. (2014). Experiences with public value capture across Europe. *Urbanistica, 154*, 147–150.

Needham, B., & De Kam, G. (2000). *Land for social housing.* Nijmegen/Hilversum: University of Nijmegen, AEDES.

Ostanel, E. (2017). *Spazi fuori dal comune* [Out of the ordinary spaces]. Milan: Franco Angeli.

Pawson, H., Lawson, J., & Milligan, V. (2011). *Social housing strategies, financing mechanisms and outcomes: an international review and update of key post – 2007 policy developments*. Report City Futures Research Centre, Sydney: Housing NSW.

Pittini, A., Ghekiere, L., Dijol, J., & Kiss, I. (2015). *The state of housing in the EU 2015*. Brussels: Housing Europe.

Plebani, F. (2010). *Housing sociale, politiche abitative e fattore tempo* [Social housing, housing policy and the time factor]. Milan: Guerini e Associati.

Poggio, T., & Boreiko, D. (2017). Social housing in Italy: Old problems, older vices, and some new virtues? *Critical Housing Analysis*, *4*(1), 112–123.

Pogliani, L. (2014). Expanding inclusionary housing in Italy. *Journal of Housing and the Built Environment*, *29*(3), 473–488.

Pogliani, L. (2016). *A new frame for social housing in Italy*. Working paper, ENHR 2016 conference. Belfast, 28 June to 1 July.

Polizzi, E., & Vitale, T. (2017). Governo collaborativo e catene relazionali di innovazione. Spunti a partire dal caso di Milano [Collaborative governance and relational innovation chains. Cues from the Milan case]. *Quaderni di Rassegna Sindacale*, *18*(2), 129–147.

Rizzica, C. (2015). A fund for social housing. In G. Ferri & L. Pacucci (Eds.), *Social housing A handbook for designers* (pp. 158–164). Milan-Turin: Bruno Mondadori-Pearson.

Torri, R. (2006). Il rischio abitativo: riflessioni fra teoria e ricerca empirica [Housing risk: Reflections between theory and empirical research]. *Rivista delle Politiche Sociali*, *3* (monografico *Case difficili: Le politiche abitative fra dimensioni sociali e dilemmi dell'agenda pubblica*), 79–98.

UrbaMonde. (2017). European Collaborative Housing Award 2017. *Urbamonde*. Retrieved from www.urbamonde.org/en/european-collaborative-housing-award-2017.

Van der Krabben, E., & Jacobs, H. M. (2013). Public land development as a strategic tool for redevelopment: Reflections on the Dutch experience. *Land Use Policy*, *30*, 774–783.

Venturi, P., & Zandonai, F. (2016). *Imprese ibride: Modelli di innovazione sociale per rigenerare valore* [Hybrid enterprises: Social Innovation models to generate value]. Milan: Egea.

Vinci, I. (2017). La riarticolazione delle politiche abitative in Italia: processi, soggetti, forme di territorializzazione [Reorganizing housing policy in Italy: Processes, subjects, territorialisation forms]. *Territorio*, *80*, 123–131.

Zanfi, F. (2015). Afterword: Getting our hands into the flesh of the contemporary city. In G. Caramellino & F. Zanfi (Eds.), *Post-war middle-class housing: Models, construction and change* (pp. 369–383). Bern: Peter Lang,.

Zangheri, R., Galasso, G., & Castronovo, V. (1987). *Storia del movimento cooperativo in Italia 1886–1986* [History of cooperative movement in Italy 1886–1986]. Turin: Einaudi.

Part II

Co-production

5 Resident participation as innovative practice

Analysing involvement within the housing association sector – UK

Tony Manzi and Charles Glover-Short

Introduction

One of the most significant innovations in contemporary, social housing practice has been the involvement of residents in decision-making processes. Across Europe, a range of initiatives has ensured a stronger resident voice in decision-making, influencing organisational strategies, and facilitating wider community empowerment (Pawson, Bright, Engberg, & Van Bortel, 2012). Participation can be defined as a "two-way process involving sharing of information and ideas, where tenants are able to influence decisions and take part in what is happening" (Cairncross, Clapham, & Goodlad, 1989, p. 19). Participation is now viewed as a policy priority in the UK, Denmark, Belgium, and the Netherlands (Pawson et al., 2012, p. 3). Whilst at times criticised as a symbolic, tokenistic response to resident dissatisfaction (McKee & Cooper, 2008), participation can play an important role in housing service delivery with residents no longer merely consulted by landlords, but closely involved as partners in establishing efficient and effective housing businesses.

The housing association sector (referring to voluntary or third sector housing organisations) in the UK has been viewed as slow to implement participation (Cooper & Hawtin, 1998, p. 11). However, since the late 1990s, it has been increasingly interested in implementing resident involvement practices, as it has assumed primary responsibility for new housing provisions and overtaken local authorities as the main provider of social housing (Pawson & Mullins, 2010). A range of initiatives has, therefore, been introduced to develop strategies for resident participation in order to demonstrate that residents are involved in decision-making processes, play an effective role in governance, and genuinely participate in wide-ranging topics (Wilson & Wilde, 2003). Moreover, recent studies have sought to demonstrate that participation is not only innovative in and of itself, but that it is possible to bring identifiable and measurable benefits. For example, research undertaken by Bliss, Lambert, Halfacre, Bell, and Mullins (2015) and Trotter, Vine, Leach and Fujiwara (2014) provides evidence of the economic value gained by organisations and residents alike from resident involvement activities.

Based on a case study of a London housing association, this chapter examines how a programme of change, which attempted to give priority to resident involvement, affected wider organisational performance. The case study provides an important illustration of how changes in governance and management, designed to introduce wide-scale resident participation, resulted in service efficiencies, performance improvements, and changes to working practices (see Manzi, Simpson, Bailey, & Glover-Short, 2016). Whilst the discussion focuses on a housing association based in England, the case study is indicative of the ways in which innovations in governance can facilitate improvements in performance and influence organisational change, illustrating how housing organisations across Europe can learn from the experience of involving residents in the decision-making process.

The institutional underpinnings of housing associations

According to Scott (2014), institutions can be classified according to three underpinning principles or pillars – comprising regulative, normative, and cultural elements. Each of these principles will have a variety of manifestations. Hence, the regulative dimension relies on rule-setting, monitoring, and sanctioning activities where the primary mechanism of control is coercion. In contrast, the normative pillar underlines the importance of a prescriptive, evaluative, and obligatory dimension, which includes preferable or desirable values and norms. The final pillar involves a cultural or cognitive dimension to consider social relations and their role in creating meaning, emphasising how processes are shaped by taken for granted understandings. However, it is important to note that these institutional pillars are mutable. As Scott (2014, p. 62) acknowledges, "Institutions supported by one pillar may as time passes and circumstances change, be sustained by different pillars." Table 5.1 indicates

Table 5.1 The three pillars of institutions

	Regulative	*Normative*	*Cultural*
Basis of compliance	Expedience	Social obligation	Taken for granted, shared understandings
Basis of order	Regulative rules (central government)	Binding expectations, good practice (board, professional institutions)	Constitutive schema (colleagues)
Indicators	Rules, laws, sanctions (legislation, threat of regulatory supervision)	Certification, accreditation (awards, performance indicators, financial stability)	Common beliefs, shared action (resident/staff satisfaction, peer group pressure)
Basis of legitimacy	Legally sanctioned	Morally governed	Comprehensible, recognisable, culturally supported

Source: adapted from Scott (2008).

the different facets of these institutional pillars and considers their application to housing associations. The empirical discussion below illustrates how they have underpinned the practice of participation within the sector.

Within housing policy, a mixed economy of service provision has produced hybrid organisations, which possess significant characteristics of more than one sector (Billis, 2010, p. 3). This hybridity has helped to transform identities and rationales within the housing sector (Mullins, Czischke, & Van Bortel, 2012); with organisations operating in a sphere between state, market, and civil society and subject to competing commercial and social influences (Muir & Mullins, 2015). The resulting challenges situate voluntary housing organisations in a "balancing act" (Blessing, 2012, p. 205) as they pursue what can often be incompatible sets of rules including the need to ensure local accountability, to access private finance, to reassure regulators, and to engage with residents.

At the same time, these tensions can also be seen as strengths. Housing associations have been described as using "chameleon-like activity" (Blessing, 2012), involving flexible goals through the idea of social enterprise (Czischke, Gruis, & Mullins, 2012) – avoiding undue dependency on public subsidy, whilst harnessing an ability to access private financial markets (Mullins & Murie, 2006). As an example, the National Housing Federation (NHF, 2016, p. 1) has stated that for every £1 invested by the government, housing associations invest another £6 from their own resources in order to build new homes. Organisational practices, therefore, involve an inevitable compromise between multiple norms (Blessing, 2012, p. 203) including the competing demands of private sector business management, civil society linkages, and public sector accountability. These pressures have presented significant challenges to voluntary sector housing organisations. For writers, such as Mullins (2006b), the core competing demands have been between the concepts of *scale and efficiency* and *local accountability*. In recent years, however, the growth and prevalence of neoliberalism within housing policy (Hodkinson, Watt, & Mooney, 2013) has, as with other policy fields, led to a private sector orientation assuming primary significance. This is supported by a regulatory agenda, which has emphasised sound financial management as the key, if not sole, criterion for success. This business relationship has assumed paramount importance in determining organisational processes and asset management strategies (Morrison, 2013), often at the expense of a social purpose, which has traditionally underpinned housing association activities. The next section considers how these processes have affected resident participation within the housing association sector.

Context: housing associations and resident participation

Following the Localism Act 2011 in the UK, tenant scrutiny was seen as an important tool in tackling a range of issues within housing management and development (Homes and Communities Agency [HCA], 2012). Co-regulation was developed as a response to this emerging agenda, referring to a process whereby residents would be fully involved in all areas of organisational decision-making (HCA, 2012). A number of claims have been made for the benefit of tenant scrutiny, such as how it can result in improved services and increased accountability (Chartered Institute of Housing [CIH], 2014). In addition, increased tenant scrutiny claims to: deliver services tailored towards resident requirements, reflecting local needs and priorities; offer better value for money and more effective targeting of resources; improve customer satisfaction; improve organisational performance (see Tenant Participation Advisory Service (TPAS)/HouseMark/CIH, undated, p. 7); remove the need for expensive external consultants; improve relationships between residents and staff; improve staff confidence; and secure wider public benefit (Centre for Public Scrutiny [CfPS], 2012, pp. 8–9).

However, there is little hard data available on the extent to which resident involvement cannot only improve satisfaction, but also promote value for money and service improvement as well. At a time when housing organisations have been placed under significant financial pressures, particularly since the global financial crisis of 2008, they are under an obligation to prioritise efficiency savings, as stated explicitly in the 2017 Housing White Paper (Department of Communities and Local Government [DCLG], 2017) and participation might, therefore, be considered an expensive luxury for organisations. For example, some have argued that resident participation is outdated and has failed residents, as they will only be interested in engaging with decision-making about local level issues (Family Mosaic, 2016).

In an attempt to provide a more robust case for the benefits of participation, a number of UK studies have attempted to quantify the value of involvement – for example Trotter et al. (2014) used a measure of social return on investment to provide an average figure for the benefits that can be achieved; Bliss et al. (2015) estimated the financial savings (calculated at £29 per property) that participation offers social housing organisations, in addition to social and community benefits. Others have stressed the benefits that residents can gain from their own participation, such as through training programmes, increased self-confidence, and developing skills such as public speaking (Channon, 2015, p. 8). However, to date, there has been little detailed analysis of the benefits of participation for housing organisations. The following sections, therefore, adopt a case study method to consider: the extent to which value for money savings can be identified from involving residents in decision-making; how far resident participation can lead to management innovation; and the extent to which participation can be embedded within an organisational culture.

Research methods

This study, conducted in 2015, utilised a case study approach to provide an in-depth analysis of an organisation called AmicusHorizon (now called Optivo). This was an organisation which had been transformed from failure to high performance over a relatively short period of time. A significant factor in this transformation was the incorporation of resident participation into the organisation's governance structure and the study analysed how this approach had affected the overall business. The material collected involved a detailed analysis of quantitative and qualitative data, including resident satisfaction surveys and data on complaints and customer contact. Detailed, semi-structured interviews were conducted with stakeholders, including three focus groups with resident representatives involving 18 residents in total and non-participant observation of three resident participation meetings. Face-to-face interviews were conducted with board members and core members of senior and lower level staff involving a total of 15 participants. The board member and staff interviews were designed to analyse how resident participation affected business processes. Questions focused on the extent to which involvement processes had facilitated organisational effectiveness, how far participation had changed the organisational culture, including relationships between residents, staff, and board members, and the extent to which service efficiencies could be identified.

Residents and board members were selected to encompass a range of roles within the organisation to provide contrasting perspectives on the governance structure and to determine how far involvement resulted in innovative practice. Additionally, interviews were conducted with external stakeholders, including TPAS, the NHF, the Department for Communities and Local Government, and local authority partners. By taking an approach which included detailed case study analysis based on a range of qualitative and quantitative data and evaluating findings in conjunction with wider analysis of how participation was affecting housing associations, the findings can provide important insights into the way in which organisations incorporate participation into existing practices and its impact upon organisational behaviour.

The case study organisation

With assets of £1.4 billion, almost 28,000 homes in management, an annual turnover of £171 million and reserves totalling £56 million, AmicusHorizon Ltd was a member of the group representing the largest housing associations in the London area (see AmicusHorizon, 2016). AmicusHorizon was formed in 2006 out of a merger between seven housing associations, but this amalgamation resulted in significant difficulties and in 2007 was placed under regulatory supervision by the Housing Corporation on the basis of failings in governance, service delivery, and a lack of engagement with residents. The Housing Corporation specified that a new board and executive team should be appointed, and AmicusHorizon Ltd was formed in 2009. Having been classified as a failing organisation and placed in regulatory supervision forced the organisation to institute wider governance and managerial changes. This failure presented an opportunity to implement a widespread programme of change with limited internal opposition, and the constraint of supervision, therefore, facilitated institutional reform.

A key principle of the new governance structure highlights how residents should be at the heart of organisational decision-making to ensure a strong, local profile and to improve performance. The structure comprised a strategic board, which included four resident members out of 12 positions, the highest proportion in the sector. This set an overall direction for the organisation. It also established a Residents' Council comprising 16 members whose role was to scrutinise service delivery and hold the board and executive accountable. A system of eight area panels, each including eight elected resident members and four independent members, was described as the cornerstone of resident governance. Arguably the most innovative feature was establishing linkages between the various groups with the Residents' Council, comprising two members from each Area Panel and with each non-resident board member assigned to an Area Panel. This ensured a horizontal and vertical flow of information so board members could have an in-depth understanding of local, as well as strategic, issues.

Additionally, residents volunteered to serve on a variety of panels and forums looking at the needs of specific services and groups. These included three repair and maintenance panels, one in each region, which met to discuss the performance of contractors and delivery of planned maintenance programmes. As with the Area Panels, residents served on interview panels when selecting new staff and could influence change and suggest improvements to service delivery.

This structure was underpinned by a sophisticated performance management system, allowing near-real-time performance monitoring, detailed breakdown of information at a regional level, and immediate access to survey comments. A further innovation was the intertwining of traditional, resident involvement with data collected through customer satisfaction surveys and CRM (customer relations management) software. The latter was used to make sure the various tiers of the Resident Governance Structure could make decisions based on a sound body of evidence. In order to analyse how these factors affected the organisation, this chapter focuses on three key areas, namely: *ensuring value for money*, *promoting innovation*, and *embedding participation*.

Ensuring value for money

The establishment of a Resident Procurement Panel was a key vehicle for delivering large savings through: identifying performance issues for existing contractors; ensuring that future contracts were neither over, nor under-specified; and drafting and evaluating tender specifications. The establishment of repairs and maintenance panels saw identified savings in the region of £2.4 million per annum as a result of renegotiating contracts following resident scrutiny of arrangements. Changes were estimated to provide savings of 30 per cent, factoring in both servicing and replacement, compared with previous providers. The role of residents in providing scrutiny of the process was seen as a key safeguard. As one manager commented, "If residents weren't involved in procurement, who would have been checking [who was] driving the agenda? Who would have been challenging … [or] doing things differently?"

Resident participation was a key element not only in identifying potential problems with contracts, but also in helping to highlight good practice, providing assurance where contracts were working well and improving satisfaction.

For example as one focus group respondent commented: 'You're actually getting voluntary people interested in value-for-money giving their honest opinion – and I think that really does make a massive difference' (Focus group respondent, 7 February 2015).

Resident scrutiny of working practices proved highly effective in identifying inefficiencies in maintenance arrangements with residents who served on repair and maintenance panels helping to produce contracts that created better quality and value for money. While some of these savings might have been identified by experienced professional staff in due course, given an effective procurement process, residents' insights played a crucial, direct role in changes that produced significant annual savings and quality improvements. Having those directly affected by decisions involved in determining the nature of repair and maintenance contracts offered a highly effective mechanism to highlight potential problems, to identify opportunities for cost savings, and to provide suggested improvements to working practices. This process was described as providing an essential "feedback loop" (Interview, chief executive, 30 January 2015) which enabled organisational learning, service improvement, and cost savings.

A further consequence of the regulative domain was to create new roles for residents. According to this view "our residents effectively have become our consultants" (Interview, senior manager, 9 January 2015). Hence "a group [of residents] that is well-resourced and sensible will often have far more impact and will do a lot of the work for you that staff were doing and free them up to do other stuff" (Interview, 9 January 2015, TPAS). As the Chief Executive commented, with resident participation "you are getting a better service, better value for money if you do more for yourself" (Interview, 16 February 2015). Residents were keen to remain as unpaid volunteers and were resistant to suggestions that they should be paid for their efforts, as "this would make us employees" and compromise their independence. The benefits of such arrangements were described in the following ways:

> There is an enormous power from having, as we have, 100 plus super-users or super-consumers out there on our estates, in our neighbourhoods, in our communities who can explain to their neighbours who are not involved why we are doing things the way we are.
>
> (Interview, 30 January 2015)

Nevertheless, when compared to other organisations the costs of participation were relatively high. Costs were calculated at a direct cost of £61 per property (reduced from £67 in the previous year). This is a significantly higher figure than those of competitor organisations where the median cost was £35 per property. However, these budgets are projected to decrease as resident involvement becomes more fully embedded into working practices and based on estimates that the social value of an engaged resident can be calculated at £8,116 (Trotter et al., 2014), 75 engaged residents would produce a wider social value of around £610,000.

Overall, savings generated from reductions in complaints and from changes to procurement practices, suggested by residents, were calculated at £2.7 million per annum. In addition, the organisation benefited from a lower level of staff turnover than other organisations and less staff sickness (see HouseMark, undated) partly due to a less antagonistic relationship with residents. As a cautious estimate, the study considered that one-quarter of the savings should be linked with resident engagement, representing annual savings of £29,000.

Ensuring innovative practice

AmicusHorizon launched an ambitious strategy in 2013 to be recognised as the best performing, large landlord in the UK by 2015/2016. Five Key Performance Indicators (KPIs), or "gold medals", were established to judge whether this objective had been achieved. The key indicators were in the areas of resident satisfaction, relet times, satisfaction with handling antisocial behaviour, satisfaction with repairs, and satisfaction with complaints handling. The gold medals were selected on the basis of analysis of customer contact data, previous survey results using key driver analysis, and reflecting local resident priorities agreed with the Residents' Council and board. Since four of the five KPIs were satisfaction measures, success rested on residents' experiences of service delivery. Staff were, therefore, compelled to design and deliver services tailored to residents' preferences. That in and of itself created an imperative to involve residents. In this way, resident involvement became key to organisational success. Table 5.2 shows changes in performance between 2010–2016, which indicate satisfaction levels that are the highest of their immediate peer group (i.e. other large housing associations) (HouseMark, undated).

Resident satisfaction with overall services in 2015/2016 was 98 per cent, compared with a peer group median of 77 per cent (HouseMark, undated). A perennial difficulty for residents and landlords was the mangement of anti-social behaviour, which frequently comprised a significant factor in resident dissatisfaction. AmicusHorizon's performance in this area had demonstrated substantial improvement, marking an increase from 83 to 98 per cent satisfaction. Residents contributed towards these performance improvements through in-depth involvement in the policy development process, specifying acceptable standards, and supplying feedback through transactional surveys. Poor survey scores were registered as expressions of dissatisfaction and logged in a system for the most appropriate team to resolve. The figure of 11.4 days relet time is also the lowest of the peer group (HouseMark, undated). Satisfaction with the repairs service of almost 99 per cent compares to a median figure of 71 per cent.

Following a review in 2009 AmicusHorizon saw a significant reduction in overall complaints. Residents helped re-design the complaint process to ensure that it became more focused on solutions. A Complaints Task Group comprising residents and staff overhauled policies and procedures in 2009/2010, which were approved by the Residents' Council and board the same year.

Table 5.2 AmicusHorizon levels of resident satisfaction and relet times, 2010–2016 (%)

	2010/2011	*2011/2012*	*2012/2013*	*2013/2014*	*2014/2015*	*2015/2016*
Overall landlord services	87.4	93.1	95.3	96.9	97.5	98.5
Tackling anti-social behaviour	82.9	92.1	93.4	94.9	96.5	98.2
Managing repairs	96.3	96.6	97.0	98.0	98.0	98.8
Dealing with complaints	69.6	92.5	94.7	94.3	95.2	97.3
Average relet times (days)	18.1	15.0	14.4	11.4	12.0	10.1

Source: AmicusHorizon, 2016.

Residents also served on panels to determine whether individual complaints should be upheld and influenced improvements to complaint procedures.

These changes resulted in a range of benefits, including savings in costs and staff time and improved relationships with residents. It was calculated that the reduction in complaints had generated annual savings of £181,000 comparing 2013/2014 to 2009/2010. These savings were achieved by attempting to resolve issues at first contact, reductions in staff time, and appointing residents as chairs of appeal panels. Involving residents not only reduced the costs of complaints dramatically, but also increased resident satisfaction with the complaints process to the highest of the relevant peer group. A total of 94 per cent of residents expressed satisfaction with complaints handled in 2013/2014, compared to a peer group median of 42 per cent.

Embedding participation

The experience of regulatory supervision provided an important, exogenous shock for the organisation with a newly appointed leadership team convinced of the merits of resident involvement. The task was, therefore, to convince staff and residents how results could be improved by investing in resident involvement. Organisational change for AmicusHorizon involved mutually agreed upon goals, as respondents commented that one of the biggest challenges had been overcoming historically low levels of trust and confidence. The establishment of one organisation from seven disparate housing associations meant that service delivery had been fragmented. The organisation was described as inward-facing, with discussions conducted between the parent company and its subsidiaries rather than between landlord and tenant. "The dialogue was in the wrong place" as the Chief Executive commented. The difficulty was expressed in the following terms:

> We had a huge job to build trust and in the first year the meetings were pretty tense, antagonistic, with lots of challenge and distrust. People were always looking for the ulterior motive. I think that residents felt that staff were self-serving rather than wanting what was right for residents.
>
> (Interview, 30 January 2015)

A central principle in the process of change was, therefore, to emphasise how the board, staff, and residents should operate as one team, working towards a common goal. This theme was repeatedly emphasised in interviews, with participation embedded "like a stick of rock" as one board member phrased it. These symbolic and ideational dimensions were claimed to have resulted in significant changes to formal and informal working practices: "Now if we see a problem emerge it is much easier to deal with it. There is now a common language … and it gives you a framework to fall back on if you are dealing with difficult topics" (Interview, senior manager, 30 January 2015).

Residents, staff, and board members undergoing identical training programmes was an important element in creating a common frame of meaning.

The decision to allocate board members to Area Panels was seen as a key change to working practices as well. Whilst, initially, many residents felt intimidated and lacked confidence in speaking to the board, "now residents are really confident contributors and even coming into the room, it isn't always obvious who is an independent Board member, who is a resident and who is a staff member" (Interview, senior manager, 30 January 2015). Resident meetings were described as more productive, less antagonistic, and more rewarding than previously, when respondents characterised the relationship following the merger as mistrustful, acrimonious, and conflict-ridden.

As mentioned earlier, a pervasive cynicism has often characterised resident involvement initiatives in the housing sector (Cooper & Hawtin, 1998), and the organisation attempted to counter this by emphasising how residents also had a vested interest in improving service delivery. As an independent board member commented "because residents want you to succeed [they] are going to come up with ideas, which will work" (Interview, 16 February 2015). A board member summarised how this culture benefited the organisation:

> If all you did was send questionnaires … you would get some information, but you're not going to get the full picture. This is consultancy … the more you coach and train them, the better they are at it. They can tell you what's not working, they can shape how to do it better, but really importantly they will tell you what matters to them.
>
> (Interview, 16 February 2015)

Informal working relationships were an important factor in embedding this culture of participation. The organisation was able to engage large numbers of residents in participation activities because residents felt their contributions were meaningful and could ultimately influence strategic decision-making. This level of influence meant many of the traditional problems in generating interest in involvement, such as apathy and low levels of interest, could be avoided. The response from one manager outlined how this approach had been successful:

> There is an endless problem in the wider sector with retention and recruitment and with burnout. We don't seem to have had those kinds of issues here. I think it might be that residents are able to see something come from [their participation].
>
> (Interview, 26 January 2015)

Similarly, from a resident perspective, one focus group participant commented, "When you see all these residents sitting here voluntarily, [you think] would *you* do that unless you were convinced that it was actually working and worth doing?" (Focus group respondent, 30 January 2015). Residents, therefore, saw themselves, and were seen by others, as a valued asset, whether through their involvement in mystery shopping, estate inspections, or as part of the formal governance process. Building a wider consensus for change was, nevertheless, seen as a difficult process. Residents pointed out that involvement by itself was not sufficient to bring about improvement and was highly dependent upon a reciprocal relationship:

> I think it's very important that we understand that it's not just residents who do this. The staff has to have the "One Team" approach and have to believe in what we do, and also we have to believe in what they do for it to work. If we didn't work together the way we do, then it wouldn't work.
>
> (Focus group respondent, 4 February 2015)

For the organisation, the benefit of this approach included how change was no longer viewed as a threat; the approach to resident engagement was described as "a relationship that drives success" (board member). As an independent observer commented of the organisation, resident involvement "is absolutely in their DNA" (Interview, 5 February 2015).

The limitations of participation and the constraints of evaluation

The research demonstrated that participation had the potential to provide a range of benefits for housing organisations, including business efficiencies and innovations in governance At the same time, the staff was keen to stress that whilst there is resident influence, they are not entirely resident-led – "We are not a housing cooperative" as one respondent commented (Interview, 9 January 2015). The limitations of participation should, therefore, also be considered. For example, contentious decisions, such as rent increases, were ultimately made by the executive team and board rather than by residents alone.

A second limitation was to ensure that participation was seen as a permanent feature of organisational strategy rather than a temporary response to a crisis situation. The narrative presented by the organisation was compelling in so far as it represented dramatic improvement from failure. However, the model adopted was highly dependent on leadership and was primarily driven by a chief executive committed to the objective of resident participation. However, if and when the leadership of the organisation changed, to what extent could this momentum be sustained in the longer term?

Furthermore, it may be understandable that some organisations are reluctant to commit fully to participation in an environment where the risks of failure are high, where specialist expertise is lacking, and where the pressure on resources is intense. AmicusHorizon had higher unit management costs than similar organisations, and respondents expressed frustration at delays when making key decisions – "Business gets done, but it gets done over a long period of time" as one respondent suggested (Interview, 9 January 2015). Moreover, there had been initial resistance over time to a more resident-led governance structure, which involved replacing staff who were hostile to the notion of resident involvement (Interview, 4 February 2015). However, the overall consequence of the changes was described in the following terms:

> You may spend a couple of extra months getting your complaints process right, but you save a massive amount of staff time by having fewer complaints and by dealing with them in a more efficient way. Enlisting residents to help … makes very good business sense.
>
> (Interview, Chief Executive, 30 January 2015)

The limitations of evaluating participation also need to be acknowledged. As one resident participation officer commented, "I know that every resident personally derives an enormous amount of value from being involved – it is lovely but you may as well count smiles" (Interview, 9 January 2015). The limitations of quantitative evaluation were expressed in the following way:

> Whatever any organisation spends is a minute fraction of their overall costs – what you get at that level of investment is really considerable. [It is about] how much goodwill, enthusiasm engagement, and excitement you get around housing. How much value are you getting there? There is a lot of payback for very, very little.
>
> (Interview, 9 January 2015)

In a wider sense, the practice of participation within the housing association sector involves a wider set of questions. The practice of empowerment can in and of itself be seen as a "relation of power and mode of subjection that endeavours to direct human conduct towards particular ends" (McKee & Cooper, 2008, p. 144). These ends are primarily designed to incorporate tenants as active citizens (Flint, 2004; McKee, 2009) with residents ultimately co-opted as surrogate managers in citizen governance. The notion that residents should act as unpaid consultants was indicative of this perspective. Similarly, Cooper and Hawtin (1998) have seen tenant participation as reinforcing and perpetuating structural inequalities and social exclusion (p. 15).

Given these more critical perspectives, it is important not to overstate the claims made on behalf of resident empowerment. Nevertheless, Pawson and Smith (2009) see new organisational forms through a process of stock transfer as having changed organisational cultures, enhanced resident influence, and led to at least partial empowerment. As McKee and Cooper (2008) have argued, participation embraces both regulatory and liberatory possibilities and, as respondents suggested, much of the value of participation can be gauged by the social benefits to residents, such as greater trust, self-confidence, and sense of belonging. Such findings are supported in Channon's (2015) analysis of how residents can benefit from participation and endorse Bradley's (2014) contention that participation has the "potential to be revelatory and transformative" (p. 55). However, the shift towards a managerial model of participation, which limits discussions of power, implies that much of the wider potential of involvement can become lost.

As mentioned earlier, Trotter et al. (2014) were able to quantify a social return on investment. However, the indicators selected fail to capture the unquantifiable benefits, which were strongly emphasised in the case study research. The emphasis on financial performance of the sector carried most influence with government regulators and it was primarily narrow indicators of social value that could provide the necessary impact for housing providers to take the idea of resident involvement seriously. The softer features of participation, therefore, tended to be overlooked in favour of harder, quantitative financial indicators. This valorisation of efficiency reflected the dominance of a wider commercial imperative within the contemporary housing association sector, indicating the primacy of market-based economic models.

Conclusions

The case study illustrated how resident participation can result in value for money, management innovation, and a changed organisational culture. The case study, therefore, supplements the evidence of earlier claims made for the organisational benefits of participation (see Bliss et al., 2015), such as providing what was described as a permanent feedback loop from residents to landlords. This level of feedback offered a thorough analysis of policies to ensure they met resident needs, removing the need to employ expensive external consultants, and improving relationships between residents and staff (CfPS, 2012, pp. 8–9).

To what extent can these conclusions be applied to the sector more widely? Whilst the research was limited to one organisation, other studies have shown how a culture of participation has become embedded within European, third sector housing organisations (Pawson et al., 2012). The example of Amicus-Horizon provided an interesting contrast to the scepticism about the wider value of participation, within an environment largely determined by resource pressures. Nevertheless, the research provides some evidence that it may take radical, external shocks to ensure that cultural change can be firmly established. For most organisations, a disproportionate emphasis on financial stability, value for money, and cost savings is likely to mean that certain objectives, such as empowerment or accountability, remained marginal aims. The exception to this rule was in cases where evidence could be provided that participation would definitively lead to long-term financial savings. A measure of caution may, therefore, be needed when discussing the scope of wider participation at a time of austerity, when the terrain for social housing is ultimately hostile, and when acknowledging the limits of over-reliance on quantitative indicators of value. At the same time, the findings from the above study indicate some of the ways in which organisational engagement in resident involvement can assist innovative housing organisations. Given the wider interest in demonstrating value for money within the public and voluntary sector, the findings will have a broader international relevance and highlight a need for further comparative study to identify how the approach taken in the case study organisation might be applied to the wider organisational field.

Acknowledgement

This work was supported by an initial grant from the Department of Communities and Local Government and AmicusHorizon Ltd.

References

AmicusHorizon Ltd. (2016). *Financial statements, 2015–16*. London: AmicusHorizon Ltd. Retrieved from www.amicushorizon.org.uk/AmicusHorizon/media/AMHMediaLibrary/Files/PDFs/Leaflets%20and%20Publications/Financial%20Statements/financial-statement-2015-2016.pdf.

Billis, D. (2010). From welfare bureaucracies to welfare hybrids. In D. Billis (Ed.), *Hybrid organisations and the third sector: Challenges for practice, theory and policy* (pp. 3–24). Basingstoke: Palgrave Macmillan.

Blessing, A. (2012). Magical or monstrous? Hybridity in social housing governance. *Housing Studies*, *27*(2), 189–207.

Bliss, N., Lambert, B., Halfacre, C., Bell, T., & Mullins, D. (2015). *An investment not a cost: The business benefits of tenant involvement*. DCLG/NTOs. Retrieved from http://nationaltenants.org/tenants-leading-change/.

Bradley, Q. (2014). *The tenants' movement: Resident involvement, community action and the contentious politics of housing*. London: Routledge.

Cairncross, L., Clapham, D., & Goodlad, R. (1989). *Tenant participation in housing management: Consumers and citizens*. Coventry: Institute of Housing/TPAS.

Centre for Public Scrutiny. (2012). *Developing tenant scrutiny and co-regulation in housing*. London: Author.

Channon, L. (2015). *Resident involvement: What's in it for tenants?* London: Housing Quality Network.

Chartered Institute of Housing. (2014). *New approaches to tenant scrutiny: Supporting organisations to pioneer new ways of working and review current and emerging practice*. Coventry: Chartered Institute of Housing. Retrieved from www.cih.org/resources/PDF/Policy%20free%20download%20pdfs/New%20approaches%20to%20tenant%20scrutiny.pdf.

Cooper, C., & Hawtin, M. (1998). Understanding resident involvement: Turning theory into practice. In C. Cooper and M. Hawtin (Eds.), *Resident involvement and community action: Theory to practice* (pp. 323–337). Coventry: Chartered Institute of Housing.

Czischke, D., Gruis, V., & Mullins, D. (2012). Conceptualising social enterprise in housing organisations. *Housing Studies*, *27*(4), 418–437.

Department of Communities and Local Government. (2017). *Fixing our broken housing market*. Cm 9352. London: Author.

Family Mosaic. (2016). *Changing focus: A new model of resident involvement*. London: Author.

Flint, J. (2004). The responsible tenant and the politics of behaviour. *Housing Studies*, *19*, 893–909.

Hodkinson, S., Watt, P., & Mooney, G. (2013). Neoliberal housing policy: Time for a critical reappraisal. *Critical Social Policy*, *33*(1), 3–16.

Homes and Communities Agency. (2012). *The regulatory framework for social housing in England from 2012*. London: Author.

HouseMark. (undated). *AmicusHorizon: Interim report*. London: TPAS/CIH/HouseMark.

McKee, K. (2009). The responsible tenant and the problem of apathy. *Social Policy and Society*, *8*(1), 25–36.

McKee, K., & Cooper, V. (2008). The paradox of tenant empowerment: Regulatory and liberatory possibilities. *Housing, Theory and Society*, *25*(2), 132–146.

Manzi, T., Simpson, I., Bailey, N., & Glover-Short, C. (2016). *Success, satisfaction and scrutiny: The business benefits of involving residents*. London: AmicusHorizon Ltd.

Morrison, N. (2013). Meeting the decent homes standard: London housing association's asset management strategies. *Urban Studies*, *50*(12), 2569–2587.

Muir, J., & Mullins, D. (2015). The governance of mandated partnerships: The case of social housing procurement. *Housing Studies*. Retrieved from http://dx.doi.org/10.1080/02673037.2014.995070.

Mullins, D. (2006a). Exploring change in the housing association sector in England using the Delhi method. *Housing Studies*, *21*(2), 227–251.

Mullins, D. (2006b). Competing institutional logics? Local accountability and scale and efficiency in an expanding non-profit housing sector. *Public Policy and Administration*, *21*(3), 6–24.

Mullins, D., & Murie, A. (2006). *Housing policy in the UK*. Basingstoke: Palgrave Macmillan.

Mullins, D., & Pawson, H. (2010). Housing associations: Agents of policy or profits in disguise? In D. Billis (Ed.), *Hybrid organisations and the third sector: Challenges for practice, theory and policy* (pp. 197–218). Basingstoke: Palgrave Macmillan.

Mullins, D., Czischke, D., & Van Bortel, G. (2012). Exploring the meaning of hybridity and social enterprise in housing organisations. *Housing Studies*, *27*(4), 405–417.

National Housing Federation. (2016) *Submission: Autumn Statement, 2016*. London: Author.

Pawson, H., & Mullins, D. (2010). *After council housing: Britain's new social landlords*. Basingstoke: Palgrave Macmillan.

Pawson, H., & Smith, R. (2009). Second generation stock transfer in Britain: Impacts on social housing governance and organisational culture. *European Journal of Housing Policy*, 9(4), 411–433.

Pawson, H., Bright, J., Engberg, L., Van Bortel, G., with McCormack, L. & Sosenko, F. (2012). *Resident involvement in the UK and Europe*. London: Hyde Housing.

Scott, W. (2014). *Institutions and organisations: Ideas, interests and identities*. London: Sage.

Tenant Participation Advisory Service/HouseMark/Chartered Institute of Housing. (undated). *Tenant scrutiny now and in the future*. TPAS/HouseMark/CIH. Retrieved from www.HouseMark.co.uk/hmresour.nsf/lookup/TenantScrutiny_lowres.pdf/$File/TenantScrutiny_lowres.pdf.

Trotter, L., Vine, J., Leach, M., & Fujiwara, D. (2014). *Measuring the social impact of community investment: A guide to using the wellbeing valuation approach*. London: HACT.

Wilson, M., & Wilde, P. (2003). *Benchmarking community participation: Developing and implementing the active partners benchmarks*. York: Joseph Rowntree Foundation.

6 Against the stream

How a small company builds affordable housing – Sweden

Stig Westerdahl

Introduction

The current housing crisis in Sweden challenges its common perception as a welfare state, where the provision of housing for the entire population is taken for granted. The shortage of affordable rental housing for low-income groups is especially problematic. More affluent groups can instead benefit from the lack of housing, when they sell their apartments and villas and prices have increased (Christophers, 2013). To provide some background to this new experience and how it contrasts with the welfare tradition, this chapter discusses current problems with affordable housing in Sweden, while the Trianon case in Malmö illustrates how opportunities emerge for other actors when historically strong institutions fail to meet the demands of disadvantaged groups.

The Swedish housing system is seen as a classic example of a "universal housing" (Fitzpatrick & Stephens, 2014; Kemeny, 2006), whereby policies do not target a particular segment of the population and are not based on means testing. Social housing has thus never existed as tenure, and is still viewed as controversial in political debate. It is seen as stigmatising and in conflict with general Swedish welfare policies, drawing on universal principles to imply that housing policies should apply to the whole population and not only target disadvantaged groups. This universal emphasis is rooted in Swedish housing policy dating back to the 1930s and still influences the housing situation today. However, the system with these historical roots is under severe pressure (Grander, 2017), as we will also discuss in this chapter.

It is important to consider Sweden's welfare ambitions after the Second World War to understand the universal housing system. The first component was the integrated housing market, creating a strong link between public and private sectors. Second, the ambition to create neutrality between different forms of tenure such as rental housing and home ownership and, third, how rent has been determined through collective negotiations with the traditionally strong Swedish Union of Tenants. Two forms of tenure have been especially important in creating the current housing stock: municipal housing companies and co-op housing societies. When the public housing companies emerged in the 1940s, they sought to protect against housing speculation and to merge housing markets with municipalities and their representatives (Bengtsson, 1995). The aim of these post-war policies was to give local politicians more control over housing conditions using specific market measures. The Municipal Housing Company was tasked with providing homes for the population, supplementing private landlords and working on equal terms with them on the housing market. Co-op housing societies with close links to the labour movement had similar goals, both in the beginning of the 1920s and later on with their expansion after the Second World War (Sørvoll & Bengtsson, 2016).

These two forms of housing provision and how they have developed in the second half of the twentieth century significantly influenced the current housing situation. This chapter also describes how a private real estate firm has identified opportunities in response to this. Trianon is a small company based in Malmö, and demonstrates a new approach to provide affordable housing in Sweden. How their model can help us better understand the current affordable housing situation in Sweden will be discussed in this chapter. We will also explore Trianon's latest developments as well as the advantages and risks of replacing municipal companies and co-op housing societies with private, for-profit initiatives to address today's housing needs. The chapter begins with a brief history of the Swedish housing system, followed by an overview of where the housing project has been built and the role of Trianon in this endeavour. It concludes with the concrete efforts that have been taken in the cooperation between this company and Malmö municipality and how these actions may affect housing policies in Sweden and beyond, placing the findings in a larger context and discussing lessons for other countries.

The chapter is based on newspaper articles and other documents disclosing the events both in Lindängen (the area where the construction has taken place) and with Trianon, a company that has grown substantially over the period described in this chapter. The more detailed information on Trianon and the work of the company is supported by a recorded interview with CEO Olof Andersson (1 March 2016), which was followed by informal (not recorded) discussions with company representatives.

Historical background

Both the rentals provided by municipal housing companies and the co-op housing societies have their origins in Swedish welfare ambitions, as reflected in the term *Folkhemmet* ("people's home") initiated by the Social Democracy in the 1930s, as well as in the shared ideal to include all segments of the population and provide housing to low-income groups. Today, public housing rental and co-op housing are two different forms of tenure with separate trajectories when adapting to a more market-oriented approach, something shown in the following.

Municipal housing companies

The emergence of Swedish public housing can be traced back to the 1930s. Industrialization led to rapid urbanization and an inadequate supply of housing to accommodate this influx. Public housing companies (also referred to as municipal housing companies) were established to provide affordable housing for the entire population. *Allmännyttan* ("for everyone's benefit") is an umbrella term for the housing sector, which contrasts with social housing based on means-testing as found in many other European countries. The public housing sector was integrated into the Swedish welfare state after the Second World War (Elander, 1991). Housing was once again in short supply during the 1960s and 1970s, due to the success of Swedish industry and its expanding workforce.

Public housing companies became a major player in the Million Homes programme, an unprecedented effort to provide affordable housing. Ironically, when this project was finalized in the mid 1970s and one million homes had been built, the industrial crisis began. Employment in shipyards, textile companies, paper mills and manufacturing industries declined, and some of their operations were moved to other countries. This resulted in vacant buildings and economic problems for many housing companies, especially in industrial areas (Turner & Whitehead, 2002).

Another important component in the history of Swedish municipal housing is Sweden's entry into the EU in 1995 (Elsinga & Lind, 2013). Before the status of Swedish public housing formally became a legal case, a national compromise was reached whereby the rental negotiation system changed and municipal housing companies lost their rent-leading position. Legislation in 2011 required companies to follow "business-like principles", resulting in municipal owners being given special directives like having to declare their companies' expected profit. This is in contrast to other municipal, non-housing companies that are managed along cost-based principles. According to the law on Swedish municipalities (SOU Prop. 2009/10: 185), municipalities are not allowed to manage companies with a profit motive. Energy companies are the only exception to this rule besides the municipal housing companies.

The current situation for public housing companies can thus be seen as a consequence both of the changes of the 1990s and legislation introduced in 2011. The shift towards market-based policies, introduced in the 1990s by the conservative government, was never altered by the subsequent social democratic governments (Hedin, Clark, Lundholm, & Malmberg, 2012). However, since then all the public housing companies have become increasingly business-oriented (Grundström & Molina, 2016). This is evident in the type of new projects being built and the lack of interest in constructing low-cost apartments (Salonen, 2015). Some municipalities have sold all or parts of their holdings since the 1990s and onwards. The most profound changes have taken place in Stockholm. The proportion of public rental flats in the city has shrunk from 32 per cent of all residents in 1990 to 18 per cent in 2010. In the inner city, the change has been even more dramatic – from 19 per cent to 7 per cent. This can be mainly explained by the conversion of rental flats in public housing companies to co-op tenure (Andersson & Turner, 2014) decided by municipal politicians. These conversions also point to the changing role for co-op housing societies, which form the other historical pillar in the history of Swedish housing.

Co-op housing societies

While the co-op housing sector in Sweden originated in the 1870s, its breakthrough came in the 1920s, slightly before the emergence of municipal housing companies (Sørvoll & Bengtsson, 2016). The co-op tenure in Sweden is an indirect housing system (Ruonavaara, 2005) where a local building society owns the apartments. Such tenure between owner occupation and renting takes many different forms internationally, and as these national versions diverge in many respects, Ruonavaara (2005) claims that comparing various tenures between countries is complex. A feature in the Swedish co-op housing system was that membership in a co-op housing society should be the result of a savings scheme, where the connection between savings and housing societies formed an important role. Future tenants could save part of their income to finance the down payment. This is why national organizations for co-op housing initially started ambitious savings schemes, which now form only a marginal part of their operations.

In regard to the law, a tenant who belongs to a building society is entitled to an apartment and a proportion of the society's assets. This implies not only the right to live in the apartment, but also a responsibility in maintaining and financially supporting the democratically organized society. Each society differs in size from a dozen members up to several thousand, and has a board to deliberate on major issues. A member does not *sell* the apartment, but can transfer the membership (at a market price), which gives the new owner the right to possess the apartment and participate in the decision-making process of the co-op.

The emergence of co-op housing societies in the 1920s was influenced by close links to the labour and tenants' movements. When more socially oriented housing policies were developed after 1945, the tenure was placed on par with municipal housing companies, emphasizing solidarity and a non-profit vision. However, price controls were abolished in 1968 after a long controversy within the two national umbrella organizations for co-op housing societies: HSB and Riksbyggen. In 1968, the co-op tenure resembled that of owner-occupied apartments and, since then, more affluent groups have been targeted (Sørvoll & Bengtsson, 2016).

The current state of the co-op tenure thus differs from its legacy. The original aim was to supply housing for larger parts of the population, especially vulnerable groups, fostering tenure based on solidarity and not the needs of individual members. The initial price controls, therefore, aimed to prevent speculation by residents or members at the expense of potential members who would suffer from higher acquisition prices.

According to Sørvoll and Bengtsson (2016), since the 1980s the co-op housing sector has expanded "through market-based appeal to consumers" (2016, p. 7). Furthermore, the boundary between organizations formed by labour and tenants' activists (HSB and Riksbyggen) in the 1920s and more recent co-op housing associations initiated by private builders has become increasingly blurred. The private Swedish Co-op Housing Centre acting on behalf of local co-op housing associations has grown quickly in the last few decades. This organization typically represents societies started by private contractors, further diminishing the affordable housing ideals rooted in the history of the co-op housing sector.

The conversion of public rental apartments to co-op societies reflects this development along with how new production has evolved. Public housing apartments in Stockholm have been converted to co-op tenure (Andersson & Turner, 2014), and private rental housing companies have sold buildings to these newly established cooperative societies. Moreover, many new developments in Sweden over the last few decades have been in this tenure and were built by large, private building companies. Upon completion, companies sell (or in legal terms, "transfer for a fee") these holdings to a co-op society, whose individual members then assume responsibility for maintenance and debt. This mirrors how co-op housing has increasingly become an attractive tenure for actors from other sectors. Self-ownership is incentivized with a 30 per cent tax reduction on interest rents for private owners – this includes co-op members. Tax benefits also apply to renovation projects. For example, the tax differences including the tax reduction for interest rates between a co-op and a rental apartment with three rooms and a kitchen is estimated to be €250 per month, an amount agreed upon by the Swedish Union of Tenants, the Swedish Association of Public Housing Companies and Swedish Property Federation (Fastighetsägarföreningen, 2017).

Statistical data

The current affordable housing shortage in Sweden has been documented by several sources (Christophers, 2013; Grundström & Molina, 2016; Kalbro & Lind, 2017), and involves actors introduced in the previous section: policymakers, public housing companies, private builders and co-op societies. The challenges can also be understood with the help of statistics. Three aspects will be highlighted: (1) how the housing stock composition has changed since 1945 and altered the relationship between different tenures, (2) how the production of new housing over the last 20 years has evolved and (3) how housing production costs have become among the highest in Europe.

Table 6.1 illustrates how co-op apartments have grown in importance at the expense of both public and private rental housing. This development has increased from 1960 onwards. An increasing number of apartments are for sale on local housing markets, which are open to everyone.

Figure 6.1 shows the sharp decline in housing production after the domestic financial crises of the early 1990s. Housing production has recovered slightly

Table 6.1 Development of housing tenures Sweden, 1945–2011

Year	*Owned*	*Co-op*	*Public rental*	*Private rental*	*Total*
1945	38	4	6	52	100
1960	34	9	14	43	100
1970	34	13	23	30	100
1980	41	14	24	21	100
1990	40	15	25	20	100
2000	39	17	23	21	100
2005	39	17	22	21	100
2011	41	22	18	19	100

Source: Bengtsson, 2015.

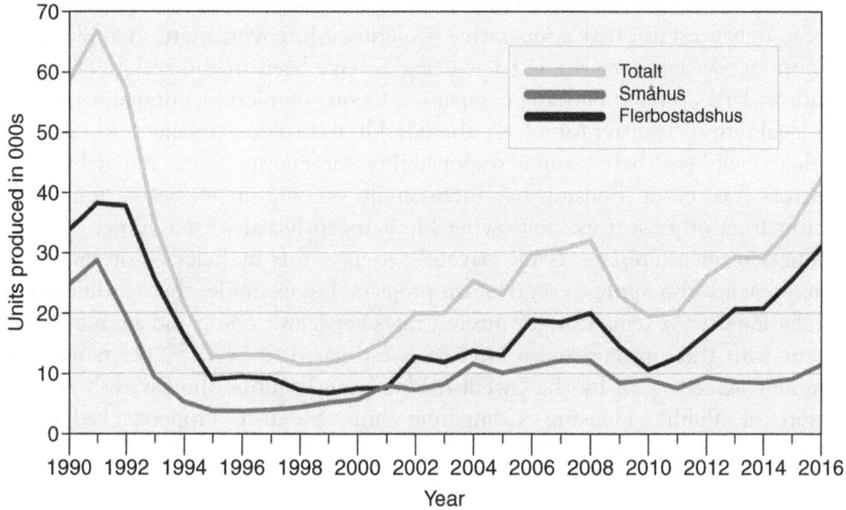

Figure 6.1 Total amount of housing produced in Sweden between 1990 and 2014.

Source: SCB, 2017a.

Note

The middle line represents the multi-family blocks built, the lower line represents detached family houses and the upper line delineates the total production.

over the past couple of years, currently reaching about 30,000 units per year. According to National Board of Housing, Building and Planning (Boverket, 2017), to reduce the shortage 80,000 new units are needed per year.

The increase of production mainly concerns an increase of multi-family units, including public and private rental housing as well as cooperative housing. The cooperative sector comprises both private producers and HSB/Riksbyggen that, as discussed earlier, have historically been connected to the co-op tenure. The sector is now dominated by private producers. From 2000, private companies built around 80 per cent of the new co-op housing (SCB, 2017b, statistics adapted by author).

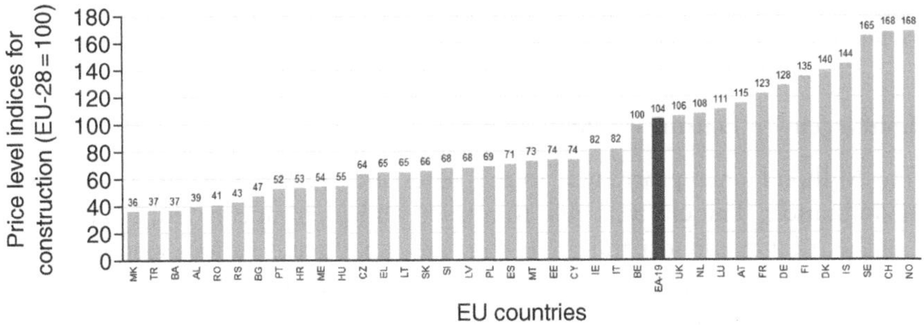

Figure 6.2 Price level indices for construction, 2014.

Source: Eurostat, 2017.

Another factor of importance for explaining the lack of affordable housing in Sweden is how production costs have increased faster than inflation, according to official sources (SCB, 2017c); these costs are now among the highest in the EU.

The causes of these high costs are much debated. Some voices in the discussion claim that strict regulations are making production more expensive, others argue instead that private constructors are making excessive profits. Regardless of these political differences, the high production costs in Sweden form part of the picture to explain the housing shortage and create additional difficulty for low-income groups.

Malmö and Lindängen

Malmö's industrial decline

Malmö is located in the south of Sweden and has 400,000 inhabitants, making it the country's third-largest city after Stockholm and Gothenburg. It has an industrial history, with textile, office machinery, building material and other factories dating back to the nineteenth century, along with a civilian shipyard employing roughly 5,000 workers that closed in 1987. The iconic Kockums Crane, visible throughout the city, was sold to South Korea and marked the end of Malmö's industrial era.

Due to these developments the city's population and employment decreased from the 1970s onwards (Billing & Stigendal, 1994). This industrial growth and decline underlies the current housing issues in Malmö and across Sweden. After Malmö's decline as an industrial centre, the city shifted its focus to becoming an intellectual hub or a "Knowledge town" (Dannestam, 2009). New upscale housing was built in desirable areas of the city, to attract high-income residents. Further developments included a university founded in 1998 and the Öresund bridge to Denmark (inaugurated in 2000), which facilitated commuting between the two countries (Holgersen, 2014). The IT industry has been a success, but at the same time, social polarization prevails (Salonen, 2012). The Lindängen neighbourhood provides an example of this.

Lindängen – a housing estate in Malmö

The Million Homes programme in the 1960s and 1970s was pivotal for Malmö's revitalization. The city was able to attract workers from Sweden, Finland and Southern Europe by expanding its shipyard, textile and various manufacturing industries (Bevelander, 2000). Several large residential areas in Malmö were built during this time, including Lindängen. These regions were easily reached – it took 15 minutes to cycle from Malmö's central station to Lindängen. The rental apartments constructed there were by then owned by the municipal housing company MKB, and completed in 1975. A co-op tenure was also built in this local application of the Million Homes programme. Co-op housing societies have historically held a strong position in Malmö's housing landscape, with close connections between private building companies and the local HSB co-op housing society (Billing & Stigendal, 1994). As a result, in 2015 public housing in Malmö made up 14 per cent of the housing sector compared to 17 per cent nationally, while co-op housing societies constitute 29 per cent of the total housing stock in Malmö compared to the national average of 22 per cent (SCB, 2017d).

The history of Lindängen

In 1985, ten years after the first inhabitants moved in, a right-wing municipal government was formed in Malmö and the MKB holdings were sold to private landlords (Karlsson, 2016). MKB suffered as a municipal company from financial problems and the political leadership felt that selling some of the holdings was necessary.

Lindängen was a suitable candidate as it had a large centre, two schools and a variety of services such as several crèches. In addition, the Motetten, a 16-storey residential building, was an impressive landmark. The idea behind the sale was to change the image of the area. Both the area itself and the connected reputation had been considered problematic since the 1980s, which prompted government projects to raise the quality of the schools and to combat segregation and poverty. The area currently has 6,500 inhabitants, more than 30 per cent of which are younger than 25. The population is increasing, and many apartments are overcrowded as a result of newly arrived refugees that are settling in Malmö. Many parents face a variety of socio-economic challenges, and their children have no quiet place to do their homework (Karlsson, 2016). The problems are mainly seen in the districts comprising rental housing, and less among the 40 per cent of the population living in co-op tenure.

A 2011 report shows that the percentage of inhabitants born outside Scandinavia is greater than average in Malmö (Karlsson, 2016). Many are refugees and migrants who have come to join their families. The inhabitants of the area generally also have a lower level of education compared to the average Malmö resident. Unemployment is higher in Malmö than the national average; few jobs are available, and many residents live on social benefits. In light of these conditions, for example, the municipality applied for EU social funds and municipal sources to improve the social situation. The application was approved, and €2.8 million were made available in 2012–2014 to target these problems. As a result, Trianon was able to conduct renovation and new housing projects in Lindängen.

Trianon

Trianon is a small real estate company based in Malmö that has focused on rental housing since 2006. It owns and manages 1,300 apartments, as well as some commercial properties, which together are valued at around €220 million. For the sake of comparison, the largest private rental company in Malmö, Stena, has 6,300 apartments in the city, and the municipal housing company MKB has more than 20,000 units. Trianon's business model is to focus on local markets, developing expertise in housing opportunities and challenges in Malmö and its surrounding regions and providing assurance when buying and selling property (O. Andersson, personal communication, 1 March 2016). In 2017, the company grew substantially after acquiring a large shopping complex in Malmö's centre. This purchase motivated the company to go public that same year; Trianon is now listed on the Stockholm Stock Exchange (Nasdaq First North).

Trianon's holdings in Lindängen are located in the area called Vårsången ("Spring Song"), and comprises 400 apartments from the Million Homes programme. Their involvement started in 2008 when Trianon took over management duties on behalf of the former owners, a Swedish private real estate company. After two years, Trianon was offered the chance to purchase the buildings at 750 €/m^2. The owners of Trianon considered this a reasonable price despite the urgent need to upgrade the buildings that were completed in 1975. While this was a large transaction for the company, it was within Trianon's financial limits and there was a considerable upside. Their financial strategy was to maintain 35 per cent solidity, however, as it was then a non-listed company with only private owners, equity was a significant concern. Trianon's growth was limited by its capacity to acquire capital within acceptable financial outcomes (O. Andersson, personal communication, 1 March 2016).

After the acquisition of existing buildings in Vårsången in 2010, the next challenge was to conduct renovations. The idea was to retain the existing residents, as Trianon regarded low-income groups in the various Million Home Programmes in and around Malmö as their primary customers and high turnover of tenants was costly. This meant that the renovations had to be carried out less expensively than other companies had managed to do, including public housing companies.

The process of determining rent levels is crucial for understanding how renovations influence the housing situation in Sweden. For decades, rents have been negotiated between property owners (often represented by their organization, the Swedish Property Federation) and the Swedish Union of Tenants. Rent-setting follows a use–value principle, as opposed to market assessments. To facilitate these negotiations, a special list is agreed upon by the two parties that identifies upgrades that justify higher rent. This means that property owners can raise fees substantially when they make substantial renovations, such as new kitchens and bathrooms. Trianon wanted to avoid this, even if it might have been profitable in the short term. This conviction was also accomplished by concentrating on improving energy efficiency and other urgent issues.

After the renovation, rents were raised from €700 to €760 per month for a three-room apartment, compared to increases between 30 and 40 per cent in many other cases (Salonen, 2015). Trianon estimates that conventional upgrades in line with the list would have led to an increase of €150 instead of €60 (O. Andersson, personal communication, 1 March 2016). Also, since Trianon bought homes in Vårsången, the yearly turnover rate has been reduced from 20 to 7 per cent (Trianon, 2016). According to the company, this was due in large part to the renovations, plans for new housing and new staff recruited among the tenants to work for Trianon.

A serious housing shortage in Sweden motivated Trianon in 2013 to transition from upgrading buildings to constructing new homes. This business initiative accompanied municipal measures in Lindängen to make the area more attractive both for existing and potential tenants and solve the social problems by creating new jobs. This was conducted through one (partly EU-funded) project addressing a lack of leisure facilities, labour-market and social issues, and contributing to housing construction and renovation projects. No new homes had been built in Lindängen in 30 years, and collaboration between builders, private property owners, who controlled most of the holdings in the area, and the municipality became a priority.

Trianon and the municipality discussed various socially minded projects in Lindängen and how renovations and new construction could be financed. Projects included homework support and summer jobs for schoolchildren, as well as employment positions for adults. Relationship building thus connected the company, the tenants and the municipality, which was instrumental in reaching agreements on renovation and new construction conditions. The municipality took a leading role, as politicians felt Lindängen had both significant concerns and considerable potential.

An important factor for deciding to build new apartments was when Trianon forecasted a demand for larger apartments. When the 400 apartments were built in the mid-1970s, the average home had three rooms. However, demand grew for an additional bedroom, which is why four-room apartments have become popular. The plan was to build mainly three- or four-room apartments, and only a few with two rooms. Trianon assumed that their current tenants wanted to move into a larger and more modern space, even if the rent was approximately €800 per month for a new apartment compared to €760 for those that were renovated.

The housing shortage in Malmö and the precarious social situation in Lindängen fuelled negotiations between Trianon and local officials. The municipality agreed to reduce the established ground rent by 90 per cent during the first year, and then reduce this rebate by 10 per cent each year until the official level was reached. Leases were usually signed for 100 years and can be sold or transferred. Owning land opens up new business possibilities, which is why the company preferred that option. Trianon promised to keep rents low and to employ ten people from the region in its construction efforts – they had already hired local tenants to assist in their daily management.

The company was contracted to build 156 apartments in four similar buildings – half of them with rental tenure and the rest co-op housing. The required tenures were crucial to the agreement, fulfilling aspirations to revitalize the image of Lindängen. The co-op flats were believed to attract more affluent residents and offer a housing career to existing rental tenants: to be able to move into a better apartment. However, the apartments were too expensive for their intended customers despite being less expensive than elsewhere in the city. When it proved impossible to sell the apartments in Lindängen, they were converted into rental flats – yet another indication that co-op housing has changed character since its introduction in Sweden.

The agreement between Malmö municipality and Trianon also included building a crèche for 100 children in Vårsången and a special site for laundry services. This type of agreement between the municipality and a property owner had never been reached before in Malmö, not even with the municipal housing company. The challenge ahead was to make the apartments attractive and affordable for their present tenants and other low-income groups. Trianon assumed that some of their existing tenants were willing to move from their current, slightly outdated apartments to newly constructed homes, provided that the rent was reasonable. This would in a following step make these empty apartments open for new tenants. Thanks to the even lower rents in the old flats, these were assumed to be attractive to people looking for affordable accommodation. However, another question was whether building companies would be willing to participate under these financial constraints.

As with the rest of Sweden, the contractors in Malmö were accustomed to building a totally different type of apartment. Their typical customers were high- to middle-income earners interested in co-op apartments in central locations. Such apartments were developed to cost between 3,500 and 4,000 €/m^2, while the range in the Vårsången project was around 1,900–2,000 €/m^2. Contractors initially said that this was impossible. However, some companies continued discussions as there was little construction work underway at this stage in 2013. Elements of the original design were modified to accommodate the desired development costs, such as scrapping or downgrading dishwashers, washing machines and tumble dryers. These features are mandatory in new co-op housing societies and are also found in more expensive rental projects, but are generally not found in apartments. Other cost-cutting measures included installing bathrooms as factory-made modules. Overall, the production was repetitive:

the apartments are identical in all four buildings, and no special requests were granted (O. Andersson, personal communication, 1 March 2016).

Another method to keep development costs in check (2,100 €/m^2) was to modify how the parking facilities were organized. According to the planning rules, Trianon would have been forced to build an underground garage at a cost of approximately 400 €/m^2. However, the company already had parking facilities available in an existing building and were thus able to avoid these costs. There was ample parking available on this property and the municipality therefore had no objections.

Most companies, including the public housing companies, usually demand higher yields in external locations and Million Homes programmes, compared to more desirable locations (Westerdahl, 2015). Yield is a ratio used by real estate firms to determine a return on investment and in this case applied to calculate whether the construction would be profitable. These requirements are usually set at 8–10 per cent in housing estates in external locations with a problematic reputation, resulting in higher rents compared to other regions. The yield for the Vårsången project was set at 5 per cent, making the profit calculation equivalent to buildings in more central locations and thus kept the rents down.

Trianon had no difficulty in setting its own yields for the investment. Most municipal housing companies, including MKB in Malmö, had a strict policy at that time. The 2011 law for these companies required "business principles" and this was interpreted by the companies as following the high yield levels determined by private valuation companies. Instead, Trianon took an independent position, believing it could adequately assess both the property values at hand and the risk level. Many public housing companies have since altered their position, lowering their yield levels and levelling them out across their holdings in a city.

Discussion: not a "not-for-profit" project

Trianon's investment in Vårsången is far from a philanthropic venture. This is reflected in its rental policies, whose conditions to obtain an apartment are stricter than the municipal company. Trianon does not consider social benefits as income, but MKB – the municipal housing company in Malmö – does. Another difference is that a suitable Trianon tenant must earn at least twice as much as the rent, while MKB only requires an income of at least 1.5 times the rent. The rationale for Trianon's stricter rental policy in this specific construction project was to attract a mix of tenants. This policy does not apply to all of Trianon's holdings.

Most of its existing tenants depend on social benefits, and the company felt that this was detrimental to Lindängen in general and especially Vårsången. Trianon offers employment to some of its own tenants to combat this, believing that a mixture of employed and social beneficiaries as tenants is preferable. None of the existing residents was affected by the stricter rental policy in the new buildings.

The role of public institutions is also important to understand the motives for Trianon, as its agreement with the municipality of Malmö was unlike any previous project. For example, the possibility of buying the land the buildings are erected on creates, as explained previously, opportunities for Trianon to construct more housing in the future.

It was agreed in negotiations between Trianon and contractors that building costs should be minimized. Trianon's overall aim was to increase the property value of its holdings in Lindängen – according to reports in 2015, its value had indeed increased by 41 per cent since 2013. This is important with respect to current accounting regulations. On the balance sheet, property assets are valued at their market value, not at the historic value it was acquired for minus any depreciation. This means that rising property values increases the total asset value, which will be reflected as greater profit on the Profit & Loss statement even if these are not sold (Westerdahl, 2015). This makes the company more creditworthy and attractive for investment. This is the result of several factors, among which is the strong demand for rental housing across Sweden as investors seek new opportunities. Another factor contributing to make this a good project for Trianon is that the original buildings were acquired at an attractive price. However, Trianon's annual financial report also suggests (albeit without substantiating the claim) that the increase of social capital in the area is contributing to growing property values (Trianon, 2016). The upgrades also result in lower management costs and improved energy efficiency. The hope is that the 156 new apartments that housed new tenants in 2017 will add further value to the company.

Conclusions

Trianon's work in Malmö confirms how social ambitions in Swedish housing policy have continually lessened over a long period. Changes in public housing companies have been ongoing since the early 1990s and the co-op housing sector attained a new character when price controls ceased in 1968. The joint outcome of changes in these two tenures is that the housing situation for poorer parts of the population can be described as a vacuum: an absence of governmental support, as well as a lack of interest from public housing companies, co-op societies and most of the private sector. Trianon has taken advantage of this vacuum by initiating the projects described here, and skilfully building relationships with the public sector. That being said, this conclusion aims to answer two questions: (1) what, if anything, was new in Trianon's approach, and (2) what are the advantages and concerns when a private, for-profit property company takes over responsibility for providing affordable housing – a task historically administered by public municipal housing companies or civil organizations in the co-op sphere? The implications for Europe and beyond follow from this second question.

To address the first question – Trianon is no pioneer, as Sweden's Million Homes programme has for a long period been of interest to private investors.

These companies typically attempted to save costs by keeping maintenance and customer interaction to a minimum with the hope of selling the holdings with a profit. Such short-term business models are rarely seen today, as Trianon, along with other companies, portrays itself as a sustainable and responsible property owner. In its goal to act locally, Trianon has been building relationships with its tenants and the municipality of Malmö. Most other companies currently operating Million Homes programmes also claim such commitment.

For Trianon, its mission is achieved by hiring staff from the area, offering homework assistance for schoolchildren and keeping rents low. This local focus helps when negotiating with officials in Malmö, as exemplified in the Vårsången case. The option to buy land instead of leasing it, may be the most remarkable part of the agreement with Malmö municipality, but other outcomes also indicate that they had positive relationships with the municipality. Examples include reduced parking requirements, gaining the right to construct a crèche and abolishing the co-op tenure when selling apartments proved difficult. Hiring local staff and using prefabricated components are not new in themselves, and neither is the idea to establish co-op housing in areas such as Lindängen. The innovation lies in how these elements were combined and systematically used to establish trust between Trianon and the municipality. This close interaction between public and private parties to create low-rent apartments is new in Sweden.

This can also be seen as a conscious strategy for Trianon; they later made similar property transactions with Malmö municipality in other problematic areas of the city. One such deal involved commercial shopping centres, where the municipality had promised to establish public operations by providing some of the rental income; a library and a crèche were about to be established in the premises of Trianon.

The favourable terms secured by Trianon can also be understood at the background of the situation for the municipal company, MKB. This public housing company has a large proportion of low-income tenants, a common pattern in the Million Homes programmes in Sweden where an increasing part of the inhabitants are poor and often migrants. This explains why MKB's new projects target more affluent customers, thus contributing to the general lack of affordable housing.

Concerning the potential innovation of providing affordable housing through private means, Trianon identified a vacuum, and due to close collaboration and relationship-building, was able to secure favourable terms for its initiative. The company has reported quick profits and increasing property values, and has announced a long-term plan with renovations and new production. This innovative approach consists of a combination of actions when first identifying a lack of affordable housing, on which Trianon has been able to capitalize.

The essence of the second question therefore focuses on the issue of whether this way of affordable housing is good or bad? The close links between local capital (Trianon) and the municipality might appear positive and in line with public–private partnerships. This positive impression is reinforced by knowledge that the interaction is intended to provide affordable housing. The expected tenants are families with two low-income workers typically employed in service sectors or public elderly care. Recently built rental apartments have rents that are too high for them, and co-op apartments require capital they neither possess nor can acquire through credit schemes. These families with two working parents are somewhere in between – those supported by social authorities (welfare recipients) on one side, and the middle class on the other side, which has become the main target group for most of the current housing production.

The main problem with a private approach is that local representatives gradually lose control of housing provision, much in the same way as national housing policies have vanished. The democratic control of housing policies is diminishing in a situation where affordable housing can only be accomplished through negotiations with real estate agencies.

Public authorities might be tempted to give more concessions financed by tax money in various forms to companies. As this Trianon case shows, such dependence on private initiatives can take various forms: options to purchase land while land rent has previously been the norm, gaining the right to build new housing, or agreements where the municipality rents premises for libraries or museums on a long-term basis, thus securing income for the private company. All of these agreements would be possible on the condition that private companies keep the actual production of affordable housing at an acceptable level.

Another risk is also clear: politicians have ownership of their own municipal housing company and are therefore likely to think long term, while new owners of a local property company could have interests that diverge from the present management. One can already see a difference between the Trianon that started the Lindängen project in 2012 and the current company structure. It was originally owned by three locals, although since 2017 the company has been listed on the Stockholm Stock Exchange, and has its sights on larger capital markets. Such expansion makes the company attractive for purchase, thus moving Malmö's affordable housing matters even farther away from local oversight.

Sweden has unique housing challenges due to its past and current policies, and the joint efforts by the city of Malmö and Trianon provide lessons for other countries in Europe and beyond. However, no partnership of this nature comes without problems, and the concessions made by the municipality demonstrate how resources and influence moved from the public to private sector. This reduces political oversight over housing something which is illustrated by the rental policy that Trianon implemented in its construction project, which was far stricter than that of the municipal housing company. Trianon required a higher minimum income and did not accept social beneficiaries as tenants, diminishing access for disadvantaged groups.

Trianon's growth since this project started may also have far-reaching implications for Swedish housing policies. The firm started as a small, locally owned company focused on one real estate market. It acquired more capital by going public, which financed its ensuing expansion as described in this chapter. Trianon's journey upward may not be finished; its property holdings may likely attract investment or purchase from a larger company. If this were to happen, what began as a simple desire to build affordable housing will have transformed into a new player in the international financial market. There remains much to be seen for affordable housing provision in Sweden.

References

Andersson, R., & Turner, L. M. (2014). Segregation, gentrification, and residualisation: From public housing to market-driven housing allocation in inner city Stockholm. *International Journal of Housing Policy*, *14*(1), 3–29.

Bengtsson, B. (1995). *Bostaden-välfärdsstatens marknadsvara* [The home: the commodity of the welfare State]. Dissertation. Uppsala: Acta Universitatis Upsaliensis.

Bengtsson, B. (2015). Allmännyttan och bostadspolitiken i går, i dag och i morgon: Institutionella förutsättningar i förändring [Public housing and housing policies yesterday, today and tomorrow: Changing institutional conditions]. In T. Salonen (Ed.), *Nyttan med allmännyttan* [The value of public housing] (pp. 25–45). Stockholm: Liber.

Bengtsson, B., Annaniassen, E., Jensen, L., Ruonavaara, H., & Sveinsson, J. R. (2013). *Varför så olika? Nordisk bostadspolitik i jämförande historiskt ljus* [Why so different? Nordic housing policies in a comparative historical light]. Malmö: Égalité.

Bevelander, P. (2000). *Immigrant employment integration and structural change in Sweden, 1970–1995*. (Vol. 15). Stockholm: Almqvist & Wiksell International.

Billing, P., & Stigendal, M. (1994). *Hegemonins decennier: Lärdomar från Malmö om den Svenska modellen* [The decades of hegemony: Lessons from Malmö on the Swedish model]. Dissertation. Lund: Lund University.

Boverket. (2017). *Beräkning av behovet av nya bostäder till 2025* [National Board of Housing, Building and Planning: Estimation of the need for new housing until 2025]. Report 2017:17. Karlskrona.

Christophers, B. (2013). A monstrous hybrid: The political economy of housing in early twenty-first century Sweden. *New Political Economy*, *18*(6), 885–911.

Dannestam, T. (2009). *Stadspolitik i Malmö: Politikens meningsskapande och materialitet* [Urban policies in Malmö: The meaning making and materiality of politics]. Dissertation. Lund: Statsvetenskapliga institutionen, Lunds universitet.

Elander, I. (1991). Good dwellings for all: The case of social rented housing in Sweden. *Housing Studies*, 6(1), 29–43.

Elsinga, M., & Lind, H. (2013). The effect of EU-legislation on rental systems in Sweden and the Netherlands. *Housing Studies*, *28*(7), 960–970.

Fitzpatrick, S., & Stephens, M. (2014). Welfare regimes, social values and homelessness: Comparing responses to marginalised groups in six European countries. *Housing Studies*, *29*(2), 215–234.

Grander, M. (2017). New public housing: A selective model disguised as universal? Implications of the market adaptation of Swedish public housing. *International Journal of Housing Policy*, *17*(3), 335–352.

Grundström, K., & Molina, I. (2016). From folkhem to lifestyle housing in Sweden: Segregation and urban form, 1930s–2010s. *International Journal of Housing Policy*, *16*(3), 316–336.

Hedin, K., Clark, E., Lundholm, E., & Malmberg, G. (2012). Neoliberalization of housing in Sweden: Gentrification, filtering, and social polarization. *Annals of the Association of American Geographers*, *102*(2), 443–463.

Holgersen, S. (2014). *The rise (and fall?) of post-industrial Malmö: Investigations of city-crisis dialectics*. Dissertation. Lund: Department of Human Geography, Lund University.

Kalbro, T., & Lind, H. (2017). *Bygg mer för fler! En ESO-rapport om staten, kommunen och bostadsbyggandet* [Increase new production of housing for more people: A governmental report on the state, the municipalities and the construction of housing]. Stockholm: Finansdepartementet, Regeringskansliet.

Karlsson, S. (2016). *Områdesbaserad politik – möjligheter till strukturell förändring: Lokalt utvecklingsarbete i marginaliserade bostadsområden i Malmö* [Area based politics – possibilities for structural change: Local development work in marginalized areas in Malmö]. Dissertation. Stockholm: Kungliga Tekniska högskolan.

Kemeny, J. (2006). Corporatism and housing regimes. *Housing, Theory and Society*, *23*(1), 1–18.

Ruonavaara, H. (2005). How divergent housing institutions evolve: A comparison of Swedish tenant co-operatives and Finnish shareholders' housing companies. *Housing, Theory and Society*, *22*(4), 213–236.

Salonen, T. (2012). *Befolkningsrörelser, försörjningsvillkor och bostadssegregation: En sociodynamisk analys av Malmö* [Movements of population, conditions for household provision and segregation of housing: A socio dynamic analysis of Malmö]. Malmö: Malmökommissionen, Malmö stad. Retrieved from http://malmo.se/download/18.d8bc6b31373089f7d9800059627/1491302726776/Det+dolda+Malm%C3%B6_Tapio+Salonen_Malm%C3%B6kommissionen_final.pdf.

Salonen, T. (Ed.). (2015). *Nyttan med allmännyttan* [The value of public housing] Stockholm: Liber. SOU 2017:725 (Swedish law on Municipalities)

Sørvoll, J., & Bengtsson, B. (2016). The pyrrhic victory of civil society housing? Co-operative housing in Sweden and Norway. *International Journal of Housing Policy*, *16*(1), 1–19.

SOU Prop. (2009/10: 185). *Allmännyttiga kommunala bostadsaktiebolag och reformerade hyressättningsregler* [Municipal public housing companies and reformed rules for rent setting]. Law proposal. Stockholm.

Turner, B., & Whitehead, C. M. (2002). Reducing housing subsidy: Swedish housing policy in an international context. *Urban Studies*, 39(2), 201–217.

Westerdahl, S. (2015). Avkastningskrav, affärsmässighet och samhällsansvar: Redovisningspraktiken i kommunalt ägda bostadsföretag [Yield, business orientation and social responsibility: Accounting practices in Municipal housing companies]. In T. Salonen (Ed.), *Nyttan med allmännyttan* [The value of public housing] (pp. 233–257). Stockholm: Liber.

Official statistics

Eurostat. (2017). Retrieved from http://ec.europa.eu/eurostat/statistics-explained/index.php?title=File:Price_level_indices_for_construction,_2014,_EU-28%3D100.png&oldid=269737.

SCB. (2017a). Retrieved from www.scb.se/sv_/Hitta-statistik/Artiklar/Bostadsbyggandet-okar-kraftigt/.

SCB. (2017b). Retrieved from www.scb.se/hitta-statistik/statistik-efter-amne/boende-byggande-och-bebyggelse/bostadsbyggande-och-ombyggnad/nybyggnad-av-bostader/.

SCB. (2017c). Retrieved from www.statistikdatabasen.scb.se/pxweb/sv/ssd/START__BO__BO0201__BO0201B/KostnaderPerLghFH2/?rxid=fbacb116-6e46-46d8-a998-08e56fc83243.

SCB. (2017d). Retrieved from www.scb.se/hitta-statistik/statistik-efter-amne/boende-byggande-och-bebyggelse/bostadsbyggande-och-ombyggnad/bostadsbestand/.

Other sources

Fastighetsägarföreningen. (2017). *Balanserade villkor* [Balanced conditions]. Fastighetsägarföreningen, SABO och Hyresgästföreningen. Revised report. Retrieved from www.fastighetsagarna.se/ProductCatalogBinaryLoader.axd?OwnerType=0&OwnerID=34a2e628-bb21-414a-856f-818b46f92846&PropertyID=3cd4819a-0214-4527-b389-d89024b98d2f.

Trianon. (2016). *Annual financial report*. Retrieved from www.trianon.se/wp-content/uploads/2017/04/TRIANON_A%CC%8Arsredovisning2017_lowres-v12-1.pdf.

7 Organizational adaptations of nonprofit housing organizations in the U.S.

Insights from the Boston and San Francisco Bay areas

Rachel G. Bratt, Larry A. Rosenthal, and Robert J. Wiener

U.S. housing nonprofits: overview[1]

The United States has a robust nonprofit housing sector. These organizations have made significant contributions toward alleviating the country's housing problems. Housing produced by various types of nonprofits comprises about 70 percent of the social housing sector, which totals about five million units. Public housing comprises virtually all the remaining 1.5 million social housing units.[2] Among nonprofits, community development corporations (CDCs) are the single largest nonprofit producer, accounting for about two million units.

The origin of CDCs dates back to the 1960s as a community-based response to urban problems. Grassroots protest and advocacy movements, which often formed around arson, redlining, displacement due to urban renewal, and housing dilapidation, transformed into a more positive set of initiatives aimed at producing new or rehabilitated affordable homes for local residents. During the 1970s and 1980s, the nonprofit housing movement began to take shape, with large numbers of organizations forming. The last national census of CDCs from the early 2000s placed their number at 4,600 (National Congress for Community Economic Development, 2005). While the net number of organizations has grown considerably during the past four decades, we also know that many organizations have gone out of business or merged with other nonprofits.

The current period, dating from the 1990s, has been marked by increasing professionalism of the sector, a greater focus on training programs, and efforts to work closely with for-profit entities, social services providers, and public officials in collaborative development efforts. Many of these efforts have been reinforced by national nonprofit intermediary organizations. The growth of nonprofits also coincided with the creation of new federal financing programs, such as the Low-Income Housing Tax Credit (LIHTC) program in 1986 and the HOME Investment Partnerships Program in 1990. The various intermediaries and public supports for CDCs at all levels of government have been characterized as part of a community development system (Bratt, 1989; Frisch & Servon, 2006; Mayer & Keyes, 2012).

Although CDCs are the single most prevalent type of nonprofit housing organization, this sector encompasses several different forms (e.g., community land trusts, mutual housing associations, and limited equity cooperatives), each of which has various attributes, strengths, and weaknesses. (For comparisons of the various approaches to social housing, see Davis, 1994 and Stone, 2006.) Even within the CDC sector, there are many different types, from small "mom and pop" storefront groups having only a few employees to large groups with hundreds of staff, serving multiple areas, or even working in several states (Vidal, 1992). As noted below, our study includes both types of organizations.

Methods and geographic coverage

This research was inspired by survey work conducted in three countries: the United Kingdom (U.K. [specifically England]), Australia, and the Netherlands (Mullins, Milligan, & Nieboer, 2017). We carried out a series of in-depth interviews between December 2015 and January 2016 with leaders of 12 high-performing nonprofit organizations in the Boston and the San Francisco Bay Areas; our interview findings form the basis of this chapter.[3]

Within each region, selected organizations met the following criteria: (1) primary focus on housing; (2) currently active in housing development/ rehabilitation; (3) at least ten years of experience; and (4) at least 200 units produced or under management. These organizations focus on housing production for rent or purchase, target the general population but also serve special-needs groups, offer supportive services, and perform work typical of the nonprofit housing sector. Six organizations were selected per region, half of them "regional" and half "local" or "neighborhood-based." Regional organizations had produced and were operating over 500 units in multiple cities, counties, or states. Local organizations work within neighborhoods in a single city or in nearby cities with smaller inventories and geographical reach.

Following the lead of colleagues in the U.K., Australia, and the Netherlands, the first phase of the research involved a written survey with approximately 100 questions employing a modified Delphi methodology (see Wiener, Bratt, & Rosenthal, 2015, for a summary of the findings of this survey). One key informant was selected per organization (e.g., Executive Director, Chief Executive Officer, or President) to form the panel. Panelists chosen to be interviewed were "reflective practitioners" known for being activists and thought-leaders.

The study's second phase involved interviews with informants completing the original survey. Interview questions addressed five organizational features: mission and values; strategic positioning; recent changes affecting the work; strategies for adapting to changing circumstances; and future directions.

Both of our study regions have accomplished, knowledgeable, and committed nonprofit organizations that are supported by a network of public and private sector entities, which, together, constitute a sophisticated nonprofit affordable housing support system. The wealth of regional experience was spurred by the national adoption of LIHTC in the mid-1980s. In addition, both Boston and the San Francisco Bay Area feature high-demand markets with rising prices and low vacancy rates. Housing-affordability challenges are pervasive. State and local governments serve as important partners, making production and preservation of low-income opportunities major policy priorities in both regions.

The city of Boston and the state of Massachusetts are innovators in affordable housing development and preservation. The housing professionals there are highly regarded for their understanding of federal housing issues and proficiency in advocacy and production. Massachusetts is one of only four U.S. states with its own state-funded public housing program. It also was one of the first states to launch its own housing finance agency, promoting homeownership and rental opportunities for lower-income households.

In 1969 Massachusetts created the Comprehensive Permit program ("Chapter 40B"), a model effort addressing exclusionary zoning practices impeding housing construction on small lots and in multifamily structures. The statute empowers the state to override such local ordinances, in order to spur affordable housing development. Chapter 40B represents one of the most successful U.S. fair-share regulatory regimes, serving as a bulwark against local opposition to development (Bratt & Vladeck, 2014).[4] Since the 1970s, Massachusetts has created innovative public–private financing and technical-assistance initiatives, nurturing the growth of over 60 CDCs, many of which are leaders in the national nonprofit movement (see, for example, Bratt, 1989).

With its global leadership in information technology, energy, and tourism, the San Francisco Bay Area features both high median incomes and great income disparities. In recent years, low-income housing construction and affordability have become marquee issues, forcing local governments to take extraordinary measures to generate new revenue from: the issuance of general obligation housing bonds; commercial linkage fees and housing impact fees (i.e., financial exactions imposed on housing developers by some municipalities); increases in sales taxes; imposition of inclusionary housing requirements; and other measures.

California has long been an innovator in housing planning and finance. Local governments exercising land-use authority must submit the Housing Element of their general plan for state-level review. Where local barriers are deemed excessive and buildable parcels insufficient, the state's housing agency can determine that a jurisdiction is out of compliance, exposing it to potential loss of state funding and lawsuits.[5] For some 40 years, California enabled the creation of local redevelopment agencies, which generated billions of dollars for affordable housing from property tax increments on new development (Lefcoe & Swenson, 2014).[6] Since 2014, the state has authorized: (1) the Affordable Housing and Sustainable Communities Program, which uses the proceeds from Cap and Trade auctions for affordable housing projects that reduce carbon emissions; (2) the No Place Like Home Program, which will bond against the proceeds from a state income tax surcharge on millionaires to generate $2 billion for housing the mentally ill homeless; (3) and a new state housing trust fund whose revenues come from a $75 per document recording fee which is charged on most real-estate transactions, raising about $250 million annually.

Structural challenges facing the nonprofit housing sector, and rationales for continued support

Research has explored the capacities CDCs need to meet their challenges, producing and managing affordable housing effectively while fulfilling their broad social missions. Some of their most compelling challenges include:

- strong leadership among boards of directors and executive teams;
- frustratingly scarce resources to support operations and fund development deals;
- complex transactions with multiple subsidy-streams and varying requirements;
- staffing demands for skilled professionals across technical areas including legal work, financial analysis, community organizing, and delivery of resident services;
- coordination across a range of public, private, and nonprofit organizations to provide the depth and breadth of services to residents;
- long project timelines and delays, forcing CDCs to address changes in the local environment; and
- advocacy for community interests while working collaboratively with financial institutions and government. (For additional details on these challenges see Bratt, 2006 and Glickman & Servon, 1998.)

Recent research has pointed out that the essence of these groups, both in the U.S. and in other parts of the world, is their hybrid characteristics, combining the agendas of for-profit entities, government, social service agencies, and community activists (see, e.g., Billis, 2010; Mullins & Pawson, 2010; Mullins, Czischke, & Van Bortel, 2012). While this adds to the complexity of these organizations, the basic concepts motivating the U.S. nonprofit housing industry are unified and consistent. The above challenges notwithstanding, we enumerate below the four major rationales for supporting the nonprofit housing sector and the ways in which our study organizations demonstrate their commitment to this agenda.

First, nonprofits have a clear mission to produce and maintain affordable housing over the long term. While it is essential that they cover their costs, desires to maximize returns and generate profits are absent. This means that their primary focus is generating positive outcomes for their residents. Yet, as our interviews revealed, social and economic imperatives are mutually reinforcing.

Second, one of the key ways nonprofits carry out their mission is using their housing as a platform for residents' social progress. This is accomplished via the delivery of wrap-around services creating greater financial security and social mobility. These services include, for example, school and community-based programs for elementary school-aged children, adult day health centers, and primary care clinics. A number of our organizations are committed to investing any surplus cash flow into these types of activities. Many interviewees view their commitment to supporting residents as a feature distinguishing their work from that of private market-rate housing developers, since the latter typically take excess cash as profit. While most groups collaborate with service providers, finding the funding to support needed services remains difficult.

Third, community-based nonprofits provide opportunities for residents and their neighbors to become deeply involved. This, in turn, not only increases the likelihood the housing will fit in with the general neighborhood, but it also promotes resident involvement and empowerment in day-to-day decision-making and, in some cases, may even provide a measure of control over how housing facilities are operated.

And, fourth, since there is no funding for new public housing development, the only way to increase the size of the social housing sector is through the nonprofit sector. As competition for housing continues to be intense in strong-market areas, social housing is a key and, perhaps, the best mechanism for providing low-income residents with security against displacement. Unless housing is separated from the private, speculative market, low-income tenants are often faced with increasing rents and the need to move.

The chapter continues with a detailed discussion of the two most compelling challenges that nonprofits in the Boston and San Francisco Bay Areas are currently confronting, as well as the adaptations they are making in response.

New challenges and adaptations

Organizations must be nimble, not only meeting new challenges and embracing new opportunities, but also realigning their internal organizational focus, operational structure, and deployment of staff and other resources. Doing nothing is not an option. Consistent with the theme of this book, this section discusses the key ways organizations are responding to the challenges they are facing. The first challenge involves dwindling financial resources to produce and maintain high quality housing affordable to lower-income households. The second relates to the competitiveness of both the Boston and Bay Area housing markets.

In response to each of these two major challenges, organizations have had to adapt. As discussed in the following sections, the agility and responsiveness of nonprofit housing producers have resulted in new innovative practices, some of which involve creative financial strategies and greater levels of collaboration in producing housing, carrying out management functions, providing resident services, and sharing governance with residents. For some producers, this has required fundamental reconceptualizations of their approach to providing affordable housing.

Adaptations to dwindling resources

Funding for federal housing and related community revitalization programs in the U.S. has undergone substantial retrenchment since the 1980s. One of our respondents noted wistfully, upon considering the organization's existing portfolio, that many of those projects simply could not be built today. LIHTCs are able to provide major financing for new construction. However, this federal subsidy typically needs to be supplemented by other resources in order to make affordable housing deals work. Moreover, although federal funding for housing has always been inadequate, the current era is likely to get much worse. With passage of new federal tax legislation in December 2017, the entire LIHTC program may be vulnerable, since reduction of corporate tax rates may now make tax credit write-offs much less lucrative to corporations. Overall, the changes in the tax code could result in significantly less tax credit equity and, therefore, less new production and less funding for building new projects and recapitalizing existing projects (Novogradac, 2017).

The current era of rapidly shrinking resources for affordable housing necessitates that nonprofits make many adaptations in order to carry out their mission. Three of the major themes arising from resource constraints, identified by nonprofits and discussed below, relate to the balancing act between social and business imperatives, the importance of strong stewardship of existing properties, and the necessity of multi-party partnerships and collaboration.

Constant re-assessment of how to balance social mission with business imperatives

The nonprofit housing organizations in our study group are committed to achieving at least a double bottom-line: ensuring financial soundness of their housing developments, while serving the needs of low- and moderate-income residents.[7] Some pride themselves on achieving true balance, but even these organizations realize that assisting the neediest residents can present a serious financial strain.

Organizations with deeper asset bases and cash flows appear to enjoy greater leeway to pursue their social housing mission. They can innovate and collaborate from a position of strength and leverage their financial position in the public interest. Other organizations may operate within tighter margins and, therefore, likely face these tradeoffs more often and in more concrete ways. All must be cognizant of what one interviewee labeled the "mission–money" matrix. Clearly, an unstable balance sheet does neither the nonprofit housing organization nor its residents and neighborhoods much good. Although the possible contradictions of the double bottom-line are easy to articulate, in the give-and-take of business management, each project and management decision must be weighed on its own merits.

One area where the mission–business tradeoff finds creative ferment is rent-setting. Many organizations operate a variety of building types and units, thereby serving different income levels with varying operational costs. Innovation lies in cross-portfolio resourcing. Organizations most actively balancing social mission and business demands may draw "excess" revenue from one building in order to ease rent conditions in another. Some interviewees emphasized the need for redirecting revenues in this fashion toward non-residential services, such as child care, health, nutrition, and other programs. The revenue needed for these expenditures may be generated from commercial spaces and facilities they operate along with their residential properties. This kind of financial strategy requires significant sophistication and organizations' efforts to achieve those upgrades represent an innovation within the sector.

A number of respondents spoke of the aggressive approaches needed to manage business situations as not being separable from the skills needed to meet public-interest housing needs more generally. One respondent noted that, while day-to-day efforts may tilt toward the business side, the mission–business tension really represents "a false dichotomy." Another characterized the balancing strategically as a "both-and" proposition. While organizations may oscillate from day-to-day or month-to-month between social and economic imperatives, the two poles are, in fact, mutually reinforcing. Few leaders of nonprofit housing organizations think of themselves solely as real-estate executives. Yet, all of our respondents recognized that real-estate prowess is a necessary ingredient for mission-oriented success. The gradual development of that prowess has been a subtle but concrete innovation in how U.S. nonprofit housing business is conducted. Even in smaller, neighborhood-based organizations, financial management has advanced to levels comparable to what has long been standard in for-profit real-estate firms.

In the wake of the global downturn and recession, it is not surprising that some organizations unapologetically place business sustainability first and foremost. In their view, they fulfill their missions primarily as real-estate professionals committed to providing affordable housing. Building and maintaining affordable housing and insuring compliance with complex regulatory requirements is demanding, labor-intensive work. Particularly for developers dedicated to operating the units they build, they wander little from the core purpose of sustaining the buildings' financial viability. This takes a sophisticated workforce and the ability to pay competitive salaries and recruit and retain talented personnel. And, since the strongest financial bottom-line translates into the greatest capacity to take on new debt, expanding the supply of lower-income housing may be dependent on this priority. Nonprofit housing organizations do not have the luxury, as one respondent observed, of running a "deficit budget."

In addition to working hard to advance their affordable-housing missions, dwindling housing resources have convinced nearly all the organizations we studied to explore new lines of business and work on more than "just housing," focusing on at least some components of a comprehensive community-development agenda. Some are expecting to expand into non-development housing activities within their target geographic areas, such as homeownership counseling and loan programs for rehabilitation or first-time home acquisition. The idea, as one interviewee put it, is to "think beyond the buildings" and to achieve "collective impacts" through a "place-making approach." These activities may also hold the promise of new revenue streams. But such innovations were not universal among our study panelists. Some were adamant about the importance of preserving core products and services and did not anticipate moving beyond rental housing development and management.

Some organizations also view their resident services programs as part of a larger community-building and engagement strategy, rather than only about providing remedial services for their residents. Programs that are focused on health, financial security, public safety, food security, after-school programming, and "getting out the vote" benefit project residents but may also include residents in surrounding neighborhoods. At least one group is contemplating forming a Community Development Financial Institution (CDFI) to finance community-based development via low-interest pre-development and seed-loans for housing, as well as commercial development, such as grocery stores in retail corridors and transit improvements. These innovations parallel the portolio-based strategies described earlier. Yet, the aim to provide services and products to project residents and the community does not characterize all organizations, and there is always the question of how to pay for services and how much staff time to devote. That said, addressing residents and their needs in "whole-person" terms is a developing focus in the housing sector.

The tradeoffs between social mission and business objectives can also sometimes play out in organizational decisions about how much resident engagement to promote in project operations. Most organizations incorporate strategies for involving residents in the management of their developments. However, a concept that was popular several decades ago involving "resident control" or extensive involvement in day-to-day management decisions and governance, has, for the most part, been replaced with various strategies for promoting resident input, engagement, and empowerment through non-management/ownership activities. If, for example, an organization provides computer and job training programs, as well as other ways that promote younger residents' preparedness for college, staff feel that they are involved in empowering residents, but not through their management functions and the operation of the housing.

This issue is far from settled for several organizations, with some staff and board members favoring more resident control and others viewing resident involvement in management as time-consuming, inefficient, and not the best use of organizational time when resources are stretched. Formal resident councils, which meet regularly with management staff, have been a common strategy for engaging residents. But, at least one organization voiced skepticism about the utility of these councils, noting that it is often the same residents management meets with every month:

> Instead of participating on resident councils, don't most residents – whether market-rate, moderate- or low-income – just want to live in their homes? Are they really interested in property-management issues if everything is going along well? We would rather have people engaged in their community than tie them into the issues involved with managing the development.

For such organizations, innovation lies in providing a sense of engagement for residents as residents, rather than experimenting with shared-control arrangements.

Finally, when an organization is interested in bringing services directly into the buildings it operates, or there is a desire to hire a resident services coordinator, the challenge is specifying which among many possible services to offer and then determining how to fund them. Organizations typically cover resident services out of the building's cash flow or through day-to-day management operations. One of the regional nonprofits in our sample is attempting to redefine the meaning of "management" to encompass far more than rent collection and basic tenant services, allowing staff to become more involved in meeting a range of resident needs. Also, they are reforming their project-planning approaches by involving building managers in financial analyses of future operations. In evaluating a potential redevelopment project, that organization analyzes the operating budget to secure stable sources for funding resident services. Another of our study organizations has decided, in the interest of greater efficiency, to change its overall approach to resident services by providing fewer services more intensely. These management decisions involve both strategic vision and adaptive thinking.

Strong stewardship of existing properties through asset management and recapitalization

Another important response to the difficulties arising from scarce financial resources involves organizations paying increasing attention to asset management and the recapitalization of properties. And, resource scarcity aside, to be strong stewards of their properties and meet funder requirements, nonprofit housing development organizations must set aside sufficient proceeds from their development budgets and project operating income for day-to-day maintenance and longer-term replacement reserves.

Respondents universally recognize the critical importance of regular building maintenance and saving for replacement. Not all own and operate older projects, and not all older projects are amenable to refinancing, but they fully subscribe to the adage that "an ounce of prevention is worth a pound of cure." One organization, in particular, spoke emphatically about the risk of being "penny-wise and pound-foolish" when it comes to rental-housing construction, rehabilitation, and management. Try as they may, however, the pressures of keeping rents low make these decisions very difficult. In many cases, organizations report they will have insufficient reserves for major repairs to units exceeding 15 years in service. They are aware that relying upon local government agencies to fund renovations is unrealistic. Consequently, recapitalization will inevitably become a significant activity center.

In some circumstances, such as when the federal Housing Choice Voucher Program is used to "mark up to market" older U.S. Department of Housing and Urban Development-insured properties having contract rents that are unrealistically low, the increased income is likely to provide the nonprofits with a more substantial financial cushion. Likewise, the Rental Assistance Demonstration (RAD) program is being used by public housing authorities, often in collaboration with CDCs, to convert public housing to a voucher-based platform with long-term rental-assistance contracts. To the extent that all these approaches provide increased revenues, the nonprofits will gain additional financial security and stability.

Recapitalization offers another revenue source for long-term property preservation through conversion to other subsidy sources, re-syndication, and refinancing of existing projects in order to retire or restructure old debt, modernize the property, increase cash flow from project operations, and pay for staff and other organizational costs. As organizations' portfolios age and resources for new construction become increasingly scarce, the pressure to recapitalize will continue to grow. The challenge, of course, is recapitalizing while preserving project affordability for current and future tenants.

Recapitalization also provides an opportunity for project-based learning. Older projects built during the 1980s and 1990s were pioneering in terms of pursuing a new model of place-based, service-enriched housing to meet the full needs of residents. However, early development budgets had very thin margins because developers were under pressure by jurisdictions and funders to control costs. Newer projects are underwritten with much higher reserves. With greater financial sophistication and knowledge of the properties, financial restructuring should enable organizations to navigate project-development better, placing them on a stronger, more sustainable financial footing. They can repair, update, and modernize with new water and energy conservation technologies and they can generate revenue to support staffing for that work and thereby reinvest in the organization.

With respect to LIHTC properties, the "limited partnership" vehicle, comprised of tax-credit investors with a 99-percent ownership interest in the property, will typically sell its interest to the general partnership in Year 15.[8] This stage marks the point when tax-credit proceeds have been exhausted and the partners are no longer at risk legally for non-compliance with program rules. When the general partner is a CDC or CDC subsidiary, in nearly all cases the general partner will continue to own and operate the property. The partnership may perform some rehabilitation at or shortly after Year 15, often in association with the change in ownership and refinancing, but the amount of work will be relatively minor. Some properties, however, will be recapitalized as affordable housing with a major new source of public subsidy, usually a new allocation of LIHTCs. In these cases, the transaction will involve a substantial program of capital improvements replacing and modernizing components of the property.

As the time for recapitalization approaches, some organizations make sure that residents are involved in identifying capital needs, since they are the people most familiar with their units and the building's common areas. If the restructuring of the ownership and/or financing will have any effect on rents and occupancy, the residents will be helped to understand capital needs assessments and repair needs. In addition, when there is a difficult subject to discuss, such as instituting a non-smoking policy for areas of a building, management teams solicit resident involvement.

Forming multi-party partnerships and collaborations

As sophisticated leaders and thinkers in the field, our interviewees were acutely aware that funding, land use, and planning decisions affecting affordable housing are inherently political, informed by divergent ideological perspectives and interests. Describing how they necessarily compete for financing with other nonprofit developers, organizations in both regions emphasized the necessity of joining federal, statewide, and regional trade associations and advocacy organizations, in order to make the case for affordable housing and build political support for supportive laws and regulations. One organization, for example, has doubled its advocacy budget within the last five years. With shrinking resources and competing demands for funding from many different sectors such as health, education, transportation, and environment, collaboration on policy and program advocacy is more critical than ever.

Cooperative strategies of working across organizational boundaries and affiliating with other nonprofit developers not only has political advantages. Many organizations report that they confer regularly with their nonprofit peers in the field, especially in the smaller Boston market, to minimize competition for sites, share peer learning, and support one another. Boston-area organizations almost never contest the same sites; they "collude" to avoid conflicts. Some have submitted joint-funding proposals to foundations. Some are joining "buyers' clubs" to reduce costs through bulk-supply purchases.

Organizations in both regions have contemplated mergers with other nonprofit developers, but most have determined such strategies to be premature so long as they remain high-performing and economically viable. One Bay Area organization, however, recently subsumed the entire portfolio of two financially troubled nonprofit organizations, essentially doubling its staff and assets. Scale advantages in large portfolios of 10,000 units or more are important for property management. That interviewee sees industry consolidation as inevitable and, in fact, a necessity for organizational and sectoral survival. By and large, however, consolidation of the industry has not occurred on the scale many predicted during the Great Recession.

The development and operation of affordable housing is at its core a highly collaborative enterprise. From project conception to completion, and through a project's useful lifetime, nonprofit developers must call upon a panoply of partnerships and coalitions to be successful. But in the current financial climate, this has become even more urgent, as groups are working to leverage available resources and to maximize the benefits they can provide. Indeed, all the organizations in the study emphasized unprecedented levels of collective action, interdependence, and holistic approaches to housing provision.

As part of the development process, organizations work closely with federal, state, and local government agencies, as well as with conventional banks, CDFIs, and equity investors that finance predevelopment, construction, and permanent take-out financing. Nonprofits also work with local governments to gain development rights and approvals and confer with neighborhood and citizens' groups to build support. Some have collaborated with churches and social service providers owning land they want to see developed for housing. While preferring to retain control, organizations have undertaken or are contemplating joint ventures with a variety of partners – faith-based organizations, high-tech companies, and for-profit developers – as co-developers and co-owners of rental housing assets. Specifically, one organization has partnered with three churches with excess land and community credibility. And, a Silicon Valley organization has been courting high-tech companies looking to house workers. In both regions, organizations working in communities with inclusionary housing mandates on market-rate developments are looking to leverage their expertise and local reputation to produce the affordable units with financial and other supports from for-profit companies.

Nonprofits often grapple with the extent to which services can or should be provided through the organization directly or by developing partnerships with local service providers. Resource scarcity is a powerful motivation behind collaboration. In addition, these efforts also have been stimulated by governmental mandates and preferences for "amenity-rich" housing. One organization which had not traditionally operated resident services programs came to understand that, to meet the residents' needs comprehensively, collaborating with the host city was necessary to increase residents' participation in municipal programs. Several organizations in both Boston and the San Francisco Bay Area are working with local health care providers to bring more health services into their buildings and exploring how they can qualify residents for Medicare, Medicaid, or private medical insurance reimbursement payments.

Adaptations to competitive housing markets

We turn from innovations and adaptations driven by growing resource scarcity in the sector toward those driven by increasingly competitive housing-market conditions. Since the organizations included in our study operate in two of the highest-cost housing markets in the country, it is not surprising that there was a great deal of uniformity in their responses: all felt that housing market pressures were an important issue. Most voiced serious concerns about the high cost of land and buildings; as a result development deals are difficult to put together and costly. Nonprofit developers and operators not only compete with one another but with for-profit firms, including investors and developers able to pay cash for developable sites and real estate.

Several organizations observed that market conditions resulted in lost opportunities in competitions with more nimble and cash-rich private investors. For example, one nonprofit developer said it was not uncommon to compete with a deep-pocket international developer able to pay cash upfront without the necessity of assessing environmental mitigation issues prior to purchasing the property. The assumption was that there would be sufficient funds, regardless of any remediation costs, to comply with environmental standards. In other words, their risk tolerance is much higher than nonprofit developers operating on thinner margins with private and public funds.

Being in a strong enough market position to dictate one's own terms is relatively unusual. Only one organization studied felt that competition with for-profit developers was not an issue, stating: "We're still in a place where we are the sought-after partner. If there is a big project, a for-profit will probably talk to us." That organization and others in our sample operate with a portfolio of existing projects and others in the development queue or pipeline. With a large enough pipeline and sufficient number of units under management, at least some organizations feel they will be quite busy for the foreseeable future.

While the previously discussed challenge – reduced federal resources – has resulted in nonprofits developing new financial models and collaborative arrangements, this challenge also has pushed nonprofits into new development realms, while also pursuing cooperative strategies of working across organizational boundaries. Despite cases where core business viability is sorely tested, the next logical step – namely, movement toward mergers and consolidations – was not observed in our study sample.

In the sections below, we discuss two adaptions to competition in the housing market – broadening the geographic focus and populations served, and development of high-density and mixed-use projects.

Broadening geographic focus and income levels of targeted households

While some of the longstanding neighborhood-based groups are still focused exclusively on their local areas, a number of organizations feel that working in a specific geographic area is less important than seizing development and rehabilitation opportunities wherever they emerge. Expanding geographic reach to contend with competitive market conditions represents a key adaptation, necessitating adaptive management innovations.[9]

Several years ago, one Boston-area group made a conscious decision to expand its geographic focus to include several neighboring towns in order to have a greater set of development opportunities and options. In fact, the organization changed its name, which had included the name of only a single city close to Boston. Its current non-location-specific name reflects its multi-city focus. Similarly, although one Bay Area organization we interviewed started out with a focus on a single neighborhood in San Francisco, it presently sees itself as a citywide agency, although it is still anchored in a gritty urban neighborhood close to downtown. With its housing now located in six additional neighborhoods, it says it is agnostic about location and will develop any site that is feasible, so long as it is in San Francisco.

Expanding even further, two Bay Area nonprofits within our study group have been working throughout California for a long time. Although some 50 percent of their pipeline is in the city of San Francisco, they also operate in other Bay Area cities, as well as much farther away – Los Angeles and Orange Counties in Southern California and the Central Valley in the interior of the state. One of these groups has projects in some 12 counties across California. Another Bay Area organization has recently followed suit and expanded its geographic reach to the City of Sacramento, to counties on the periphery of the Bay Area, and into Southern California.

An organization in the San Francisco Bay Area acknowledged that pursuing deals close to the urban cores of Oakland and San Francisco is impossible due to the high costs of land, existing properties, labor, and local government fees. Instead, it now seeks opportunities in locations that are "in front of the wave – before anyone else wants to buy there. If we are able to develop nice homes, then others will want to live there." Another Bay Area organization specializing in suburban projects has changed its acquisition program, seeking to buy and bank more land more quickly while it is available and affordable.

One Boston-based organization, which has been developing in a number of states for years, is looking to increase its housing stock in 70 neighborhoods in 30 cities where it already has a presence to an additional 20 neighborhoods. Another organization in the Boston area has had a citywide focus since its inception, but is now interested in expanding throughout Massachusetts to take advantage, in part, of a state program known as "40T," which gives the state a right-of-first-refusal on the redevelopment of "expiring-use" properties.[10] These are affordable housing projects developed by profit-motivated entities with time-limited public subsidies that are at risk of termination.

The choice to expand income-eligibility toward better-off households is another adaptation to market pressures and seems, in part, to also be politically driven. A plea often echoed in American cities involves the need for workforce[11] housing for "essential" employees, such as teachers, public safety workers, or nurses. This preference is demonstrated in a number of recent state and local funding initiatives specifically supporting mixed-income projects with higher average income-eligibility guidelines. In general, communities appear less resistant to workforce housing; opposition is often strongest when projects target only the neediest households.

Moreover, the higher allowable incomes translate into lower financial burdens for the organization, since there is a decreased need for subsidies to produce and operate the new units. That factor alone makes this approach more financially feasible. Though it creates tensions relative to these organizations' missions, broadening income-eligibility in this fashion represents an adaptation that some nonprofits are considering in the highly competitive market environments that we studied.

Taken together, these circumstances are making it less practicable for our respondents' organizations to serve residents at or below 50 percent of area median income levels. Tenants with fewer assets, unsteady employment, and serious illness or disability face enormous housing challenges or even the risk of homelessness, particularly in places like Boston and the Bay Area.

One strategy mentioned by a few organizations as a way to continue to serve lower-income populations involves moving toward larger-scale projects. The more units in a new development, the greater the opportunity to spread costs, layer income-eligibility levels, and take advantage of cross-subsidy economies. The impediments to success in such efforts, however, are formidable, since finding larger-scale buildable sites in dense urban neighborhoods is an enormous hurdle. Alternatively, groups may be able to spread costs throughout multiple projects. Generally, organizations with greater operating margins due to strong asset bases are better able to maintain deeper affordability. In short, the organizations studied here are committed, in principle and in practice, to their core missions of maximizing assistance and targeting households with the greatest need and they regularly analyze opportunities and fashion strategies to tackle these challenges.

Increasing density and mixed-use development

Compounding the high cost of land is the current emphasis in state and local housing policy on higher-density development near existing urban services, particularly public transportation. Such policies strive to meet smart growth and sustainability goals and are able to achieve reduced land costs per unit. One Bay Area organization observed that "a lot of communities are now very aggressive about density. Part of the density strategy involves creating a mixed-use setting, combining offices with residential development." A Boston-area organization holds the view that higher density is the only way to get the necessary approvals from the city. The City of Cambridge, for example, is looking to create zoning overlay districts to encourage more affordable housing development.

Given the extremely high costs of new construction in the areas in our study, a number of our organizations are looking for opportunities to acquire and stabilize existing buildings as a way to continue serving lower-income residents and preserve affordable housing that is under threat. As housing markets in these two regions strengthen – reaching price levels comparable to or exceeding those seen in the real estate "bubble" and the run-up to the mortgage meltdown – the conversion of affordable housing to market-rate units, neighborhood gentrification, and displacement of the poor are reaching a state of crisis.

In the U.S. system of time-limited, rent-restricted contracts, an entire movement dedicated toward *preservation* of affordability has long been underway (see, for example, Fields, 2015). In this struggle, we see how mixing in moderate-income households in reconfigured buildings may help facilitate the infusion of new resources necessary to make the effort feasible. But such income-mixing also raises questions about how to find replacement housing in the event that deeply affordable units are lost in the process.

Final thoughts

This chapter presents several important and innovative adaptations that are being made by a small group of high-performing nonprofit affordable housing development organizations in the U.S. in response to pressing challenges. The challenges discussed here – dwindling financial resources and competitive and high-demand housing markets – may be similar to those in many other cities in Europe and elsewhere. This chapter suggests that *inward-facing* adaptations are integral to the survival of these nonprofits and that strategic collaboration has been the norm for many years.

Not surprisingly, constraints on financial resources, from the federal government level down to the local government level, have resulted in organizations making a number of adaptations involving financial strategies. Organizations are constantly assessing their work in terms of balancing their social and economic goals. The chapter underscores that the use of currently available financial mechanisms, whether new or existing, demands high levels of proficiency in real estate development and management, a thorough understanding of federal, state, and local housing programs, continuous professionalization and training, and involvement in advocacy efforts at every level of government. The growth in the sophistication of these groups makes many of them as savvy and technically capable as for-profit real-estate firms, if not more so.

At the same time, the strain on financial resources has increased the importance of asset management and recapitalization of existing, older properties. A genuine tradeoff rests within the pressures of pursuing new construction while maintaining and recapitalizing each organization's existing portfolio. The structure of subsidy in the U.S. places time limits on assisted-rent protections. The more an organization's capacity is stretched in order to extend and preserve existing units and their affordability to low- and moderate-income residents, the less that organization can risk in the name of expanding its portfolio.

This situation is particularly worrisome for the social housing sector in the U.S., generally, as the flow of subsidy continues falling well short of genuine need for affordable rental housing as a whole. Larger organizations with broader portfolios may be able to survive the vicissitudes of public policy and the market by shifting from development to asset management during lean times, while others will be hard-pressed to keep staff and remain viable. Here, as with other issues, the strategy and vision of the organizations in this study perpetuate inclusive ambitions, notwithstanding the severity of the financial tradeoffs and risks.

Respondents in our study group were strongly committed to organization-led initiatives that are aimed at using housing as a platform for promoting residents' economic security, facilitating resident involvement and empowerment, and increasing the fit of an affordable housing project within the neighborhood. Although their organizations typically rely less on collaborative, resident-led involvement in housing management activities than in some housing models, they often provide residents with opportunities to provide feedback, identify capital needs, and determine the amenities and services that add the most value.

This chapter also demonstrates that resource scarcity is a powerful incentive for inter-organizational collaboration. All the organizations in the study emphasized the importance of collective action, interdependence, and holistic approaches to housing provision. Indeed, with affordable housing in the U.S. most often resulting from the efforts of sophisticated and hybrid networks, including nonprofit and for-profit developers, as well as government at all levels and national nonprofit intermediary organizations, the study of the U.S.

nonprofit affordable housing sector demonstrates a high level of inter-sectoral cooperation and collaboration.

Dwindling resources and intensely competitive housing markets have also precipitated adaptations in housing product types, geographical focus, and income targeting. In many cases, there has been an increase in project density, unit numbers, and the development of mixed-income and mixed-use projects that include commercial activities. These are responses to financial pressures to maximize revenue from new development and perhaps cross-subsidize lower-income residents, but also to scoring preferences for denser, transit-oriented, and more sustainable development in state and local government housing programs. These pressures are also forcing organizations to consider serving a higher-income population and expanding into new geographical areas with more development opportunities.

Our study shows that these efforts are as demanding as they are rewarding. Nonprofit housing development in U.S. metropolitan areas, such as Boston and San Francisco, is not a career for the faint of heart. Our interviewees represent a rare breed. These leaders are sage observers of their "industry." Agility and strategy are at a premium; they must be deft forecasters of business conditions and policy change. Many have deep experience across a range of firms and business perspectives. Whether in smaller community-oriented or more regionally minded organizations, they also share a commitment to improving the lives of working families and the poor. They see the interconnections between these regions' growing economies and widening income disparities. And they are ever mindful of the need to balance housing development with community development, inclusion, and neighborhood preservation. The pursuit of innovation and adaptation is continuous. Ultimately, they are responsible for the survival of their organizations and the fostering of their teams' livelihoods and careers.

Based on our study and our overall knowledge and work with the U.S. nonprofit housing sector, we see both an organizational commitment to traditional values and savvy questioning of unexamined assumptions. Nonprofits wish to empower residents, but not necessarily in ways which complicate property management excessively. They wish to operate with a nonprofit mindset, while thriving in highly competitive business and subsidy environments. They question the addition of new functions and capacities in-house when partnerships with outside providers may be preferable. And, they are making the most of housing's increasing prominence on state and local policy agendas. As for the latter, community-based developers are able to specialize in select locations proximate to one another, while regional groups must navigate numerous, diverse political settings simultaneously across the projects in their pipelines.

Moving forward, one of the signature challenges will be balancing the need to ensure a pipeline of new units in construction with the need to maintain and upgrade nonprofits' existing inventories. What undergirds the system of affordable housing finance in the U.S. is relatively short-term subsidies that may be renewable in some instances but are often time-limited in others. Organizations constantly face the prospect that at some future juncture they will have to restructure the underlying financing and recapitalize the property in order to retire existing debt, renegotiate the terms of new financing, and modernize older units, all while keeping rents at pre-existing low levels. To the extent organizations must devote resources to preserving their current portfolios, the fewer resources they may be able to devote to expansion. At the same time, the flow of capital and rental subsidy continues to fall. Larger organizations are more strongly positioned to withstand the shocks of public policy and the economy and transition from development to asset management during lean times, but smaller organizations may struggle to survive.

Moreover, the large-scale withdrawal of federal support for affordable housing, amplified by the election of Donald Trump in 2016, has challenged some states to step into the vacuum and create new and innovative financing tools. These state-level programs are encouraging and are already spurring greater levels of innovation across the nonprofit housing sector.

In Massachusetts, creation of the Donation Tax Credit in 2016 has provided a credit against state income-tax liability for owners donating existing housing properties and structures. And state policy favors transfer of for-profit-owned affordable housing to qualified nonprofits committed to long-term affordability. In California, to offset the loss of local redevelopment agency funding, the state is devoting 20 percent of the proceeds from Cap and Trade auctions from polluting industries to affordable housing projects that reduce dependence on fossil fuels. An ingenious plan to bond against the proceeds of revenue from the state's income tax on millionaires for mental health services will raise billions for housing the mentally ill homeless. A new fee on most private real estate transactions creates a recurring revenue source for affordable housing.

Based on our survey and interviews, we are confident that nonprofit housing organizations will continue to adapt and innovate in order to survive and be in a position to address the housing needs of the communities within which they operate. But, if financial survival means a new focus on serving higher-income populations and diversifying into non-housing activities, traditional commitments in the public interest to assist people and communities in the greatest need may be compromised.

Notes

1 Most of this section is excerpted from Bratt, 2017.

2 This includes about 1.2 million federally subsidized units, 300,000 units operated by the Department of Defense, and 60,000 public housing units produced by several state and local governments across the U.S. For additional information on how these estimates were derived, see Bratt, 2017.

3 We are indebted to the individuals who were interviewed, as follows: *Boston Area*:
Peter Daly, Homeowners' Rehab, Inc.
Ann Houston, The Neighborhood Developers
Chrystal Kornegay, Urban Edge
Bart Mitchell, The Community Builders
Jeanne Pinado, Madison Park Development Corporation
Amy Schectman, Jewish Community Housing for the Elderly

San Francisco Bay Area:
Don Falk, Tenderloin Neighborhood Development Corporation
Matt Franklin, MidPen Housing
Lisa Mandolini, Eden Housing
Dan Sawislak, Resources for Community Development
Doug Shoemaker, Mercy Housing California
Joshua Simon, East Bay Asian Local Development Corporation

4 Interestingly, our study panel's Boston-area organizations serve cities already surpassing Chapter 40B's minimum affordability thresholds, exempting those places from the fair-share law.

5 Notwithstanding California's Housing Element law, the California Environmental Quality Act gives local citizens the right to challenge residential projects on environmental grounds, which has, unfortunately, been used to stall, or prevent entirely, projects and resulted in increased costs.

6 Following action by the Governor and California Legislature to deauthorize redevelopment agencies to help reduce the state's budget deficit, later validated by the California Supreme Court, these agencies were dissolved in 2012. Many have since called for restoring the ability of local governments to create redevelopment agencies and use tax increments for affordable housing.

7 It has also been suggested that many nonprofits are committed to meeting a Quadruple Bottom Line, which also includes "sensitivity to the way the housing fits into the larger fabric of the neighborhood and contributes to neighborhood viability" and a commitment to making the housing "as environmentally sensitive and sustainable as possible, which involves minimizing the use of nonrenewable energy resources and striving to reduce transportation needs" (Bratt, 2012).

8 Although restrictions officially end in Year 15, there is a strong expectation that the developments will remain affordable to households below 50 percent or 60 percent of area median income (AMI) for at least an additional 15 years.

9 Similarly, a 2014 survey of large nonprofits carried out by the Housing Partnership Network revealed that, over the following three years, more than twice as many groups were planning on expanding their geographic focus compared with those that were anticipating focusing on a specific locality (Walsh & Davidson-Sawyer, 2014).

10 In contrast to public housing, the original private for-profit owner can opt out of the contractual obligations with the federal government, which commits the owner to retaining unit affordability for a specified number of years. Under 40T, nonprofits have the first opportunity to buy these properties and keep them affordable with government subsidies.

11 Often, the term "workforce" housing is used to describe housing for politically more "desirable," moderate-income populations, although lower-income households are also in the workforce. It raises longstanding questions in the social policy literature about the extent to which resources should be targeted to the "deserving" poor (i.e., low-wage workers) or to the "undeserving" poor (i.e., those on welfare).

References

Billis, D. (2010). From welfare bureaucracies to welfare hybrids. In D. Billis (Ed.), *Hybrid organizations and the third sector: Challenges for practice, theory and policy* (pp. 3–24). London: Palgrave Macmillan.

Bratt, R. G. (1989). *Rebuilding a low-income housing policy*. Philadelphia, PA: Temple University Press.

Bratt, R. G. (2006). Community development corporations: Challenges in supporting a right to housing. In R. G. Bratt, M. E. Stone, & C. Hartman (Eds.), *A right to housing:*

Foundation for a new social agenda (pp. 340–359). Philadelphia, PA: Temple University Press.

Bratt, R. G. (2012). The quadruple bottom line and nonprofit housing organizations in the United States. *Housing Studies*, *27*(4), 438–456.

Bratt, R. G. (2017). The role of nonprofits in meeting the housing challenge in the U.S. *Urban Research and Practice*. doi: 10.1080/17535069.2017.1341951.

Bratt, R. G., & Vladeck, A. (2014). Addressing restrictive zoning for affordable housing: Experiences in four states. *Housing Policy Debate*, *24*(3), 594–636.

Davis, J. E. (1994). Beyond the market and the state: The diverse domain of social housing. In J. E. Davis (Ed.), *The affordable city: Toward a third sector housing policy* (pp. 75–106). Philadelphia, PA: Temple University Press.

Fields, D. (2015). Contesting the financialization of urban space: Community organizations and the struggle to preserve affordable rental housing in New York City. *Journal of Urban Affairs*, *37*(2), 144–165.

Frisch, M., & Servon, L. J. (2006). CDCs and the changing context for urban community development: A review of the field and environment. *Community Development Journal*, *37*(4), 88–108.

Glickman, N. J., & Servon, L. J. (1998). More than bricks and sticks: Five components of community development corporation capacity. *Housing Policy Debate*, *9*(3), 497–539.

Lefcoe, G., & Swenson, C. W. (2014). Redevelopment in California: The demise of TIF-funded redevelopment in California and its aftermath. *National Tax Journal*, *67*(3), 719–744.

Mayer, N., & Keyes, L. (2012). City government's role in the community development system. In J. DeFilippis and S. Saegert (Eds.), *The community development reader* (pp. 158–166). New York: Routledge.

Milligan, V., Hulse, K., & Davison, G. (2013). *Understanding leadership, strategy and organisational dynamics in the not-for-profit housing sector* (AHURI Final Report No. 204). Melbourne, Australia: Australian Housing and Urban Research Institute.

Mullins, D., & Pawson, H. (2010). Housing associations: Agents of policy or profits in disguise? In D. Billis (Ed.), *Hybrid organizations and the third sector: Challenges for theory and practice* (pp. 197–218). London: Palgrave Macmillan.

Mullins, D., Czischke, D., & van Bortel, G. (2012). Exploring the meaning of hybridity and social enterprise in housing organisations. *Housing Studies*, *27*(4), 405–417.

Mullins, D., Milligan, V., & Nieboer, N. (2017). State directed hybridity? The relationship between non-profit housing organizations and the state in three national contexts. *Housing Studies*. doi: 10.1080/02673037.2017.1373747.

National Congress for Community Economic Development. (2005). *Reaching new heights: Trends and achievements of community-based development organizations (5th national community development census)*. Washington, DC: Author.

Novogradac, M. (2017, December 17). *Final tax reform bill would reduce affordable rental housing production by nearly 235,000 homes* [Blog comment]. Retrieved from www.novoco.com/notes-from-novogradac/final-tax-reform-bill-would-reduce-affordable-rental-housing-production-nearly-235000-homes/.

Stephens, J., & Fulton, W. (2012). A quickie divorce: Local government and redevelopment agencies in California. *Planning and Environmental Law*, 64(8), 9–10.

Stone, M. E. (2006). Social ownership. In R. G. Bratt, M. E. Stone, & C. Hartman (Eds.), *A right to housing: Foundation for a new social agenda* (pp. 240–260). Philadelphia, PA: Temple University Press.

U.S. Office of Management and Budget. (2017). America first: A budget blueprint to make America great again. Washington, DC: Author.

Vidal, A. C. (1992). *Rebuilding communities: A national study of urban community development corporations*. New York: Community Development Research Center, Graduate School of Management and Urban Policy, New School for Social Research.

Walsh, D., & Davidson-Sawyer, J. (2014). *U.S. CEO future strategy survey results*. Boston, MA: Housing Partnership Network (unpublished manuscript).

Wiener, R. J., Bratt, R. G., & Rosenthal, L. A. (2015). Housing organizations' adaptations to change in the U.S.: Preliminary findings from the San Francisco Bay Area and Boston. Presented to the European Network of Housing Research Conference, Lisbon, Portugal (unpublished manuscript).

8 Two modes of co-production in social housing

Comparing UK and Australian experience

David Adamson

Co-production in housing services

This chapter is concerned with the evolution of co-production in the social housing system. The discussion will explore the recent emergence of two very distinct patterns of co-production in the United Kingdom and Australia. The co-production patterns identified are innovative responses to housing management that build on early tenant participation models. They have emerged to meet rising levels of social disadvantage and consequent social need in social housing communities. The social housing systems in the United Kingdom and Australia share many key features, but also demonstrate critical differences in the housing service model (Adamson, 2016a). The differences have led to contrasting patterns of tenant relations that can be termed co-production.

As in other service areas, the social housing trajectory towards co-production has a long history. It is only recently that the term co-production has been applied to the models of social housing service delivery that have evolved from early practices of tenant participation and tenant engagement. From the earliest uses of the term co-production in the work of Elinor Ostrom in the 1970s (Ostrom, Parks, Whitaker, & Percy, 1978, as cited in Alford, 2014), the concept of co-production has gained increasing currency in social policy design and in the delivery of a range of personal and social services (Alford 2009, 2014). It has become a core component of public service reforms and the central pillar of the operational delivery of a range of public services (Osborne & Strokosch, 2013). Bovaird (2007) defines co-production as: 'The provision of services through regular, long-term relationships between professionalized service providers (in any sector) and service users or other members of the community, where all parties make substantial resources contributions' (p. 847).

The critical point in this definition is the inclusion of service users in the co-production definition. It is this involvement of service users that is central to the analysis presented here. This is distinct from a more limited conception of co-production as the engagement of third or social sector organisations in the co-design and co-delivery of what in the past have been government services (Pestoff, Osborne, & Brandsen, 2006). This *co-management* of public services (Brandsen & Pestoff, 2006) is related to, but distinct from, the *co-production* explored in this chapter, which identifies the role of social housing tenants in the co-production of the housing service. We are centrally concerned with the involvement of service users in the design and implementation of services.

In a broad sense any recipient of a public service is engaged in its production (Alford, 2009). Alford illustrates this view with reference to the service user role in the production of health, education and police services. Without user engagement, their conformity to required behaviours and compliance with regulations, a service cannot be effectively delivered. In social housing, simply to be a tenant is to agree to a range of regulations and comply with general behaviours in order to maintain the tenancy. However, Bovaird's definition (2007) introduces the role of the service user as a contributor of resources. In the social housing field this implies at least an investment of time and energy in the cleanliness and maintenance of the property. In a later article, Bovaird refines the definition to extend the meaning beyond this potentially, relatively passive role for the service user, to include outcomes emerging as a result of the co-production relationship rather than the simple co-delivery of a service (Bovaird & Loeffler, 2012). Consequently, co-production can be associated with better social outcomes or reduced costs as an added value deriving from the relationship between service provider and service user. This also represents the development of 'public services *BY* the public' rather than 'public services *FOR* the public' (Bovaird & Loeffler, 2012, p. 1121).

Voorberg, Bekkers and Tummers (2015) further elaborate on the concept of co-production by reference to the related term 'co-creation'. More associated with commercial product development, co-creation involves the consumer in a design role. Consumer participation informs the eventual product design. This co-creation of products or goods appears distinct from the co-production of a service, which is primarily a role in the implementation, particularly of public services. In reality, in their systematic review of the literature, they find the uses of these terms are inter-changeable and that the use of the term co-production can include different levels of involvement in all stages of service design and implementation (Voorberg et al., 2015). In the field of social housing it can be argued that the physical fabric of the house itself is co-produced through the collaboration of tenant and social landlord.

> In the public housing case, the tenants on the estates in question received a mixture of goods and services. On the services side, to the extent that tenants organize themselves to work with estate management to discourage vandalism or anti-social behaviour, they co-produce a service: safety, social amenity, and/or privacy. But on the goods side, their rental payments entitle them to fixed term possession of a set of tangible assets: the concrete, timber, and other physical elements making up the structure of their apartment.
>
> (Alford, 2014, p. 307)

However, the focus of this chapter is on the co-production of a comprehensive housing service rather than housing goods. It will explore the extent to which the tenants are engaged in a co-production of additional outcomes and added value that are the direct result of the co-production relationship.

This emergence of the concept of co-production reflects a general trajectory of increased service user engagement growing from the passive models of post-Second World War welfare interventions, to the more client-focused models of social and human services evolving in the 1990s. Co-production did not appear overnight and has multiple origins in service delivery. Its shape and form is consequently path dependent and the term has different meanings to different professional groups, in turn shaping their relationships with service users and the patterns of user engagement. Osborne and Strokosch (2013) identify two over-arching perspectives on co-production; the public service perspective and the service management perspective.

The public service perspective delineates a transition from public services, operated on behalf of users by professionalised service providers, towards a more collaborative model. In the New Public Management of the 1990s, service users were recast as consumers and customers (Pawson & Wiesal, 2014; Suszynńska, 2015) within a reform agenda grounded in creating competition between providers. The same period saw the outsourcing of public services to third and private sector providers to release the service improvements and improved outcomes that competition was perceived to provide. In this perspective, service improvement and added value derived from the consumer client exercising choice between competing providers, thereby driving change. This 'choice' based approach positions co-production as an optional service element deployed in pursuit of effectiveness and improved outcomes in the service system (Osborne & Strokosch 2013).

In contrast, in the service management perspective, co-production is seen as intrinsic to service delivery. 'Its basic premise is that co-production is an essential and inalienable core component of service delivery: you cannot have (public) service delivery without co-production' (Osborne & Strokosch, 2013, p. 36). This characteristic derives from the simultaneous production and consumption of services. It is the dual experience of the producer and the consumer that defines the interaction. More importantly, it is the consumer's expectation and experience of the service that determines the outcomes of the service model. Co-production in this perspective is unavoidable and exists the moment a service is delivered and received. In this model, service improvement is secured by *voice* in which service users are able to influence the pattern of services they receive through their everyday interaction with service providers (Pawson & Wiesal, 2014). In more 'enhanced' versions of co-production this may involve service users in formal representative roles in the management and governance structures of the service provider, creating opportunity for co-production to 'challenge the existing paradigm of service delivery' (Osborne & Strokosch, 2013, p. 37).

The extent of co-production can vary between services and is dependent on the level of interaction between provider and service user. The provision of social housing services involves a high degree of co-production. To establish and maintain a tenancy requires a significant degree of collaboration, negotiation and compliance on both sides. The housing provider is required to comply with national regulatory frameworks, including financial management, service quality and tenant satisfaction criteria. The tenant is required to comply with tenancy rules, behavioural codes and financial payments in order to maintain the tenancy. The consequence is a close and elaborate relationship between tenant and housing provider in which a degree of co-production is inevitable.

I will now identify the activities and practices that exist in the social housing field in which tenant and landlord engage in a service model that extends beyond the simple provision of housing. These practices include a range of added programmes and services to enhance the quality of tenants' lives. This is the terrain of co-production and it is difficult to conceive of these activities developing over time without active involvement of significant numbers of tenants.

A typology of housing-led social and economic interventions

The following typology is derived from the author's academic and, professional practice working with housing organisations in Wales and Australia, engagement with UK and Australian peak bodies and advisory roles to Welsh Government (Adamson, 2010a, 2010b; Adamson & Bromiley, 2013; Adamson, 2016a). This experience includes periods of policy development during secondments to government where the author worked for extended periods as a member of the government policy team. The experience drawn on here also includes funded and commissioned academic research, and sector leadership as a CEO of a Centre for Regeneration Excellence. The typology has been developed through a reflective review of personal professional practice in the field of housing-led regeneration in Wales and most recently Australia.

The elements of the typology are presented as increasing levels of complexity with Levels Four and Five requiring similar levels but differing patterns of co-production. They denote increasing degrees of co-production as the service model becomes more comprehensive and elaborate.

Whilst this typology is not exhaustive it identifies the core activities that have emerged and continue to develop. Levels One to Three have evolved over an extended period with early tenant participation and engagement activities in the 1980s maturing in the more comprehensive patterns of co-production evident in tenant empowerment and community development practices. These were a response to the emerging patterns of poverty in social housing communities in the UK throughout the 1990s and 2000s (Adamson, 2010a, 2010b). Levels Four and Five are recent innovations and the primary focus of this chapter. They are a suite of innovative approaches developed in the social housing sector to meet the increased social needs of tenants. The level of social need experienced by social housing tenants has increased with the process of residualisation whereby increasingly impoverished and disadvantaged

Table 8.1 Co-production patterns in social housing

Level	*Types of intervention*
Level One Tenant engagement and participation	Improved tenant consultation and participation structures including: • Estate forums • Survey and focus group consultations • Street representatives
Level Two Tenant empowerment	Tenant involvement in governance and decision-making including: • Training tenant advocates • Tenant Board membership • Development of tenant scrutiny roles • Tenant co-design of stock improvement • Choice-based letting
Level Three Community development (CD)	Enhancing community cohesion and integration through CD activities including: • Events-based community engagement • Play and youth schemes • Elder support programmes • Community capacity development training and personal development opportunities • Provision of community hubs and associated activities
Level Four Community regeneration	Development of local economic opportunity and tenant capacity to participate in the economy including: • Social procurement strategies • Targeted recruitment and training of tenants • Development of social enterprises • Low carbon retrofit • Raising housing standard through housing renewal • Provision of public buildings including community centres, schools, health facilities • Improved public realm and estate condition
Level Five Support provision	Provision of a range of support services meeting the needs of a diverse range of tenants including: • Tele-healthcare services • Gardening and handyman support services • Vocational training • Energy use advice and support • Debt management and loan facilities • Parenting support • Counselling services

populations are housed in social housing (Lee & Murie, 1999). This residualisation process is discussed later in this chapter.

In all these activities tenant participation is an essential component and increasing levels of tenant collaboration and resource contribution are required. In all but Level One an enhanced level of co-production is required (Osborne & Strokosch, 2013). This co-production plays a significant role in challenging the public housing paradigm in which the tenant was perceived as a passive service user. That view prevailed in the earliest days of post-1945 housing provision and is, to a considerable extent, maintained in systems dominated by continued state provision of social housing, for example in the public housing sector in Australia.

With this typology available to inform an examination of patterns of co-production in the UK and Australia we now turn to an analysis of the evolution of co-production in each jurisdiction.

Housing service co-production in the UK

In the UK, public housing emerged in the municipal sector and was largely provided by local councils to house lower-income, working-class families. In the post-1945 welfare settlement the provision of good quality homes for returning soldiers and their families was a critical element of physical reconstruction in major settlements. Furthermore, it was a core component of the ideological settlement found in concepts of equality and social justice (Murie, 1997). The large-scale building programme was also a major economic stimulus that was a key component of the economic recovery that created the affluent working class. Living in a high quality 'council' house, built to the Parker Morris standard (Parker Morris Committee, 1961) and acquiring consumer durable goods and car ownership were critical to the working-class lifestyle and culture of the 1960s. Much of the rise of the 'affluent worker' (Goldethorpe, Lockwood, Bechhofer, & Platt, 1967) could be attributed to the improved housing standards of the municipal sector and the role of city authorities in eliminating the 'slum' dwellings of the pre-war period.

Council management of housing was a command and control model with a passive service user response expected of tenants. Tenants were not allowed to repair, decorate or manage the property in any way. The organised tenant movement offered resistance to that centralised control and initial engagement of tenants in municipal housing management structures can be identified from the 1970s onwards (Bradley, 2008). However, regulation of tenant behaviour and freedom in their home was strict with clear guidelines for behaviour, property care and internal decoration. This model prevailed until the 1980s when housing associations were established by the Conservative Government. Their creation was in part from a concern with delivery standards, in part from an interest in reducing the influence of large municipal authorities and in part from a desire to introduce some level of contestability and competition into the social housing system (Nygaard, Gibb, & Berry, 2007). The patterns of governance associated with the new housing associations accelerated tenant involvement and tenant board membership became the norm, with up to one-third of housing association directors drawn from the tenant community by the early 2000s (Bradley, 2008).

Housing associations grew rapidly in number and scale in the 1990s, a process accelerated by large-scale housing asset transfer from local authorities (Smyth, 2012). From the first large-scale transfer in 1988, the strategy became mainstream, at first in England (Malpass & Mullins, 2002,) followed by Scotland and Wales to become the core strategy to meet the need for social housing. The outcome was a not-for-profit housing sector operating at significant scale. This major restructuring of the social housing market was dependent on highly favourable Treasury concessions on debt write-off, gap-funding and stock valuations to provide an attractive asset class to institutional lenders (Smyth, 2012). This provided housing associations with considerable borrowing capacity, grounded in asset transfer with title, guaranteed rental income, paid directly to landlords in the form of housing benefit, and a rigorous regulatory environment to provide security to institutional lenders.

This policy environment was consolidated with favourable social policy, especially during the Labour administrations of 1997 to 2010. Complementary policies included urban renewal programmes such as the Strategy for Neighbourhood Renewal and the New Deal for Communities. Parallel programmes in Wales (Communities First) and Scotland (Communities Scotland) also supported urban renewal (Adamson, 2010b).

In this wider context of urban regeneration policy, housing associations were critical partners in many of the targeted disadvantaged communities (Card & Mudd, 2006), where significant concentrations of social housing were the norm. Their contribution included repair and renovation projects and a modest improvement of social housing supply. Their role was also fundamental to the achievement of new housing quality standards such as the Decent Homes Standard in England and the Welsh Housing Quality Standard (WHQS). Much of the motivation for asset transfer was to create organisations and an asset class that could secure funding from institutional lenders to enable the achievement of the new housing quality standards. Their local authority predecessors were prevented from borrowing by UK Government Treasury rules and asset transfer to housing associations became the primary route to repair and renewal of social housing in the UK.

It was also the case that housing services evolved to meet the pressing social needs of an increasingly residualised tenant population. Rising levels of poverty during the 1980s and 1990s had created neighbourhoods where poverty and social exclusion had become the norm (Adamson, 2010b). Management of social housing had to contend with tenants whose lived experience included long-term economic inactivity, poverty, social exclusion and increasing levels of anti-social behaviour. For Stephens and Leishman (2017, p. 1054), *social renters* were between 1.5 and 2 times more likely to experience poverty than their wider sample, with most experiencing 'chronic' poverty. The response on the part of social housing providers was to tackle communal levels of poverty through programmes targeting community level solutions, including community development activities.

Often encapsulated in the term 'more than bricks and mortar', (e.g. Communities First Support Network, 2011; Kanter & North, 2012) an increasing number of housing organisations developed social interventions that were intended to improve the quality of life of their tenants. Interventions have evolved from simple community development activities into the arenas of urban regeneration, health improvement, education and training provision and the promotion of employment opportunities. Whether to deliver social regeneration activities or not is an organisational choice and organisations that take this route are usually those with a strong social enterprise and not-for-profit culture and ethos. The Centre for Local Economic Strategies (CLES) identifies such organisations as 'progressive' housing providers who as organisations can identify their regenerative capacity.

> For some, this diversification is part of a progressive approach to neighbourhood management which considers the wider role that RPs (*Registered Housing Providers*) can have in enabling thriving places. RPs have important roles to play in local economies, drawing together communities through social networks and providing support for tenants to access opportunities for their personal development. This is about going far beyond a focus on just homes and thinking about the broader role that RPs can have in supporting the lives of their residents.
>
> (CLES, 2013, p. 1)

By the mid-1990s this pattern of provision had attracted the *Housing Plus* label to describe a general approach which was nevertheless characterised by a wide range of interventions. A 1997 Joseph Rowntree review of Housing Plus activities on five London estates (Kemp & Fordham, 1997) identified the following approaches being adopted:

- improved tenant participation and consultation;
- development of multi-agency partnerships;
- provision of social facilities including play areas, mother and toddler clubs and youth facilities/workers;
- vocational training;
- revised letting policy to improve social mix.

Practices of this kind became widespread in the UK housing movement, including in the devolved housing regime in Wales. In response, the then Federation of Welsh Housing Associations convened a Community Development interest group to identify good practice and promote the Housing Plus agenda. In the context of housing stock transfer, community regeneration activities became established as a key element of the 'transfer offer' to tenants. Would-be housing association recipients of transferred stock were aware of the critical need to address social as well as housing issues. In this they were also able to build on longer-term community development practice by housing associations to develop community regeneration approaches which tackled the full range of social problems evident in social housing communities.

In the current post-transfer context there has also been a developing interest in providing economic and employment opportunities for residents of social housing communities. The achievement of the new Housing Quality Standards in England and Wales ensured that there was significant expenditure in the very poorest communities. The opportunity to link this to the training and employment of local people was identified early in this process. Consequently, a range of social procurement practices have emerged from the desire to ensure that the money spent on achieving new housing standards would have direct economic benefit in the communities where the money would be spent.

To support innovative procurement practice, the Welsh Government established an arm's-length organisation called i2i (Chartered Institute of Housing, 2010). There an expert team developed the legal frameworks for innovative procurement practice, which ensured local employment, targeted recruitment and training and the creation of apprenticeships as core contract requirements of any companies providing services to achieve the WHQS. This produced the *Can Do Toolkit* (Chartered Institute of Housing, 2010) which gave clear legal guidance to commissioning agencies on the development and enforcement of effective social clauses in all WHQS contracts. This has been enthusiastically embraced by the stock transfer sector, which has also adopted wider practices of community-based regeneration through tenant participation, energy efficiency and community activity programmes.

The context described above provides fertile ground for the evolution of a co-production of the housing service. Community development, engagement and participation programmes are commonplace, as is the representation of tenants in governance and management of Housing Associations. From board memberships to scrutiny panels and mystery shopper roles, tenants are actively involved in the design, delivery and improvement of housing services in all jurisdictions in the UK. The following case study provides a typical illustration of how a Housing Association and its tenants co-produce their housing service.

A UK case study: the Bron Afon Community Housing Mutual

The ballot for the transfer of the Torfaen Local Authority Housing stock of just under 10,000 homes took place in 2007 and a new Community Housing Mutual (CHM) organisation was established in March 2008 to receive the transferred stock. Tenant turnout in the transfer ballot was 68 per cent with a majority vote of 59 per cent for transfer. The *offer* document included a strong recommendation for transfer from the local authority and was clear that without transfer the WHQS would not be achieved and that the quality of housing services could not be maintained. The newly established CHM was quick to establish its credentials as a *social enterprise* with a clear commitment to improvement of services and a major regeneration approach to tackle the endemic poverty of the housing communities it served.

An early emphasis was on creating employment opportunities by developing its own direct labour force to support both its repairs service but also the achievement of WHQS. This involved retraining the labour force inherited from the local authority, alongside the creation of new apprenticeships.

Its second major emphasis has been on tenant engagement. Alongside the basic CHM pattern of tenant board membership, it has developed extensive tenant participation approaches in all aspects of housing services. An extensive programme of tenant training has been made available and many tenants have been assisted into very active roles within the organisation as energy wardens, secret shoppers and sub-committee members. The organisation also facilitates voluntary activity in befriending projects, family support services, digital inclusion, employment support and environmental projects. Full training is provided to volunteers and the activities are promoted as stepping-stones to employment.

Specific co-production example

Bron Afon founded a Youth Forum to support the many failed tenancies involving young tenants who were not in education, employment or training (NEET) in 2009. Now with 170 registered users this self-managed forum initiates projects and directly participates in the management of Bron Afon CHM, for example by participating in interviews for all new staff. To recognise the role of young people, Bron Afon has reduced the minimum age of membership of the CHM to 11 from the originally required 16 years. The forum determines future actions and establishes Task and Finish Groups to deliver them. Current projects are:

- **Own Two Feet:** an eight week training course to prepare homeless young people for a tenancy with the organisation.
- **Sport That Works:** a sport orientated employability programme in partnership with statutory employment agencies to prepare young people for work.
- **Go Girls:** a project to improve the confidence of young women around issues of employment, domestic violence and body image.
- **Ty Cyfle:** from recognition by the forum of a need for forms of intermediate tenancy for young people, a derelict block of flats has been repaired by young people and self-managed with appropriate professional support to create eight one-bedroom apartments.

All projects have been conceived and designed by members of the forum and supported by appropriate agencies to achieve effective delivery. The Youth Forum has been recognised nationally through housing sector awards.

The core characteristic of this model of intervention is *community empowerment*. Central to this has been the engagement of tenants in the management and coordination of housing services. Building on a long evolution of community development approaches, the interventions by UK housing associations typified by the case study are generally targeted at whole communities. Individuals benefit by their participation in communal approaches to economic and cultural change. The emphasis is on changing the lived experience of tenants through communal provision. This represents an *enhanced* (Osborne & Strokosch, 2013) approach to co-production with tenants having influence in a wide range of operations of the housing organisation.

Housing service co-production in Australia

Social housing in Australia initially follows a similar trajectory to the UK. An initial rapid phase of development post-1945 saw a major building programme create 670,000 new homes between 1955 and 1956 (Troy, 2012). A similar economic stimulus to the UK was achieved and did much to create the 'lucky country' reputation of Australia. As in the UK, the primary beneficiary of this programme was the working class population employed in the new services and manufacturing industries. In Australia, the housing was managed by the separate state governments, with funding provided by Federal Government in a series of partnership agreements. These have varied in form and nomenclature but prevail until today (from 2017 termed the National Housing and Homelessness Agreement).

However, despite this early commitment a *bifurcation* of housing policy (Jacobs, Atkinson, Peisker, Berry, & Dalton, 2010; Jacobs, 2015) occurred with a 1956 decision to allow tenant purchase of public housing. The result has been a social housing stock of declining number since that time (Pawson & Wiesal, 2014). There has been a clear policy preference towards homeownership as a key component of the *Australian Dream*. From a 50 per cent homeownership level in 1947, this increased to a peak figure of 70 per cent in the 1966 census (Troy, 2012). Homeownership is supported by a range of Federal and State provided subsidies (Grudnoff, 2016), with a combination of Capital Gains Tax exemptions and general tax concessions for properties that are 'negatively geared' where investment costs exceed rental income. This is currently fuelling a housing price 'bubble' in the major cities. Policy settings favour property investors over first time purchasers and renters in the housing market as well as in Federal housing policy (Heaton, 2016; Gurran & Phibbs, 2015; Jacobs, 2015). In contrast, social housing has been: 'Chronically underfunded, neglected, stigmatised … kept afloat in the twenty-first century only by ongoing asset sales and deferral of essential works' (Pawson & Wiesal, 2014).

In Australia, the term social housing refers to a combination of state provided homes and those managed by the community housing sector (Yates, 2013). In 2015 there were 394,844 social housing households with 80 per cent in state owned housing and 17 per cent in the community sector. The remainder is State Owned and Managed Indigenous Housing (SOMIH) (Australian Institute of Health and Welfare (AIHW), 2015). New stock development is almost non-existent and acute shortages of social housing prevail. Current national waiting lists stand at *circa* 200,000 (AIHW, 2015).

Currently 4.8 per cent of the population meet their housing needs from social housing and, despite the stigmatisation of social housing in the Australian media and wider culture, social housing in Australia plays a significant role in housing low-income families, with highly positive benefits for their overall lived experience. For example, 95.3 per cent of tenants in public housing and 93.7 per cent of tenants in community housing felt better able to manage their rent and finances. Some 88 per cent felt more able to cope, and over 80 per cent reported enjoying better health since moving into social housing (AIHW, 2015). In qualitative studies, tenants' evaluation of public housing has been very positive in terms of the impact on their lives and their sense of social inclusion and 'belonging'. This in contrast to the often negative social exclusion focus of much of the social housing literature (Mee, 2007, 2009).

However, in the face of unmet demand and acute social need it is inevitable that a significant residualisation process is occurring as social housing allocation is largely on the basis of acute need. The socio-economic profile of Australian social housing tenants is similar to those in the UK in that they are low-income households. However, there is a high incidence of mental illness, physical disability and addiction behaviours. Allocation of social housing is almost entirely based on need and there is no parallel process to choice-based letting systems as in the UK. With only 4.8 per cent of housing supplied by the social sector, the service is inevitably 'rationed' to those with greatest need. This may include tenants with significant health challenges or those with poor tenancy performance in the private sector, which has effectively eliminated them from future private sector tenancies (Wiesel, 2012).

In a recent review of a New South Wales (NSW) social housing community, over 95 per cent of tenants allocated in the previous year were designated as having high or very high needs, with 42 per cent of them housed directly from homelessness or risk of homelessness (Adamson, 2016b). This has prompted the description of Australian social housing as an 'ambulance service' (Fitzpatrick & Pawson, 2014) and a growing perception of social housing as 'welfare housing' (Yates, 2013). Jacobs and Manzi (2017) see this as an inevitable consequence of the declining political and popular support for welfare and social security spending within the wider neo-liberal 'punitive management of poverty' (Jacobs & Manzi, 2017, p. 28). Social outcomes for Australian tenants are low with high levels of economic inactivity and much current policy focuses on improvement of tenant health and educational outcomes to create employment trajectories that can support a transition from social housing to the private rental sector.

In further contrast to the UK, there has been little asset transfer to the community housing sector. A Council of Australian Governments (COAG) agreement in 2010 (Commonwealth of Australia, 2010) agreed to transfer up to 35 per cent of public housing to the community sector. However, in the majority of states little progress has been made towards that level of asset transfer. The exceptions are Tasmania and NSW where major transfer programmes have been initiated. NSW state has recently concluded the transfer of 14,000 properties. However, the transfers that have occurred have been management transfers and have not included title to enable the benefits of stock transfer realised in the UK (Pawson, Milligan, Wiesel, & Hulse, 2013). This has restricted the borrowing capacity of the sector and prevented meaningful growth. Consequently, a 'large' community housing provider in Australia would have around 5,000 properties in management, with very few directly owned. This is despite a recognised capacity to innovate and expand operations and diversify housing models (Gilmour & Milligan, 2013; Milligan, Hulse, Pawson, Flatau, & Liu, 2015).

The only exception to this wider policy framework occurred following the Global Financial Crisis which prompted an economic stimulus programme by the 2007 Rudd administration (Groenhart, 2013). This saw the re-establishment of the role of Minister for Housing, the launch of the National Rental Affordability Scheme (NRAS) in 2008 and the Social Housing Building Initiative within the Nation Building Economic Stimulus Plan (Milligan & Pinnegar, 2010). However, this policy did not challenge the predominance of subsidy for home ownership and itself had a limited target to build 50,000 homes (Jacobs et al., 2010).

In this more marginalised Australian context of social housing, there has been no significant emergence of the patterns of co-production identified above in the UK housing system. Key parameters of a collective approach to comprehensive tenant co-production through participation in service design, delivery and governance has not emerged.

However, innovative approaches of tenant support have emerged to assist tenants maintain their tenancy. As in the UK this innovation has occurred over the last five to ten years and represents a major departure from the 'bricks and mortar' provision of housing. Furthermore tenants are directly engaged in co-production of their individual tenancy. This is especially true where challenges to the tenancy exist and the housing provider secures tenant collaboration with support services in order to maintain the tenancy. Tenants can be comprehensively involved in programmes of 'wrap-around support' that ensure they meet personal challenges and maintain their tenancy. There has been considerable innovation in the provision of support services and despite reluctance on the part of community housing providers to accept a 'case management' role, they are actively engaged in securing support for tenants with a range of needs.

Case study: Compass Housing Services, community housing provider

Compass Housing Services is based in Newcastle, NSW with additional operations in Queensland and New Zealand. With 4,200 properties it is one of the largest community housing providers in Australia and is recognised as an industry leader in the sector. Evolving from a small local community provider with origins in the 1980s it employs over 140 staff with offices in urban, rural and remote regions. It provides housing management services to the NSW and Queensland state governments and has been relatively successful in securing transfers of state housing assets. This has accelerated in recent years as the NSW state housing department has engaged in several periods of asset transfer, culminating in an overall transfer of 14,000 properties in 2017. Compass Housing will receive 1,827 of this latest tranche of transfers.

Compass regards itself as a 'socially regenerative' housing provider with a mission and associated values to improve social outcomes for its tenants. This has engaged the organisation in the development of a range of social interventions and community development activities. Central to this is a 'specialist tenancy management model' that conducts wellbeing assessments of its tenants at the time of the six monthly physical inspections of properties. Deploying the Community Star Outcomes Assessment™ method, tenants are assessed in terms of their personal wellbeing and social integration. Declining profiles at personal levels are targeted by referral to appropriate support agencies to assist the tenant overcome any personal difficulties that may prejudice their ability to maintain the tenancy. Compass has formal Memoranda of Understanding and cooperation agreements with over 50 support agencies. Key issues for tenants are physical disability, mental illness, addictions and anti-social behaviours.

Where a housing complex is demonstrating increased levels of anti-social behaviours and deteriorating social cohesion, a range of community development methods are delivered to provide opportunities for developing social capital and community cohesion. In areas of concentrated social housing with high levels of economic disadvantage and social exclusion, Compass uses the Deep Place method of community renewal developed in the UK to address long-term, structural poverty (Adamson & Lang, 2014).

The focus of these interventions is to provide a supportive environment and to ensure that tenants are connected to and engage with relevant third-party support providers. Referrals are made to partner organisations and the tenant is supported to engage with the relevant provider. This engages Compass as the landlord and the individual tenant in a collaborative framework to ensure that the tenancy is maintained. This form of co-production differs considerably from the more communal approaches evident in the UK.

Specific co-production example

In new tenancies established under the NSW Government Social and Affordable Housing Fund (SAHF), Compass will provide formally defined 'tailored support coordination services'. This will require a formal needs assessment of the tenant and all family members over the age of 16. A Support Plan will be co-produced with the tenants to define and deliver the patterns of social support required by the family to improve social outcomes in health, education and employment. Reassessment will occur at the anniversary of tenancy commencement. The tenants will be supported to access the support agencies identified in the Support Plan. The policy identifies an 'opportunity' cohort of tenants with potential to improve social outcomes to enable a transition to the private rental sector, or even homeownership.

In this programme the tenant is most directly involved in the co-production of their tenancy. There are high levels of compliance required and conformity to an agreed programme of support is the underpinning collaboration between the housing provider and the tenant. This approach is a form of 'coordinated support' rather than case management but engages the tenant and the organisation in a close collaboration to maintain the tenancy. Compass, as housing provider, will appoint specific support staff, but the tenant will be directly engaged in co-production of the outcomes.

Conclusion: two modes of co-production

In examining the contrasting patterns of co-production in Wales UK and NSW Australia two modes of co-production can be identified.

- **Service co-production**: an 'enhanced' pattern of co-production in which the general approach is communal and deploys engagement of tenants in managerial and governance processes of the organisation itself. The emphasis is on a relationship between the tenant collective and the housing provider.
- **Tenancy co-production**: a support model in which tenants are supported at communal and personal levels to maintain the behaviours required to sustain a tenancy. The emphasis is on the relationship between individual tenants and the housing provider.

Two factors have influenced the evolution of these distinct modes. The first is the higher levels of residualisation evident in the Australian housing system. Residualisation of social housing is a long-recognised issue in social housing policy. The term refers to ways in which rising levels of poverty and an associated spatial distribution of social exclusion has been concentrated in social housing communities (Lee & Murie, 1999). In the UK, social housing constitutes some 18 per cent of all housing (Clarke & Monk, 2011) while in Australia it is 4.8 per cent. In the UK whilst needs-based allocation is historically a component of residualisation (Clarke & Monk, 2011), it is offset by elements of choice-based letting and conscious policies to promote more mixed social housing communities.

Earlier, we identified the almost exclusively needs-based allocation to social housing in Australia and increased perception of the social housing provision as an 'ambulance' service (Fitzpatrick & Pawson, 2014). Social housing in Australia is provided to those experiencing the highest levels of need in society (Morris, 2015). This suggests that social housing in Australia is limited to the most socially excluded sections of the population, who are likely to experience lower educational attainment, a wide range of physical and mental illnesses and limited social capital. Their general capacity to engage actively as tenants in the patterns of co-production evident in the UK is limited by this level of residualisation. In the UK jurisdiction, the tenant population is more likely to include people who are employed and able to redirect generic skills and competencies to the role of active tenant. Inevitably, in Australia, a housing cohort with severe social and wellbeing challenges is less likely to participate in the governance structures of the housing organisation. Hence in Australia tenants tend to be co-producers of their personal tenancy rather than co-producers of the housing service itself.

This does not negate their role as co-producers. Indeed, it may be a more demanding role. In the Australian case study presented above, tenants may variously be engaged in regular attendance at appointments with multiple support providers, active engagement with educational opportunities and access to volunteering or employment activities. This involves potentially radical lifestyle change.

The second major factor determining the patterns of co-production is the regulatory environment. In the UK there has been a long-standing regulatory requirement to engage tenants in service provision. With variations between devolved administrations, there is an overall high evaluation of the contribution that tenants can make to the provision of housing services. This is recognised for example in the Homes and Communities Agency approach to 'involvement and empowerment' requiring involvement in:

> a. the formulation of their landlord's housing-related policies and strategic priorities
> b. the making of decisions about how housing-related services are delivered, including the setting of service standards
> c. the scrutiny of their landlord's performance and the making of recommendations to their landlord about how performance might be improved
> d. the management of their homes, where applicable
> e. the management of repair and maintenance services, such as commissioning and undertaking a range of repair tasks, as agreed with landlords, and the sharing in savings made, and
> f. agreeing local offers for service delivery.
>
> (2017, para. 1.2.1)

The Australian National Regulatory Scheme for Community Housing (NRSCH) has no similar expectations. The only comparable requirement to earn or maintain national recognition is the reporting of results from a tenant and resident satisfaction survey (NRSCH, 2015). Compliance with contractual requirements of state departments can impose additional criteria but have historically not included any characteristics of co-production.

In NSW, the primary jurisdiction of operation of the Australian case study, the primary policy environment sees social housing as a 'pathway'. The NSW *Future Directions* (NSW Government, 2016) policy framework encourages community housing providers to work with their tenants to achieve better social, educational and employment outcomes for themselves and their family members. In the recently developed SAHF programme, additional resources have been provided to community housing agencies to deliver 'tailored support coordination services' to tenants housed under the scheme. The policy objective is for tenants to make the transition from social housing to the private rental sector. The SAHF strategy has set a 5 per cent target for tenants transitioning to private rental. This is a significant policy innovation that both recognises existing support practice developed by community housing providers and seeks to develop it further and require it from housing providers who are yet to provide such services.

NSW state policy will in the future be based on a co-production of the tenancy and improved social outcomes rather than co-production of the housing service. There is currently no financial, regulatory or cultural incentive to engage tenants in the design, delivery and review of housing services.

In the UK 'housing service co-production' has become embedded in the practice of Housing Associations and has a corresponding recognition in organisational roles and professional training. It constitutes an element of the regulatory environment and the self-assessment procedures of individual organisations. In Australia, the 'tenancy co-production model' has become a common aspect of service delivery and routine form of professional practice. In NSW it has become an element of the primary policy environment for social housing. The innovations that have occurred in both jurisdictions are consequently structurally positioned to be consolidated and developed further. Their long-term influence is to change the conventional 'bricks and mortar' social housing paradigm and the role of social housing providers.

For housing providers in each jurisdiction, the consolidation, development and extension of the relevant mode of co-production has become an important part of the operational environment. Their future role as housing providers will, in part, be dependent on their abilities to deliver the expected outcomes. However, there is also considerable opportunity to enhance each model by adoption of the alternative approach in a hybrid model.

Towards a hybrid model

In summary, the two distinctive models of housing co-production identified in this chapter are not contradictory but could be highly complementary if adopted in combination. This would create a very comprehensive co-production model that would benefit tenants of all capacities and levels of interest, and the organisations that house them.

Levels of tenant engagement in design, governance, delivery and evaluation of housing services in Australia is minimal. Despite the additional barriers to tenant engagement presented by a more highly residualised population than evident in the UK, the adoption of practices developed in the UK would be of considerable benefit. Currently, there is little opportunity for tenants to influence the pattern and quality of the housing services they receive. Compass Housing, the subject of the Australian case study presented here, has recently established a Compass Tenant Involvement Panel (CTIP) that reports directly to Board and is in the process of developing three regionally based Tenant Assessment Panels to report on the housing service from a tenant perspective. New South Wales Federation of Housing Associations is also supporting two trial studies of Tenant Service Assessor schemes, funded by the State Government, Family and Community Services Department under its Housing Industry Development strategy. This suggests that there is an emerging Australian interest in greater tenant involvement in 'service co-production'.

Similarly, tenant support systems are rare in the UK. Generally, 'wrap around' family support is seen as a social service provision and such approaches are regarded as exceptional in the housing field. Where they have occurred, they have attracted considerable interest (Shelter UK, 2007), but have not led to a general adoption by housing providers. Central government has developed its Troubled Families Programme to work with the most marginalised 400,000 families nationally. The initial evaluation report identifies successes, but also difficulties maintaining family progress once the family exits the programme (Department for Communities and Local Government, 2017). The Australian experience suggests that the close relationship between families and social housing providers can establish a strong platform on which to deliver stable patterns of family support. The development of a 'hybrid' model focused on service co-production and tenancy co-production would create a comprehensive model and further opportunities for different patterns of tenant involvement that reflect tenants' interests, capacity and competence.

References

Adamson, D. (2010a). Community empowerment: Identifying the barriers to 'purposeful' citizen participation. *International Journal of Sociology and Social Policy*, 30(3–4), 114–126.

Adamson, D. (2010b). *The impact of devolution: Area-based regeneration policies in the UK*. York: Joseph Rowntree Foundation.

Adamson, D. (2016a). *Towards a national housing strategy*. Hamilton: Compass Housing Services.

Adamson, D. (2016b). *A deep place study of Muswellbrook, NSW*. Hamilton: Compass Housing Services.

Adamson, D., & Bromiley, R. (2013). Community empowerment: Learning from practice in community regeneration. *International Journal of Public Sector Management*, 26(3), 190–202.

Adamson, D., & Lang, M. (2014). *Towards a new settlement: A deep place approach to equitable and sustainable places*. Merthyr Tydfil: Centre for Regeneration Excellence Wales.

Alford, J. (2009). *Engaging public sector clients: From service-delivery to co-production*. Basingstoke: Palgrave.

Alford, J. (2014). The multiple facets of co-production: Building on the work of Elinor Ostrom. *Public Management Review*, 16(3), 299–316.

Australian Institute of Health and Welfare (AIHW). (2015) *Housing assistance in Australia 2015: Social housing dwellings. Online and supplementary data tables*. Retrieved from www.aihw.gov.au/housing-assistance/haa/2015/.

Bovaird, T. (2007). Beyond engagement and participation: User and community co-production of public services. *Public Administration Review*, *67*, 846–860.

Bovaird, T., & Loeffler, E. (2012). From engagement to co-production: The contribution of users and communities to outcomes and public value. *Voluntas*, *23*, 1119–1138.

Bradley, Q. (2008). Capturing the castle: Tenant governance in social housing companies. *Housing Studies*, *23*(6), 879–897.

Brandsen, T., & Pestoff, V. (2006). Co-production, the third sector and the delivery of public services: An introduction. *Public Management Review*, 8(4), 493–501.

Card, P., & Mudd, J. (2006). The role of housing stock transfer organisations in neighbourhood regeneration: 'New localism' and social networks. *Housing Studies*, *21*(2), 253–267.

Centre for Local Economic Strategies (CLES). (2013). *The CVLES 10. The vital things to know: Progressive housing associations*. Manchester: Author.

Chartered Institute of Housing (CIH Wales). (2010). *The can do toolkit*. Retrieved from www.cih.org/i2i/candotoolkit.

Clarke, A., & Monk, S. (2011). Residualisation of the social rented sector: Some new evidence. *International Journal of Housing Markets and Analysis*, 4(4), 418–437.

Commonwealth of Australia. (2010). *Regulation and growth of the not-for-profit housing sector: Discussion paper*. Canberra: Commonwealth of Australia.

Communities First Support Network. (2011). *More than bricks and mortar: The Welsh housing quality standard – implications and guidance for Communities First*. Cardiff: author.

Department for Communities and Local Government (DCLG). (2017) *Troubled families programme: Evaluation overview policy report*. London: Crown Publisher.

Fitzpatrick, S., & Pawson, H. (2014). Ending security of tenure for social renters: Transitioning to 'ambulance service' social housing. *Housing Studies*, 29(5), 597–615.

Gilmour, T., & Milligan, V. (2013). Let a hundred flowers bloom: Innovation and diversity in Australian not-for-profit housing organisations. *Housing Studies*, *27*(4), 476–494.

Goldethorpe, J. H., Lockwood, D., Bechhofer, F., & Platt, J. (1967). The affluent worker and the thesis of embourgoisement: Some preliminary research findings. *Sociology*, *1*(1), 11–31.

Groenhart, L. (2013). Reflecting on a decade of Australian social housing policy: Changes in supply and geography, 2001–2011. *Geographical Research*, *51*(4), 387–397.

Grudnoff, M. (2016). *CGT main residence exemption: Why removing the tax concession for homes over $2 million is good for the budget, the economy and fairness*. Canberra: The Australia Institute.

Gurran, N., & Phibbs, P. (2015). Are governments really interested in fixing the housing problem? Policy capture and busy work in Australia. *Housing Studies*, 30(5), 711–729.

Heaton, A. (2016, 3 February). *Is Australia's housing policy debate built on myths?* Retrieved from https://sourceable.net/m/single/?name=australias-housing-policy-debate-built-myths.

Homes and Communities Agency. (2017). *Tenant involvement and empowerment standard*. London. Crown Publishers.

Jacobs, K. (2015). The 'politics' of Australian housing: The role of lobbyists and their influence in shaping policy. *Housing Studies*, 30(5), 694–710.

Jacobs, K., & Manzi, T. (2017). The party's over: Critical junctures, crises and the politics of housing policy. *Housing Studies*, 32(1), 17–34.

Jacobs, K., Atkinson, R., Peisker, V. C., Berry, M., & Dalton, T. (2010). *What future for public housing? A critical analysis. Final Report 151*. Melbourne. AHURI.

Kantor, K., & North, J. (2017). *More than bricks and mortar: Responding to the housing crisis – theologically, morally, practically and politically*. Joint Public Services Team. Retrieved from www.jointpublicissues.org.uk/wp-content/uploads/2012/12/BricksAndMortar.pdf.

Kemp, G., & Fordham, R. (1997). *Implementing 'Housing Plus' on five housing association estates*. Housing Research Findings No. 219. York. Joseph Rowntree Foundation.

Lee, P., & Murie, A. (1999). Spatial and social divisions within British cities: Beyond residualisation. *Housing Studies*, *14*(5), 625–640.

Malpass, P., & Mullins, D. (2002) Local authority stock transfer in the UK: From local initiative to national policy. *Housing Studies*, *17*(4), 673–686.

Mee, K. (2007). 'I ain't been to heaven yet? Living here this is heaven to me': Public housing and the making of home in inner Newcastle. *Housing, Theory and Society*, *24*(3), 207–228.

Mee, K. (2009). A space to care, a space of care: Public housing, belonging and care in inner Newcastle, Australia. *Environment and Planning*, *41*, 842–858.

Milligan, V., & Pinnegar, S. (2010). The comeback of national housing policy in Australia: First reflections. *International Journal of Housing Policy*, *10*(3), 325–344.

Milligan, V., Hulse, K., Pawson., Flatau, P., & Liu, E. (2015). *Strategies of Australia's leading not-for-profit housing providers: A national study and international comparison*. Melbourne: AHURI.

Morris, A. (2015). The residualisation of public housing and its impact on older tenants in inner-city Sydney, Australia. *Journal of Sociology*, *5*(2), 154–169.

Murie, A. (1997). The social rented sector, housing and the welfare state in the UK. *Housing Studies*, *12*(4), 437–461.

National Regulatory System for Community Housing (NRSCH). (2015). *NRSCH compliance: Provider guide 2015*. Retrieved from www.nrsch.gov.au/__data/assets/file/0005/335057/Provider_Compliance_guide_Oct_2015.pdf.

New South Wales Government. (2016). *Future directions for social housing in NSW*. Sydney. Retrieved from www.socialhousing.nsw.gov.au/?a=348442.

Nygaard, C., Gibb, K., & Berry, M. (2007). Ownership transfer of social housing in the UK: A property rights approach. *Housing, Theory and Society*, *24*(2), 89–110.

Osborne, P. S., & Strokosch, K. (2013). It takes two to tango? Understanding the co-production of public services by integrating the services management perspectives and public administration perspectives. *British Journal of Management and Public Administration*, *24*, 31–47.

Ostrom, E., Parks, R. B., Whitaker, G. P., & Percy, S. L. (1978). The public service production process: A framework for analysing police services. *Policy Studies Journal*, *7*, 381–389.

Parker Morris Committee. (1961). *Homes for today and tomorrow*. London: Her Majesty's Stationery Office.

Pawson, H., & Wiesal, I. (2014). Tenant agency in Australia's public housing transfers: A comparative assessment. *International Journal of Housing Policy*, *14*(4), 344–367.

Pawson, H., Milligan, V., Wiesel, I., & Hulse, K. (2013). *Public housing transfers: Past, present and prospective*. Final report No. 215, Melbourne: AHURI.

Pestoff, V., Osborne, S. P., & Brandsen, T. (2006). Patterns of co-production of public services. *Public Management Review*, *8*(4), 591–595.

Shelter UK. (2007). *Shelter inclusion project. Managing anti-social behaviour in the community: five years on*. London: Author.

Smyth, S. (2012). The privatization of council housing: Stock transfer and the struggle for accountable housing. *Critical Social Policy*, *33*(1), 37–56.
Stephens, M., & Leishman, L. (2017). Housing and poverty: A longitudinal analysis. *Housing Studies*, *32*(8), 1039–1061.
Suszynńska, K. (2015). Tenant participation in social housing stock management. *Real Estate Management and Valuation*, *23*(3), 47–53.
Troy, P. (2012). *Accommodating Australians: Commonwealth government involvement in housing*. Sydney: Federation Press.
Voorberg, W. H., Bekkers, V. J. J. M., & Tummers, L. G. (2015). A systematic review of co-creation and co-production: Embarking on the social innovation journey. *Public Management Review*, *17*(9), 1333–1357.
Wiesal, I. (2012). Mobilities of disadvantage: The housing pathways of low-income Australians. *Urban Studies*, *51*(12), 319–334.
Yates, J. (2013). Evaluating social and affordable housing reform in Australia: Lessons to be learned from history. *International Journal of Housing Policy*, *13*(2), 111–133.

9 Monumental mural design

The outcome of interactive urban storytelling – France

Lionel Toutain Rosec and Jean-Pierre Schaefer

Introduction

Over the last 50 years in France, the relatively standardised architecture that has been a feature of urban construction often disconnected from town or city centres and has made the population living in social housing more vulnerable. This vulnerability is characterised by lower participation in the life of society and a higher incidence of related evils, including low neighbourhood attractiveness, rapid deterioration of the built heritage, and disconnection from social activities and urban culture (Dubedout, 1983). Numerous participatory and collaborative initiatives have been taken to offset or even reverse this trend (Région Aquitaine, 2014). For 30 years, proactive public policies have focused on investing in redesigning these neighbourhoods in both functional terms (e.g. major renovation and reconstruction) and social terms, with a view to help residents retake ownership of their living areas and to revive a virtuous economic and social dynamic (CGET, 2017). In this chapter, we explore the example of the CitéCréation Company; for 40 years, through its "Monumental Mural Design" approach,[1] it has been working in these neighbourhoods on crafting a new urban heritage narrative using a participatory approach involving the residents.

The stories told on refurbished facades of the buildings refer to the local stories of the inhabitants and turn these districts into open books.

After starting slowly in the first half of the twentieth century, the production of social rental housing in France increased significantly between 1955 and 1975 (Scanlon, Whitehead, & Arrigoita, 2014). With this high growth came the use of an architectural vocabulary inherited from the principles of the modernist movement, but in a simplified form, featuring the economy of technical means and architectural repetitiveness (Driant, 2017). Providing light and open spaces for all inhabitants was achieved through the construction of towers and blocks of flat far from the traditional urban fabric. The pressure of housing demand and a centralised decision-making system left little room for consultations with residents. The scale of property developments and the dimensions of the buildings were disproportionate compared to existing urban fabrics. Depending on land availability, new neighbourhoods were built either in isolated areas or integrated into existing urban areas, but in a totally different style from the surrounding buildings. By remaining true to its hygienist objective of the modernist movement, this approach produced limited dense spaces, featuring well ventilated plots that were completely different from the traditional urban landscape. Some attempts were made at landscaping the public realm, but there were no financial means to ensure proper long-term maintenance (Fourcaut, 2004).

Most of the construction was in the form of apartment blocks. While most new neighbourhoods (three-quarters of them) were dedicated to social rental housing, some buildings with flats for private ownership were also included (a quarter of the housing units in these neighbourhoods). Apart from some slight improvements (e.g. balconies and better designed entrances), their architectural appearance was like social housing blocks. Based on decisions made by the central government, these neighbourhoods were designed as coherent wholes whose site plans were definitive, i.e. not destined to change (Noyé & Lelévrier, 2009).

From the 1980s onwards, new housing production in France remained active (350,000 units per year on average); however, compared to previous decades, the housing was more diversified, notably due to the growing share of single-family homes. The size of the buildings and of the new neighbourhoods was reduced. Resident consultation procedures became mandatory. The production of social rental housing continued, accounting for between 15 and 25 per cent of housing production. However, for the last 25 years, the social rental, private rental, and homeownership sectors in France have renewed their architectural forms. The architecture of the new housing production (e.g. dimensions of buildings, balconies, and height) was designed on an improved human scale. Without passing judgement on the quality of the architecture, we can say that social housing became very similar to the rest of mainstream housing production. However, this led to a deepening of the territorial divide between the new neighbourhoods and those built before the 1980s – all the more so because for 25 years, between 1980 and 2004, none of the eight million new housing units was built in the neighbourhoods developed before the 1980s. These areas remained unchanged until the National Urban Regeneration Programme (PNRU) started in 2005. Although the stock of approximately one million social housing units built before the 1980s now represents only a quarter of the total supply of social rental housing, it remains a significant symbol of poor-quality housing that is associated with the social sector (Le Goullon, 2014). While remaining affordable, the asset value of this stock has depreciated compared to all other types of housing (Schaefer, 2014). This depreciation in the collective minds of people has also greatly and adversely affected its image in the eyes of the tenants concerned. The modern (sanitary) comfort that it represented 40 years ago is now widespread. In addition, the more recently built housing units have extra features, such as larger houses on the outskirts of the housing estates and apartment blocks with balconies in the inner areas, which are well integrated into the urban fabric or located in better designed districts (TNS Sofres, 2013).

Older social rental housing units generate lower rents than recently produced social housing. The former is therefore more attractive to lower-income households. Older social housing units are also generally profitable for property managers, even though their decline in quality may lead to a rise in tenant turnover (due to the departure of middle-income households) or to higher vacancy rates (with locations becoming unattractive even to low-income households). The original loans for older social housing units have been amortised and the rents paid contribute to the managing entity's total housing portfolio. These funds are used to finance the supply of new social rental housing units. Thus, in spite of their generally negative image, these social housing areas retain real functional and financial value; housing providers hesitate to demolish them, despite their negative image. They prefer to refurbish these properties and closely involve the residents to better understand their discontent and try to address it.

Consequently, participatory initiatives and co-production approaches are becoming central to the housing refurbishment processes in order to capture and enhance the heritage value of social housing estates, while also taking into account the impact on the surrounding urban area as a whole.

Recent urban regeneration policies in France

The PNRU, launched in 2004 by the French government, combines actions to improve the quality of housing and neighbourhoods with interventions to address economic and social issues (ANRU, 2007). To improve the image and identity of these areas, actions should be visible to neighbourhood residents, as well as to people in the surrounding area. Major investments have been made (€40 billion over the 2004–2018 periods) under this programme for demolition and rehabilitation works and for constructing new housing and neighbourhood facilities (ONZUS, 2013).

This urban regeneration programme is partially financed by the state, local government authorities, and businesses (through the 1 per cent *Action Logement* payroll tax to fund employee housing support) (ANPEEC, 2013). However, most of the funding is provided by a special financial institution (Caisse des Dépôts) in the form of low-interest, long-term loans. These loans will be reimbursed by social housing landlords (companies and offices). Thus, the final payer is still the tenant. Consequently, the urban regeneration programme needs to be financially feasible. Thus, the question is the following: how can the value of the housing stock be enhanced again in technical, symbolic, and use terms for the benefit of the residents, but also in terms of market value?

French urban regeneration policy focused on priority neighbourhoods and involves the state, local government authorities, landlords, and other local partners and funders. The legal framework for PNRU is provided by a city contract (*contrat de ville*) with provisions relating to economic development, employment, social cohesion, the living environment, and urban regeneration. Economic development comprises support for job-seeking, training, and entrepreneurship. Social cohesion is strengthened by measures to improve social, cultural, and sports amenities, as well as the support of local, non-profit voluntary organisations. The PNRU also aims to strengthen education, healthcare, and public safety. The city contracts target some 400 priority neighbourhoods across France to be transformed with a view to enhance social diversity and improve relations with the rest of the town or city.

Resident participation in neighbourhood regeneration

Resident consultation in housing rehabilitation began in the early 1990s. Consultation is mandatory[2] and must allow the nature of the required works and their effects on rents and service charges to be discussed with residents, making them a serious participant in regeneration projects. This is even more important in the event of a demolition project involving the rehousing of residents. Although assessing the financial benefit of consultation is no easy matter, the absence of consultation may create high subsequent costs due to worksite failure or a rapid deterioration in completed projects.

Under the laws and regulations governing urban development policy in France, all schemes are managed with the involvement of the residents concerned. Established in 2015, citizens' councils provide places for exchanges between residents and represent them in all the decision-making bodies set up under a city contract. The councils offer scope for initiatives based on residents' needs. Thus, more than ever, residents are considered as decision-makers, and this promotes participatory initiatives to improve their living environments.

The emergence of CitéCréation

The gradual process of empowering residents to take control of the changes in their built environments through concerted action is not new in France. Resident involvement has been supported by a very diverse range of civil society associations and networks. In this context, several students at the School of Fine Arts in Lyon started CitéCréation in 1978 as a cooperative business focused on the design and production of monumental and enduring wall paintings or murals, advocating the importance of shared urban storytelling.

A large part of CitéCréation's activities has been focused on the social housing sector, developing its expertise in participative engineering focused on residents. Through their contacts with residents and social landlords, CitéCréation consultants had often observed the disappearance of a shared local identity that has been stifled by uniform and standardised architecture. The residents were no longer aware of the local identity of their neighbourhood and failed to "put down roots" in their living areas. In addition to the residents' loss of the sense of belonging to their neighbourhoods, there were growing economic and social problems, such as uncontrollable vacancy and tenant turnover rates, rising charges and damage to property, the lack of festivities or collective events, high levels of unemployment, social isolation, and early school withdrawal.

The "monumental mural design" approach developed by CitéCréation is grounded in its early experiences with social housing projects and contacts with residents. The core element in this approach is the belief that the monumental aesthetic response must come from the local human and natural history, co-constructed, and then shared with the residents. It is indispensable that residents retake ownership of their living spaces and redevelop social ties. Consequently, each project can craft an urban narrative that is shared and approved by the users of the local area.

The distinguishing feature of monumental mural design is to use drawing and painting to depict narratives that tell the stories of neighbourhoods. This approach is different from wall paintings conceived first and foremost as cultural works of art. Monumental mural design is a heritage-enhancing initiative of the highest aesthetic and technical quality. It is a long-term project lasting several decades, i.e. as long as the structures on which the work of art is painted last. Such works of art adapt to the constraints imposed by the public spaces used in terms of robustness and warranty.

The monumental mural design approach takes into consideration the different stakes of French urban regeneration policy by focusing on resident participation. It is integrated into refurbishment programmes and must feed consultations and citizens' councils. These contributions become reality with the construction period and change the image of the district; they also increase the confidence of the tenants, as well as the feeling of belonging in the community.

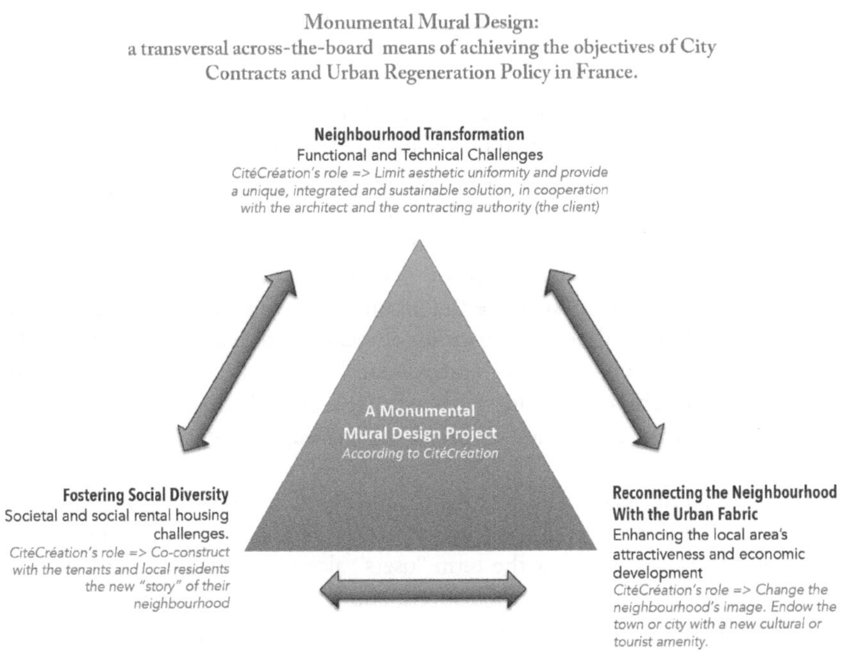

Figure 9.1 Monumental mural design aims according to CitéCréation.

The role of CitéCréation: approach and critical success factors

The success of a project depends on good coordination between the stakeholders at every stage. The participatory approach is conducted without making any unreasonable promises, but with a commitment to consider collectively validated elements. Under the overall responsibility of the contracting authority (the client), several stakeholders are involved with CitéCréation at different stages of a project:

- The social landlord and the tenants are the project's key actors. The social landlord must promote a robust and innovative heritage strategy, be well organised, and must maintain constructive relations with residents.
- Good relationships with local political actors (e.g. elected officials, technicians, and voluntary associations) are also essential.
- Other stakeholders can come into play depending on the context of a project, such as the National Urban Regeneration Agency (ANRU), Caisse des Dépôts (public interest financial institution), regional authorities, EU funds, and public and private sector businesses.

A monumental mural design project is based on a methodology focused on co-creation throughout the design and implementation phases:

- The *design phase*, which lasts six months on average, is structured around four creative workshops for tenants and jointly organised by CitéCréation and the social landlord. During this time, several presentations are made: principles underpinning the monumental mural design, the design concepts, artistic models based on local and individual stories. This procedure can also be activated locally and simultaneously on social networks to reach users who are often absent from these meetings, such as economically active people and young adults. This design phase has a dual purpose: first, to compose a robust corpus of documents (testimonies, pictures, video reports, items, etc.), to create the urban narrative and work on artistic creation and, second, to allow a group of residents to emerge that are capable of acting as the project's "ambassadors". Parallel to this, CitéCréation works with the contracting authority (the client), the architect, and the project management team on preparing the implementation for the overall project.

  Designing specifically highlights an interest in users and their environment. Residents are at the forefront with their lives, cultures, residences, habits, dreams, etc., but the term "users" also includes, among others, visitors, tourists, voluntary organisations, and businesses. Designing also implies understanding the local heritage in terms of its buildings (e.g. architecture, urban scale, and history), urban environment (e.g. neighbourhood layout, connections with the town or city centre, traffic flow analysis), and natural features (e.g. flora and fauna, and landscaping issues). Designing means taking an interest in all the human, technical, and natural data relating to a specific local area in order to decipher the issues and find the appropriate response in terms of urban storytelling.

"Designing" is also related to "drawing", i.e. producing an aesthetic and visual response that is comprehensive, balanced, and elegant. This entails the production of works of art that meet the residents' concerns regarding the attractiveness of their local area and their pride in it. The act of drawing also implies a storytelling dimension. The image exposed in a public location tells a story to those who look at it. This story should be understood by the great majority of audiences, which means the work of art should meet the requirement for universal aesthetics, i.e. be relatively figurative. Its content should convey a message linked to local history.

- The *implementation phase* runs throughout the project. The completed mural works reveal on a monumental scale the aesthetic participatory urban narrative. A new and better quality and more sustainable image of the neighbourhood emerges in the eyes of residents and visitors.

The projects may help to significantly improve the quantitative and qualitative performance indicators of the landlords, even though it is still sometimes difficult to measure all outcomes in the monitoring and follow-up studies. Generally speaking, it is necessary to take multiple indicators into consideration.

The partial rehabilitation projects carried out between the 1980s and the 1990s sometimes used stereotyped or fragile technical solutions (e.g. cladding). New investments amounting to €8,000 per housing unit (representing 8 per cent of the value of the homes) did not suffice to avoid a decline in the attractiveness of this housing stock. The current projects envisage investing amounts three to five times larger. A monumental mural design project represents between 2 and 10 per cent of this overall budget, depending on the landlord's aesthetic and participatory ambitions.

Urban storytelling: three cases

The core of the monumental mural design concept consists of giving life to the facades of urban buildings with murals depicting unique local stories shared by the local community. The local urban area is seen as a book, and each social housing building within this area is seen as a blank page on which to write a chapter of the story. The sum of these pages tells the story in a way that is consistent with all the perspectives that characterise the neighbourhood. This blank page may not necessarily be a gable, as it may occupy the outside of an entire building. Artistic mural painting is a medium that allows great freedom of expression in terms of unique aesthetic responses while making it possible to achieve a high level of durable technical quality on walls of any type (e.g. stone, concrete, brick) or on all kinds of cladding (e.g. aluminium, metal, wood, stone, glass).

This section presents three cases where CitéCréation was involved in the creation of monumental mural designs. The cases contain the narratives of some residents and other actors closely involved in the rehabilitation project.

Case 1: Tony Garnier Urban Museum, Lyon rehabilitation rewarded by UNESCO

In 1985, *Grand Lyon Habitat*, Lyon's main public sector social landlord, undertook a vast project to rehabilitate one of its oldest heritage sites, namely the housing estate known as *Cité Tony Garnier*. The estate was built in the early 1930s by Tony Garnier, a local architect and city planner who was known as the father of "hygiénisme" (sunlight for every dwelling, winds analysis driving construction programmes, and integration of free spaces and urban vegetation) and of the ideal industrial city (*Cité Industrielle*). This complex of 1,500 housing units for over 3,000 residents was in a pitiful state. The social landlord was considering the option to partly demolish the complex. However, a group of residents made a concerted effort to prevent this to keep local history alive. Supported by the expertise of CitéCréation, this initiative gave birth to the Tony Garnier Urban Museum, located in this social housing neighbourhood, featuring an urban trail of 24 monumental murals or frescoes that highlight the thinking and achievements of Tony Garnier as architect and city planner. This urban narrative, initially created with the help of residents, now welcomes tens of thousands of tourists every year.

"A lasting change of image"

In 1985, Eddie-Gilles di Pierno was the very young president of Cité Tony Garnier's tenants' association and of a local committee:

> In 1985, our neighbourhood, built in the early 1930s by Tony Garnier, was close to the end of its useful life. After an initial phase of very complex and costly rehabilitation works, the landlord had concluded that it would be easier to demolish and rebuild what remained. As for "Maestro" Tony Garnier, everybody had forgotten about him, including the residents and the politicians. At the age of barely 20, I became the president of the local neighbourhood committee. I was surrounded by dozens of ladies in their 60s who were proud of their neighbourhood, with its history, and were determined to fight to prevent its disappearance. At a time when we were looking for any means of drawing attention to this situation, Michel Roz, an architect from Lyon, organised an event on the Tony Garnier site, highlighting the exemplary nature of Garnier's work on the Industrial City. As a result, Tony Garnier regained recognition of his importance and we saw an opportunity to enhance the value of this neighbourhood.
>
> In order to force the landlord to rehabilitate the rest of our housing estate, the tenants' association committee then asked CitéCréation to think

Figure 9.2 Picture 1: Tony Garnier Urban Museum facade, by CitéCréation.

about how to make our gloomy homes more attractive by having monumental murals painted on them. In 1987, CitéCréation came up with the concept of the Tony Garnier Urban Museum, to tell the story of Tony Garnier's vision, research work and completed projects using monumental murals painted on neighbourhood buildings. At first, not more than 40 tenants thought that this strategy would save our neighbourhood. It was

Figure 9.3 Tony Garnier's residents, by CitéCréation.

> also necessary to check (and demonstrate) that it was in everybody's collective interest to live in Tony Garnier's utopia. So, we rolled up our sleeves and visited over 400 homes to persuade other tenants. And the support we got was overwhelming.
>
> In 1988, with the most highly-motivated tenants and Mr Christophe Pawlowski, an expert on Tony Garnier, we imagined a trail of 24 monumental heritage murals of buildings designed by Tony Garnier to be painted on our buildings. The project was launched in 1989. In the wake of this, the demolition of the housing estate was abandoned, and the comprehensive rehabilitation of the neighbourhood began and continued for 10 years. The entire monumental mural trail was completed in 1995, but as early as 1993, UNESCO rewarded this project, and its residents, for its exemplary nature as part of the World Decade for Cultural Development.

Eddie-Gilles di Pierno, president of Cité Tony Garnier's tenants' association, continues:

> What evidence do we have of the success of this project? First, the incredible way the tenants took ownership of it; by the end of the 1990s, we had up to 600 "project ambassadors." Thousands of visitors came to admire the

Figure 9.4 Picture 2: Tony Garnier Urban Museum facade by CitéCréation.

murals without a single act of vandalism. Neighbouring schools showed an interest in them. Tony Garnier definitively recovered his prestige and all the residents (over 3,000 people) knew all about his life. Furthermore, the project's success was reflected in the press and in the number of tourists walking around our buildings. Very soon, as early as in the late 1980s, the image of the neighbourhood changed completely. References to our neighbourhood switched from the "general news" section of the press to the "heritage and culture" pages. Throughout the 1990s, the media coverage increased, and articles appeared in the French press (*Le Figaro*) and international media.

"An unquestionable success"

Catherine Panassier, President of Grand Lyon Habitat, the largest social housing body in Lyon:

Figure 9.5 Tony Garnier Urban Museum facade latest inauguration, by Michel Djaoui.

> The project was an unquestionable success in terms of promoting the neighbourhood and opening it up to the outside world, but also in terms of strengthening social ties. Furthermore, the fact that the rehabilitation of the social housing buildings by Grand Lyon Habitat coincided with monumental mural design project restored the residents' pride in living in this neighbourhood.

Thirty years later, the Tony Garnier urban museum and the social housing buildings have aged. The collective momentum that had given birth to the museum has diminished and the housing units no longer meet contemporary standards of energy efficiency and comfort. Hence, the decision by Grand Lyon Habitat to launch a new and ambitious rehabilitation programme, which will respect the quality of the heritage buildings and, at the same time, will restore the wall paintings on the same themes as before, i.e. utopias and the ideal city.

Case 2: "Art'mosphere by DOMANYS", Yonne County, Burgondy-Franche Comté

Domanys is a public housing authority for Yonne County in the Burgondy-Franche Comté region of France. As the main local manager of social housing, Domanys manages 10,000 homes and employs over 200 people. In 2015, the management of Domanys decided to undertake an innovative rehabilitation programme, and entrusted CitéCréation with a monumental mural design project for a heritage site with 110 homes in the town of Tonnerre.

"Traditional rehabilitation does not work"

Karine Lascols, General Manager, explains the project, its challenges, and its preliminary results:

> This programme to rehabilitate 110 apartments in the small town of Tonnerre poses many challenges. The residence in question, which comprises four apartment blocks built in the 1960s, no longer meets the housing needs and expectations of our clients. It's an urban enclave disconnected from the town and nobody wishes to go there. Furthermore, this area suffers from a negative image due to the social vulnerability of its residents and the related sense of insecurity. The vacancy rate exceeds 20%, so we're looking for solutions to enhance the attractiveness of this heritage site. We have observed that traditional rehabilitation programmes do not develop social ties. Also, no matter how attractive the programme may be, people do not settle in a neighbourhood in which they feel insecure. We realised that we would have no chance of enhancing the attractiveness of the site if the residents themselves did not "sell" their residence. So, we incorporated into the rehabilitation programme an innovative initiative aimed at durably recreating social ties.

First, we had to persuade the tenants to support the innovative monumental mural design approach, which was completely new to this neighbourhood, but we also had to convince our own internal heritage management teams! During its feasibility study, CitéCréation presented its engineering project to the Domanys teams, who embraced the concept with its participatory and aesthetic dimensions. Staff members became magnificent ambassadors for the project in the eyes of the tenants. The attendance rates at the creative workshops run by CitéCréation for the residents reached 30 to 40%, whereas only 5 to 10% of residents attended our rehabilitation consultation meetings. We also launched a digital version of these workshops via Facebook and Instagram, which are social networks, and were accessible within a radius of 25 kilometres around the town of Tonnerre. During the four-month consultation period, these physical and virtual channels of communication reached over 500 people, i.e. more than twice the number of tenants in the residence! The leverage provided by the social networks enabled us to communicate with both the economically active and the young sections of the population whom we failed to interest in our project. During the consultation and co-design phase, the residents showed their great interest in being listened to and participating in the process of designing an aesthetic concept. The people from beyond the neighbourhood also appreciated the interest shown in them. In other words, at this stage of the monumental mural design project, although the rehabilitation work had not begun, and the murals had not been painted, the residents' perception of their neighbourhood was already changing.

Figure 9.6 Domanys, by CitéCréation.

> The rehabilitation works started in March 2017 and are due to last for 18 months. The first rehabilitated building featuring a monumental mural design has been visible since the end of May. Although most of the project remains to be implemented, we have already observed that the images of the neighbourhood in the eyes of our tenants and the way they use the residence have changed. The project has strengthened social ties. Today, instead of criticising our local teams, people begin by making positive comments, such as stating that the feelings of insecurity and isolation are diminishing. The local law enforcement personnel have much less work to do than before! Town councillors also express their satisfaction at the positive feedback they get from the citizens of Tonnerre who are already visiting the residence.

General manager Karine Lascols:

> We would have liked more people to participate in the consultation phase. We also noted how many participants are afraid to express their views and give their opinions. We all have our doubts about how long people will show respect for the monumental murals. That said, a different and positive image of the neighbourhood is emerging, and our sales people are optimistic about the improving trend in the vacancy rate. So, I'm confident that this project will rise to the economic challenges of rental housing in this part of the town.

Case 3: So'Fresk by Vilogia, Lyon

In 2015, the *Vilogia* housing group launched a project for the improvement of 450 heritage housing units in the Vallonniere suburb of Lyon. This project formed part of a rehabilitation programme that aimed to bring together residents from different generations whose residence (three buildings) was laid out in such a way as to separate them from each other. Vilogia commissioned CitéCréation for a monumental mural design project that focused on strengthening social cohesion in the area.

"We are now part of the story"

Charha Chikhi and Maurice Ruffier, the building caretakers, talk about this project, which was implemented in close cooperation with the residents:

> At the beginning of the project, the residents appeared to be a little apprehensive. What would be put on the walls and who would pay? Bear in mind that on this estate, we house over 1,500 residents with very different backgrounds and representing a broad range of age groups. Although the elderly residents remembered the construction of this residence and the state of the neighbourhood in the 1960s, many of the other residents did

Figure 9.7 Picture 1: So'Fresk Vilogia, by CitéCréation.

not. CitéCréation clearly explained that it was up to them to tell their stories and develop the new narrative that would be shared by all. Residents participated in local workshops. There was a lot of discussion between the meetings and residents could also participate via the internet. People came to us in our caretaker quarters to ask for more detailed information on the

Figure 9.8 Picture 2: So'Fresk Vilogia, by CitéCréation.

next stages of the project. Little by little, the degree of trust increased and, above all, residents who were unacquainted began to speak to each other. Not only did they discover the story of their neighbourhood, but they also contributed to the emergence of a new narrative about all of us.

Today, as the monumental mural design project enters its last phase, everybody is very enthusiastic and is impatient to see what comes next. Even the young residents like the project. The tenants have understood that this project enhances the value of their buildings, to which they refer by naming the murals painted on them. They move around between the buildings to discover and compare them and ask for explanations. Others have begun to visit them.

As for us, the caretakers, this project has enabled us to change our positioning in relation to the residents. We've started to engage in a new kind of dialogue with them and to say positive things, even though rehabilitation periods are never easy. In addition, we too are now part of the story!

Discussion

Any monumental mural design project requires good coordination between local stakeholders and strategic decision-makers. It should enable all stakeholders to achieve their objectives and legitimise their action; the residents should be able to co-create the embellishment of their residences; local housing staff, such as caretakers, should give new meaning to their community action; social housing managers should be able to implement a unique and innovative project that affects only a fraction of their assets; and local voluntary organisations should generate more synergies by participating in the project. In addition, for social landlords, such an approach helps to improve internal cohesion between, for example, the management teams and the technical teams involved in the rehabilitation project.

Numerous issues need to be addressed as part of each monumental mural design project:

- In terms of the landlord's *strategic governance*, will the project enhance the sustainability and profitability of the heritage asset? A project involving an ageing asset whose construction cost has been amortised generates equity capital, but reinvesting diminishes these returns of funds, at least during the lifetime of the new loans. So, a financial equilibrium is not easily achieved.
- In terms of the landlord's *operational governance*, is the project manageable at a local level? Does it involve voluntary and economically motivated local players? Does it provide local professionals (maintenance staff, caretakers, site managers, etc.) with an opportunity to have positive contacts with tenants?
- Regarding *user participation*, do the tenants and residents accept such an approach?
- Regarding *political governance*, does the project give a favourable image of the local area? Does it generate material for a shared urban narrative based on the local area's history, sociology, and culture?
- Regarding the *architects and city planners*, do they accept including an aesthetic non-academic feature in the urban space?

CitéCréation gives a precise example of a fully integrated monumental mural design actor. It is able to implement variable sized projects with a long-term return on experience.

However, as a newly innovative approach integrated into refurbishment programmes, monumental mural design is not easily fitted to the administrative circuits of social landlords and policy makers. Specific insurance, maintenance, and financing are new issues to be tackled. Some landlords might still be hesitant in determining if the approach is a real investment or one of pure expenditure.

Another limit concerns architectural trends that see facade design as nonsense. Thus, the participatory approach about facade design with tenants is not acceptable. As well, some elected representatives that think urban storytelling should not be integrated into lasting realisations. Finally, because of a lack of identified professional actors, participatory mural design interventions stay confined to small associations or associated with street-arts family projects.

Brought by the new legal obligations given by the French government and the emergence of citizen councils, such participatory approaches are developing in France. Private and public players have the obligation to implement it into their programmes. However, without the emergence of strong professional actors to absorb the demand, the risk is to see the development of improvised participatory design projects that will intensify the stigmatization of social neighbourhoods into the French urban landscape.

Conclusion

This chapter described how monumental mural designs help to open up and regenerate social housing neighbourhoods and increase social cohesion. The monumental expression of a shared urban narrative enables residents to retake ownership of their neighbourhoods, while endowing the local areas concerned with new cultural and tourist amenities to reconnect these marginalised urban spaces with the rest of the town or city. For over 30 years, this approach has been successfully deployed in various locations not only in France, but also in Germany, Austria, and Sweden. This success is based on the requirement to produce long-lasting high-quality works of art to tell a shared story, using a participatory methodology that follows a rigorous procedure while being adaptable and transferrable to other countries, target groups, and contexts. In whatever country, the mission of monumental mural design remains the same: to mitigate the impact of growing urban standardisation and the loss of heritage of places and people.

Notes

1 In this chapter, the monumental mural design approach applied by CitéCréation is used as an example of an innovative participative method that has developed and matured over the years.

2 Mandatory under Circular 93-60, dated 6 August 1993 and extended by the Solidarity and Urban Renewal law of 13 December 2000 to any property transaction that impacts rents or charges.

References

ANPEEC. (2013). *Rapport d'activité 2012* [Activity report 2012]. Paris: ANPEEC.

ANRU. (2007). *Les enjeux de la concertation avec les habitants* [Residents consultation issues]. Retrieved from anru.fr/index.php/fre/Mediatheque/Publications/Les-enjeux-de-la-concertation-avec-les-habitants.

CGET AMADEUS CDC. (2017). Développement économique local en quartiers prioritaires [Economic development in priority neighbourhoods]. Saint-Denis, France: CGET.

CitéCréation. (1999). *Musée Urbain Tony Garnier, des HLM que l'on visite* [Tony Garnier Urban Museum: a visited social housing district]. Lyon: éditions Lyonnaise d'Art et d'Histoire.

CitéCréation. (2014). *Les fresques des bords de Loire* [Frescoes on the banks of the Loire river]. Lyon: Éditions La Simarre & CitéCréation.

CitéCréation. (2011). *Les fresques des Noirettes, une aventure humaine* [Noirette's frescoes, a human adventure]: Lyon: éditions CitéCréation.
Driant, J-C. (2017). Les politiques du logement en France [Housing policies in France]. Paris: La Documentation française.
Dubedout, H. (1983). Ensemble refaire la ville [Together, lets' build the town again]. Paris: Documentation française.
Fourcaut, A. (2004). Le monde des grands ensembles [The world of large scale real estate]. Paris: CREAPHIS.
Le Goullon, G. (2014). Les grands ensembles en France, genèse d'une politique publique 1945–1962 [The history of large scale real estate]. Paris: Editions CTHS no. 56.
Noyé, C., & Lelévrier, C. (2009). *Diversification de l'habitat, diversification fonctionnelle* [Housing diversification]. Paris: IAU.
ONZUS. (2013). *Dix ans de PNRU, bilan et perspectives rapport d'évaluation.* [Assessment of ten years of urban renewal] Saint Denis, France: Editions du CIV.
Région Aquitaine. (2014). *Panorama régional des démarches participatives en politique de la ville.* Bordeaux: Région Aquitaine.
Scanlon, K., Whitehead, C., & Arrigoita, M. (2014). *Social housing in Europe.* London: Wiley.
Schaefer, J-P. (2014). Quartiers en renouvellement urbain: La valorisation de l'immobilier est-elle mesurable? [How to measure real estate value in urban renewal areas?]. Paris: Réflexions immobilières IEIF, no. 69.
TNS-Sofres. (2013). *Baromètre image du logement social* [Barometer of social housing]. Paris: Union Sociale pour l'Habitat.

Part III

Housing finance models

10 "Wiener Wohnbauinitiative"

A new financing vehicle for affordable housing in Vienna, Austria

Alexis Mundt and Wolfgang Amann

Introduction

Austria has a long tradition of supply-side housing subsidies directed at individual families developing their own single-family housing and, in the multi-apartment sector, Limited-Profit Housing Associations (LPHAs). These associations construct and manage mainly rental apartments with long-term leases, based on cost-rents and targeted at low- and middle-income households. By this channel, the nine Austrian regions were able to set up a large and internationally acknowledged social rental housing sector (Lawson, Gilmour, & Milligan, 2010; Deutsch & Lawson, 2012; Mundt & Amann, 2010; Reinprecht, 2014).

As for Vienna, which is the Austrian capital and a region in its own right, this traditional subsidy scheme was lately expanded by a new scheme, the so-called *Wohnbauinitiative* (WBI), initiated by the municipality of Vienna in 2011 and continued in a new programme in 2015. It is meant additionally to encourage multi-apartment housing construction and address overshooting housing demand in the city.

The background for this initiative is strong population growth and increasing pressure on the general rent level. Vienna is growing much stronger than previously planned and housing construction targets are periodically scaled up: in 2011, when the WBI was started, the quantitative aim was calculated at 7,500 new dwellings each year, a noticeable increase on former targets. In 2016 the quantitative aim was raised to 13,000 new dwellings per year, out of which some 9,000 are planned to be subsidised units and the rest market-financed projects (Stadt Wien, 2016). With these ambitious quantitative targets, the city's administration is reacting to a strong increase in housing demand due to household formation, and internal and external immigration into the city (Prenner, 2014). Likewise, it shows an ongoing commitment to a high share of subsidised units in overall construction (Lawson, 2010; Reinprecht, 2014). Vienna nowadays is a rental city with an internationally extraordinary large share of social housing. According to the microcensus 2014 (on main residency dwellings), some 20 per cent of all tenures are owner-occupied houses and flats, some 76 per cent are rental flats and 4 per cent are other tenures. The rental sector is formed by privately rented flats (32 per cent), LPHA rental flats (19 per cent) and the still large stock of municipal rental flats (25 per cent). The last two categories can be considered the social rental sector, that is 44 per cent of all tenures (see Mundt & Amann, 2010). With this large market share of social housing, the Austrian, and especially the Viennese, rental market comes close to what Jim Kemeny (1995; Kemeny, Kersloot, & Thalmann, 2005) has identified as a "unitary rental market", a market where the non-profit housing segment is competitive, provides good market coverage and, therefore, shows a rent-dampening influence on the overall rent level. In a "unitary rental market" the private and the social market segments compete with each other, because they both address large population groups, provide similar qualities and reach sufficiently large volumes. How these interrelations are realised in the Austrian rental market has recently been demonstrated by Mundt and Amann (2010). The book chapter at hand will address how the municipality of Vienna reacts to current challenges to a "unitary rental market" in Austria that are emerging due to insufficient new social housing construction and a widening gap between social and private market rents.

Rental costs are lower in the social housing sector than in the private rental market. They are usually based on historic construction costs. Municipal rental flats in 2015 cost on average 6.4 €/m², LPHA rental flats 6.7 €/m² and private market rents 8.7 €/m² (Statistik Austria, 2016, p. 46). Especially market rents have increased very strongly during the last ten years and the availability of affordable rents on the market has lessened considerably. This has created an insider–outsider problem on the rental market: while long-term resident households still benefit from low historic rents and secure contracts, newcomers to the rental market face prohibitively high private market rents and fewer social housing options. Access to new LPHA housing is often restricted by high capital contributions demanded from future tenants. These contributions are repaid if the tenant moves out (minus 1 per cent p.a.), but, as many social tenants have few savings, constitute a considerable barrier to LPHA housing. They can reach a level of 100–500 €/m². The municipality of Vienna offers individual low interest loans to households who struggle with meeting required capital contributions. Income limits to qualify for these loans are however very low and only a limited number of households receives them.

The WBI was initiated in 2011 to quickly expand housing construction by adding housing units that receive some, but compared to existent regional schemes, less public subsidies. It demands less capital contributions from future tenants. The scheme was reinitiated in 2015 when quantitative targets for housing completions were further expanded. From its very beginning, the scheme was designed to widen, and not to replace, existing regional subsidy schemes. It adds another layer to housing supply, focusing on middle-income households and a mid-price range, as will be described in detail below.

This contribution builds on our analyses of available data and documents on the WBI. Additionally, several personal interviews with policy practitioners and builders were conducted to retrieve important information on the functioning and organisation of the WBI, and to be able to present some current housing projects. Also, the interview partners were asked about their views of pros and cons of the WBI.

Context and governance framework

From a historical perspective, it is typical that the share of subsidised units in overall completions is very high. This is true for all Austrian regions and especially for Vienna (Amann, Jurasszovich, & Mundt, 2016). Out of some 9,500 overall completions in 2014, some 6,500 units were subsidised (roughly two-thirds), including some 800 units within the WBI scheme. Looking at the total housing stock in Vienna, the city claims that 62 per cent of the Viennese population lives in subsidised housing of various types (Förster & Menking, 2016, p. 7).

In 2004, Vienna city council stopped building new housing projects directly through municipal companies (municipal housing was re-introduced in 2016 as another measure to abate housing shortage) and relied more on organisations of the private sector to construct affordable rental housing. First and foremost, these are the LPHAs. But also (national and international) commercial developers have access to subsidies if they comply with stipulations of the Viennese Housing Construction Subsidy Law (from 1989 in its current form of 27 February 2017), especially concerning restricted access (income limits), ecological standards and other quality criteria.

Competition between developers increased since 1995 with the implementation of *Bauträgerwettbewerbe*, public housing development competitions organised by the *Wohnfonds Wien*, the Vienna fund for housing construction and urban renewal. These competing bids, often for large-scale projects on land provided by the fund, are open to all developers. Smaller housing projects may also be submitted by all developers to the *Grundstücksbeirat* (Land Advisory Board), which assesses the projects according to a point system on four major categories: economic aspects (land costs, total building costs, user costs and contract conditions etc.), ecology (climate- and resource-friendly construction, diversity of use of green and open spaces, etc.), architecture (structure of the building, design, etc.) and social sustainability (suitability for day-to-day use, cost reduction through planning, living together in communities, etc.). This competitive assessment of applicant projects is known as the four-pillars-model (wohnfonds_wien, 2015; Förster & Menking, 2016). The emergent projects are characterised by very high quality standards, e.g. concerning energy efficiency; often higher than in commercial new construction (Amann, Hüttler, & Mundt, 2012). The International Building Exhibition in Vienna in 2022 (*Internationale Bauausstellung*, IBA) will address the Viennese model of urban development and the role limited-profit housing plays within it.

In spite of the strict stipulations of the call for tender, competition in the tender procedures is fierce since there are fewer and fewer projects to compete on. Lately, the functionality of the existent two instruments has decreased, due to a general reduction of available subsidies and the difficulties for developers obtaining building plots that meet the maximum price requirement of the land advisory board (Mundt, 2013). The Vienna fund for housing construction and urban renewal still has considerable reserves, but only releases them to the competitions step by step (Förster & Menking, 2016).

The WBI was introduced as a new subsidy scheme with easier access criteria. At the same time, it keeps up public influence on the quality and price level of housing projects. The WBI dwellings add a new layer to the variety of subsidised housing completions in Vienna.

Table 10.1 depicts the different layers of new multi-apartment housing completions in Vienna and summarises the existent subsidy programmes and market-financed housing completions in dependence of the achieved rent level, tenants' capital contribution and access criteria. The figure focuses on multi-apartment new construction, where most new construction takes place. Only a much smaller part is single-family houses and new dwellings in existing buildings.

The middle layer of new construction is formed by the "regular" subsidy programmes, projects selected by the land advisory board or housing development competitions. Income limits are fairly high in order to enable a strong social mix. They are €44,700 net yearly income for a single person and €66,610 for two adults (2017). The fairly recently introduced construction layers below the middle layer consist of different subsidy schemes in which an additional loan by the administration enables lower rents for households that fall into lower income brackets (*Superförderung*). Most of these apartments are in the SMART format: these are small apartments with efficient floor plans and capital contributions that are much lower than in the regular schemes. Access criteria are stricter and income limits are lower if the full subsidy is claimed. Also, urgent housing need has to be proven, similar to municipal apartments. New municipal apartments receive the highest subsidy and enable the lowest rent level in new construction. As an additional benefit, there are no capital contributions for future tenants.

Social mix being a fundamental aim of the Viennese planning and housing administration, it is nowadays general practice that different layers of housing construction are realised within the same building. Projects usually combine different subsidy schemes with some market-financed apartments.

Market-financed new construction by commercial developers and by LPHAs has increased strongly in the last years. If LPHAs build without public subsidies and rely fully on market finance, they also have to charge cost-rents, but these will reach a higher level compared to subsidised projects. Commercial developers cover mainly the prime segment: rent levels will nowadays be clearly above 12 €/m². There are usually no capital contributions.

The large share of subsidised new apartments in overall output requires continuous and large public support. On average between 2010 and 2014, Vienna spent some €570 million on housing subsidisation within its regional housing budgets each year. Some 46 per cent of these expenses are loans for subsidised multi-apartment construction, some 39 per cent go to subsidised renovations

Table 10.1 Layers of multi-apartment housing completions in Vienna

Layers of multi-apartment housing completions in Vienna	*Rent level (gross), €/m² approx.*	*Tenant contribution €/m² approx.*	*Income limits and access criteria*	
Market financed (commercial developers)	12–25	0	No	↑
Market financed (LPHAs)	9–12	approx. 500	No	
Wohnbauinitiative 2011 (variant 1)	9.30	150	No, but 50% of new allocations through city administration	
Wohnbauinitiative 2011 (variant 2)	7.70	500	No, but 50% of new allocations through city administration	Tendency to higher rents, and at the same time less public subsidies
Subsidised apartments in "regular" subsidy schemes (land advisory board or housing development competitions)	7.5–8.00	max. 500	Fairly high	
Subsidised apartments with "Superförderung"	8–8.50	69.21	Fairly high, lower if income dependent additional subsidy	
Subsidised apartments with "Superförderung" (SMART)	7.50	max. 60	As above + proven urgent housing need	
New municipal housing construction	7.50	0	As above + proven urgent housing need	

Sources: own depiction based on housing construction, regional subsidy statistics; Personal communication – Teschl, 1 March 2016; Liske and Liske-Weninger, 14 April 2016; Aigner-Tax, 22 April 2016; Langmann, 28 April 2016; Glaser, 10 May 2017; Welzig, 15 May 2017.

Note
The gross rent level includes all rents, overhead building charges, taxes, but no energy costs.

and refurbishments. Thirteen per cent are means-tested housing benefits and only some 2 per cent are subsidised loans to households building their own single-family housing. Over the last decade there has been a shift of housing policy expenses towards a stronger focus on multi-apartment buildings, on new construction and refurbishments. The years 2011 and 2012 were exceptions because Viennese housing subsidy expenses were much lower than on average (Amann, Jurassovich & Mundt, 2015). This short-term reduction in subsidy expenses was also reflected in the number of subsidised new units in the multi-apartment stock: from an average level of around 6,300 yearly subsidised units between 2007 and 2010, there was a decline to only 2,500 units in 2011 and 4,800 units in 2012. During these two years, austerity measures had to be taken by the city council that also affected subsidised housing output. Since then, the number has increased again, to the highest level in the past 20 years in 2014, with over 9,100 subsidised units (Amann et al., 2016).

A large part of this recovery can be attributed to the WBI dwellings, which entered the statistics with 3,300 subsidised dwellings in 2013 and 2014. In coming years, more WBI dwellings will be completed and a sum of around 6,300 dwellings will be reached.

Other than the regional subsidy expenses, the WBI loan the city provided was not financed out of yearly regional budgets but came from an additional loan. In 2011, Vienna, in its capacity as a municipality, took out a loan of €300 million via the Austrian Treasury which was earmarked for the WBI and passed on to the participating consortia.

What is the innovation and how does it work?

The WBI is a subsidy scheme by the municipality of Vienna which provides medium-term, low interest loans and/or cheap building land for housing construction. It is an addition to the general regional housing subsidy schemes, in place in Vienna for many decades. It encourages new construction in the mid-price range, granting financial benefits in exchange for limited-term social obligations by the developers concerning rent levels and access criteria.

The WBI encourages innovative elements in subsidy arrangements: the orientation on both commercial and LPHA housing providers, the inclusion of capital from institutional investors, municipal building plots and medium-term municipal loans, and the limited-term nature of rent control for new contracts.

The first wave of the WBI was initiated in 2011. It was addressed at consortia of developers (LPHA and/or commercial) and financial institutions (banks, insurance companies), with the aim fostering co-financing of social housing by financial institutions. The main idea is to use beneficial finance conditions granted to the City of Vienna, as a low-risk, highly rated borrower, towards building consortia, which then pass on the benefit to tenants through cheaper than market rents and long-term secure rental contracts.

The City of Vienna stipulated the requirements for participating in the scheme in its 2011 call for tender (MA 50, 2011):

- Some municipal building plots would be sold to the consortia at a below-market price (around 235 €/m^2). The market rate is at least double that price. These plots are additional to the reserves held by the Vienna fund for housing construction and urban renewal which are designated for the regular regional subsidy schemes (housing-development competitions and land advisory board) (Stadt Wien, 2011).
- Loans of 800 €/m^2 usable floor space would be provided by the municipality, in the form of bullet loans and with an interest of 3.9 per cent for ten years (fixed term). These loans would be second rank in banking collateralisation, making additional commercial loans cheaper (see section below on finance).

In exchange for these privileges, the participating consortia would meet the following requirements:

- Own equity by the developers has to be at least 350 €/m^2 usable floor space.
- Financial partners have to invest at least €75,000 per completed dwelling.
- During the loan term (ten years) rent levels and capital contributions by future tenants are limited. There are two variants: 6.10 €/m^2 net rents and maximum 150 €/m^2 capital contributions by tenants (repayable minus 1 per cent p.a. when the tenant moves out); or 4.75 €/m^2 net rents and maximum 500 €/m^2 capital contributions by tenants.
- The allocation of 50 per cent of all completed dwellings, and 50 per cent of all re-allocations of dwellings during the loan term will be conducted by the general allocation agency for subsidised housing, the *Wiener Wohnberatung* (Vienna housing helpdesk). It allocates the dwellings according to social criteria and general waiting lists. However, there are no income limits as in other subsidy schemes (see Table 10.1).
- The remaining 50 per cent of allocations will be carried out by the developers themselves. However, all rental contracts have to be of an unlimited term. For sitting tenants, during their tenancy, rental rates will only be valorised with overall inflation as measured by the consumer price index. Only for new allocations, and after the public loan term of ten years has expired, can commercial developers charge higher market rents. They can also offer these dwellings for sale then. LPHAs who build WBI apartments have to charge cost-rents throughout the entire existence of the building.

The initial call was set up for some 6,300 new dwellings following this scheme to be built between 2012 and 2015. Overall investment would account for approximately €1 billion (Stadt Wien, 2012). Due to good experience with the new subsidy scheme, a second wave of the WBI was initiated in 2015 (see below).

The city's influence on the quality of submitted projects is secured through a special advisory board that evaluates the projects and proposes improvements, much like in the other subsidy programmes (WBI advisory board, see below).

Altogether the WBI 2011 will yield some 35 projects. The project size ranges from 13 units to around 450 units. More than two-thirds of all WBI 2011 projects are already completed, the others are still in the pipeline. The projects are located throughout the city with larger projects mainly in the current urban development areas, with a focus on "Seestadt Aspern" (see below).

Who is involved?

Region and municipality of Vienna

Vienna holds a special position as it is a region and a local entity (municipality) at the same time. Therefore, in addition to the regional housing subsidy agendas, it has special leeway to apply municipal measures as well as regional policy instruments. For example, other regions often do not hold land banks as Vienna does, only some municipalities in certain regions apply that instrument. The WBI is also a "municipal" measure in addition to the regular housing subsidy schemes that fall in the "regional" competence of Vienna. Vienna was the main player in the WBI scheme: it proposed the WBI, initiated the call for tender, financed the subsidy part of the scheme and provided cheaper than market building plots.

Consortia of developers and financial investors

To participate in the first round of the WBI, participants had to be consortia formed by housing developers and financial investors. It was the intention to activate the national financial industry (banks and insurance companies) to play a stronger part in the financing of affordable housing construction. The plan was successful in as much as six consortia of housing developers and financial investors emerged and participated in the call.

The consortia were formed of one or more LPHAs or commercial developers together with at least one bank or housing construction bank (Stadt Wien, 2011). These consortia qualified for participating in the WBI scheme, i.e. partly receiving cheap municipal building land and additionally qualifying for the subsidised municipal loans.

The involved developers are mainly LPHAs, but also their commercial daughter companies, and/or commercial developers. Since the Global Financial Crisis, social housing has become more interesting as a long-term and low-risk investment with relatively low, but stable yield. Institutional investors have gained importance in financing social housing construction in several European countries (Oxley et al., 2015).

Limited-profit housing associations

LPHAs in Austria date back to the early twentieth century and continuously gained importance since the 1950s. The main idea is the setting up of a long-term social housing stock at below-market cost-rents directed at large parts of the population (Mundt & Amann, 2010). Today, 189 LPHAs are active in Austria, some as co-operatives others as limited-profit companies, but within a common legal scheme and supervisory structure. Currently 53 of all LPHAs have their headquarters and main focus of activity in Vienna. LPHAs have continuously increased their importance and have incremented their tenure share due to strong construction output. The LPHA housing stock plays a crucial role as affordable housing choices throughout the lifespan of households (Deutsch, 2009).

LPHAs have to focus on housing construction, refurbishment and housing management. In fact, it is a strong incentive for high construction quality and social balance if housing associations function as long-term managers. LPHAs are private sector enterprises that are geared towards fulfilling the demand for affordable housing, but which nevertheless act in an economically rational manner (Ludl, 2007; Lawson et al., 2010). Profits have to be reinvested in the sector. LPHAs have to be registered and are strongly audited. The sector itself conducts a first auditing procedure on a yearly basis, the respective regional governments are auditing authorities on a second level. LPHAs nowadays mainly build rental apartments, partly with a right to buy (after 10 or 15 years). In Vienna, they nowadays also build without regional subsidy loans but with market finance. Cost-rents apply nevertheless. For market-financed activity, some LPHAs have also set up commercial daughter companies (Pech, 2014).

Housing Construction Banks (Wohnbaubanken)

Taking up activity in 1994, their main task is to provide developers of affordable housing with medium- to long-term low-interest loans. Housing Construction Banks refinance themselves by the issuance of Housing Construction Convertible Bonds (HCCB) directed at private investors. These bonds benefit from tax advantages and are highly popular due to security of investment. Placing of the bonds continuously increased between 1994 and 2004 and peeked in 2004 and 2007. In 2007 €2.3 billion could be raised by the placement of HCCB. Since the Global Financial Crisis, HCCB have lost some appeal and new emissions bottomed in 2012, gaining importance again in 2013. Finance raised by HCCB has to be invested in subsidised housing projects. Most subsidised housing projects were therefore co-financed by these funds (Schmidinger, 2008, p. 264; Amann, Lawson, & Mundt, 2009; Lawson, Milligan, Yates, Amann, & Kratschmann, 2012). At the end of 2012, the volume of outstanding loans was around €14 billion. There are six Housing Construction Banks active in Austria today. Housing Construction Banks also participated in the consortia of the 2011 WBI call and also channelled additional finance raised through HCCB into WBI projects. This is yet another example of how the WBI initiative fits into an existent institutional framework which seems to contribute to the scheme's success.

WBI advisory board

The City of Vienna has had good experiences with implementing advisory boards for safeguarding the quality of subsidised housing projects. These advisory boards come in various forms and sizes, but usually include experts from different fields, some strongly linked to the city council and its various departments others more independent (architects, urban and land-use planners, building experts, ecologists, etc.) (Brech, 2012).

The WBI advisory board is with six standing members relatively small compared to advisory boards in other subsidy schemes but includes partly the same people. It is headed by a representative of the housing subsidy department of the city council (Brech, 2012, p. 120).

The WBI advisory board's sessions are rather flexible and the board can convene on short-term notice, which is also seen as a big benefit as it speeds up the process (Personal communication Liske & Liske-Weninger, 14 April 2016). The feedback of the advisory board to the developers and planners is more personal and immediate than in the more formalised advisory board sessions of other subsidy schemes. Necessary amendments and possible improvements are communicated directly after the sessions. A civil engineering consulting company (DI Herbert Liske) is in charge of organising and documenting the board's sessions and pre-evaluating the submitted projects.

As in the regular housing construction schemes, WBI projects are evaluated following the mentioned four-pillars-model (economic aspects, ecology, architecture, social sustainability). The economic aspects are however evaluated less competitively than in the other subsidy schemes because participants do not compete on overall construction costs but fulfil the requirement of economic efficiency if the proposed projects meet the above-mentioned criteria of maximum rents and capital contributions. This is seen as a main advantage and functions as an incentive for participants, who are reluctant or unable to take part in the highly competitive development competitions of the regular regional subsidy schemes (Personal communication Liske & Like-Weninger, 14 April 2016; Personal communication Langmann, 28 April 2016).

Finance

Table 10.2 summarises the cornerstones of the WBI schemes and their financial elements. All loans are bullet loans and have to be repaid at the end-term of the loan including interest, similar to a bond (Stadt Wien, 2011). Interest payments are included in cost rents starting with the first year. However, maximum rents are limited during the loan term.

WBI loans are cheap money for the developers and help them in the building process. The fact that the city's loans are secured only in second rank, makes additional market finance less expensive. Banks can secure their loans in first rank and also interpret the city's involvement as a guarantee of the projects' financial soundness. The city's scrutiny of subsidised projects throughout the

Table 10.2 WBI volumes and financial details

	Volume of (municipal) loans	*Dwellings*	*Interest rate*	*Loan term*	*Refinancing*
WBI 2011	c. € 230 million	6,300	3.9% fixed, bullet loan	10	Extra loan through Austrian Treasury (OeBFA)
WBI 2015	c. € 100 million	t.b.d. approx. 1,800	2.5% fixed, bullet loan	10	Taxes, i.e. regional budget

Source: personal communication – Teschl, 1 March 2016 and Liske and Liske-Weninger, 14 April 2016; MA 50, 2011.

quality procedures encourages the involvement of financial investors and banks as it adds security.

The city itself refinanced the loan via the Austrian Treasury, which manages public sector debt, with the same interest rate it passed on to the consortia (including liability fees) (Personal communication Teschl, 1 March 2016).

While the loan conditions sounded very promising in 2011 when the call was initiated, a strongly declining international interest rate environment increased the availability of even cheaper market loans for housing developers. This led to the fact that not all developers in the end took up the offered municipal loans. The remaining €70 million that were not taken up by the consortia were used to refinance existing housing construction loans, which for historic reasons still had very high fixed interest rates (Personal communication Teschl, 1 March 2016).

In the new wave of the WBI, which was agreed in 2015, the parameters of the loans were adapted to reflect the recent interest rate development. Now the loans will charge a fixed annual interest of 2.5 per cent for ten years. At the same time, the maxima of capital contributions and rent levels were left unchanged and not adapted to inflation. The first projects of the WBI 2015 were realised similar to WBI 2011 projects (Personal communication Teschl, 1 March 2016). However, there are considerations to integrate the new format into the regional subsidy schemes and thus to become a regular subsidy arrangement.

As the City of Vienna channelled cheap finance to housing developers, the city itself is responsible for loans being paid back in due time and that the risks involved are minimised. The following elements reduce these risks:

- The call was directed at consortia, so that risk is spread across more developers and financial institutions (Personal communication Langmann, 28 April 2016; Personal communication Teschl, 1 March 2016). At the same time, financial involvement is less pronounced if discounted building land is provided by the city itself.
- Many LPHAs are involved. They have a very high credit rating due to the LPHA housing sector they are embedded in (Amann et al., 2009).

After the sector's own auditing and control framework for all LPHAs, the City of Vienna is the second supervisory body over all LPHAs based in Vienna. The city therefore has a very clear idea of their financial situation. There is no additional formal guarantee or underwriting from the City of Vienna.

- The completed dwellings are usually cheaper than the market and in the current situation, allocation and marketing of the dwellings is not an issue, reducing thus the risk of vacancies. Most WBI dwellings are highly popular with clients and quickly taken up (Personal communication Aigner-Tax, 22 April 2016). The developers can advertise and allocate 50 per cent of all completed dwellings on their own account.

Table 10.3 summarises differences in costs and finance components between typical WBI projects as opposed to strictly market-financed projects. Building plots are much more expensive under market conditions and also construction costs are higher, due to usually smaller construction sights and missing incentives to keep construction costs low. Since WBI loans are not available, commercial loans play a much larger part in financing the construction. Such loans show less favourable and longer terms than WBI loans. Own equity by developers usually cover building plot costs, while tenants' capital contributions are usually higher in market-financed projects than in WBI schemes. As a result, rents in market-financed projects are much higher than in WBI projects. Differences vary across specific projects and locations but can easily amount to 2 €/m^2 (monthly rent) (Personal communication Stephan Langmann, 13 March 2018).

The WBI has had repercussions on federal housing policy as the federal state of Austria initiated a similar scheme, much inspired by the Viennese WBI. A federal *Wohnbauinvestitionsbank* (WBIB), a housing construction investment

Table 10.3 Financing examples

	Example WBI project: costs and finance based on m² useable floor space	*Example market-financed project: costs and finance based on m² useable floor space*
Building plot (incl. preparation)	€350	€900
Construction costs	€1,750	€2,300
Overall costs	**€2,100**	**€3,200**
Own equity developer	€350	€900
WBI loan	€800	€0
Tenants' capital contribution	€400	€500
Other loans (housing construction banks and commercial banks)	€550	€1,800
Overall finance	**€2,100**	**€3,200**

Source: personal communication Langmann, 13 March 2018; own calculation.

bank, was set up in autumn 2016. Once in operation, it will finance the planned "federal housing construction initiative" with a volume of €5.75 billion. In this process, the bank will channel €700 million of funds from the European Investment Bank into affordable housing, and necessary infrastructure, throughout Austria. Long-term low and stable interest rates for housing construction are the main drivers.

Examples of the innovation

Seestadt Aspern

Seestadt Aspern is Vienna's most dynamic urban development area and among the largest in Europe. It is located at the north-eastern part of the city on and around the site of a former airport and measures 240 ha. It is conceived for 20,000 inhabitants and around 8,000 housing units. The general development plan was designed by the Swedish architect Johannes Tovatt and approved by the municipal council in 2007.

Seestadt Aspern will be realised in three stages (see Figure 10.1) (MA 18, 2012):

- first stage (2009–2017): planning and greenspace completion, centrally located lake, technical infrastructure including a new metro line, first building phase with 2,500 dwellings and 300 student homes, offices, commerce.
- second stage (2017–22): further development areas on the northern part of the lake, with housing and mixed usage, access to the train station.
- third stage (from 2022): increase in density and urbanisation around the train station, settling of further businesses, cultural and leisure infrastructure.

The first phase of construction is already completed (especially the southern part). The main idea was to combine different regional subsidy schemes and market-financed housing construction in the area to attract different income groups and foster social inclusion and social mix. The completed dwellings will belong to different layers of housing supply as outlined in the section on "Context and governance framework", above: from more expensive, completely marked-financed housing to highly subsidised and much cheaper housing, originating from housing-development competitions. The mix of social and functional qualities, the prioritising of public transport and climate neutrality through renewable energy (solar, photovoltaic panels) are driving ideas of the master plan (Förster & Menking, 2016, pp. 104–109). From the very beginning, the planning process was very inclusive and involved several stages (Brech, 2012). While experts, architects, city planners and the general public were involved during the planning phase, the ongoing participation process also involves the resident population and potential future inhabitants.

A large part of the new dwellings will originate from the WBI. There are some 14 projects with altogether around 1,600 dwellings, i.e. around 27 per cent

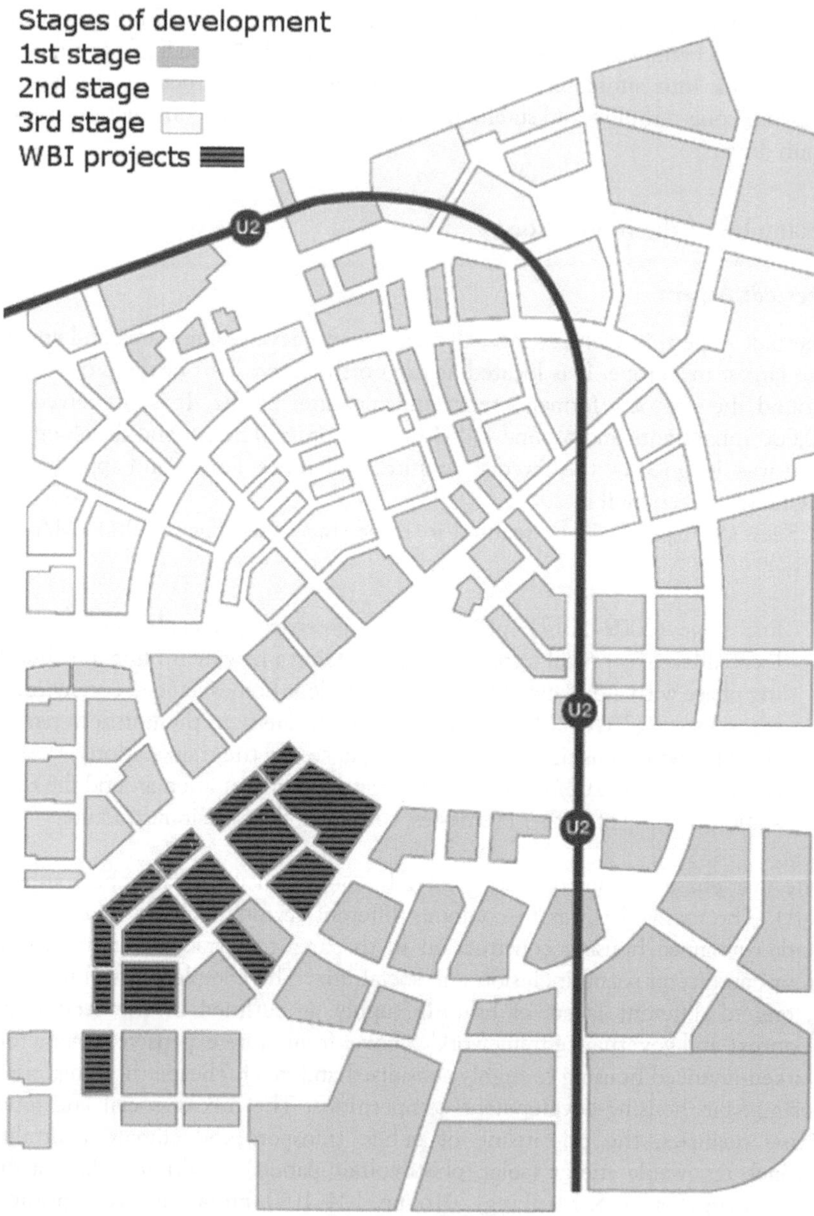

Figure 10.1 Stages of development in Seestadt Aspern.

Sources: MA 18, 2012, p. 105, own additions based on Brech, 2012 and personal communication – Teschl, 1 March 2016.

of all WBI 2011 dwellings will be completed in Aspern. In addition, there are 760 subsidised units from the regular subsidy schemes, some 300 units for student housing and 150 units in co-housing projects.

Waldmühle Rodaun

The Waldmühle Rodaun was realised by a consortium of four LPHA developers (ÖSW AG, Familienwohnbau, WBV-GBA, Wien-Süd) and two financial investors (Raiffeisen, S-Wohnbaubank). For the project a special joint venture company was set up, with each developer participating at 25 per cent. The same consortium also builds other, smaller WBI projects (Personal communication Langmann, 28 April 2016).

The project Waldmühle Rodaun includes 450 rental units in several buildings grouped around a central park of 12,000 m² (Figure 10.2). Around 80 of the units will be barrier-free "assisted living" units. The project is located at the western fringe of Vienna, bordering the neighbouring region of Lower Austria and set in the middle of the Vienna Woods, which covers large parts of the Western city surface and continuous in the neighbouring municipalities belonging to the region of Lower Austria (Figure 10.3).

The project was realised at the former site of a cement factory, out of operation since 1995, which had to be demolished. "Urban mining" recycling technologies were applied as a special feature of the project. Around three-quarters of the material from the former factory was used in the construction of "Waldmühle Rodaun" (Personal communication Langmann, 28 April 2016). Other elements

Figure 10.2 Overall layout of Waldmühle Rodaun.

Source: Waldmühle Rodaun Betreuungsgesellschaft mbH, permission to reprint.

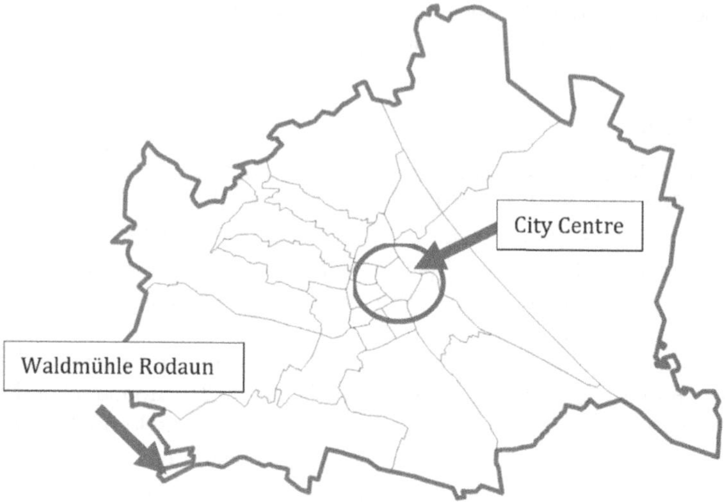

Figure 10.3 Location of the project Waldmühle Rodaun in Vienna.
Source: own depiction.

guarantee a high ecological standard for the project: central gas heating and warm water for the whole project with additional solar-collectors and thermal pumps. All dwellings have sizes of 59–125 m², and have either a balcony, terrace or own garden. Social infrastructure includes supermarkets, a common swimming pool and a kindergarten. The project was completed in late 2017.

Applicant tenants were able to choose from both financing variants which were a prerequisite of the WBI 2011 (see the section on "Context and governance framework", above).

As an example, a three-room dwelling, 82 m² usable floor space, 12 m² balcony, cost at completion:

1 variant 1: tenant capital contribution: €12,900; monthly gross rental costs: €790 (i.e. 9.6 €/m²);
2 variant 2: tenant capital contribution: €43,000; monthly gross rental costs: €663 (i.e. 8.0 €/m²).

Some dwellings in the more luxurious "villa"-sized buildings are slightly more expensive. There is some cross-subsidisation across all dwellings to reach the rental maxima stipulated in the WBI 2011 call. The gross rent levels mentioned here are in line with the net rents stipulated in the call after considering overhead building charges, a reserve fund contribution for maintenance, taxes, inflation adaptation since 2011, and the additional balcony.

The project's finance elements include the WBI loan, tenant capital contributions, own equity by the developers (especially for the building plot, see

Table 13.2) and financial involvement of the consortium partners: housing construction bank *S-Wohnbaubank* and the commercial bank *Raiffeisen*. The building plot was brought in by the developers and did not belong to the city, contrary to many other WBI projects.

The main challenge in completing the project was its particular location at the fringe of a natural reserve at Vienna's borders to neighbouring municipalities (Personal communication Langmann, 28 April 2016). Special cooperation and coordination between the administrations of all involved municipalities was necessary.

Considering the remote location of the project, demand and interest for the dwellings was less than in other more central WBI locations. Marketing for the project had to focus on families due to the relatively large dwelling sizes. A right to buy option after ten years was introduced to make the project more attractive. Some pictures of the project's construction stages are presented in Figures 10.4. Further images, floor plans and short videos with information on the project are available on the project's homepage (www.waldmuehle-rodaun.at).

Figure 10.4a Waldmühle Rodaun: pictures of construction stages – cement factory before construction.

Figure 10.4b Waldmühle Rodaun: pictures of construction stages – difficult construction works.

Source: Waldmühle Rodaun Betreuungsgesellschaft mbH, permission to reprint.

Figure 10.4c Waldmühle Rodaun: pictures of construction stages – completed project.

Source: Waldmühle Rodaun Betreuungsgesellschaft mbH, permission to reprint.

Outcomes, relevance, transferability

The main advantages of the WBI scheme can be summarised as follows:

- it pushes supply in a heated market,
- it provides a new tier of affordable housing in the mid-price range,
- it opens up new financing sources as it attracts institutional investors,

- it is less costly for the Viennese budget than other schemes,
- it uses existent elements of quality control for new buildings,
- it contributes to social mix and inclusion.

In addition to all available material, the interviews have highlighted some benefits of the WBI in relation to other subsidy schemes and to non-subsidised housing construction: the established subsidy schemes in Vienna are very high-profile with standardised procedures and strong competition between applicants. The process usually takes a long time and is highly formalised, e.g. concerning the quality councils' sessions, notifications, periods allowed for resubmissions and amendments for tendered projects. The WBI takes two steps back from the very ambitious and administrative complex existing subsidy schemes. It is more flexible, quicker and calls for slightly less strict requirements. It has less administrational costs for participation and follows a speedier process (Personal communication Liske & Liske-Weninger, 14 April 2016; Personal communication Teschl, 1 March 2016; Personal communication Langmann, 28 April 2016). On the other hand, the WBI is a good alternative to completely market-financed new construction, the quality of which cannot be influenced by advisory boards or competitive assessment. Also, with the WBI scheme, the City of Vienna maintains a certain influence on the social character of the subsidised dwellings, albeit only for a limited period.

The main advantages of the WBI scheme and its innovative components are also confronted with drawbacks and criticism:

- Social obligations will only last for ten years. This is a major difference from the general Viennese subsidy approach, focused on the long-term cost-rent structure and social allocation criteria of the LPHAs and the municipal housing stock. Commercial developers will be allowed to raise the rent level after ten years (only for new tenants) to a possibly higher market level. LPHAs, on the other hand, have to stick to cost-rents throughout the existence of the buildings. Since the scheme is very new, the long-term effects cannot be assessed yet.
- There are no formal income limits, even though 50 per cent of allocations are carried out by the Vienna housing helpdesk. Also, main residence is not a precondition, as it is in the other regional subsidy schemes. Overall, social targeting is not as strong as in other schemes.
- The financial benefit did not materialise to the intended extent, because the beneficial conditions passed on from the municipality to the developers lost clout with the decline in the market interest rate which happened during the time span of the scheme. Therefore, the conditions offered in the initial WBI were less attractive two years after the call then had been intended. The WBI of 2015 already offers more favourable conditions. The framework of the WBI will be more successful in a constant or increasing interest rate environment.

- Public building plot reserves were a crucial element in the WBI's success. The financial benefit alone would not have such a decisive effect on overall costs.
- The WBI helps to encourage additional affordable housing construction, but compared to the highly ambitions current output targets, this will not be enough.

The transferability of the WBI scheme to other countries and cities is more pronounced than in the other Austrian housing subsidy schemes because the constraints and requirements are less strict and the application process is speedier. Social obligation concerning maximum rents and the social allocation of half the dwellings through the city's agency last only for ten years. Thus, the subsidy scheme is also attractive for commercial developers and financial investors looking for a low-risk stable investment, but without unlimited social obligations.

However, the institutional and regulatory context of Vienna is important for the WBI's success. The scheme can build on an existing framework (advisory boards to safeguard quality, LPHAs, supervisory structure over LPHAs, city's land reserves, additional finance by Housing Construction Banks, etc.). The scheme also heavily depends on the availability of building plots that the municipality provided. The risks involved due to the financial position of developers and financial partners have to be minimised through adequate mechanisms.

An application of this or a similar scheme is possible in European countries where cities enjoy good financial ratings and can refinance themselves cheaply on the capital market. The Austrian federal initiative to set up a federal housing construction investment bank was designed after the WBI example. Though not yet in operation at the moment this chapter was finalised, the WBI investment bank will be able to channel funds from the European Investment Bank into affordable housing projects all over Austria.

Overall, the success of the Austrian social housing sector shows many elements that can serve as a role model for international applications and the WBI appears to be one of them.

References

Amann, W., Hüttler, W., & Mundt, A. (2012). Austria: Social housing providers at the forefront of energy efficiency. In N. Nieboer, S. Tsenkova, V. Gruis, & A. van Hal (Eds.), *Energy efficiency in housing management: Policies and practice in eleven countries* (pp. 151–175). Abingdon, New York: Routledge.

Amann, W., Jurassovich, S., & Mundt, A. (2015). Berichtsstandard Wohnbauförderung 2015 [Standard report housing subsidies 2015]. Study commissioned by the City of Vienna, Department for Housing Research and International Relations. Vienna, Austria: IIBW.

Amann, W., Jurasszovich, S., & Mundt, A. (2016). Berichtsstandard Wohnbauförderung 2016 [Standard report housing subsidies 2016]. Study commissioned by the City of Vienna, Department for Housing Research and International Relations. Vienna, Austria: IIBW.

Amann, W., Lawson, J., & Mundt, A. (2009). Structured financing allows for affordable rental housing in Austria. *Housing Finance International*, June, 14–18.

Brech, J. (2012). *Neue Wege der Planungskultur: Das Kooperationsprogramm der Wohnbauinitiative für die Seestadt Aspern* [New pathways of planning: The cooperation programme of "Wohnbauinitiative" at Seestadt Aspern]. Retrieved from www.wohnbauforschung.at/Downloads/Praesentation_Brech_fin.pdf.

Deutsch, E. (2009). The Austrian social rented sector at the crossroads for housing choice. *European Journal of Housing Policy*, 9(3), 285–311.

Deutsch, E., & Lawson, J. (2012). *International measures to channel investment towards affordable rental housing: Austrian case study*. Study by the Australian Housing and Urban Research Institute on behalf of the Government of Western Australia. Melbourne, Australia: AHURI.

Förster, W., & Menking, W. (Eds.). (2016). *Das Wiener Modell: Wohnbau für die Stadt des 21. Jahrhunderts* [The Vienna model: Housing for the twenty-first-century city]. Berlin: Jovis.

Kemeny, J. (1995). *From public housing to the social market: Rental policy strategies in comparative perspective*. London: Routledge.

Kemeny, J., Kersloot, J., & Thalmann, P. (2005). Non-profit housing influencing, leading and dominating the unitary rental market: Three case studies. *Housing Studies*, *20*(6), 855–872.

Lawson, J. (2010). Path dependency and emergent relations: Explaining the different role of limited profit housing in the dynamic urban regimes of Vienna and Zurich. *Housing, Theory and Society*, *27*(3), 204–220.

Lawson, J., Gilmour, T., & Milligan, V. (2010). *International measures to channel investment towards affordable rental housing*. AHURI Research Paper. Melbourne, Australia: AHURI.

Lawson, J., Milligan, V., Yates, J., Amann, W., & Kratschmann, A. (2012). *Housing supply bonds: A suitable instrument to channel investment towards affordable housing in Australia?* Melbourne, Australia: AHURI.

Ludl, H. (2007). *Limited-profit housing associations in Austria*. Vienna, Austria: GBV.

MA 18. (2012). *Stadt bauen: Beispiele für und aus Wien. Werkstattberichte Stadtentwicklung Nr. 124*. [Building a city: Examples for and from Vienna. Lab report city development, number 124]. Vienna, Austria: Author.

MA 50. (2011). *Call Wohnbauinitiative Wien 2011* [Tender Call Wohnbauinitiative Wien 2011]. Vienna, Austria: Author.

Mundt, A. (2013). *Housing supply in Austria: Providers, motivation, competition*. Conference Paper presented at the WIFO 6th Geoffrey J.D. Hewings Regional Economics Workshop. Vienna, Austria: WIFO.

Mundt, A., & Amann, W. (2010). Indicators of an integrated rental market in Austria. *Housing Finance International*, Winter, 35–44.

Mundt, A., & Springler, E. (2016). Milestones in housing finance in Austria over the last 25 years. In J. Lunde & C. Whitehead (Eds.), *Milestones in European housing finance* (pp. 55–73). Oxford: Wiley-Blackwell.

Oxley, M., Tang, C., Lizieri, C., Mansley, N., Mekic, D., Haffner, M., & Hoekstra, J. (2015). *Prospects for institutional investment in social housing*. Study commissioned by the Investment Property Forum Research Programme. London: Investment Property Forum.

Pech, M. (2014). Gründung und Entwicklung gewerblicher Tochtergesellschaften gemäß § 7 (4b) WGG [Founding and development of commercial daughter companies according to § 7(4b) WGG]. In W. Amann, H. Pernsteiner, & C. Stuber (Eds.), *Wohnbau in Österreich in europäischer Perspektive* [Housing construction in Austria in a European perspective] (pp. 275–283). Vienna, Austria: Manz.

Prenner, P. (Ed.). (2014). *Wien Wächst: Herausforderungen zwischen Boom und Lebensqualität* [Vienna is growing: Challenges between boom and quality of life]. Vienna, Austria: AK-Wien. Retrieved from http://media.arbeiterkammer.at/wien/PDF/studien/Stadtpunkte12.pdf.

Reinprecht, C. (2014). Social housing in Austria. In K. Scanlon, C. Whitehead, & M. Fernández Arrigoitia (Eds.), *Social housing in Europe* (pp. 61–73). Oxford: Wiley Blackwell.

Schmidinger, J. (2008). Wohnbaubanken und gemeinnützige Bauvereinigungen: eine Partnerschaft für nachhaltig günstiges Wohnen [Housing construction banks and limited-profit housing associations: A partnership for affordable housing] In K. Lugger & M. Holoubek (Eds.), *Die österreichische Wohnungsgemeinnützigkeit: ein europäisches Erfolgsmodell* [Limited-profit housing in Austria: A European best practice model] (pp. 259–267). Vienna, Austria: Manz.

Stadt Wien. (2011). Pressemitteilung: Wohnbauinitiative 2011 bringt den WienerInnen rund 6.250 neue, qualitätsvolle und kostengünstige Wohnungen [Press release: Wohnbauinitiative 2011 will bring 6,250 new, high-quality and affordable apartments to the Viennese population]. Vienna, Austria: Author.

Stadt Wien. (2012). Pressemitteilung: Wohnbauinitiative: Startschuss für 1.600 Wohnungen in Aspern [Press release: Wohnbauinitative: Take-off for 1,600 apartments in Aspern]. Vienna, Austria: Author.

Stadt Wien. (2016). Pressemitteilung: 13 Bauträgerwettbewerbe mit mehr als 11.000 Wohneinheiten [Press release: 13 building competitions with more than 11,000 dwellings]. Vienna, Austria: Author.

Statistik Austria. (2016). *Wohnen 2015: Tabellenband* [Housing 2015: Tables]. Vienna, Austria: Author.

Wohnfonds_wien. (2015). *Beurteilungsblatt 4-Säulen Modell* [Evaluation sheet 4-pillars model]. Vienna, Austria: Author. Retrieved from www.wohnfonds.wien.at/downloads/lgs/beurteilungsblatt.pdf.

List of interviews

- Dietmar Teschl, City of Vienna, Head of housing subsidy department, MA50, 1 March 2016.
- Herbert Liske & Patricia Liske-Weninger, Zivilingineurbüro. Organiser of the WBI Advisory Board sessions and pre-tests of submissions, 14 April 2016.
- Gabriele Aigner-Tax, Housing Helpdesk Vienna (Wohnberatung Wien), 22 April 2016 (telephone).
- Stephan Langmann, Managing director "Waldmühle Rodaun", 28 April 2016 and 13 March 2018.
- Daniel Glaser, City of Vienna, Department for Housing Research and International Relations, 10 May 2017 (telephone).
- Alexander Welzig, Housing Helpdesk Vienna (Wohnberatung Wien), 15 May 2017 (telephone).

11 The carrot and the stick

Sustaining private investment in affordable rental housing – USA

Anita Blessing

Introduction

This chapter addresses growing interest within European urban development in mobilising investment from private financial institutions in order to improve affordable rental housing supply. It draws on longstanding US experience for insights of relevance to European debates. While strong state interventions helped address affordable housing supply in many of Europe's cities during the twentieth century, neoliberal reforms over recent decades have changed the state of play. National public and social housing systems have been scaled back, based on claims that they distort commercial competition and expose states to risk during times of austerity. In the US, these same claims were used by the real estate lobby in the late 1940s to negotiate provisions in the first federal public housing legislation that would restrict the quality of housing built and ensure it would never compete with private sector rentals (Hays, 1995).

In both Europe and the US, state austerity has also provided a rationale for 'localism', with certain powers and responsibility devolved to local communities, a key objective being to mobilise resources from local civil society and commercial actors (Swyngedouw, 2005). This shift, occurring earlier in the US than in Europe, has brought state, market and civil society actors with differing organisational goals into ongoing negotiation over local housing and urban development outcomes. While 'triangular' forms of governance that encompass state, market and civil society participation have been promoted as a means of giving voice to local communities in Europe, significant power asymmetries between actors remain unaddressed (Jacobs & Manzi, 2013). Private not-for-profit providers of affordable rentals, prioritised by the state in many settings, rely increasingly on private finance to supplement dwindling state support. As a result, private investor decisions bear increasingly on their ability to meet housing need.

Currently, low and moderate income renters are being priced out of high demand European rental markets, including urban cultural and financial centres. This has implications for both social justice and socio-spatial cohesion (Habitat for Humanity, 2015). At question in Europe is how private investment from financial institutions such as pension funds and banks may be motivated to increase affordable housing supply. More specifically, stakeholders are asking how this might be accomplished under conditions of state austerity, liberalising property markets, and 'localism', premised on local participatory governance. State agencies, in particular, are asking how incentive measures and tailored investment products might stimulate private investment. Ultimately, they seek the Holy Grail – sustained large-scale flows of low-cost private capital for socially beneficial projects as state support is pulled back (Blessing & Mullins, forthcoming).

In the years since the recent financial crisis, a contracting securities market and diminishing yields on competing investments have increased the pool of private capital willing to back affordable rental projects in European cities. While access to finance remains uneven around Europe, successful use of bond finance on the part of social banks and large social housing associations in some locations has made the 'Holy Grail' seem more attainable. Simultaneously, European investors developing social impact investment strategies in response to changing social expectations have started to consider affordable housing as an impact investment. To tap into impact investment, not-for-profit stakeholders in affordable rental housing have recognised the need for clear ways to measure and report on the social and economic benefits that quality affordable rentals can bring to urban communities (see Garnier, 2016).

In this context, state housing agencies and not-for-profit providers are attempting to develop and sustain win/win relationships based on investors providing steady flows of capital on terms that support affordability, in order to attain a blend of modest low-risk returns and reputational benefits. While recent academic studies suggest that such win/win relationships are indeed being achieved in certain settings (see Tang, Oxley, & Mekic, 2017), this is occurring under conditions of low interest rates and loose monetary policy that have boosted the appeal of residential real estate relative to other investments (Garnier, 2016). Despite the fact that investors are claiming they are motivated by reputational gains, it remains unclear exactly how such reputational gains connect to their core goals, such as profit maximisation.

Theories of corporate social responsibility, implicit in investors' claims that they finance affordable rentals out of social duty, position firms as social actors regulated by social norms (Crouch, 2012; Carroll & Shabana, 2010). Despite ample attention to how regulation of not-for-profit housing providers impacts institutional investment in their projects, the significance of how investors are publicly regulated remains underexplored in debates on affordable housing finance in Europe. While investors can be expected to pursue strong returns for their shareholders or members, less is known about how other non-financial considerations, including 'reputation', influence their investment decisions. However, as the EU attempts to transition to a financial system that will support sustainable urban development, the role of regulatory drivers for sustainable investments is beginning to receive policy attention (European Commission, 2018).

To speak to developing European interest in this issue, the chapter explores US experience in motivating investment in affordable rental housing. It draws insights into how private commercial investment in affordable rental housing may be motivated by the state, using both incentive and regulatory frameworks. Rather than advocating direct policy transfer between settings as different as Europe and the US, the aim is to understand the investment relationships between key actors in US affordable rental housing finance, and to gain insights into how they are governed or institutionally structured. Here, institutions are understood as social norms: the sets of rules, but also the practices that regulate a field of human interaction (Ruonavaara, 2005, p. 214). For the purposes of this chapter, we focus on formal policy and legislative structures, but also on the institutionalised processes of negotiation and deliberation that key actors employ to pursue their various goals. From this discussion of key US actors and institutions, 'middle-range' generalisations about cross-sectoral investment relationships are drawn. Such generalisations are by nature tentative, based on the recognition that social phenomena are unique and thus may not be replicable. These generalisations are then used to consider whether similar institutional settings and governance mechanisms could help structure cross-sectoral investment relationships in Europe (see Bengtsson & Hertting, 2014).

The 1986 federal Low Income Housing Tax Credit (LIHTC) programme, which accounts for the majority of affordable rental housing generated in the US, provides the 'case' of a long-standing incentive mechanism. Despite significant international interest in implementing similar approaches (Blessing & Gilmour, 2011), the research that supports this chapter suggests that the programme is not a 'stand-alone' piece of policy. Its long-term success in mobilising private finance for affordable rentals is partially due to the Federal Community Reinvestment Act (CRA) 1977, which helps to drive demand for investment opportunities in affordable rental housing and a range of other socially beneficial categories. This legislation requires many types of banks to demonstrate service to low and moderate income constituents in communities where they take deposits, or risk being denied permission for planned mergers or acquisitions. Specific types of investment that contribute towards compliance with the Act may be justified at lower rates of return. These include financing new affordable rental housing supply and preserving existing supply.

In describing the 'carrot' of tax incentives and the 'stick' of community reinvestment legislation that helps tax incentives function, attention is given to how the governing mechanisms within these structures take effect and shape the politics of investment in US affordable rental housing. The concluding analysis reflects on some of the key risks and benefits of the tax credit approach as a means of incentivising investment. While the programme is used nationwide – the interest here is how it works in high demand urban rental markets where low and moderate income households are being priced out. Accordingly, the research that informed this chapter draws on grey (policy) literature and academic studies at the federal level, as well as on similar material specific to New York City. As a global cultural and financial centre, New York City is known as a high-pressure rental market with severe affordability problems, but also as a pioneer in housing policy and advocacy. The research is informed by original interviews with experts in the New York City affordable housing industry conducted in late 2016 about the significance of low-income housing tax credits and how they take effect in local markets.

Drawing on recent academic and policy research, the chapter starts by reviewing trends in institutional investment in rental housing, and considers efforts in Europe to connect affordable rental housing projects to emerging forms of social impact investment. The chapter then provides some context on housing policy in the US, and describes US policy and legislative structures. Finally, the chapter links the discussion back to European debates and sets out new directions for research.

Affordable rental housing and social impact investment in Europe

Institutional investment in rental housing: a double-edged sword?

Since the recent financial crisis, institutional investment in rental housing has been alternately framed in policy debates around Europe as a sought-after prize that will boost new affordable supply, and as a potential threat to existing supplies of affordable rentals. Recent successes on the part of large not-for-profit housing providers, social banks and municipalities in raising bond finance for new social and affordable rentals have strengthened policy interest in motivating sustained flows of investment. While some academic commentaries have waxed optimistic about this prospect, others have cited risks, such as not-for-profit providers becoming 'over-leveraged' or debt-burdened to a point where they have trouble meeting their operating costs and potentially place social housing assets and tenancies at risk. Effectively, there is a risk of organisational 'financialisation', wherein financial metrics and values penetrate and dominate their operations, undermining their social purpose (Wainwright & Manville, 2017; Aalbers, Loon, & Fernandez, 2017).

Moreover, reliance on private market-oriented investment appears to be a double-edged sword in that the same conditions favouring investment in new-build affordable rental projects may also create new challenges around preserving existing low-income housing stock. Liberalising European property markets have recently seen waves of bulk purchases of existing low-rent dwellings by large institutional investors and their intermediaries. Many acquisitions have come as financially pressured social housing providers or municipalities have divested stock, or rent controls have been weakened. Significant changes in the ownership of rental housing stock in Germany, Spain and elsewhere in Europe have triggered concerns about the need to preserve existing stocks of low-rent housing in high demand urban areas, where gaps between current and potential rents are considerable (Fields & Uffer, 2016). Patterns of 'renovictions' – where new owners renovate and raise rents beyond sitting tenants' means – and other forms of tenant displacement, have brought the issue of investors' social conduct in European urban housing markets into the spotlight.

A further risk of reliance on private capital to fund new affordable rental projects is that macro-economic conditions that favour such investment are subject to change. Without regulatory or incentive stimuli to keep investment relationships in place, the capital now willing to back projects with a social purpose may flow into other, higher yield investments. While the importance of state regulatory frameworks in encouraging local investments has long been recognised (see Smith, 1904, IV.2.6–2.9), this issue has recently resurfaced in urban policy debates. Recent studies have questioned the benefits of 'competitive city' strategies that ask cities to compete for the business of globally active footloose firms, in favour of more 'grounded' urban development that asks corporates and financial institutions to contribute to the cities where they do business and have members, employees and customers (Engelen, Froud, Johal, Salento, & Williams, 2016; Clark, 2000).

Regulatory frameworks for 'responsible' investment

In tandem with the EU Single Market, the European Commission has rhetorically promoted Corporate Social Responsibility (CSR), including socially beneficial investment on the part of financial institutions in disadvantaged communities (European Commission, 2001). As the rationale of fair commercial competition in the Single Market has prompted European directives for social housing providers to narrow their range of property market activities and target low-income households, Europe has simultaneously asked commercial actors to embrace broader societal missions. Recent EU initiatives have encouraged 'social finance', a general term signalling the use of private finance resources to create public, social or environmental value or impact alongside a financial return (Daggers & Nicholls, 2016). The current EU Sustainable Finance initiative aims to transition to a financial system that will support sustainable development and circular urban economies. It also advocates improved transparency so that Europe's citizens actively engage with sustainable finance issues (European Commission, 2018).

The European Investment Bank has emerged as an important source of low-cost debt finance for not-for-profit and municipal providers of affordable and energy efficient housing. Further specific regulatory and incentive frameworks for private investment in affordable rental housing remain a topic of strong policy interest at the EU level. To date, national regulatory frameworks, particularly the implicit state and intra-sectoral guarantees enjoyed by strong national not-for profit housing sectors, have been most effective in mobilising private investment. However, these mechanisms continue to be controversial with respect to European Competition Policy (Mullins, Milligan, & Nieboer, 2018). A further development of relevance to affordable rental housing finance has been the rise of 'impact investment' amongst financial institutions and other firms, which refers to investments made with the intention of generating a measurable, beneficial social or environmental impact alongside a financial return (Matthews, Sternlicht, Bouri, Mudaliar, & Schiff, 2015).

While the trend of impact investment is more advanced in the US, where corporate philanthropy has long been established as a funding source for socially beneficial urban development, it is gaining traction in Europe, along with innovations in green bond finance that are pushing Europe into a global leadership position in this field (European Commission, 2018). Gradual top-down regulatory changes to motivate socially beneficial investments within the EU are to some extent being met by bottom-up efforts from civic actors. Not-for-profit housing providers, social banks and consultants in European property markets have launched initiatives to make affordable rentals more visible as social impact investments, for example by developing measurable indicators of the social, neighbourhood and health impacts of affordable housing that investors can report on (NWB, 2017). Within this environment new forms of negotiation over affordable rental housing investments and outcomes are emerging between state agencies, civic sector actors and commercial investors, and it is here that the relevance of the US experience becomes more apparent.

Affordable rental housing finance in the USA

US housing need and housing assistance

The US is often portrayed having an ultra-capitalistic marketised economy, and typified as an archetypal liberal welfare state, based on minimum levels of means-tested assistance for the households in highest need (Harloe, 1995). However, US welfare spending on middle-income groups rose from the 1980s, while spending on the poorest households fell (Blessing, 2016). US public housing is supplemented by multiple programmes for privately financed 'affordable' rental housing that often target low- to moderate-income working households in tight rental markets, rather than welfare recipients. The participation of varying types of not-for-profit housing providers, including local neighbourhood-based Community Development Corporations (CDCs), has been pivotal to affordable rental housing supply. This is particularly the case in urban areas, with the sector accommodating over 1.5 million households by 2009 (Bratt, 2009). With some exceptions, federal funding has taken a 'sector agnostic' approach enabling commercial providers of affordable rental housing to compete for key sources of funding alongside not-for-profits.

The recent financial crisis had severe impacts on housing conditions in the US, with over seven million people losing their homes to foreclosure. Homeownership fell from close to 70 per cent in 2004 to 63.4 per cent in 2015. Over the same decade, the number of people renting grew by nearly nine million. An oft-cited statistic is that there is no state in the US where a minimum wage worker can afford a one-bedroom apartment at fair market rent (Office of U.S. Senator Maria Cantwell Hart, 2017). Based on an affordability standard of no more than 30 per cent of gross income spent on housing, nearly one-third of all households in the country and nearly half of all renters spend more than this limit and are therefore 'cost burdened'. More than one-quarter of renters is severely burdened, spending at least half of their income on housing (O'Regan, 2017). Low rates of housing construction and wage stagnation have heightened housing affordability problems.

Currently, public housing comprises less than 1 per cent of all dwellings nationally, and affordable rentals provided privately through programmes such as the Low Income Housing Tax Credit take this up to 5 per cent of all housing (Schwartz, 2011). Yet in large cities, concentrations of affordable rentals are significantly higher, and patterns of state intervention diverge somewhat from those normally associated with liberal welfare states (see Harloe, 1995). In New York City, around 5 per cent of all dwellings are in public tenure, with roughly another 7 per cent comprising privately owned affordable dwellings (Ellen & Weselcouch, 2015). When various forms of rent-regulated units are included, nearly 50 per cent of rental dwellings are subject to some kind of state imposed affordability control. Given that only 32 per cent of dwellings are owner-occupied in New York City, these various types of affordable or rent-regulated units comprise roughly a third of all dwellings. Despite this, affordability problems remain severe.

The majority of US federal support for housing targets those able to buy a home and, currently, slightly less than 65 per cent of dwellings around the US are owner-occupied. As measured in 2014, the annual federal government spend of US$52 billion on housing assistance for low- to moderate-income households in the rental sector was dwarfed by the $130 billion in support provided to wealthier households, primarily through relief on mortgage interest payments and property tax. Federal spending on public housing and LIHTC, and grants for state and local government housing programmes stands at around $7–8 billion for each of these categories. While public housing funding is spent mainly on operating costs and maintenance, the LIHTC programme provides new affordable supply. Demand side assistance in the form of tenant-based and project-based 'Housing Choice Vouchers', which subsidise rents in the commercial sector, commands a larger spend of around US$30 billion (Congressional Budget Office, 2015). In New York City, bond finance generated by the Housing Development Corporation, a state-established development company, provides additional support for affordable rental housing, yet industry professionals stress the continuing importance of federal funding through the LIHTC programme.

The carrot: financially incentivising institutional investment in affordable rental housing

Described by the US Federal Department of Housing and Urban Development as the most important resource for creating affordable housing in the United States today, the LIHTC was introduced in 1986 amidst cuts to spending for public housing and promotion of private alternatives. At an annual cost of around US$8 billion, the programme has yielded over 2,970,000 privately provided affordable rental dwellings, more than exist in US public housing, and has leveraged over $100 billion in private investment (US Department of Housing and Urban Development (HUD), 2017; Office of U.S. Senator Maria Cantwell Hart, 2017). Tax credits are a familiar part of the affordable housing finance landscape, and are known colloquially as LIHTCs, pronounced 'Ligh-tecks'. The current US Federal Administration's enthusiasm for corporate tax cuts has negatively impacted recent LIHTC yields; however, the approach has widespread support and 2017 saw the introduction of a bipartisan bill to expand and improve it (O'Regan, 2017). Tax credits are used in the US to encourage various publicly desirable investments, including the preservation of heritage buildings and area-based revitalisation and economic development. Since the resource used is forgone future taxes, credits escape the radar of some traditional ways of measuring public expenditure, yet they still represent an annual loss to the public purse.

As a tradable credit that can be resold, the LIHTC is of value to not-for-profit and commercial developers alike. The programme has attracted significant international policy interest as a successful instrument that pursues a publicly defined mission in a commercial market context (see O'Brien, 2014; Oxley, 2013). From the point view of an international onlooker, it may appear to be running successfully on market signals alone. Yet, as this discussion will show, administration and compliance requires significant government resources, and the state also has a role in stimulating demand.

How the LIHTC works

LIHTCs are reductions in the dollar amount of federal taxes owed by individuals or organisations in exchange for investment (development equity) in low-income rental housing. Credits may be claimed by a holder with a tax liability annually over a ten-year period, however annual redemption is directly tied to the proportion of eligible tenants currently living in the housing produced. Credits are allocated each year to state governments or large municipalities on a per capita basis (US$2.35 in 2017). They are then awarded via competitive tender to affordable rental housing proposals that best fulfil national and local assessment criteria.

Proposals for either the construction or the substantial rehabilitation of housing may be submitted by not-for-profits, for-profit developers or mixed consortia. Once a developer has won tax credits for a designated scheme, they may be retained for direct use over a ten-year period, providing the developer has a tax liability. More typically though, they traded via a syndicator in return for capital that covers a significant proportion of development costs and thus reduces the cost of debt finance for the remaining proportion. While commercial developers may use a combination of LIHTCs and conventional loans, not-for-profits are more likely to layer different types of grants, loans and credits within a single project in order to reach specific needs groups.

'Sales' of the credits are typically facilitated through the syndicator's structuring of a limited partnership between the developer and the investor. In a typical configuration, the developer serves as the general partner, taking a majority of the cash flow, while the investor takes profits, losses, depreciation and tax credits. The investor is not involved in the development process or the ongoing management of the rented project, and is not permitted to withdraw from the partnership until the end of the compliance period, during which units produced must be made available at affordable rents. Syndicators, many of which are not-for-profit organisations, have an important role in placing credits with investors seeking specific locations, including banks regulated under the Community Reinvestment Act; as explained in the following section. More than just connecting parties financially, some not-for-profit tax credit syndicators have become important intermediaries in the affordable rental housing industry, providing expert knowledge, but also undertaking research and developing indicators to promote green, healthy and sustainable urban development. While investment structures used to trade LIHTCs are complex and may vary, Figure 11.1 gives an overview of some typical patterns of allocation and trade.

LIHTC affordability and targeting

LIHTC programme rents are geared to the local Area (gross) Median Income (AMI). In settings of extreme income inequality such as the New York City metropolitan area, additional subsidies may be needed to reach low-income households. At the Federal level, the scheme began with an initial 15-year 'compliance period' wherein rents were capped at 30 per cent of AMI, which

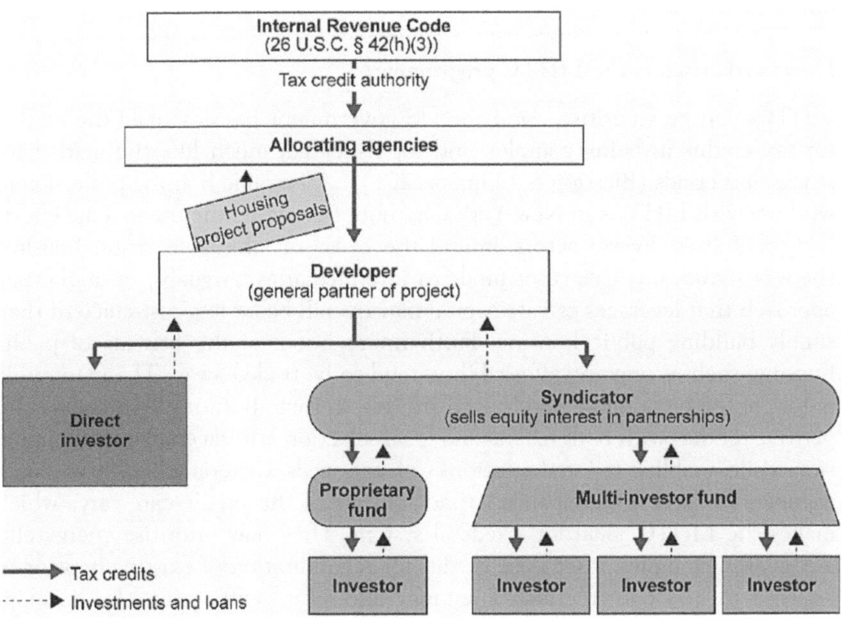

Figure 11.1 Overview of the low-income housing credit process.

Source: US Government Accountability Office, 2017.

was later extended to 30 years, and 50 years in New York State. After this, investors may exit, potentially resulting in the withdrawal of properties from the affordable housing sector. In New York City, the widespread use of rental housing programmes with time-limited affordability requirements, including the LIHTC has led to an impending crisis in 2020 when many are expected to expire. In the City's current housing plan, 60 per cent of the affordable units to be 'delivered' will constitute preservation of existing units, whilst 40 per cent are new build. In this light, the orientation of developers, which usually continue as general partners, emerges as significant. While some commercial developers may choose to preserve affordability not-for-profits follow a social mission that encourages them to do this.

The LIHTC programme enables mixed-income developments, but allocates credits only for units designated for eligible tenants – those earning up to either 50 per cent AMI, in which case a minimum of 20 per cent of units must be set aside, or those earning up to 60 per cent AMI, in which case at least 40 per cent of the units must be set aside. The credits' tradability and the role of syndication enables both large and smaller scale housing projects to be financed, and while most are built in dense, urban, areas, LIHTCs are also used in rural locations. Tenants with rising incomes are not evicted from LIHTC projects, and developers may be incentivised to target the working poor, rather than those in highest need of assistance (McQuarrie & Guthrie, 2007 p. 258). Groups likely to be housed in LIHTC projects include older people, key workers and veterans.

How marketised is the LIHTC programme?

LIHTCs can be securitised, and the US government has described the market for tax credits as being complex and sophisticated, much like the market for stocks and bonds (Blessing & Gilmour, 2011). Affordable housing professionals working with LIHTCs in New York City note that while the programme effectively mobilises diverse actors around the cause of affordable rental housing, there is significant leakage of funds to intermediaries. Arguably, a marketised approach that leverages private capital may overall be far less cost-efficient than simply building public housing. Furthermore, some of the benefits of public housing, such as ongoing affordability, tend to be traded away. The marketised nature of the programme also has advantages, in that allocating credits via competitive tenders with both federal and local selection criteria encourages innovation while enabling tailored solutions to local needs. Criteria added by the state agencies or large municipalities that administer the credit can vary, which makes the LIHTC ideal for a federal system. They may prioritise energy efficiency, for example, or set aside credits for rehabilitation of existing housing as opposed to new construction. They may also award extra points for developments designed for transition to tenant ownership after the affordability period passes. The tradability of LIHTCs helps mobilise a wide range of actors and encourages long-term collaborative relationships across sectors.

While the LIHTC programme has highly marketised elements, state agencies still play a strong role in bureaucratic administration and compliance, and a high degree of transparency is maintained with respect to housing outcomes. Local administrators of LIHTCs are required to serve the lowest income families for the longest possible period of time, and must also set aside at least 10 per cent of tax credits awarded to not-for-profit developers. The US Federal Department for Housing and Urban Development (HUD) maintains a public database with detailed information on every LIHTC project ever undertaken, including address, number of units, tax credits provided and other sources of finance. Geocoding of the database has enabled academic research on the geographical distribution of projects and on their neighbourhood impacts. Further programme requirements govern investors. Within an LIHTC limited partnership, any breaches of these requirements are reported to the federal tax authority (Inland Revenue Service), so that investors can only claim credits for a given year if the relevant housing project is in compliance. Here, syndicators have an important role alongside state agencies in monitoring and substantiating compliance to ensure that investors can claim credits.

Stimulating demand for tax credits: local markets for social impact investment?

When it was launched in the late 1980s, the LIHTC programme was originally a temporary structure aimed at individual property owners, and initial uptake was slow. During the 1990s, community development professionals saw an opportunity to mobilise far larger streams of capital from corporate investors that could claim depreciation (tax benefits related to the cost and maintenance of a rental property apportioned over its useful life), as well as tax credits. As these professionals began to market LIHTCs to corporate investors via favourably structured deals, the programme gathered momentum and was eventually made permanent (McQuarrie & Guthrie, 2007). Large financial institutions, primarily banks, now make up the majority of investors. However other 'non-financial' companies such as large tech and communications firms have turned to LIHTC deals at times when yields on other investments are low. As tax-exempt organisations with specific long-term liabilities, US pension funds are not drawn to LIHTCs, but instead favour long-term debt investment such as long-term loans, encouraged in some instances by state guarantees. In New York, bond finance issued by the City's Housing Development Corporation provides one of a variety of ways to mobilise pension fund capital.

Investors in tax credits do not necessarily pay the syndicator a full dollar for each dollar of tax credits lost to the public purse. In line with the programme's marketised nature, demand for credits rises and falls. During the financial crisis, demand fell and projects stalled, prompting government intervention. Early in the programme's development, less than half of each tax dollar foregone went into new housing, while 2006 saw close to full dollar returns, a trend that has continued over recent years. Significantly for this discussion, credits may trade at rates higher than a full dollar depending on local market conditions. Leading US scholars explain this apparent anomaly in terms of 'non-financial considerations' (Schwartz & Melendez, 2008, p. 267); specifically, they highlight the local market impacts of federal regulatory measures that we explore in the next section.

The stick: state regulatory stimuli for investment in affordable housing

The federal CRA was passed during the 1970s as civic activists from multiple cities collectively sought to counter 'redlining'; systemic discrimination in the form of geographically based exclusion from mortgage finance and other forms of investment. 'Redlining' refers to the practice of colour coding maps, with red indicating perceived high credit risk, prompting lenders to withhold – or to overcharge for – credit, even where individual applicants are creditworthy. Begun in the private sector, and institutionalised in the 1934 Federal Housing Act, redlining patterns typically reflected the race or ethnicity of residents, with the result that certain communities, including many in New York City, experienced catastrophic disinvestment during the 1970s economic slowdown. While redlining was formally institutionalised in the US, the process has global relevance, and similar exclusionary practices have been observed in Europe (Aalbers, 2009).

The CRA applies to all banks classified as 'holding companies' – typically retail banks that take deposits. However, wholesale banks also have responsibilities under the Act that relate to community development. The Act states that 'depository institutions have a continuing affirmative obligation to meet the credit needs of the communities in which they operate, including low- and moderate income neighbourhoods, consistent with safe and sound operations' (Federal Reserve Bank, 2014). It works in tandem with the 1975 Home Mortgage Disclosure Act, which requires banks to make public their lending patterns, with online data broken down by neighbourhood, income and race or ethnicity of the borrower. Described by civil society organisations as a 'greenlining' mechanism, the CRA is enforced via biannual exams covering both qualitative and quantitative assessment criteria. Smaller banks may be assessed less frequently. State agencies play key roles in implementing the CRA, including departments of the Federal Reserve Bank, housing finance agencies and federal tax agencies (Schwartz & Meléndez, 2008).

CRA regulated financial institutions are required to demonstrate adequate reinvestment within the categories of 'lending', 'community development' and 'service'. The community development test, which covers goods with a societal purpose such as affordable housing, is challenging to comply with, but purchasing LIHTCs provides a relatively simple means. Accordingly, the CRA drives demand for tax credits amongst regulated investors, which purchase the majority of LIHTCs traded around the nation (Lindsey, 2009). Bank performance is graded relative to other local CRA regulated banks, which sparks competition between banks, and this is another key mechanism that makes the CRA take effect and stimulate demand for socially beneficial investments in a given local assessment area. The service test, comprising 25 per cent of the CRA exam, considers the adequacy of branches and ATMs, but it also analyses 'the extent and innovativeness of [a bank's] community development services', in relation to the local 'performance context', including 'the performance of similarly situated lenders' (Barr, 2005, p. 112). As well as driving inter-bank competition, the imperative of CRA compliance encourages coordination between banks to reduce information costs. This has spurred the development of multi-bank initiatives to develop best practices.

Localism in action?

A given bank's 'CRA assessment area' must include one or more US census tracts, geographic regions designed for the purpose of taking a census, with an average of 4,000 residents. The assessment area generally encompasses the census tracts where the bank's headquarters and branches are located, but also surrounding geographies where the bank has taken substantial deposits from low- and moderate-income customers. In practice, the CRA takes effect in low-income neighbourhoods, but it also provides credit and services for lower-income groups in high-demand, gentrifying areas. Because several banks usually have CRA responsibilities within a given area, some of the risk of investment is removed. This spatial dimension within CRA assessment enforces local societal responsibilities and, arguably, puts localism to use to provide a balancing role between the conflicting logics of profit and social purpose. Signalled by the phrase 'safe and sound operations' in the Act, CRA assessment criteria incentivise safer forms of credit and penalise loans deemed deceptive (Taylor & Silver, 2009). Local contact plays a part in mitigating risk, with some CRA-eligible loans and grants administered through not-for-profit Community Development Financial Institutions (CDFIs) that work closely with local recipients. This has facilitated some of the more old-fashioned, face-to-face lending that used to be done by local banks on the basis of local knowledge. Lending to CDFIs attracts CRA credit, as do certain forms of financial support for not-for-profit housing providers.

Monitoring of bank CRA performance in New York City shows that considerable local reinvestment responsibilities apply to both large retail and wholesale banks of US origin such as Capital One, Bank of America and Citibank, and US-based affiliates of European banks, such as Santander, Deutsche Bank and HSBC (ANHD, 2014). While commercial investment firms have not traditionally fallen under the jurisdiction of the CRA, some, including Goldman Sachs and Morgan Stanley, took on holding company status in 2008 in order to gain access to emergency lines of finance. However, as these giant globally active footloose firms drew on the taxpayer-funded web of support, including deposit insurance reserved for local retail banks, they were pulled into the regulatory radar of the CRA, and this mobilised significant new streams of CRA-eligible investments that count towards CRA compliance.

In order to comply with the CRA and to achieve high ratings, many large banks develop a distinct unit or department for CRA-related activities. By the late 1990s, over 70 per cent of large CRA regulated banks had developed such a unit, using local expertise to engage community actors and develop appropriate local loan products and risk mitigation procedures. CRA exams reward banks for foreclosure-prevention efforts, as well as for counselling, modifying loans and investing in funds that finance loan modification (Taylor & Silver, 2009). Within their broader organisations, CRA compliance units tend to face profitability challenges because their loans are smaller and more complex. However, lending and investment activities that are CRA eligible may in some cases be justified at lower rates of return than may otherwise be sought (Willis, 2009).

The CRA's source of regulatory powers

While CRA investments are frequently presented by banks as 'double bottom line' initiatives within their CSR or impact investment strategies (i.e. financial and social return), professionals in New York affordable rental housing finance stress that the relatively steady investment flows collectively generated by the LIHTC and the CRA must be at least partially attributed to strong regulatory 'teeth' embedded in the CRA. Banks with inadequate CRA ratings risk being denied approval by the US Federal Reserve Bank to undertake proposed mergers or acquisitions. CRA enforcement is to some extent triangular, in the sense that it provides civil society groups, often highly organised advocates, with the opportunity to comment on performance and to challenge major corporate plans. To avoid such challenges, banks pursue high CRA ratings by pledging and making local area investments, often devising five or ten year plans for an area. CRA commitments inevitably include some investments that would occur without the Act, yet overall they are significant to urban community development. The value of CRA local area investment plans made between 1977 and 2009 alone is estimated at over US$6 trillion, with single bank pledges running well into the billions (Lindsey, 2009; Schwartz, 2012; Taylor & Silver, 2009).

The publicly released results of CRA exams have evolved into a sophisticated source of data for community groups and activists. In New York City, the membership organisation for not-for-profit CDCs monitors and reports on local bank reinvestment activities. Their annual publication 'The State of Bank Reinvestment in New York City' (see ANHD, 2017) demonstrates CRA impact at the neighbourhood level and enables stronger qualitative comparison of individual bank performance than facilitated by federal CRA exams. It also promotes strong performers as industry standard setters. Not-for-profits in community development also play a strong advocacy role through their member-body, routinely submitting comments during CRA exams. Accordingly, New York City industry participants describe the Act itself as 'necessary but not sufficient' for channelling investment into affordable rental housing. While the CRA makes powerful use of the mechanism of disclosure, the local impacts of this unique national institutional construct are at least partially determined by the active and strategic participation of not-for-profit civic sector participants in the housing market. This varies across the US; however, local actors are assisted by nationally active community reinvestment not-for-profits, some of which are also active in syndicating tax credits.

Not-for-profit affordable housing developers emphasise the importance of the CRA in driving demand for LIHTCs (Blessing & Gilmour, 2011; ANHD, 2014). Many describe a synergistic effect – albeit one that was unplanned by the designers of the two separate institutional structures. While both structures took time to take effect, the CRA alone motivated little institutional investment in urban housing and community development until the launch of the LIHTC. From the late 1980s, the mutually reinforcing effect of the two instruments, the 'stick' of federal legislation and the 'carrot' of the tax credit, gave significant momentum to bank involvement in low-income housing markets, and 'brought banks, corporations, community developers, and local governments together to build the market for low-income housing' (McQuarrie & Guthrie, 2007, p. 250).

As a form of market intervention that ostensibly extends credit to parties often denied loans, the CRA has attracted controversy for contributing to the financial crisis (Lindsey, 2009). However recent studies have found that only around 6 per cent of sub-prime loans occurred under the Act, and most sub-prime lending targeted middle- or higher-income households, with delinquency rates fairly consistent across all income groups (FCIC, 2011; Canner & Bhutta, 2008; Aalbers, 2009). The CRA has also been widely credited for turning around patterns of neighbourhood decline in US cities and improving banks' dealings with low-income communities (McQuarrie & Guthrie, 2007; Olsen, Chakrabarti, & Essene, 2009). Given its role in stimulating markets for local societal investments, its effect may best be understood in terms of 'quasi-market' forces. Its 'regulatory teeth' threaten lost market opportunities. Disclosure of CRA exam results and requirements to consider comments from community groups during merger approval processes help connect bank performances to evolving societal expectations. Although the Act is rarely used to block corporate plans, the threat is substantial, and CRA compliance is arguably a prerequisite for maintaining basic organisational legitimacy (see Dart, 2004).

The normative foundation of the CRA

An 'oft-cited rationale' for the CRA is 'quid pro quo' (Olsen et al., 2009). Civil sector commentators describe a social compact between the state and the banks that provide crucial economic and community services. Recent research has shown that implicit government backing gives larger banks a market edge in allowing them to pay out lower interest on large deposits (ANHD, 2014). Based on this 'quid pro quo' reading of the CRA, proposals have been made to extend it to other financial institutions and industries that enjoy taxpayer support (Olsen et al., 2009). Proposed revisions of the CRA under the current federal administration, however, appear likely to weaken demands made on regulated banks (Ensign & Tracy, 2018).

Regardless of the Act's future, the culture of transparency, reciprocal societal responsibilities and public negotiation that the CRA promotes has encouraged local actors in US urban policy to assert power in new ways. A number of major US cities have recently passed additional layers of responsible banking legislation. Since 2012, for example, the City of Los Angeles requires commercial and investment banks seeking to manage shares of its $30 billion asset portfolio to participate in its Responsible Banking Investment Monitoring Programme. The aim is to stimulate community reinvestment by the City's financial partners by considering their performance alongside the usual financial indicators when financial partners are selected. Participants must regularly detail local community development and affordable rental housing loans and investments, participation in the City's foreclosure prevention and home loan principal reduction programmes, and, where applicable, the institution's CRA score (City of Los Angeles, 2015).

While CRA-related investment should not be confused with voluntary social impact investments, this 'quid pro quo' rationale connects into the social impact investment ethos. However, unlike impact investment, which seeks to influence certain outcomes or behaviours in measurable ways, the CRA gives credit for particular classes of investment, rather than investment impacts. Proposals to modernise the Act, which was instituted at a time when banking was very different, have called for more attention to the impacts of investments, as well as for regulation of a wider range of institutions.

Conclusions

The CRA and the LIHTC programme, both federal policy and legal structures, have been credited with creating a cross-sectoral 'organisational field' that helps connect local opportunities for investment in affordable rental housing with investors' organisational goals. This chapter examined these two key institutional structures and considered how they are used by key actors in affordable housing provision and community development. It aimed to draw insights of relevance to the problem of affordable rental housing finance in European cities, amidst state austerity, but also increased emphasis on localism. The CRA arose from local patterns of civic activism in response to systematic race and space-based discrimination around access to finance. It has strong links to the US civil rights movement and subsequent programmes of affirmative action, and this makes it difficult to connect to European experience. Indeed, the principle of affirmative action diverges from long-held values in some continental European settings, such as universal access to welfare. Yet in the context of neoliberal reforms that restrict state support to the socially disadvantaged, its relevance for Europe is growing.

With regard to identifying specific policy tools or programmes that might be replicable in Europe, a look at the US approach seems to offer only negative lessons. What seems to be a successful marketised system of channelling private investment into social projects emerges as highly bureaucratic and reliant on state regulatory powers. Incentive tools for institutional investment in affordable rental housing may not work in settings lacking the 'stick' of community reinvestment laws. Furthermore, the interaction between the CRA and the LIHTC programme was unplanned. The 'quasi' market forces unleashed by this synergy were slow to gather momentum. International lessons may also be negative in the sense that LIHTC affordable housing outcomes are weaker than traditional social or public housing outcomes, and not necessarily desirable.

However, with respect to middle-range generalisations about the problem of motivating, but also sustaining private investment in a class of assets that are often non-profit maximising, there is much to learn. US experience highlights the power of regulatory frameworks in achieving flows of what otherwise may seem to be investments motivated by modest returns and reputational benefits alone. By activating the mechanisms of public disclosure, voluntary local monitoring, regulatory power and competition between target investors, the CRA has proven to be a significant game-changer. The Act stimulates local markets for the type of investment that an LIHTC deal can easily provide. While these two structures were not designed to work together, they nonetheless achieve this, to the benefit of affordable rental housing finance. However, the strategic participation of civil society actors in both advocating for and negotiating community reinvestment helps determine the local effectiveness of both the CRA and the LIHTC programme in meeting emerging and continuing housing needs.

Considering how the CRA works to stimulate local markets for tax incentives may help to point out powers of governance that are still untapped in Europe, and to raise new questions about the kinds of relationships between key actors and institutions that could address severe socio-spatial inequalities and underpin sustained flows of community investment, even as market conditions shift. Overall, the CRA is a small part of financial regulation that neither radically challenges the societal power of financial institutions, nor corrects serious societal injustices associated with financial markets. Yet within the US competitive banking sector, it finds powers in the mechanisms of public disclosure, and in the regulatory muscle to frustrate plans for major corporate moves.

Disclosure provisions empower civic sector actors, such as not-for-profit community development professionals to participate in regulation. Rather than simply asking local civic sector stakeholders to negotiate with commercial investors, it helps address power asymmetries between them. Arguably, the CRA provides an example of how state legislation can help not-for-profit affordable rental housing providers that follow social missions to deal with the challenges presented by neoliberal reforms, state austerity and reliance on local participatory forms of governance. The CRA–LIHTC synergy is unique to the US, yet it could inspire policymakers to activate similar mechanisms amongst similar constellations of actors in other settings.

The current Sustainable Finance initiative on the part of the European Commission not only asks how private investment can be harnessed to fund sustainable urban development, but also how citizens and civic sector actors may be better informed about – and empowered to participate in – financial systems

(European Commission, 2018). Yet Europe lacks some of the societal conditions that the US attaches to the taxpayer support and other benefits enjoyed by its banks. The CRA, which offers the prospect of creating local markets for socially beneficial investments through formalised reciprocal social responsibilities for financial institutions, may provide inspiration for Europe on how to achieve a more sustainable financial system.

Acknowledgements

Research for this chapter was enabled by a Marie Skoldowska Curie European Fellowship.

The author thanks the following organisations for their generosity in speaking to me about their work in New York City Affordable Housing Provision: the New York City Housing Authority, the Association of Neighbourhood and Housing Development, the Local Initiatives Support Corporation, Enterprise Community Partners, JOE NYC and Mr M. Jahr.

References

Aalbers, M. B. (2009). Why the Community Reinvestment Act cannot be blamed for the subprime crisis. *City and Community*, 8(3), 346–350.

Aalbers, M. B., Loon, J. V., & Fernandez, R. (2017). The financialization of a social housing provider. *International Journal of Urban and Regional Research*, *41*(4), 572–587.

Association of Neighbourhood and Housing Development (ANHD). (2014). *The state of bank reinvestment in New York City*. Retrieved from www.anhd.org/wp-content/uploads/2011/07/2014-REPORT-Single_Page-NoBleed_FINAL.pdf.

Barr, M. S. (2005). Credit where it counts: The Community Reinvestment Act and its critics. *New York University Law Review*, 80, 513.

Bengtsson, B., & Hertting, N. (2014). Generalization by mechanism: Thin rationality and ideal-type analysis in case study research. *Philosophy of the social sciences*, *44*(6), 707–732.

Blessing, A. (2016). Repackaging the poor? Conceptualising neoliberal reforms of social rental housing. *Housing Studies*, *31*(2), 149–172.

Blessing, A., & Gilmour, T. (2011). The invisible hand? Using tax credits to encourage institutional investment in social housing. *International Journal of Housing Policy*, *11*(4), 453–468.

Blessing, A., & Mullins, D. (forthcoming). Organisational hybridity in affordable housing finance. In D. Billis & C. Rochester (Eds.), *Handbook on hybrid organisations*. Cheltenham: Edward Elgar.

Bratt, R. G. (2009). Challenges for nonprofit housing organizations created by the private housing market. *Journal of Urban Affairs*, *31*(1), 67–96.

Canner, G., & Bhutta, N. (2008). *Staff analysis of the relationship between the CRA and the subprime crisis*. Memorandum, Board of Governors of the Federal Reserve System. Retrieved from www.federalreserve.gov/images/20081203_analysis.pdf.

Carroll, A. B., & Shabana, K. M. (2010). The business case for corporate social responsibility: A review of concepts, research and practice. *International Journal of Management Reviews*, *12*(1), 85–105.

City of Los Angeles. (2015). *Responsible banking investment monitoring program*. Retrieved from http://cao.lacity.org/RBO/.

Clark, G. L. (2000). Moral sentiments and reciprocal obligations: The case for pension fund investment in community development. *Ethics, Place and Environment*, 3(1), 7–24.

Congressional Budget Office. (2015). *Report: Federal housing assistance for low-income households, September 9, 2015*. Retrieved from www.cbo.gov/publication/50782.

Crouch, C. (2012). Sustainability, neoliberalism, and the moral quality of capitalism. *Business and Professional Ethics Journal*, *31*(2), 363.

Daggers, J., & Nicholls, A. (2016). *The landscape of social impact investment research: Trends and opportunities*. Said Business School, University of Oxford.

Dart, R. (2004). The legitimacy of social enterprise. *Nonprofit Management and Leadership*, *14*(4), 411–424.

Ellen, I., & Weselcouch, M. (2015). *Housing, neighborhoods, and opportunity: The location of New York City's subsidized affordable housing*. New York: NYU Furman Center.

Engelen, E., Froud, J., Johal, S., Salento, A., & Williams, K. (2016). *How cities work: A policy agenda for the grounded city* (CRESC Working Paper, No. 141, p. 115). Retrieved from http://hummedia.manchester.ac.uk/institutes/cresc/workingpapers/wp141.pdf.

Ensign, R. L., & Tracy, R. (2018, January 10). Trump administration seeks to change rules on bank lending to the poor: Regulators plan to revamp rules governing banks under the Community Reinvestment Act. *Wall Street Journal*.

European Commission. (2018, January 31). *Final report of the high-level expert group on sustainable finance, financial stability, financial services and capital markets union*. Brussels: Author.

European Commission, Directorate-General for Employment. (2001). *Promoting a European framework for corporate social responsibility: Green paper*. Brussels: Office for Official Publications of the European Communities.

Fields, D., & Uffer, S. (2016). The financialisation of rental housing: A comparative analysis of New York City and Berlin. *Urban Studies*, 53(7), 1486–1502.

Financial Crisis Inquiry Commission (FCIC). (2011). *The financial crisis inquiry report: Final report of the national commission on the causes of the financial and economic crisis in the United States*. Washington, DC: Author.

Garnier, S. (2016, December). *Responsible housing finance in Europe: Less gambling, better investments, blog for Housing Europe*. Retrieved from www.housingeurope.eu/blog-849/responsible-housing-finance-in-europe.

Glickman, N. J., & Servon, L. J. (1998). More than bricks and sticks: Five components of community development corporation capacity. *Housing Policy Debate*, 9(3), 497–539.

Habitat for Humanity. (2015). Housing review 2015: Affordability, livability, sustainability. Retrieved from www.habitat.org/sites/default/files/housing_review_2015_full_report_final_small_reduced.pdf.

Harloe, M. (1995). *The people's home? Social rented housing in Europe & America*. Oxford: Blackwell.

Hays, R. A. (1995). *The federal government and urban housing*. Albany, NY: SUNY Press.

Jacobs, K., & Manzi, T. (2013). New localism, old retrenchment: The 'Big Society', housing policy and the politics of welfare reform. *Housing, Theory and Society*, 30(1), 29–45.

Lindsey, L. B. (2009). The CRA as a means to provide public goods. In P. Chakrabarti, D. Erickson, R. S. Essene, I. Galloway, & J. Olson (Eds.), *Revisiting the CRA: Perspectives on the future of the Community Reinvestment Act* (pp. 160–166). New York: Federal Reserve Banks of Boston and New York.

McQuarrie, M., & Guthrie, D. (2007). Houses for the poor and new business for banks: the creation of a market for affordable housing. In V. Kashturi Rangan, John A. Quelch, Gustavo Herrero, & Brooke Barton (Eds.), *Business solutions for the global poor: Creating social and economic value* (pp. 249–258). Hoboken, NJ: Jossey-Bass.

Matthews, J., Sternlicht, D., Bouri, A., Mudaliar, A., & Schiff, H. (2015). *Introducing the impact investing benchmark.* Cambridge Associates and the Global Impact Investing Network. Retrieved from https://thegiin.org/assets/documents/pub/Introducing_the_Impact_Investing_Benchmark.pdf.

Mullins, D., Milligan, V., & Nieboer, N. (2018). State directed hybridity? The relationship between non-profit housing organizations and the state in three national contexts. *Housing Studies*, *33*(4), 565–588.

Nederlandse Waterschapsbank N.V. (NWB). (2017). *Affordable housing bond framework.* Retrieved from www.nwbbank.com/download/nwb-affordable-housing-bond-framework.

O'Brien, V. (2014). Funding affordable housing: Low income housing tax credits in the USA and their potential in the UK. Study funded by the Winston Churchill Memorial Trust. Retrieved from www.wcmt.org.uk.

O'Regan, M. (2017). America's affordable housing crisis: Challenges and solutions. Katherine M. O'Regan, Professor of Public Policy and Planning, NYU's Robert F. Wagner Graduate School, Faculty Director, NYU Furman Center for Real Estate and Urban Policy, Before the Committee on Finance, United States Senate, Tuesday, August 1, 2017.

Office of U.S. Senator Maria Cantwell Hart. (2017). *Meeting the challenges of the growing affordable housing crisis: Expanding and improving the housing tax credit.* Senate Office Building, Washington, D.C. 20510.

Olson, J., Chakrabarti, P., & Essene, R. (2009). A framework for revisiting the CRA. In In P. Chakrabarti, D. Erickson, R. S. Essene, I. Galloway, & J. Olson (Eds.), *Revisiting the CRA: Perspectives on the future of the Community Reinvestment Act* (pp. 2–7). New York: Federal Reserve Banks of Boston and New York.

Oxley, M. (2013, December 9). How America and France increased affordable housing supply. *Guardian*.

Ruonavaara, H. (2005). How divergent housing institutions evolve: A comparison of Swedish tenant co-operatives and Finnish shareholders' housing companies. *Housing, Theory and Society*, *22*(4), 213–236.

Schwartz, A. (2011). The credit crunch and subsidized low-income housing: The UK and US experience compared. *Journal of Housing and the Built Environment*, *26*(3), 353–374.

Schwartz, A. (2012). *Housing policy in the United States*. New York: Routledge.

Schwartz, A., & Meléndez, E. (2008). After year 15: Challenges to the preservation of housing financed with low-income housing tax credits. *Housing Policy Debate*, *19*(2), 261–294.

Smith, A. (1904). *An inquiry into the nature and causes of the wealth of nations*. Edited with an introduction, notes, marginal summary and an enlarged index by Edwin Cannan. London: Methuen. Retrieved from www.econlib.org/library/Smith/smWN.html.

Swyngedouw, E. (2005). Governance innovation and the citizen: The Janus face of governance-beyond-the-state. *Urban Studies*, *42*(11), 1991–2006.

Tang, C. P., Oxley, M., & Mekic, D. (2017). Meeting commercial and social goals: Institutional investment in the housing association sector. *Housing Studies*, *32*(4), 411–427.

Taylor, J., & Silver, J. (2009). The Community Reinvestment Act: 30 years of wealth building and what we must do to finish the job. In P. Chakrabarti, D. Erickson, R. S. Essene, I. Galloway, & J. Olson (Eds.), *Revisiting the CRA: Perspectives on the future of the Community Reinvestment Act* (pp. 148–159). New York: Federal Reserve Banks of Boston and New York.

US Department of Housing and Urban Development (HUD). (2017). Office of policy development and research: Low income housing credit dataset. Retrieved from www.huduser.gov/portal/datasets/lihtc.html.

US Government Accountability Office. (2017). US low-income housing tax credit: The role of syndicators. February 16. GAO-17-285R. Publicly released: March 1, 2017. Retrieved from www.gao.gov/assets/690/682890.pdf.

Wainwright, T., & Manville, G. (2017). Financialization and the third sector: Innovation in social housing bond markets. *Environment and Planning A*, 49(4), 819–838.

Willis, M. (2009). It's the rating, stupid: A banker's perspective on the CRA. In P. Chakrabarti, D. Erickson, R. S. Essene, I. Galloway, & J. Olson (Eds.), *Revisiting the CRA: Perspectives on the future of the Community Reinvestment Act* (pp. 59–70). New York: Federal Reserve Banks of Boston and New York.

12 Innovative affordable housing finance delivery model in England

Nicky Morrison

Introduction

The housing crisis in England is well documented, with the gap between housing demand and supply underpinning many of the housing challenges facing the country. The government in its Housing White Paper published in February 2017 acknowledged that: 'the housing market in this country is broken and the cause is very simple: for too long, we haven't built enough homes' (DCLG, 2017a). The Department of Community and Local Government's live tables highlight that 142,600 homes were completed in 2017, which represents a shortfall of between 84,500 and 134,500 homes required per annum (DCLG, 2017b).

As demand far outstrips supply, housing has become less affordable. On average, house prices are now almost seven times household income in England, and in London the figure is over 13 times. Excessive house price inflation not only makes homeownership out of reach for first time buyers but also feeds into rent inflation. In 2000, 10 per cent of the UK population privately rented, in 2015 it was 19 per cent. Yet escalating private rental increases, estimated at 5 per cent per annum, results in rising household debt, arrears and evictions (Savills, 2018). Those in greatest housing need are the most vulnerable to the growing unaffordability of house prices and rents. Key indicators of housing stress in England's housing system include growing waiting lists for subsidised social rental housing and rising homelessness numbers (Shelter, 2018). The housing crisis also has commensurate negative impacts on labour mobility, economic competitiveness and productivity in localities where stress is greatest but also it has well documented negative ramifications nationally (Gibb, O'Sullivan, & Glossop, 2008).

The UK government has stated that 'England needs net additions of around 225,000 to 275,000 homes per annum'. The Chancellor of the Exchequer's Autumn Budget 2017 set out a commitment to 300,000 new homes to be built a year (HM Treasury, 2017). The government also recognises that it is imperative to find innovative housing delivery partnerships to help fix the 'broken' housing market. Increasingly and across the country, local authorities are looking for innovative new models where they can take the lead again in delivering affordable homes in their area (Hackett, 2017). Moreover, the government acknowledges that local authorities should be part of the solution to fixing England's 'broken' housing market. It has therefore begun to loosen regulatory restrictions in order to allow entrepreneurial local authorities to innovate and explore these different delivery models. Rather than working alone, there has been a recent surge in local authorities' interest in setting up joint ventures with not-for-profit housing associations (HAs), particularly as they are able to access sources of private funding that are not available to local authorities.

The purpose of this chapter is to outline how the UK government framework has changed and how this innovative joint venture works between a local authority and an HA with a particular focus on how the innovation relates to finance. To do so, the chapter draws on the example of Brighton & Hove City Council that has set up a joint venture with Hyde Group Limited in October 2017. This type of joint venture is the first of its kind in England. It acts therefore as a trailblazer and can provide early lessons for other English local authorities keen to adopt this delivery model. There is also considerable transferable relevance to other countries equally interested in exploring this type of innovative funding arrangement as a way to deliver new affordable homes.

The context and UK government framework

The UK government acknowledges that those in the greatest housing need are the worst hit by the housing crisis. Yet at the same time it has also dramatically reduced its subsidy for new affordable homes over time (The Housing Finance Corporation (THFC), 2016). Government capital-grant allocations were halved from £8.8 billion to £4.4 billion in the Homes and Communities Agency's (HCA) 2010–14 Affordable Homes programme and to £1.7 billion in the HCA's 2015–18 programme. An 'affordable' rent model was also introduced in April 2011, whereby rents on re-lets and new affordable homes built must be a maximum of 80 per cent of local market levels and let on fixed-term tenancies (Morrison, 2016).

The government's withdrawal of funding has had immediate knock-on consequences, with the number of homes built in England falling year-on-year (Chartered Institute of Housing (CIH), 2018). In 2015/16, affordable housing delivery hit a 24-year low, with around 32,000 built, compared to 66,600 in 2014/15. The government measures to link rents more explicitly to market levels have also altered the affordable housing mix in HAs' development programmes across the country. Of the affordable homes built, only 6,550 of the new homes were for social rent (i.e. around 45–65 per cent of market level). In 2016/17, the overall number of affordable homes (at 80 per cent of market level) increased to around 41,500. The amount of social rental homes, however, fell further still to 53,809 (DCLG, 2017b).

The policy landscape for housing and planning has started to change. Following the UK government's 2017 Housing White Paper, there has been a shift from a dominant narrative and a focus on homeownership and planning deregulation to recognition that more social and affordable homes are needed (Town and Country Planning Association (TCPA), 2017). The government, however, is still seeking to reduce its financial commitment to subsidising their construction. In response to growing pressures to find alternative funding sources, the Greater London Authority (GLA) (2017) established a *Homes for Londoners* Board to investigate new delivery models to drive up an increase in affordable housing provision.

The key finding that arose from the GLA Board's investigation was that the availability of finance is not the principal problem in achieving the necessary housing numbers needed, particularly in London (GLA, 2017). Additional funding capacity exists in the English HA sector to finance the delivery of large numbers of affordable homes across the country. The HCA's *Sector Risk Profile* (2017) confirms that the year 2016 saw the HA sector access an unprecedented variety of sources of funding. The largest HAs are also asset rich, having a combined turnover of £20 billion, end of 2017 (Stothart, 2018). The GLA (2017) therefore argues that the key barrier to housing delivery is in fact the difficulties in accessing land. The HA sector cannot allocate additional financial resource capacity to deliver new affordable homes where they are needed the most as they are constrained by limited land availability. The sector is in effect prevented from achieving its maximum capacity.

In contrast, local authorities across England have access to council-owned land but face significant government restrictions that limit their ability to build new affordable homes on their own on these sites. In the past, local authorities received government capital grants and were able to directly build, therefore making a major contribution to the number of new homes built per year. During the 1980s, local authorities built over 88,500 council homes in a single year. This figure is currently less than 2,000 council homes per year (TCPA, 2017). Local authorities now face considerable restrictions on their ability to borrow from institutional investors and they cannot use their Housing Revenue Account to fund council housing development. They also have to comply with government rules on the use of receipts from sales of council housing stock through the Right to Buy. They therefore cannot access this additional income source to provide affordable housing replacements in their local areas (Hackett, 2017).

Although local authorities can obtain finance from selling off their council-owned land to private house builders, the New Economics Foundation (2017) highlights, however, that as little as 7 per cent of the land sold off, to date, was used for social rental housing. The pace of private sector development also remains at an all-time low in the UK and cannot be relied upon to scale up delivery and meet the government's ambitious housing targets (Pettifor, 2018). In contrast, the TCPA (2017) advocates that local authorities should instead hold on to their own land and enter into new partnerships with HAs to deliver social and affordable rental homes.

Local authorities establishing innovative joint venture partnership arrangements with asset rich HAs therefore offer a win–win solution to resolving the funding and land barriers that the different partners respectively face in their quest to scale up affordable housing delivery in specific localities. Moreover, the UK government has begun to recognise the role that local authorities can play in delivering new homes, particularly through these types of innovative partnership arrangements. The UK Government (2017) Housing White Paper includes a section on 'Backing local authorities to build', stating that:

> Local authorities' role in delivering new housing goes beyond using their planning powers. They also have an important role in delivering homes themselves. We want to make sure that they have the tools they need to get homes built where the market isn't coming forward with enough. … There are a number of good examples (including) joint venture models … We welcome innovations like these, and want more local authorities to get building.
>
> (paras 14 and 3)

This new government stance has stimulated ambitious local authorities to be much more proactive in their approach to affordable housing delivery, with many now exploring innovative funding partnership arrangements with HAs. The local authority that has led the way in developing such joint ventures is Brighton & Hove City Council, which forms part of Sussex coast housing market in the south east of England. Both the GLA *Homes for Londoners* Board and the TCPA showcase this joint venture as exemplary for other local authorities and HAs to follow (GLA, 2017; TCPA, 2017). The way the innovation works is outlined below.

What is the innovation and how does it work?

Brighton & Hove Council has established a new Limited Liability Partnership (LLP) with Hyde Group Limited (HA) on a 50:50 basis, which is called *Homes for the City of Brighton & Hove*. This special purpose vehicle, through an LLP, allows the local authority and HA to work together in a structure that ring-fences the project and limits the liability of both parties. The joint venture's governance arrangement entails a 50:50 board representation, with three members from either side. Before entering an agreement with the HA, the council performed a thorough due diligence of the HA management and development track record. Both partners need to ensure that there is sufficient expertise in the new LLP's Board and at both their Executive levels to manage the new enterprise.

The £120 million joint venture was given final council approval in October 2017 to build 1,000 homes, half of which will offer rents linked to the National Living Wage. The rest of the homes will be shared ownership, ring-fenced initially for local residents (see below).[1] There is also the potential for more affordable housing to be built through this LPP, which would be supplemented by sites sought by Hyde in the market, at a later date (Cross, 2018).

There are a number of key organisational principles underlying this type of special purpose vehicle. The LLP holds the housing stock outright. It is not leased or transferred to either partner or a third party. Hyde Group Limited, i.e. the HA's parent registered provider, is the 'investing' partner, along with Hyde New Build, a subsidiary of the HA group. The hybrid organisational structure will become more pronounced, following plans to set up a subsidiary design-and-build company with service agreements with Hyde and the council. This subsidiary will also provide asset and housing management services once the housing stock is built (Hyde, 2017). There is a lot of management time required to set up and run a joint venture project of this nature. By establishing a separate subsidiary, this enables the project to have dedicated staff managing it and also keeps the joint venture ring-fenced, thus protecting the two partners from any undue risk. As Oxley et al. (2015) stress, there needs to be a strong understanding of the interdependencies between all parts of the LLP including where there are guarantees or cross default clauses between the registered HA entity and the non-registered elements of the LPP, in order to avoid excessive risks.

The risks associated with this type of joint venture investment revolve around the HA's ability to plan, build and deliver the budget and timescale agreed with the local authority. The finance raised is not secured against either partner's assets and instead against the revenues to be generated from the project in order to ensure that the local authority and the HA's balance sheets are protected. There is a need to fill and manage the properties ensuring that rental voids and management costs are kept at an acceptable level. Yet given high levels of housing need in the local authority area, tenant demand is likely to be guaranteed. Households registered on Brighton & Hove's waiting list will have first choice in the allocation of the social rental properties.

There are a number of benefits to this model for both partners. The key benefit to the local authority is that it is able to operate outside its traditional Housing Revenue Account route and free of government restrictions. The main aim of the project is the provision of lower-cost rental housing, with the potential to generate a long-term income for the council through funding returns. The local authority also gains access to the HA's technical and commercial developer skills, and benefits from the HA's supply chain arrangements and volume buying power. Both LLP members benefit from the pooling of funding and resources, and sharing of risk (GLA, 2017). They share the cost and risks, but also the rewards from entering this joint venture arrangement. The joint venture structure also mitigates the risk of the local authority building 1,000 homes itself (Cross, 2018).[2]

The key benefit to the HA is access to the council-owned land for development. As the HA is working with a local government, this also means there is more transparency around delivery and adherence to key performance indicators. The LLP is required, for example, to model a property downturn into their business forecasts, which has to be tested to show that there would be no loss to either the local authority or HA if such an event occurs. The HCA (former) Regulator of the HA sector stresses that joint ventures must not give rise to recourse to social housing assets and/or create an impairment risk. It is critical that transparency and due diligence mitigate risk for both parties in order to avoid problems in the future (cited in Hilditch, 2018).

Finance

Both the local authority and the HA (the LLP members) provide equity to fund the project, with the funds provided to the LLP as non-interest bearing loans. Hyde Group Limited has the ability to provide equity capital from its reserves whilst Brighton & Hove Council's equity component equates to its land provision, which was valued by Savills (property agents) and provided at best consideration. Each partner has put around £60 million of equity on this basis into the 50:50 LLP. The model is predicated on an undisclosed internal rate of return.

The joint venture partners deliberately did not seek government grant funding through the HCA Affordable Housing Programme allocations. This allows the LLP to maintain control over lettings and sales. A key benefit to being self-funding is that it also removes the government requirement for the housing to be sold through Right to Buy legislation. This gives a lot of flexibility to both partners and frees them of restrictive government regulations.

Each LLP member is expected to receive a commercial rate of return on its equity investment from the profits generated in the LLP. They benefit from a stable long-term index-linked revenue stream, with the rental growth on the social rental properties linked to the consumer price index (CPI). Rents on the shared ownership properties carry the standard link to the Retail Price Index plus 0.5 per cent (Cross, 2018). The shared ownership investment also provides the potential for capital growth, through house price inflation linked to staircasing receipts (GLA, 2017). The partners have also managed to save 10–15 per cent on construction costs through the design, along with economies of scale, and are now exploring the use of modular build to make costs and speed of delivery as efficient as possible (Hyde, 2017).

While there are no initial plans to seek further investment, this type of inflation-linked liability-matching affordable housing joint venture could appeal to institutional investors (Cross, 2018). There are no plans, to date, to take more equity or gear up with debt, as the 1,000 homes are fully funded. In the future, the option exists, however, to gear up and develop more or bring in third party funding or equity. This type of investment opportunity is likely to appeal potentially to institutional investors as it matches up relatively well with pension fund long-term liabilities that are index linked.

Once built and let, the social rented homes are likely to be more attractive to investors than the private rented sector as they offer a very secure income rising in line with inflation. Tenant demand will remain strong so void periods are predicted to be very low (Brighton & Hove, 2016b). For Cross (2018), this type of 'light-touch' management will also make 'the gross to net "very efficient" … the types of homes being delivered in the locations and at the prices set will make them a "fairly liquid asset" for buyers' (p. 1). The returns for the investor are potentially strong in the term of the capital gains from the social rented housing assets as well as access to the cash flows (rental income) that are long dated inflation-linked (Oxley et al., 2015).

Examples of innovation: offering bespoke rents

A key principle behind this joint venture is to create a bespoke affordable housing delivery model, with the housing product tailored to the specific housing needs that exist within Brighton & Hove local authority area. Both partners are keen to challenge the government's existing definition of affordability, where rents are set at 80 per cent market level. As the local authority argues, this model has not worked in the local area, providing only 500 new affordable homes since the government introduced the affordable rent model in 2011 (Brighton & Hove, 2016a, 2016b).

The two partners have instead established a discounted rent model, whereby rents will be tailored to National Living Wages to meet the needs of local people on low incomes rather than being linked to the housing market price levels (Brighton & Hove, 2017a, 2017b). By creating this bespoke affordable housing model tailored to local incomes, average rents will equate to less than 60 per cent of local market rents. This rent calculation ensures that they are genuine affordability for low income working households from the local authority area (Hyde, 2017).[3] In 2016, medium annual incomes of households in the local area were at £29,000 (Brighton & Hove, 2016b). Qualifying persons for this subsidised rental housing must comply with Brighton & Hove Council's household income thresholds used to allocate council-owned and HA housing. To date, this equates to those households on the area's lowest income quartile. As demand far outstrips supply, a point system is used, including other eligibility criteria, e.g. the applicants need to be aged 18 or over, in housing need and fit the local connection criteria of five years' residency.

The shared ownership homes, meanwhile, will be ring-fenced for a period of time for local buyers in the area. The cost of a mortgage, rent and service charge for the proposed shared ownership housing is predicted to be less than the cost of local private market rents for comparable homes, and has been calculated to ensure that the properties are affordable to households earning average local incomes in the local authority area. There are 21,000 people on the council's housing register in Brighton and Hove, to date, of whom 10 per cent would be able to afford shared ownership (Hyde, 2017). Hyde also has a very strong shared ownership resale record, with more than 80 per cent of re-sales kept as social rental housing (Cross, 2018). As this single innovative case study is still in its infancy, the long-term benefits for tenants and buyers cannot be proven, to date. However, given both partners' firm commitment to retaining the principle of investment into affordable housing in perpetuity, the long-term sustainable outcomes of this new collaborative arrangement seem promising.

Discussion: outcomes, relevance, transferability

Joint ventures are an established concept in many European cases and are increasingly common in the English HA sector. Examples to date, however, have centred on HAs entering joint ventures with equity financiers and primarily been set up to deliver market sales housing through the HA's non-registered subsidiary. There has also been a growing trend in England for HAs to also set up joint ventures with institutional investors in order to diversify into market rental housing products (see Morrison, 2016). Under this type of joint venture arrangement, the HA fully manages all aspects of the properties and the institutional investor is in essence a 'silent investor', providing capital and accepting the risks and returns of the investment.

Whilst these activities add value and resources to the HA to be used as a substitution of government grant, there are a number of risks in HAs setting up new un-registered special purpose vehicles to carry out these non-core commercial activities. Mitigation action, break clauses and exit strategies need to be put into place to manage these risks placed on social housing assets for any market housing built or unsold or un-let properties. An awareness of the external political and economic environment, access to general housing market research for the services provided, and specific local housing market research is also essential (Morrison, 2016). For Manzi and Morrison (2017), operating effectively in one housing market does not necessarily mean that an HA will automatically do so in another. The key criticism of joint ventures predicated on non-core commercial activities is that the LLP becomes vulnerable to housing market fluctuations. Delays in initiation and completion of schemes, slowdowns in sales, reductions in market prices and failures to achieve projected sales incomes create real threats to an HA's business plan assumptions and its ability to comply with loan covenants.

Whilst joint ventures between local authorities and HAs are less common in England and Europe, there is a number of distinct benefits for both partners. The example of Brighton & Hove joint venture with Hyde HA offers a template for other local authorities and HAs across Europe to consider. The format would by necessity be tailored to specific government regulatory frameworks and aligned to local circumstances and priorities. Already Brighton & Hove Council has received a considerable amount of enquiries from other English councils on how to set up such a joint venture with active HAs in their local area (Cross, 2018). Although it took a two-year process to establish this pioneering local authority/HA joint venture, there is clear scope to reach a sign-off in a much shorter time frame and bring the projects on stream more quickly.

The lower-cost rental housing approach adopted by Brighton & Hove joint venture with Hyde HA clearly has the potential to be adopted elsewhere in Europe too. Tailoring rents to income meets the needs of local people on low incomes, who otherwise would be spending a considerable proportion of their earnings on rent and housing costs. Ring-fencing the project and not being reliant on government grants provides considerable scope to be flexible in rent setting. By taking back control on determining rents, this provides a means to challenge governments' definition of affordability. The same principle of gaining autonomy in rent setting can equally be applied across Europe. Moreover, by combining council-owned land and the use of an HA's internal resources, the potential to generate a long-term income for each partner through funding returns is also clearly evident. A strong business case therefore can be made.

Whilst local authorities and HAs are not always aligned culturally, they do match in relation to their transparent governance structures, committee approval processes and duty to provide housing (TCPA, 2017). This is the case across Europe too. The attraction of local authorities and HAs working together is the opportunity to combine skills, expertise and funding to deliver development, with the local authorities' main resources being council-owned land. They are therefore natural partners to enter into a joint venture arrangement. There are also more immediate benefits to a joint venture than if a local authority launched its own local housing company. As Hackett (2017) noted in the English experience, it can take five years or more to see any significant housing output through this route. Local authorities do not have the same resources, systems and supply chains in place as many developing HAs. By ring-fencing the joint venture, the local authority is in turn free of government regulations on its ability to act (TCPA, 2017). Although restrictions on municipal authorities vary across Europe, red tape exists in the majority of jurisdictions, albeit to different degrees, which could be eased through setting up these special purpose vehicles.

Local municipalities across Europe have become ever challenged by their governments to show that they have a supply of new housing land, as part of their local plan preparations. Untapped sources of local authority-owned land also exist in most European municipalities, thus this collaborative financing arrangement has wider applicability here too. Using local municipal-owned land and establishing joint ventures with not-for-profit housing providers provides the respective partners with a means to take more control over the development process. Rather than relying solely on the private sector housing delivery, these innovative partnerships give local authorities the ability to influence the timing of new development coming on stream. Both partners can directly respond to evidence of housing need, with delivery becoming less predicated on housing market cycles. They can act counter-cyclically, providing a steady and guaranteed stream of affordable housing output.

These innovative joint ventures also enable local authorities to play a much more proactive role in the long-term stewardship of their local area. For TCPA (2017), they can ensure high-quality public realm and the connectivity and cohesion of new housing schemes within the existing urban area, therefore creating a much more holistic approach to regenerating areas. By taking the lead and working jointly with HAs, there are also valuable indirect benefits for the local authority and its local area. These include social and economic benefits from the inward investment into the provision of new housing and also through increased council tax revenues (Cross, 2018).

Conclusions

Local authorities across England are beginning to take proactive new approaches to delivering affordable homes, in response to a lack of private sector delivery and a desire to be freed of government restrictions (Hackett, 2017). Brighton & Hove Council has taken the lead and established a first-of-its-kind innovative joint venture with the HA, Hyde Housing Group, to provide 1,000 affordable homes in the local area (Hyde, 2017), setting the rents to National Living Wages guarantees that the housing will be genuinely affordable for low-income households. The shared ownership properties will also be ring-fenced for local buyers in the area. Moreover, there is a strong business case to be made in setting up this LLP, which innovatively pools resources and shares the costs, risks and financial rewards, as outlined above.

Other local authorities are keen to learn how to set up similar joint ventures with active HAs in their local areas (GLA, 2017). Specific LLPs can be set up to acquire, fund, develop and own discounted rental and shared ownership homes, which reflect the local authorities' different circumstances and priorities. The joint venture structure also mitigates the risk of a local authority building homes by itself, particularly if they lack skills and have a shortage of people and resources. There is considerable potential to translate this innovative joint venture funding model into the European context. As the TCPA (2017) contend, for this innovation to take place, a strong political and corporate leadership within the local authority is necessary. Moreover, it also takes strong government backing for local authorities to take back the lead in building homes again (Hackett, 2017). Having this necessary central and local government support applies across Europe too. Further collaborative research is therefore needed to explore the transferability potential and to assess the costs and benefits of these new types of housing delivery models in more depth.

Moreover, there is a large number of innovative permutations to use joint ventures that have the potential to be explored further too. These include not just joint ventures between a local authority and one HA but also multiple stakeholder participation could occur. Given the potential appetite from institutional investors, these types of joint ventures can bring in equity investors at the outset or at a later date. The benefits to all parties are strong (Oxley et al., 2015). It could also entail more than one HA in the LLP agreement, with the nature of the structure adapted accordingly. For smaller HAs, particularly those with limited scope for providing equity capital from their own reserves, this would enable them to benefit from institutional investor's ability to raise equity and debt funding (THFC, 2016; Tang, Oxley, & Mekic, 2016).

In England, there are growing debates over how to bring more equity investors into the HA sector (Lyons, 2018). Joint ventures that focus not only on non-core commercial activities but also on affordable housing provision need to be at the forefront of these discussions. These types of index-linked investments are likely to appeal to institutional investors who also gain returns from property management fees and access to experienced property management services provided by the local authority and the HA's management company set up in the LLP. The local authority and HA equally retain an equity interest in the joint venture and a financial interest to manage the social rental properties well. Joint ventures also allow the risks and returns to be ring-fenced from each of the partner's operations. They remain safeguarded, with defined return and risk boundaries (Oxley et al., 2015).

As innovative delivery models between local authorities and not-for-profit housing providers take off across Europe, this provides a way to bring new funding sources to affordable housing delivery. Initially these joint ventures would combine council-owned land and HAs' resources, but later private equity finance could be drawn in, with each partner in the LLP sharing the risks and rewards. This model of development enables local authorities to address local patterns of housing need much more effectively. But also it allows them to secure value increases of land for future reinvestment (TCPA, 2017). Retaining these socio-economic benefits in the local area are considerable. Selling land on to the open market creates a lost land and affordable housing opportunity. Operating through a special purpose vehicle also provides an effective means for both local authorities and HAs to set their own rents, thus critically challenging government definitions of affordability. They also become less beholden to government restrictions on their activities. As public and not-for-profit organisations work more closely together across each country, they in turn take control of the pace of new housing development. They become less affected by private house building industry practices that are driven by profit and vagaries of the housing market. By doing so, they start to play a greater role in scaling up affordable housing delivery and helping to fix 'broken' housing markets witnessed across Europe.

Notes

1 Shared ownership properties entail a household part renting and part buying a property, normally starting on a 50:50 basis, with the household having the ability to staircase up to 100 per cent full ownership.
2 The LLP members' agreement does not constitute a public contract for the purposes of UK's Public Contract Regulations 2015 and selection of either local authority/HA does not require an EU-regulated procurement process.
3 The affordable rents tailored to income are currently linked flat to the CPI, which the local authority is keen to maintain to ensure homes remain 'genuinely' affordable (Brighton & Hove, 2017a).

References

Brighton & Hove City Council. (2016a). *City plan: Part one Brighton and Hove City Councils development plan*. Retrieved from www.brighton-hove.gov.uk/sites/brighton-hove.gov.uk/files/FINAL%20version%20cityplan%20March%202016compr.

Brighton & Hove City Council. (2016b). *City plan: Part one annex housing implementation strategy*. Retrieved from www.brighton-hove.gov.uk/sites/brighton-hove.gov.uk/files/FINAL%20annex%203%20%28mar%202016%29.pdf.

Brighton & Hove City Council. (2017a). *Key stage in delivery of 1,000 affordable homes.* Press release, 26 September. Retrieved from www.brighton-hove.gov.uk/content/press-release/key-stage-delivery-1000-affordable-homes.

Brighton & Hove City Council. (2017b). *Minutes from the Policy Resources & Growth Committee meeting*, 12 October. Retrieved from https://present.brighton-hove.gov.uk/Published/C00000912/M00006704/$$ADocPackPublic.pdf.

Chartered Institute of Housing (CIH). (2018). *More than 150,000 homes for social rent lost in just five years, new analysis reveals.* Retrieved from www.cih.org/news-article/display/vpathDCR/templatedata/cih/news-article/data/More_than_150000_homes_for_social_rent_lost_in_just_five_years_new_analysis_reveals.

Cross, L. (2018). *Hyde and Brighton Council sign off £120m joint venture.* Retrieved from www.socialhousing.co.uk/news/news/hyde-and-brighton-council-sign-off-120m-joint-venture-53753.

Department for Communities and Local Government (DCLG). (2017a). *Fixing our broken housing market.* Retrieved from www.gov.uk/government/uploads/system/uploads/attachment_data/file/590464/Fixing_our_broken_housing_market_-_print_ready_version.pdf.

Department for Communities and Local Government (DCLG). (2017b). *Live table on house building 241: 'Permanent dwellings completed, by tenure, United Kingdom, historical calendar year series'.* Retrieved from www.gov.uk/government/statisticaldata-sets/live-tables-on-house-building.

Gibb, K., O'Sullivan, A., & Glossop, C. (2008). *Home economics: How housing shapes city economies.* London: Centre for Cities.

Greater London Authority (GLA). (2017). *New delivery models.* Retrieved from www.london.gov.uk/what-we-do/housing-and-land/housing-and-land-publications/new-delivery-models-homes-londoners-sub.

Hackett, P. (2017). *Delivering the renaissance in council-built homes: The rise of local housing companies.* London: The Smith Institute.

Hilditch, M. (2018). *Joint ventures fertile territory in the future says former regulation chair.* Retrieved from www.socialhousing.co.uk/news/joint-ventures-fertile-territory-for-problems-in-the-future-says-former-regulation-chair-54521?

HM Treasury. (2017). *UK government autumn budget 2017.* Retrieved from www.gov.uk/government/publications/autumn-budget-2017-documents/autumn-budget-2017.

Homes and Communities Agency (HCA). (2017). *Sector risk profile.* Retrieved from www.gov.uk/government/publications/sector-risk-profile-2017.

Hyde. (2017). *Brighton-Hove to get 1,000 affordable homes.* Retrieved from www.hyde-housing.co.uk/news/building-homes/brighton-hove-to-get-1-000-affordable-homes/.

Lyons, J. (2018). *The evolving relationship between housing associations and equity providers.* Retrieved from www.socialhousing.co.uk/comment/comment/the-evolving-relationship-between-housing-associations-and-equity-providers-54124.

Manzi, T., & Morrison, N. (2017). Risk, commercialism and social purpose: Repositioning the English housing association sector. *Urban Studies.* DOI: 10.1177/0042098017700792.

Morrison, N. (2016). Institutional logics and organisational hybridity: English housing associations' diversification into the private rented sector. *Housing Studies*, *31*(8), 897–915.

New Economics Foundation. (2017). *Selling public land is making the housing crisis worse.* Press release, 3 May. Retrieved from http://neweconomics.org/2017/03/selling-public-land-making-housing-crisis-worse-new-research/.

Oxley, M., Tang, C., Lizieri, C., Mansley, N., Mekic, D., Haffner, M., & Hoekstra, J. (2015). *Prospects for institutional investment in social housing*. London: Investment Property Forum.

Pettifor, A. (2018). Why building more homes will not solve Britain's housing crisis. *Guardian*. Retrieved from www.theguardian.com/commentisfree/2018/jan/27/building-homes-britain-housing-crisis.

Savills. (2018). *UK housing market update 2018*. Retrieved from www.savills.co.uk/research_articles/213153/226532-0.

Shelter. (2018). *Why we campaign: The housing crisis*. Retrieved from http://england.shelter.org.uk/campaigns_/why_we_campaign/the_housing_crisis/what_is_the_housing_crisis.

Stothart, C. (2018). *Largest associations grow turnover to £20bn in 2017*. Retrieved from www.socialhousing.co.uk/insight/largest-associations-grow-turnover-to-20bn-in-2017-53498.

Tang, C., Oxley, M., & Mekic, D. (2017). Meeting commercial and social goals: Institutional investment in the housing association sector. *Housing Studies*, *32*(4), 411–427.

The Housing Finance Corporation (THFC). (2016). *Investing in affordable housing*. London: Author.

Town and Country Planning Association (TCPA). (2017). *How can councils secure the delivery of more affordable homes? New models, partnerships and innovations*. London: Author.

UK Government. (2017). *Fixing our broken housing market housing white paper*. Retrieved from www.gov.uk/government/publications/fixing-our-broken-housing-market.

13 Energy performance fee to cover investments in the energy efficiency of affordable housing

The Netherlands

Anke van Hal, Maurice Coen and Eefje Stutvoet

Introduction

The Dutch 'National Energy Exploration 2015' (Nationale Energieverkenning 2015; Schoots & Hammingh, 2015), showed a remarkably optimistic view on the future energy quality of the existing housing stock of housing associations. Despite the fact that at the moment of publishing the housing associations seemed not able to reach their ambitions, the authors expected housing associations to accelerate their activities and reach the goal of an average energy-index of 1.25 in 2020 (or, described in the former standard, an energy label B).[1] The report shows that this optimism is based on the investment prognoses for housing associations and their applications for financial incentives for energy efficiency. The authors also expect a successful continuation of the initiative 'Stroomversnelling' (Acceleration programme). This initiative has the goal to transform 100,000 existing dwellings into so-called 'zero-on-the-meter' homes: houses with a very limited energy use, before 2020. A cornerstone of this programme is an innovative way of financing: the Energy Performance Fee (EPF). In this chapter, we describe the background and impact of this EPF.

Methodology

The EPF was introduced in 2016. Due to the short period of existence knowledge about the effects of an EPF is limited. As a result, this chapter largely describes the theoretical functioning of the financial system. Early experiences with the system are described too, as well as discussions that occurred during the process of introduction. A set of knowledge papers about the background and theoretical functioning of this system, written by two of the three authors of this chapter (Coen & Stutvoet, 2016a, 2016b, 2016c, 2016d), forms the basis of this text. The information these papers contain results from a problem analysis, based on experiences in several energy ambitious renovation projects, interviews with experts and desk research of relevant information. Concepts of the papers were sent to experts for a final check. The papers are updated annually to incorporate recent experiences and developments.

Barriers to investments in energy efficiency

An innovative way of financing renovations with far-reaching energy ambitions was necessary because of the split-incentive dilemma where landlords have no incentive for making energy efficiency investments from which their tenants will have the main benefits, and where tenants have no incentive to invest in the landlord's property. Landlords often will only invest when they are assured of reimbursement by their tenants (Faber & Hoppe, 2013). Also, the 'Landlord Levy' (*verhuurdersheffing*; Priemus, 2014), a new tax provision for housing associations, is a barrier for housing associations to invest in renovation projects with high energy ambitions (Aedes, G4, G32, Woonbond & VNG, 2016). As well is the housing allowance cap introduced in 2016 (*aftoppingsgrens*; National Housing Federation, 2017). Since 1 January 2016, households with a right to rent allowance (*Huurtoeslag*) must, in principle, be allocated a home with a rent under this cap: around €600, depending on household size and age (Witjes, 2017). All these measures reduce the investment capacity of a housing association.

An innovative approach

A government-initiated innovation programme called 'Energy Leap' (Energiesprong) created the opportunity for six housing associations and four building companies to overcome these barriers to investment. Energy Leap was an innovation programme, initiated by the Ministry of Interior and Kingdom Relations (BZK). The programme was active from 2010 to the end of 2016 with the goal to create a transition towards an energy neutral built environment in 2050. To reach this result, the market was challenged, and opportunities were taken to create a transition (Energiesprong, 2017).

These six housing associations and four building companies launched an innovative idea based on the use of money that could not be used before. This is money that is paid by residents for their energy bill. In return for the investment in the energy efficiency of their home, tenants get a guaranteed energy performance of their homes. This means that the amount of energy for an average household during an average climate-year equals the energy production of the dwelling. Tenants are also supposed to pay a monthly 'Energy Performance Fee' to the housing association. The energy costs of the tenant should not increase so the fee (combined with an energy bill in case the tenant uses more energy than average) cannot be higher than the tenant's former energy bill. The fee as an additional income enables housing associations to invest in energy efficiency measures. This innovative way of thinking creates a potential flow of funds around €13 billion annually for the existing Dutch housing stock. This is the amount of money that Dutch households on average spend on their energy bills. As we will explain later in this chapter, a transition in the traditional way of working of building companies and housing associations is necessary to make the EPF a success.

Transition

The 'Energiesprong' programme formed the basis for the 'Stroomversnelling' initiative ('Acceleration' programme) and the EPF. 'Energy Leap' stimulated the development of innovative technological and process-oriented concepts, and the integration of these concepts in the built environment in constantly growing numbers (SEV, 2010). These concepts consist of prefabricated facades and roofs that transform existing terraced houses into homes that hardly have any energy use within a few days. The energy-saving techniques are usually integrated into the heavily insulated facade. Illustrations of innovative processes related to these concepts are new ways of procurements and the industrial way of working, based on prefabrication (for an explanation, see later in this chapter). The programme is organized around pilot homes in which the technological concepts of 'de Stroomversnelling' are tested (see Figures 13.1 and 13.2, for examples). These technological concepts create the opportunity to transform standardized developed existing dwellings into brand-new-looking dwellings that hardly have an energy demand for heating within several days. Based on the findings of these pilot-homes, process innovations were developed. In addition to changes in the procurement method also ways of cooperation and financing fundamentally changed to promote a large-scale application of the technological concepts (for an explanation, see later in this chapter). These process changes represent a break with previous energy efficiency programmes, which were also oriented on the existing housing stock. Programmes like Energiesprong and 'de Stroomversnelling', with the aim of creating a transition,

Figure 13.1 Pilot project of the technological concept of 'de Stroomversnelling' in Nieuw Buinen.

Figure 13.2 Pilot project of the technological concept of 'de Stroomversnelling' in Arnhem.

are characterized by system changes; changes in the context in which innovation development and scale-up take place.

The Energiesprong-approach, and in the extension thereof the approach of 'de Stroomversnelling', are largely based on the model of transition of Rotmans (2003). There are other theoretical insights too that are used as a source of inspiration for the programmes but, in this chapter, we restrict ourselves to the relationship with the work of Rotmans. In their first-year plan Energiesprong used Rotmans' definition of system innovation: 'System innovations are innovations that transcend the organization level and radically change the relationship between enterprises, organizations, and individuals' (2003, p15). According to Rotmans and Horsten (2012) conditions for successful transitions are based on a number of linked trends (macro level), adequate social pressure on the current structure of rules, procedures and ways of thinking and acting (micro level) and enough drive for internal change and sufficient opportunities to innovate (both on a meso level). Energiesprong tried to bridge the gap between the different levels and is derived from the meso level, because its original goal was to create 'innovation space' (the creation of conditions, like a change in legislation, in which innovation can take place; Versteeg, Poolen, Van Rijn, & Opstelten, 2009). The experiments characterize the micro level (e.g. change in cooperation between the parties, and the development of technological concepts). However, they aim to create movement at the meso level too (for example by adapting regulations and financial systems of housing associations). These experiments also have to cope with both opposing and supporting social trends. By using these supporting social trends as a momentum, the upscaling of the concepts can be promoted (a relation with macro level). For example, the crisis in the building industry and the introduction of the Landlord Levy created support for innovations and transition. The introduction of the EPF can be seen as meso level; technological concepts are developed and have to be facilitated by a change in the financial system.

The EPF and its consequences

In this section, we follow the reasoning behind the introduction and up-scaling of the technical concepts of 'de Stroomversnelling'. The core rationale behind the EPF consists of four elements. (1) The introduction of the EPF created a flow of funds for housing associations based on the money that is paid by residents for their energy bill (see next subsection 'The EPF'). (2) To make it possible for housing associations to invest this flow of funds in energy efficient technological concepts, building companies have to reduce their prices by industrializing the production of these kind of concepts (see subsection 'Price reduction'). (3) As a result of this industrialized approach, the cooperation between housing associations and the building companies changes fundamentally. Instead of being performers of detailed assignments on-site, building companies become suppliers of standardized prefabricated technological concepts (see subsection 'Cooperation between housing association and building company'). (4) The prefabricated renovation concepts only become affordable if widely adopted. To become widely adopted, residents must become attracted to the concepts. For that reason creating enthusiasm amongst residents for the energy efficient technological concepts is an important challenge (see subsection 'Creating enthusiasm amongst residents').

The EPF

The EPF is a monthly fee that can be charged by housing associations to their tenants if his or her dwelling is equipped with a technological concept that makes it plausible that the amount of energy for an average household during an average climate-year equals the energy production of that dwelling. These houses are called zero-on-the-meter homes, and their energy performance is guaranteed by the building company. The EPF replaces the costs of the energy bill and is charged in addition to the rent and service costs.

In the past it was not possible for the housing association to generate a flow of energy-related money to finance their energy investments because the possibilities for rent increases were limited. To make this revenue stream possible, rent regulation was adjusted (Blok, 2016). The revised legislation was adopted in May 2016, and the regulation came into force in September 2016. Originally, these changes applied only to dwellings which, as a result of the adjustments, would no longer use natural gas as a source of energy. However, in February

2017, in response to protests, the law was changed again to make it possible to also use the EPF for zero-on-the-meter homes that are still connected to the natural gas network (Blok, 2017). In these cases a compensation of energy flows is required which means that gas consumption must be compensated by a quantity of renewable energy generated on or at the home.

The EPF is part of the allowance that can be asked by the housing association from the tenants if their home is transformed into a zero-on-the-meter home. This allowance consists of the following four components (but not necessarily all four):

1 a fee for home improvements (e.g. renovation of the kitchen and/or bathroom) as part of the rent;
2 an allowance for energy in the form of an EPF – this allowance is not part of the rent or service charges;
3 compensation for energy-efficient household appliances as part of the service charge (if these are integrated into the technological concept);
4 heating costs – these are the costs related to the delivery of heat under the Heat Law (*Warmtewet*),[2] and these are no part of the service costs.

In order to use the EPF, the homes must meet some basic conditions.[3] The amount of the fee that may be requested by the housing association from the tenants can be found in the EPF regulation (Staatsblad, 2016). Table 13.1 shows the basic table for dwellings that are not connected to a heating network and for that reason do not need to comply with Heat Law regulation.

The EPF has several advantages. First, as a result of the changes in regulation, housing costs can stay neutral. The total energy costs and rent won't change which means that tenants pay the same as they used to pay or, with new tenants, tenants don't pay more than they would have had to pay for a comparable home. As a result, the homes remain available for low-income groups. The second advantage is the reduction of the energy demand and the introduction of sustainably produced energy. Third, the housing association and building company can create an economically viable business case. Furthermore, no significant additional (administrative) costs are needed, and the development of innovations is stimulated.

There are, however, also disadvantages. Urgenda and Balanshuis, for example, warned in an open letter for the limited application of the EPF for buildings with historical value (Federatie Ruimtelijke Kwaliteit, 2016). The EPF is focused on a strong reduction of the energy demand of a building instead of on minimizing the use of non-renewable energy sources. This results in a focus on insulation which often requires a change in the appearance of buildings and could be detrimental to the heritage value (Federatie Ruimtelijke Kwaliteit, 2016). Another complaint relates to the requirement that all energy should be sustainably produced on, in or at the home. This makes impossible the application of collective district-level energy and heating solutions, like a collective biogas plant fed with green waste, or a wind turbine at the edge of the

Table 13.1 Illustration of a Staatsblad (Blok, 2016) (translated): the maximum energy compensation for a dwelling heated by renewable energy that is generated in the dwelling

Net heat demand for space heating (kWh_th/m²) per year	*Minimal sustainably generated heat for space heating and domestic hot water (kWh_th/m²) per year**	*Minimal production renewable energy for tenant use (kWh/m²) per year, per dwelling ≥ (Ehelp + 1,800) but not > (Ehelp + 2,600)***	*Maximum fee (€/m²/month)****
0 < Net heat demand ≤ 30	Net heat demand + 15	Ehelp + 26	1.40
30 < Net heat demand ≤ 40	Net heat demand + 15	Ehelp + 26	1.20
40 < Net heat demand ≤ 50	Net heat demand + 15	Ehelp + 26	1.00****

Notes

* This concerns the net amount of heat generated for space heating and domestic hot water (it is the output of an installation which generates heat, seen over a year, and at average climatic conditions).

** This concerns the energy generated for an average electricity consumption of the residents in a year.

Ehelp concerns the building-related electrical energy that is necessary for the operation of installations such as ventilation systems, cooling systems, and systems for measurement and monitoring. Also, the electricity required for the functioning of installations that use heating sources like air, water and soil are seen as Ehelp and should also be generated sustainably. Energy for lighting is not supposed to be Ehelp. Energy for lighting is covered by the amount of energy that the tenant may use (a minimum of 26 kWh/m² produces by the dwelling per year).

*** The EPF is an amount of money per square metre space per month. The heat demand and the amount of in or on the house generated renewable energy are expressed in kilowatt-hours per square metre per year. In addition, the assumptions were made that the heat does not exceed 50 kWh/m² per year. The amount of renewable energy for hot water is at least 15 kWh/m² per year, and the amount of renewable energy that is available for the tenant is at least 26 kWh/m² per year.

**** An EPF is not possible if the heat demand is higher than 50 kWh/m² per year and/or if the amount of renewable heat produced is less than the net heat plus 15 kWh/m² per year and/or if the renewable energy that is available for use by the tenant is less than 26 kWh/m² per year.

neighbourhood. Also, the method of calculation is not yet sophisticated enough according to specialists, and the EPF is sensitive to future developments. For example, trend analyses show that it is likely that the cost of electricity will decrease but energy performance compensation cannot decrease because the EPF ensures that there is a healthy business case. A lower EPF makes the business case less attractive. Also, the possible elimination of the set-off regulation[4] may have far-reaching negative consequences in the near future (Goes, 2016). Broadening the EPF regulation to include homes with a natural-gas connection has been met by strong resistance from Stroomversnelling participants stating that the revised system contains too little incentives for innovation (Stroomversnelling, 2016).

Price reduction

The EPF creates a new and additional financial flow to housing associations because money that was previously paid to energy companies becomes available for them. This financial flow creates the possibility of spending more resources on renovations with high energy ambitions. Also the expansion of the lifespan of the dwellings, as a result of renovation activities, increases the amount of money that can be invested. Calculations, based on the EPF and an extension of the lifespan by 40 years, determine the amount of money available to invest and, consequently, also the maximum price of the innovative technological concepts (see Table 13.2).

There are various models to determine investment capacity. Energiesprong uses the net discounted cash flow calculations model. In this model, the value of a dwelling is calculated by creating the net cash value of all income and expenses over the remaining lifespan of the dwelling against an internal rate of return requirement. It is also possible to calculate the investment opportunities based on market value. According to the Housing Act 2015, housing associations must value their property based on this value, and such calculation leads to other outcomes (Buffing, Achterveld, & Conijn, 2016). However, because of the requirement of the 'Social Housing Guarantee Fund' (*Waarborgfonds Sociale Woningbouw*) that guarantees social housing financing, to use the net discounted cash flow calculations model Energiesprong uses this calculation model (WSW, 2016). For an average Dutch terraced house calculations based on this model make it possible to invest €70,000 in a 'zero-on-the-meter' renovation (see Table 13.2).

The prospect of this investment capacity attracted the six housing associations and four building companies to become part of the initiative 'de Stroomversnelling'. The result was the agreement that, if the six housing associations were willing to renovate 11,000 dwellings, the construction companies would offer a zero-on-the-meter renovation for €60,000 per dwelling after a prototype phase of about 1,000 dwellings. In most cases, the zero-on-the-meter renovation also included a new bathroom, kitchen and toilet because, when the house is

Table 13.2 Example of the calculation for an average Dutch terraced house

Example		*Operating term*	*Net present value*	*Investment capacity*
Rent (month)	€550	Lifespan 15 years	€40,000	
Energy (month)	€120	Lifespan 25 years	€60,000	€20,000
Maintenance (year)	€1,300	–		
Management (year)	€1,300	Lifespan 40 years	€80,000	€40,000
Charges, fees (year)	€500	EPF over 40 years		€30,000
Residual value	€5,000	**Total investment capacity**		**€70,000**
Internal rate of return	5.25%			

Note
* Amounts in table are rounded off.

updated, it can be rented again for decades. Residents often appreciate these new facilities more than energy saving measures (Sijpheer et al., 2016).

In a parallel programme for private owned houses, the bar was placed at €45,000. This amount is roughly equivalent to the present value of the energy bill of the average Dutch household over the mortgage period (the period within which the loan for the property must be paid). A new bathroom, kitchen and toilet are not included in this price.

The first technological, prefabricated and integrated, zero-on-the-meter concepts that were developed, according to what later became the criteria of the EPF, see Table 13.2, were still significantly more expensive than €60,000. Jan Willem van de Groep (2013), one of the initiators of the 'Stroomversnelling', stated that 'The stakes are high: the price should be 30/40 percent lower than in previous experiments [...]. The scale [of 11,000 dwellings] makes it possible for the building companies to follow through.' He points out, however, that not only the scale but also the working processes of the building companies have to change. 'Better stuff at lower prices with guaranteed performance [...] cannot be done in the traditional way! Innovation and industrialization are key concepts.' All this has far-reaching consequences for the building companies. As Leen van Dijke, chair of the association of 'de Stroomversnelling', stated in an interview (Van Mil, 2016):

> All building elements must be prepared in a prefabricated way to make it possible that a renovation can be realized in one or several days. This requires a transformation of the business, which we should not think of too lightly.

Undeniably, 'de Stroomversnelling' is a major challenge for construction companies. That building companies are taking the initiative to offer complete prefabricated products (integrated renovation concepts) instead of responding to traditional tender processes is a big change. Tendering processes, based on detailed specifications and drawings, are replaced by the marketing of products by building companies. A building company that used to be a contractor has become a provider of concepts, products and technological solutions. This has far-reaching consequences for the cooperation between building companies and housing associations.

Cooperation between housing association and building company

As we have demonstrated previously, the EPF makes it possible to invest a certain amount of money. To meet the EPF criteria for this amount, building companies have to reduce the price of their technological solutions by integrating a diversity of energy-efficiency measures into prefabricated technological concepts that are suitable for similar houses. They have to sell their products on a large scale to recoup their investments, and housing associations, who own large quantities of similar houses, are their preferred clients.

Purchasing these technological concepts can be very attractive for housing associations too. Compared to the traditional tendering processes this way of working is much easier for them. Many of the responsibilities shift towards the building companies. The housing associations still have to know exactly what kind of renovation concept they are looking for. Ideally, if all needs and requirements are known, housing associations start the search for suitable prefabricated technological concepts, offered by building companies. If a fitting product is found, housing associations buy the product and shift all responsibilities towards the building company that sells the product.

However, due to the lack of enough technological concepts at present (about 20 for terraced houses and some for multi-apartment buildings) building companies often have to develop and offer concepts based on the location-specific needs and requirements of the housing association. This requires a temporary – intermediary – form of cooperation between the building company and the housing association that is different from the past but also different from the envisaged future. Together they have to create a technological concept that meets the requirements of the EPF, the specific requirements of the housing association and that suits houses of other housing associations too.

When the dwellings are uninhabited the phases of implementation, execution and delivery are easy for the housing association because the building company creates and delivers. But if the dwellings are occupied, the building company and the housing association have to make agreements with residents about the renovation process. The building company can, as part of the concept, offer all kind of services to reduce the nuisance for the residents. They can promise, for example, to finish their work before weekends or they can offer residents a quiet place to drink coffee or do homework during the building activities. In these cases, the building company has direct contact with the residents. This is a new experience for housing associations. They are no longer the only party that communicates with the residents. This is a big change that often takes a lot of effort from all sides. Good coordination of the communication activities of the housing association and the building company is essential.

In order to meet the requirements of the EPF, building companies also have to guarantee the energy performance of their renovations, including the period of use. As a result, they are also responsible for the maintenance of the renovated dwellings for several decades, and as a result they have to stay in touch with the residents over this period. Buying prefabricated zero-on-the-meter renovation concepts, made possible by the introduction of the EPF, is attractive for housing associations but also has far-reaching consequences. Especially with regard to contacts with residents. Enthusiasm about the transformation of their home towards a zero-on-the-meter home is important for the housing association because they are responsible for the quality of the homes they rent to their tenants. Also for the building companies, enthusiasm by residents about their renovation concepts is important. They have to sell large numbers of these concepts and benefit from positive stories. In other words, the opinion of residents is extremely important. However, many of them have different needs, priorities and interests from energy efficiency.

Creating enthusiasm amongst residents

The EPF resulted in the development of prefabricated renovation concepts that become affordable if widely adopted. To become widely adopted, residents have to become attracted to the concepts. Practice shows, however, that the interest of residents in energy efficiency is limited (Schoots & Hammingh, 2015; Van der Werf, 2011). Dutch initiatives, like the 'More-with-Less' programme (*Meer-met-Minder*), with the goal to insulate 300,000 houses a year in a way that improves the energy quality with two Dutch label steps,[5] were not successful (Vringer, van Middelkoop, & Hoogervorst, 2014) Also, activities of municipalities, mainly focused on privately owned houses, are not reaching their goals (Huisman, De Jong, Van Duin, & Stoeldraijer, 2013). Even housing associations are not as successful as expected. An evaluation shows that the current target of Aedes (the umbrella organization for Dutch housing associations) to bring the housing stock of their members up to an average of energy label B, will not be reached if the current pace of the progress holds (Vringer et al., 2014).

One of the main reasons for the unsatisfactory results is that many residents are not taking the step to a combination of measures (van Hal, 2016). This is caused by the fact that for residents this is a complex decision where many aspects have to be taken into consideration. The behavioural model for energy saving behaviour of tenants and homeowners (see Figure 13.3) shows the complex interplay of factors (from the perspective of the government) that has to be taken into account (Vringer, van Middelkoop, & Hoogervorst, 2016).

The model clearly shows that there are several motives for tenants and homeowners to decide to (or to decide not to) take energy efficient measures (e.g. comfort, money savings, certainty, safety and care for the environment and several emotional motives). There are also many physical and social issues that

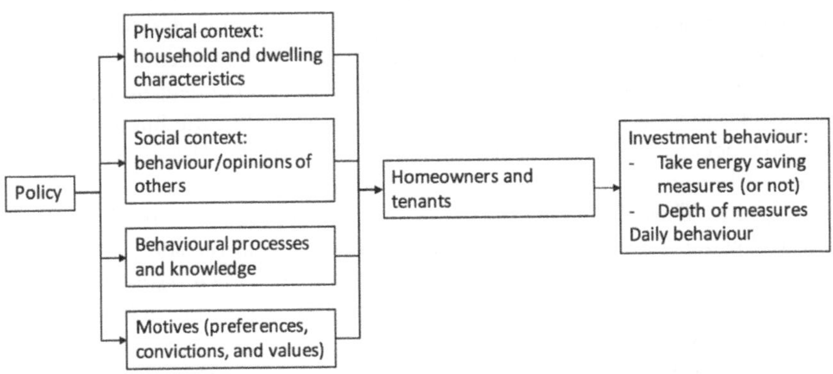

Figure 13.3 Behavioural model for energy saving behaviour of tenants and homeowners.

affect the decision (e.g. age and energy performance of the dwelling, savings and income of the residents, opinion of neighbours and family; Vringer et al., 2016). Some practical questions will come up, such as: 'Will I be living here long enough to benefit from this financially?' and 'Are the adjustments to my dwelling easy to implement or not?' But also more emotional considerations can play a part, such as: 'Will my neighbours be doing the same?' and 'Am I going to spend my money on saving energy or on a new kitchen?' Some considerations can even be very emotionally charged, like: 'I'd want to, but I'm afraid of the mess and nuisance' and 'I don't want strangers in my house' (van Hal, 2016). These last two issues introduce another factor that complicates the decision making: professionals often assume that residents make rational decisions. Despite the fact that most governmental policies are based on the idea of a rational and calculating 'homo economicus', decisions are also influenced by behavioural processes such as loss aversion and fear for nuisance. Decisions are not always rational (Vringer et al., 2014).

Renovation professionals should be well prepared to handle these two aspects (complexity and emotional behaviour). To do so, it is important for renovation professionals to realize that energy efficiency (and sustainability overall) is not an important issue for most residents (Schoots & Hammingh, 2015). This means that it is not enough to bring up good arguments for energy saving measures. More is needed. To compete with other products, incorporating energy efficiency measures in homes has to awaken enthusiasm. In the Netherlands, research that combines knowledge from human sciences with energy efficient renovation experiences, the development of new educational methods and a search for success stories, has been part of joined efforts to find ways to create this enthusiasm. A national knowledge platform called 'HomeMates' has been established to bundle and share all these findings (van Hal, 2016).

Discussion: first experiences

At the moment of writing this chapter, the EPF has only been recently introduced. The number of practical experiences is limited. One of the few zero-on-the-meter renovation projects that is thoroughly evaluated is a project in the municipality of Heerhugowaard (Sijpheer et al., 2016). Residents were asked if they would recommend the renovation project. Yes, 65 per cent of the respondents said. However, the satisfaction is often not rooted in the improved energy performance. Residents consider it more important that the house is 'up to date' again. They are happy with their new bathroom and kitchen and with the beauty of it. They also appreciate the improved comfort (comfortable warm, no wind blowing through cracks anymore, less noise from outside), and that, of course, is related to the improved energy performance. The residents in Heerhugowaard also often expressed their appreciation for the induction stove (Sijpheer et al., 2016).

With regard to the financial aspects, the reactions are more diverse. There were no specific questions about this aspect in the Heerhugowaard study, but the residents spontaneously said something about it in 12 of the 32 interviews that were part of the research. The main problem was that some residents, contrary to what was promised, paid more for their energy expenses after the renovation than before. The difference was often small, but for people with lower incomes, every penny counts. This problem has two reasons. First, advances on the final energy account, charged by the energy suppliers, were not adapted to the new situation. There seemed to be a lack of knowledge among the energy suppliers about the zero-on-the-meter concept and the EPF. This sometimes resulted in a refusal to change advances on the final energy account to zero. As a consequence, the residents have high costs in the first year, because they also pay the housing association the EPF. After the first year, residents get a refund from the energy supplier. In the meantime, however, financial problems may arise for people with the lowest incomes. Until the energy company refunds the monthly advance, tenants feel uncertain and often 'stressed'. To solve this problem the housing association and building company attempted to mediate with the energy suppliers, but, in many cases, this was not successful. In Heerhugowaard, the housing association (Woonwaard) offered some residents a month of deferred rent to remove the (temporary) financial pressure (Sijpheer et al., 2016).

The second reason behind the problem of 'paying too much' lies in the calculation, made for every household, to determine how much the EPF could be (the amount of the EPF and the new preliminary energy bill should be no more than the previous energy bill). These calculations proved complex, partly because of the different contracts that people had with energy companies. This also complicated insight into the difference between the payment for and after the renovation.

The evaluations of other zero-on-the-meter renovation projects (Sijpheer, Cozijnsen, Leidenmeijer, Borsboom, & Van Vliet, 2015) reveal little about the financial aspects. However, it is clear that lack of trust is an important reason for residents not to agree with housing association plans. Especially plans involving a rent increase and uncertain energy savings, result in uncertainty and resistance among tenants with a low income. For these residents, almost all long-term benefits (like protection against the increase of energy prices) are not relevant as a result of their focus on their expenses in the short term.

Conclusion

In this chapter we presented the far-reaching consequence of the EPF, both in positive and negative terms. The most positive effect is that the EPF allows parties to invest in renovations with challenging energy ambitions, such as zero-on-the-meter renovations. These investment opportunities lead to an innovative form of product development in the construction sector and profound changes in cooperation between professionals, and between professionals and residents as a result. The EPF arrangement and all its consequences are, however, vulnerable for future developments, like decreasing electricity prices and elimination of the set-off regulation. Maybe it will not always be possible to keep energy expenses the same. There are already housing associations that increase the rent for new tenants. However, even if the price of electricity goes down and the set-off regulation disappears, it is not expected that the rationale underpinning the EPF will disappear too. The idea of using the saved energy costs as a financing mechanism seems to be rooted in practice already. Banks and other parties are also looking for ways to process this principle in their offers (see for example wocozon,[6] 2017).

Notes

1 The energy efficiency of existing homes can be determined in the Netherlands via two different methods: the energy label and the Energy Index. The Energy Index is based on approximately 150 characteristics of the home, the energy label on the ten most important characteristics. With the Energy Index, the energy performance of a home can be calculated more accurately (RVO, 2018).

2 The Heat Law was introduced 1 January 2014, to protect consumers against excessive costs for the supply of heat. This is because research showed that providers of district heating often charge too much due to their monopoly position. The law protects by limiting the costs that can be charged for heat (Koedam, 2014).

3 Basis conditions include: (1) the guaranteed maximum for net space heating must fall within standards set by governmental decree (see Table 13.1), (2) the energy, needed for the heating of space and an average amount of hot water, should be produced in or on the dwelling and (3) the guaranteed minimum production of renewable energy should fall within official standards (see Table 13.1).

4 Off-setting means that the resident can set off the energy returned to the grid with received energy from the grid.

5 The energy performance of buildings in the Netherlands, is expressed in 'labels', ranging from A (energy efficient) to G (very energy inefficient). An improvement of two label steps could, for example, entail a move from label D to label B.

6 Wocozon organizes and finances solar power projects for housing associations in a separate company and gives the housing association control over strategy, return and price policy. The corporation does not become an energy supplier, but can use the cash flow as a result of the energy savings.

References

Aedes, G4, G32, Woonbond & VNG. (2016). *Reactie op De Staat van de woningmarkt.* Brief aan de Tweede Kamer, 7 December.

Blok, S. A. (2016, 31 August). Besluit van 23 augustus 2016, houdende regels omtrent de mogelijkheid voor verhuurder en huurder een energieprestatievergoeding overeen te komen (Besluit energieprestatievergoeding huur). Staatsblad van het Koninkrijk der Nederlanden.

Blok, S. A. (2017, 20 January). Regeling van de Minister voor Wonen en Rijksdienst van 17 januari 2017, nr. 2017-0000025902 houdende wijziging van de Regeling energieprestatievergoeding huur in verband met de mogelijkheid voor verhuurder en huurder om een energieprestatievergoeding overeen te komen voor een woning met een aansluiting op het gasnet. *Staatscourant.*

Buffing, S., Achterveld, W., & Conijn, J. (2016). *Handboek modelmatig waarderen marktwaarde vastgoed in verhuurde staat.* Rotterdam: Ortec.

Coen, M. C., & Stutvoet, E. N. M. (2016a). *Kennispaper 'Comfortabel wonen met Nul op de Meter'*. Den Haag: Energiesprong.

Coen, M. C., & Stutvoet, E. N. M. (2016b). *Kennispaper 'Wetgeving Energieprestatievergoeding'*. Den Haag: Energiesprong.

Coen, M. C., & Stutvoet, E. N. M. (2016c). *Kennispaper 'Nieuw businessmodel voor corporaties'*. Den Haag: Energiesprong.

Coen, M. C., & Stutvoet, E. N. M. (2016d). *Kennispaper 'Van aanbesteden naar afnemen'*. Den Haag: Energiesprong.

Energiesprong. (2017). *Over Energiesprong*. Retrieved from www.energiesprong.nl.

Faber, A., & Hoppe, T. (2013). Co-constructing a sustainable built environment in the Netherlands: Dynamics and opportunities in an environmental sectoral innovation system. *Energy Policy*, *52*, 628–638.

Federatie Ruimtelijke Kwaliteit. (2016). *Isolatie vaak te duur en ongeschikt*. Retrieved from www.omgevingsweb.nl/nieuws/isolatie-vaak-te-duur-en-ongeschikt.

Goes, R. (2016). *Haken en ogen aan de energieprestatievergoeding*. Retrieved from www.energieoverheid.nl/2016/02/23/energieprestatievergoeding.

Huisman, C., De Jong, A., Van Duin, C., & Stoeldraijer, L. (2013). *Regionale prognose 2013–2040: Vier grote gemeenten blijven sterke bevolkingstrekker*. Statistics Nederland/Planbureau voor de Leefomgeving.

Koedam, A. (2014). *Handreiking Warmtewet voor woningcorporaties, versie 2.0*. Den Haag: Aedes.

National Housing Federation. (2017). *Local housing allowance cap and supported housing*. Retrieved from www.housing.org.uk/topics/supported-housing/local-housing-allowance-cap-and-supported-housing/.

Priemus, H. (2014). Is the landlord levy a threat to the rented housing sector? The case of the Netherlands. *International Journal of Housing Policy*, *14*(1), 98–106.

Rotmans, J. (2003). *Transitiemanagement: Sleutel voor een duurzame samenleving*. Assen: Van Gorcum.

Rotmans, J., & Horsten, H. (2012). *In het oog van de orkaan: Nederland in transitie*. Boxtel: Aeneas.

RVO. (2018). *De Energie-Index en het Energielabel*. Retrieved from www.rvo.nl/onderwerpen/duurzaam-ondernemen/gebouwen/wetten-en-regels-gebouwen/bestaande-bouw/energie-index/verschil-energie-index-en-energielabel.

Schoots, K., & Hammingh, P. (2015). *Nationale Energieverkenning 2015*. Petten: Energieonderzoek Centrum Nederland.

SEV. (2010). *Uitvoeringsprogramma InnovatieAgenda energie Gebouwde Omgeving | Jaarplan 2010*. Rotterdam: Stichting Experimentele Volkshuisvesting.

Sijpheer, N., Cozijnsen, E., Leidelmeijer, K., Borsboom, W., & Van Vliet, M. (2015). *Resultaten uit monitoring: over tevreden bewoners*. Den Haag: Energiesprong/Platform31.

Sijpheer, N., Borsboom, W., Leidelmeijer, K., Van Vliet, M., De Jong, P., & Kerkhof, H. (2016). *Resultaten uit monitoring: Bewonerservaringen en meetresultaten uit Nul op de Meterwoningen in Heerhugowaard* (BAM). Den Haag: Energiesprong/Platform31.

Stroomversnelling. (2016). *EPV, ja! Gas, nee! Een rem op versnelling*. Retrieved from http://stroomversnelling.nl/epv-ja-gas-nee-een-rem-op-versnelling/.

Van de Groep, J. W. (2013). *Vijf mythen over de Stroomversnelling ontrafeld*. Retrieved from https://janwillemvandegroep.com/2013/11/10/vijf-mythen-over-de-stroomversnelling-ontrafeld/.

Van der Werf, E. N. M. (2011). *Bewonersbelangen bij renovatie in bewoonde staat*. Delft: TU Delft.

Van Hal, A. (2016). *The third success factor of renovations with energy ambitions*. Paper presented at SBE16-conference, Toronto.

Van Mil, R. (2016). *NOM is de nieuwe norm. Page 5. Installmedia juni 2016*. Retrieved from www.installmedia.nl/845457/-NOM_is_de_nieuwe_norm.pdf?v=4.

Versteeg, F., Poolen, M., Van Rijn, D., & Opstelten, I. (2009). *Innovatieagenda Energie – Gebouwde Omgeving – Uitzicht op energieneutrale nieuwbouw en duurzame bestaande bouw*. Den Haag: Interdepartementale Programmadirectie Energietransitie.

Vringer, K., Van Middelkoop, M., & Hoogervorst, N. (2014). *Energie besparen gaat niet vanzelf. Evaluatie energiebesparingsbeleid voor de gebouwde omgeving*. De Bilt: RIVM.

Vringer, K., Van Middelkoop, M., & Hoogervorst, N. (2016). Saving energy is not easy: An impact assessment of Dutch policy to reduce the energy requirements of buildings. *Energy Policy*, 93, 23–32.

Witjes, B. (2017). *Vragen en antwoorden over passend toewijzen*. Retrieved from www.aedes.nl/artikelen/klant-en-wonen/huurbeleid/passend-toewijzen/norm-passend-toewijzen-geldt-per-1-januari-2016.html.

Wocozon. (2017). *Wat doen we?* Retrieved from http://wocozon.nl/wat-doet-wocozon/.

WSW. (2016). Corporaties: borgstelling en leningen. Retrieved from www.wsw.nl/corporaties/borgstelling-en-leningen/.

14 Keeping prices down with government support and regulation

Affordable housing in Germany

Michael Neitzel, Susanne Juranek, and Janina Kleist

Introduction

After years of stagnation and decrease, the population in Germany has been growing since 2010. However, population growth is concentrated in large cities and metropolitan areas, while, in rural areas, the trend of a shrinking population continues. Large cities, metropolitan areas, and medium cities with large universities have been the primary destination of migration movements – from within Germany as well as from abroad (Körner-Blätgen & Sturm, 2016).[1] In rural municipalities the number of households decreased by 17 per cent since 2000, while in large cities (more than 500,000 inhabitants) the number of households rose by more than 20 per cent (Müller, 2017, p. 3). At the same time, the completion of new dwellings has been lagging behind. After a decade of little construction of new housing, since 2011 building activities have been on the rise again (Held & Waltersbacher, 2015, pp. 15–16). Still, between 2012 and 2015 only 800,000 new dwellings were completed, while the number of private households increased by 1.3 million at the same time (Müller, 2017, p. 4). Thus, for the following years, the need of new dwellings is estimated at 350,000–400,000 apartment units per year (Bundesministerium für Umwelt, Naturschutz, Bau und Reaktorsicherheit (BMUB), 2017).

Due to housing shortages, rents have been on the rise, especially in large and medium-sized cities with important universities, raising questions about the affordability of housing even for households with average incomes. Prices for new rental contracts increased by 10.4 per cent from 2011 to 2016, and by 18.3 per cent in a ten-year-perspective (Forschung und Beratung für Wohnen, Immobilien und Umwelt GmbH (F+B), 2017, p. 2). These are average numbers for the whole of Germany, taking also into account rural and areas with a shrinking population. High price increases and the overall high rent levels in economic power zones (the so-called *Big Seven*: Berlin, Hamburg, Munich, Cologne, Frankfurt/Main, Stuttgart, and Düsseldorf) make it more and more difficult for low- and middle-income households to find adequate housing in these areas.

New instruments and innovative approaches are needed to provide affordable housing in Germany's housing market hot spots. This chapter will first briefly discuss traditional demand and supply side instruments of housing policy and will then elaborate on new approaches to support and regulate affordable housing in Germany.

Traditional demand and supply side government support

The provision of affordable housing is considered to be the responsibility of the German government and public authorities (Deutsche Bundesregierung, 2013, p. 114).[2] German affordable housing policy is traditionally based on a twofold approach: demand side and supply side support.

Supply side support

On the supply side, subsidy programmes for social housing have a long tradition in Germany (Bundesinstitut für Bau-, Stadt- und Raumforschung (BBSR), 2011a).[3] The objective is to support households that cannot afford adequate housing at market conditions. In the years 2001/2002, legislation for social housing programmes underwent deep reform, and, since then, the authority lies exclusively on the level of German federal states (BBSR, 2011b, pp. 4–5).[4] This is to take into account and react on the regionally diverse housing markets, so that subsidies can be issued more flexibly with regard to the local situation. Support is granted – usually in form of loans (BBSR, 2011b, p. 14)[5] – to new housing construction as well as to investments in the existing building stock, e.g. modernization, energetic improvements or senior-friendly modifications. As a condition for the subsidies, accommodation costs and rents are restricted to a certain level and apartments may only be rented to specific target groups, e.g. low-income households, families and other households with children, single parents, the pregnant, the elderly, the disabled, the homeless, or other persons in need.

These traditional housing policy instruments have not been able to sufficiently accommodate the large influx of new residents into urban areas. Sluggish construction activities, as described above, point to shortcomings on the supply side of housing. Obstacles to more construction activities are a lack of suitable building sites, lengthy planning and permit procedures, and sometimes local resistance of residents in the neighbourhood against new buildings (BBSR, 2017a). Moreover, high construction costs are a detriment to affordable housing: they directly influence the rents that have to be realized by the investor for the investment to be cost-effective (BMUB, 2015a, pp. 6–7).

Demand side support

Public transfer payments (i.e. demand side support) are an essential feature of the German welfare state that is laid down in the German constitution. German social legislation includes provisions to secure housing for the weakest groups in society that are unable to pay the costs of accommodation of their own means. Public transfer payments either cover the total amount of accommodation costs (recipients of Social Assistance[6] and of Unemployment Benefit II[7]) or allowances are paid if necessary (Housing benefit). Support is given not only to German citizens but to all persons living in Germany including refugees and asylum seekers.

Housing benefit (*Wohngeld*) is a tax-free allowance to support low-income groups that do not receive Social Assistance or Unemployment Benefit II, in covering accommodation costs, i.e. rents as well as the costs of owner-occupied residential property (BBSR, 2016, p. 4). Eligibility and the amount granted depends on the size of the household, income, the amount of rent or the burden of accommodation costs (for home owners), as well as the general level of rents of the district (BBSR, 2016, p. 4). Housing benefit does not directly take into account energy costs (BBSR, 2015, p. 95).[8] Rising energy costs have been indirectly considered in the latest housing benefit reform of 2016, with the adaption of the parameters in the formula for calculating the sum of the housing benefit allowance (BBSR, 2016, pp. 6–9). After the reform of 2016, approximately 870,000 households are eligible for housing benefits, resulting in expected government expenses of €1.5 billion annually (BMUB, 2015b). The new idea to include a 'climate component' into housing benefit will be discussed below.

Innovative approaches to affordable housing in Germany

Taking into account the limitations of traditional housing policy instruments to create much needed housing and to keep rental prices down, policy makers are under pressure to find new solutions. This section will discuss new trends and innovations in German housing policy, their results, and effects. Four new instruments are explored: (1) rent control to limit the increase of rents in strained markets, (2) a climate component for housing benefits to make energy efficient housing more affordable for low-income groups, (3) special subsidy programmes to support specific target groups, and (4) 'concept procurement' to allocate land according to the quality of the development concept.

Rent control

With strained housing markets and rising rental prices, new construction of affordable housing is desperately needed to satisfy the high demand. This will tackle the root of the problem, but it is time-consuming to expand housing supply through new construction. Rent control (or rental cap, in German *Mietpreisbremse* 'rental price brake') is devised to limit the rise of rental prices for new rental contracts in high demand markets in a short-term perspective and with quick effects.

The regulation states that the rent stipulated in the rental contract may not exceed the reference rent customary in the locality for the respective dwelling by 10 per cent. The 'rental price brake' only applies if federal states define areas with strained housing markets by ordinance until 2020 with a maximum duration of five years.

A housing market is considered to be strained if a sufficient supply of adequate rental dwellings is at risk. In order to specify these vague legal concepts, criteria were defined to determine an insufficient supply situation. Among these are:

- rent increases are considerably higher than the German average;
- the average burden of rental costs for households is above the German average;
- increasing population without the new construction of necessary housing;
- low vacancies and high demand at the same time.

In the discussion about the draft bill, housing federations,[9] representing the interests of housing providers, emphasized the importance of rent control only being applied in cases with well-founded evidence of strained markets. As rent control merely treats the symptoms of a deficit in supply but does not eliminate the cause, federal state governments are to explain which other measures are taken to provide relief.

As of January 1, 2017, 12 of the 16 federal states have made use of the regulation. In Berlin and Hamburg, rent control is applied for the whole city. It is moreover applied in the city state of Bremen, with Bremerhaven excluded. In East Germany, besides Thuringia, the federal state of Brandenburg has made use of the regulation because the communities of the affluent Berlin suburbs have seen a rise in rents due to the pressure of high demand.

Traditional rent control mechanisms

As for pricing theory, rent control is a price cap that is a large intervention in the formation of rental prices on housing markets. Before, there were regulations in German tenancy law established in the 1960s and 1970s for the adjustment of rents in existent rental contracts. In first time letting of an apartment and in renewed letting subsequent to an ending tenancy, there was in general no fixed price cap.

There were two protective provisions against the excessive increase of rental prices and usury: an excessive increase of rental prices (according to the Economic Offences Act, *Wirtschaftsstrafgesetz*) means exceeding the usual prices by 20 per cent, usury (based on the German Criminal Code) according to jurisdiction means exceeding the usual prices by more than 50 per cent. These protective provisions required additional elements of offence that were difficult to prove in practice. In case of an excessive increase of rental prices, the tenant had to prove that there was a shortage of comparable dwellings, which the landlord used to his advantage. The landlord on the other hand was allowed to ask for higher prices, if they could justify that the extra rent was needed to cover running costs. In case of usury, the landlord for example would have to be found guilty of exploiting the tenant's predicament. In these cases, the tenant owes the landlord only the payments customary in the locality and could reclaim the excessive rent also for past periods of time. Consequently, these protective provisions proved ineffective against high rents.

Rental price brake

The 'rental price brake' is a new instrument that was introduced by the federal government to protect tenants from high rents in regions with strained housing markets. For public authorities, this instrument has the advantage that it does not incur direct costs for public budgets. There are also some disadvantages, though, because a rise of rents sets strong incentives for investors to invest in the construction of new apartment buildings. By capping the prices of newly concluded rental contracts, this incentive is considerably weakened. That means the investor has to rely on current rent increases in existing rental contracts that are dependent on a rise of the rents customary in the locality documented in rent indexes.[10] By introducing rent control, it was suspected that the rise of local rent levels would be curtailed. Thus, rent control would worsen investment conditions, in particular for new housing construction, and that would intensify the problems. Therefore, in the discussions of the federal government's draft bill, newly constructed homes let for rent for the first time and comprehensively refurbished apartments are exempt from the regulation. Likewise, a higher rent of a previously existing rental contract may still be charged.

Rent control has moreover the disadvantage that it does not have a targeted effect. Rental prices are not 'controlled' for particular target groups that are not able to find affordable housing. Price advantages as a result of rent control also benefit higher income tenant groups. Housing markets analysis has shown that the rise of rents moves mostly in accordance with the rise of average purchasing power. That means that it is (still) related to the general development of incomes. As for the competition for high-demand city centre locations, if there is a price cap by rent control, landlords will choose different criteria for selecting tenants. They have many options due to the high demand and will thus prefer tenants that have advantages for them, e.g. those with a high degree of creditworthiness. Those groups of tenants that are particularly affected by high rents – low-income groups and large (family) households – will still not find an apartment. Rent control cannot eliminate or ease the shortage of housing.

With lower rents, households with higher incomes in particular, would likely show an increased demand for apartments in the city centre, possibly resulting in a process of gentrification in some high-demand urban districts. At the same time, the balance between the owner-occupied and rental housing market shifts, because the owned housing market is not regulated and it is in a position to pay higher land prices in the competition for available land.

Another controversial aspect of rent control is that landlords have ways of circumvention, for example because they can charge additional payments for furniture or garages and parking spaces. From the tenants' side, it is criticized that excessive rent is not refunded for the past, but only from the point of complaint.

Considering the negative effects that result from rent control, the focus should be on other instruments for elimination of the causes of rental price rises, i.e. the construction of additional housing. The temporal limit of rent control is also for gaining time to initiate the additional construction of housing.

About two years after the first federal states introduced rent control in 2015, there are first experiences, which do not paint a consistent picture. Various studies tried with different approaches to define the effectiveness of rent control and came to the conclusion that the desired effects have mostly not (yet) occurred (Neitzel, Klöppel, & Dylewski 2014; Bodelschwingh, Dettmann, & Schlichting, 2016; Bundesministerium für Justiz und Verbraucherschutz (BMJV), 2017; Kholodilin, Mense, & Michelsen, 2018). Policy makers will further discuss whether the regulations of rent control have to be adjusted and tightened.

Integrating a climate component into the housing benefit support system

The federal government pursues ambitious energy and climate policy objectives. It has formulated several measures to this end in the *Klimaschutz 2020* Climate Action Programme, which aims to reduce greenhouse gas emissions by at least 40 per cent compared to 1990 levels (BMUB, 2014).

A 'climate component' in the housing benefit (*Wohngeld*)[11] support system would help low-income households rent housing with higher energy efficiency standards, or remain in their current home after energy efficient modernization and a subsequent increase in the rent. Thus, the climate policy goals would be supported by an extension and accentuation of an existing social-political instrument. The effects of this climate component were explored in a feasibility study conducted by InWIS (Institute for Housing, Real Estate, Urban and Regional Development) and the German Economic Institute (IW) (BBSR, 2017b).[12]

Normally, apartments with higher energy efficiency standards are rented out at a higher price. In the housing benefit support system, the entitlement payment increases to compensate for the higher rent. Thus, there is already an incentive for residents to rent an apartment with higher energy efficiency standards, as long as the price remains below the maximum amount of eligible rent.

Increasing the maximum amount of eligible rent, which only applies insofar as certain energy efficiency standards are met, is an accurate and easy-to-manage option for integrating a climate component into the housing benefit system. This is because separate funding for housing benefit households is only necessary if the rent for an apartment with higher energy standards is greater than that of a comparable apartment.

Adjusting the maximum amount for which housing benefit is granted for an apartment has the additional advantage that all other social policy aspects that are considered by housing benefit (e.g. number of household members, amount of income) remain in place.

Determining the energy efficiency standards or a specific parameter to base the climate component on is challenging, considering the ambitious climate policy goals, the energy standard of the building stock, the modernization measures, and the living situation of the households with low income. Climate policy is effectively supported when higher standards are agreed upon.

The specific level and structure of the climate component, i.e. the figure by which the maximum amount of eligible rent must be adjusted, lies in an area of tension between the higher rent for apartments with higher energy efficiency standard and the achievable energy savings by a household (see Figure 14.1), and varies greatly depending on the housing market conditions. In strained housing markets, a higher rent can often be achieved for homes with higher energy efficiency standards or from modernizing a home. However, the energy savings in general do not depend on the housing market situation. In order to create appropriate incentives, the feasibility study mentioned above recommends that the climate component should not be set too low, and should be gradually staged according to rent levels (*Mietenstufen*).[13] For the upper limit of the climate component, it is important that the additional amount of housing benefit is no higher than the additional net rent for the increased energy efficiency minus the achievable energy savings. This ensures that no double funding occurs.

The feasibility study showed that in the scenario with the largest effects on recipients, the extra costs for public budgets[14] would increase by around €40 million. Households eligible for the climate component (existing housing

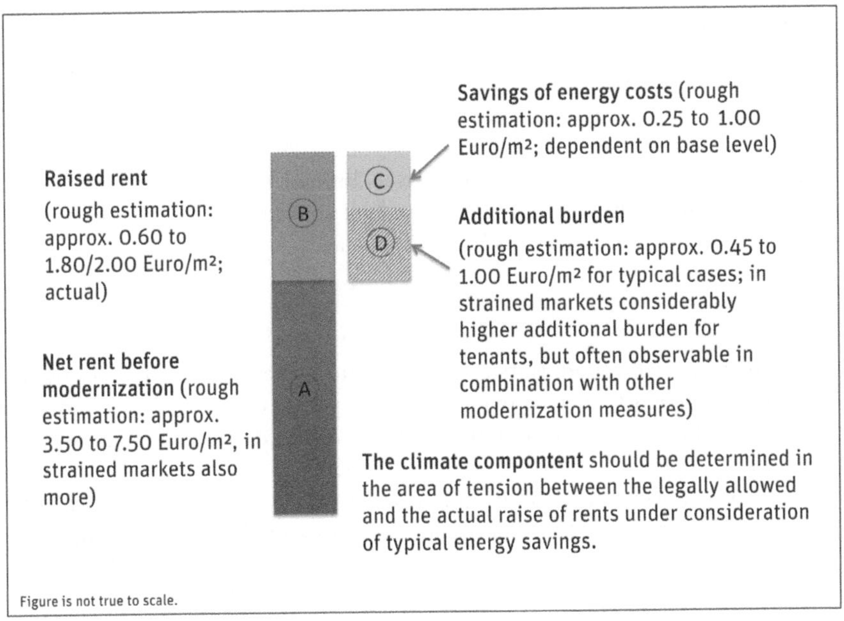

Figure 14.1 Relationship of higher net rent and savings of energy costs.

Source: own figure.

benefit households and additional recipients) would receive, on average, an additional €60 housing benefit per month, with an increase of eligible rent of €81.

The study further demonstrated that including a climate component into housing benefit makes it possible to support higher rent for an apartment having a higher energy standard within the already existing housing benefit support system. Adjusting the maximum amount of eligible rent is a relatively easy way to implement a climate component that retains the hitherto intended effects of the social policy of housing benefits.

To follow up on this work, the German federal government has commissioned a study to determine precise energy standards for the climate component. In the draft of the coalition agreement for the nineteenth legislative period (2017–2021), the integration of a climate component into housing benefit was supported. However, a final decision has not yet been made.

Although the simulations conducted in the feasibility study resulted in a relatively low number of households that would benefit from the climate component, it is important to note that higher energy standards are not yet widespread. Hopefully a climate component can incentivize low-income households to rent an energy efficient home.

Special subsidy programmes for specific target groups

While disadvantaged groups have long been the focus of housing policy and subsidy programmes in Germany, there remains a lack of adequate housing for all who are in need. Moreover, current subsidy programmes address all vulnerable groups as one, without considering each group's special needs. Thus, subsidy programmes were created for specific groups, with special consideration for those who were most in need of support. These target groups consist of the elderly, students, and refugees, all of whom have limited resources, special housing requirements (e.g. small units), and often lack appropriate housing. This is particularly the case in cities with a housing shortage.

Elderly

In an ageing society, there is increasing demand for senior-friendly housing that cannot be sufficiently met by existing subsidy programmes. By 2035, almost 30 per cent of the population in Germany will be older than 65, and almost 9 per cent will be at least 80 (BMUB, 2016).[15] In 2009, it was estimated that only 5 per cent of seniors (individuals 65 and older) would live in senior-friendly homes (BBSR, 2014, pp. 33–35).[16] As a result, the German federal government started the first programme[17] for converting dwellings into senior-friendly[18] homes (BBSR, 2014, p. 13). An evaluation of the programme from 2009–2013 found that it was effective in mobilizing investments for the conversion to senior-friendly homes. However, significantly more resources would be required to meet the projected senior-friendly housing demand in 2030 (Prognos, 2014, p. 80).[19]

The programme was subsequently extended in 2014 to include two options: subsidized credits and grants (Tchouvakhina & Brüggemann, 2014, p. 3).[20] Further modifications were introduced in 2015 and 2016: credits can be supplied with annual interest rate of 0.75 per cent for up to €50,000 per home; grants cover up to 12.5 per cent of eligible costs with a maximum of €6,250 per home (KfW, n.d.). Support is provided for housing organizations, homeowners and tenants (pending approval of the landlord).

Students

Similar to the elderly, students also have specific housing requirements. Affordability is key as students are likely to have limited income and are on a tight budget. They usually live in single-person households, and thus have no need for large apartments. In metropolitan regions with universities, the influx of students creates further strain on housing markets (BMUB, n.d.). In November 2015, the German Federal Ministry for the Environment, Nature Conservation, Building and Nuclear Safety started a new funding programme for student apartments. In a pilot phase until 2018, subsidies totalling €120 million will be provided for innovative sustainable and affordable housing projects for students and trainees (BMUB, 2015c).

The so-called 'Vario' ('Vario' is derived from various) apartments were to be high quality and able to accommodate various target groups, such as students and (later) elderly people (BMUB, 2015c). They are small apartments in city centres, and should provide a comfortable space to live and study. Rent is limited to €260 per month, with a maximum of €280 in cities with strained housing markets (BMUB, 2015c). Out of 40 proposals, 20 were selected to fund new buildings as well as conversions of existing units. An overview of the projects can be found online (see BBSR, n.d.).

In addition to this federal programme, there are also new initiatives at the regional level to create more affordable housing for students. In 2015 and 2016, subsidy programmes were introduced in Bavaria, Hamburg, Rhineland-Palatinate, and Hessen. In North Rhine-Westphalia, such programmes have already been in existence since 2013.

Refugees

Subsidy programmes at the regional level were also introduced to promote housing for refugees. Since 2014, the development bank for North Rhine-Westphalia, NRW.BANK, has provided loans to municipalities for the acquisition, construction, and modernization of such housing centres (NRW.BANK, 2016a). In addition, the *Förderung von Wohnraum für Flüchtlinge* ('funding for housing for refugees' programme) for housing providers started in 2016 to accommodate the increasing number of refugees. The programme funds apartments for rent, which may include shared spaces and cooperative apartments. Eligible building activities include the construction of brand new housing, the creation of housing within existing stock (construction costs >650€/m²), and other renovation activities (construction costs <650 Euro/m²). Funded homes have to be used as refugee accommodation for 10 to 25 years. Rent is limited to 4.25 and 6.25 €/m² per month according to the average rent of the municipality. The rent may be increased by 1.5 per cent p.a. (NRW.BANK, 2016b).

Even though similar programmes are set up in other regions, e.g. Baden-Württemberg and Rhineland-Palatinate, funding programmes for refugee housing could be extended, especially in regions with strained housing markets.

'Concept procurement' – allocating land according to the quality of the development concept

Substantial new construction is necessary to meet the high demand of affordable housing in large cities and university towns. Municipalities have to devise their own strategies to systematically develop additional building areas that can be provided to the market at reasonable prices. On the one hand, this conflicts with the sustainable development goals of the German federal government, who since 2002 have sought to limit the additional demand for land for residential and traffic areas to 30 hectares per day until 2020 (Technische Universität Darmstadt & ISP Eduard Pestel Institut für Systemforschung e.V., 2016, pp. 43ff.). While the demand for land can be reduced by adding floors to existing buildings, it is nevertheless necessary to allocate more land, even though this means that the maximum land use target set by the German federal government cannot be reached (Technische Universität Darmstadt & ISP Eduard Pestel Institut für Systemforschung e.V., 2016).

On the other hand, the high demand for construction areas has considerably increased prices for land in large cities in general, particularly in the city centre. In attractive regions, such as Munich, the standard value for a one square metre plot is valued at 3,000€/m² and above (Neitzel & Walberg, 2016, pp. 26ff.). At this level, it is not possible to develop affordable housing, and other measures to reduce capital expenditure are thwarted. For example, reducing construction costs or making subsidies available.

Given the high demand and high prices of land, less expensive building areas are hardly available. If, for example, municipalities own plots that they could offer at low prices for social policy-related reasons, they nonetheless have to sell them at the highest price possible due to budgetary restrictions.

In recent years, some cities have developed new models, called 'Concept Procurement' (*Konzeptvergabe*), or procurement with conditions, in order to allocate land based on a qualitative assessment and to absorb the planning-related increase of land value mostly for public purposes. What does this mean in this context? When land is allocated as building land, it increases in value. This planning-related profit is distributed between the investor(s) and the municipality, which absorbs the amount to cover the planning costs as well as the costs for urban development and social or ecological objectives. While this partial absorption of the planning-related profit is an established practice of municipalities, it has never before been combined with new procurement rules. Municipal plots can be sold according to the quality of the concept at lower prices than usual, based on which concept will best implement the predefined objectives in a comprehensive way.

Such new models, also called models of 'Cooperative Building Land Development', are used for non-municipal plots to incorporate development rights into contracts for urban development. This includes certain quotas for subsidized or lower priced housing, or to further social, urban development, or ecological requirements (BMUB, 2015d, p. 4).

As investors bear the costs of development rights for social infrastructure, public green spaces, and compensation measures, municipal budgets are spared and building areas can be developed more quickly.

Munich can be considered a pioneer of such models. Already in 1994 it had established the *Sozialgerechte Bodennutzung* model ('socially just land use', *SoBoN*) due to the high demand for social housing. The objective was to let the costs of developing access roads, green spaces, social infrastructure for children, compensation measures, and planning be paid for by those who profit from establishing development rights. The model included a 30 per cent quota for subsidized rental and owner-occupied housing. From 1994 to 2016, the model was applied in 150 legally binding land development plans. In total, 46,250 apartment units were built, 11,990 of which were subsidized (muenchen.de, n.d.).

For years, such models were hardly used elsewhere. However, given the rising demand for affordable housing since 2010, more cities have introduced such models based on Munich's example.

The *Innenentwicklungsmodell* ('inner development model', *SIM*) was established in Stuttgart in 2011, and extended in 2014 after a successful track record. Due to geographic conditions – Stuttgart is located in a circular, deep valley – developing additional building areas is difficult. In Stuttgart, 20 per cent of new residential floors have to be dedicated to subsidized housing. Either the owner or the investor cedes the areas to the municipality at a reduced value, or enters an agreement to build the apartments on their own. One-third of the subsidized apartments are dedicated to subsidized social housing with a limited rent of 7.50€/m^2, another third to rental housing for middle-income groups with a limited rent of 8.50€/m^2, and the last third to inexpensive, owner-occupied housing. In regards to the additional land value, one-third of the value generated by development rights is kept by the investor as an incentive for further investment, and two-thirds are absorbed by the municipality to secure quality standards for urban development and to cover the planning costs of subsidized housing. That means that the city of Stuttgart also offers its own subsidy programmes within the framework of this model, which are financed by the planning-related increases in land value (Landeshauptstadt Stuttgart, n.d.).

Following the same pattern, the Cooperative Building Land Development model was employed in Cologne towards the end of 2013. A citywide quota was established requiring subsidized housing in at least 30 per cent of new housing developments (Stadt Köln, 2014). Currently, these models are increasingly used (e.g. in Berlin, Bonn) to develop much-needed building sites, and ensure that affordable housing is built, particularly for the subsidized housing market.

Investors, who want to acquire and develop building land for housing, criticize such models if the conditions do not allow for profitable development. A typical example is the requirement to include 30 per cent (subsidized) social housing, 30 per cent reduced rent housing for the 'middle market' (those ineligible for social housing, but unable to pay market rental prices), and 40 per cent privately financed housing. Depending on the scope required of subsidized or reduced rent housing prices, and the level of the rental or other price cap, a project can only be carried out if the privately financed housing covers the deficit. This increases the costs of the privately financed housing without any rental or other price caps, significantly limiting the return on investment and therefore any interest to invest in the first place.

Given the high demand for housing in many growing German cities, Cooperative Building Land Development models and concept procurement are important instruments to make additional building areas available and to construct additional housing. This is particularly the case for subsidized housing and for the lower priced rental sector. For this 'middle market', that is neither served by social housing nor by the private market, it is currently the only supply side instrument to construct adequate housing in Germany.

Conclusion

Given the high demand for housing in many parts of Germany, social housing policy is experiencing a renaissance. In order to develop units in the affordable (rental) housing sector, and to minimize the financial burden for existing low-income rental households, new instruments were developed and some of them are already in use. They address the following issues:

- Rent control serves to limit rent increases for new rental contracts. Its effects are controversial and it is often called ineffective.
- The climate component for housing benefits links social and energy policy objectives. The details of its conditions are still being discussed – it is expected to be introduced by 2019.
- Subsidy programmes for specific vulnerable groups allow for the adjustment of funding conditions to suit the needs of the target groups.
- The procurement of building land based on the quality of the development concept allows municipalities to develop building areas faster, and to use the planning-related increase in land value to cover public costs and to ensure the construction of subsidized or affordable housing.

Thus, the social and housing policy tool box has been expanded. However, it is clear that the application of these concepts has not yet succeeded in meeting the demand for housing, or limiting the increase in housing costs. Housing policy has to combine all available instruments and apply them consistently in order to ensure affordable housing for all.

Notes

1 For details on the impact these migration movements have had on the demographic structure of cities, see Körner-Blätgen and Sturm (2016).
2 The high quality of living and housing is detailed as an important policy objective in the coalition treaty of the Third Merkel Cabinet 2013.
3 The first act regarding housing in the Federal Republic of Germany was passed in 1950, the second in 1956, which was in effect (with amendments) until 2001.
4 With a transition period until 2007.
5 Grants are also possible in special cases, when other financing options fail due to low cost effectiveness, but the purpose is desirable with regards to policy objectives.
6 Social assistance is a basic security payment. It is determined according to German Social Code Book Twelve (SGB XII). People in need who are unable to work or over the age of 65 are eligible.
7 Unemployment Benefit II, often referred to as Hartz IV – the reform concept for the German labour market – is an income replacement benefit that is paid according to the German Social Code Book Two (SGB II) to employable people in need. It is an insurance benefit financed from the contributions that employees pay into unemployment insurance.
8 Between 2009 and 2010, a lump sum was included for heating costs.
9 For example, GdW, the Federal Association of Housing and Real Estate Companies, or BFW, the Federal Association of Free Real Estate and Housing Companies.
10 A rent index or a representative list of rents is an overview over the rents effective in a locality for comparable apartments.
11 *Wohngeld*, as described earlier in this chapter. A 'climate component' would be added to the complex formula that is used to calculate the amount each recipient is eligible for.
12 This section follows with additions and modifications to the English Management Summary of the research report (BBSR, 2017b). The following questions were decisive for the implementation of the study. Which approaches exist for integrating a climate component into the housing benefit, and which incentive effects are anticipated? From which energy standards should the climate component be granted, and how can this standard be verified? How many households would be reached by it? In what amount should the climate component be granted, and which costs and effects are associated with this?
13 When calculating the maximum amount of housing benefit, local rent levels are taken into account. All German municipalities are assigned a grade (*Mietenstufe*) from I–VI, which reflects a percentage deviation from the German average. The idea is that an apartment of comparable size should be equally affordable for recipients all across Germany, independent of local rent levels.
14 The costs for housing benefit are covered one half by the federal government, the other half by regional governments.
15 In 2012 the shares were at 20.7 per cent and 5.4 per cent, respectively.
16 Based on interviews conducted in 2009.
17 This is a programme of KfW (Kreditanstalt für Wiederaufbau), the promotional bank of the Federal Republic of Germany and a public law institution originally established in 1948.
18 Senior-friendly means that there are no barriers to move within the apartment, i.e. no stairs, sufficiently wide doors and sanitary areas, and a walk-in shower.
19 In 2013, there were around 700,000 senior-friendly homes in Germany, 17 per cent of which were converted with support of the KfW programme. Up to 2.9 million more homes will be needed by 2030.
20 The grant option was already in place between May 1, 2010 and December 31, 2011.

References

Bundesinstitut für Bau-, Stadt- und Raumforschung (BBSR). (2011a). *Wohnraumförderung der Länder* [Regional subsidy programmes for housing]. Bonn: BBSR. Retrieved from www.bbsr.bund.de/nn_821088/BBSR/DE/WohnenImmobilien/RahmenbedInstrumente/ProjekteFachbeitraege/Wohnraumfoerderung/wohnraumfoerderung.html.

Bundesinstitut für Bau-, Stadt- und Raumforschung (BBSR). (2011b). *Fortführung der Kompensationsmittel für die Wohnraumförderung: Endbericht* [Continuation of the funds of compensation for housing subsidies: Final report]. Bonn: BBSR. Retrieved from www.bbsr.bund.de/BBSR/DE/WohnenImmobilien/RahmenbedInstrumente/ProjekteFachbeitraege/Wohnraumfoerderung/Fachgutachten_Wohnraumfoerderung.pdf?__blob=publicationFile&v=2.

Bundesinstitut für Bau-, Stadt- und Raumforschung (BBSR). (2014). *Potenzialanalyse altersgerechte Wohnungsanpassung* [Potential analysis of senior-friendly adaption of housing]. Bonn: BBSR. Retrieved from www.bbsr.bund.de/BBSR/DE/Veroeffentlichungen/Sonderveroeffentlichungen/2014/DL_potenzialanalyse_altersgerechte_wohnungsanpassung.pdf?__blob=publicationFile&v=2.

Bundesinstitut für Bau-, Stadt- und Raumforschung (BBSR). (2015). Wohnsituation und Wohnkosten von Haushalten im Niedrigeinkommensbereich [Housing situation and housing costs of low-income households]. *BBSR-Online-Publikation*, (8). Bonn: BBSR. Retrieved from www.bbsr.bund.de/BBSR/DE/Veroeffentlichungen/BBSROnline/2015/DL_ON082015.pdf?__blob=publicationFile&v=3.

Bundesinstitut für Bau-, Stadt- und Raumforschung (BBSR). (2016). Wohngeldreform 2016: Mikrosimulationsrechnungen zur Leistungsverbesserung des Wohngelds [Reform of housing benefit 2016: Microsimulation calculations for the improvement of housing benefit]. *BBSR-Online-Publikation*, (6). Bonn: BBSR. Retrieved from www.bbsr.bund.de/BBSR/DE/Veroeffentlichungen/BBSROnline/2016/bbsr-online-06-2016-dl.pdf?__blob=publicationFile&v=3.

Bundesinstitut für Bau-, Stadt- und Raumforschung (BBSR). (2017a). *Trendwende beim Wohnungsneubau ist eingeleitet: Interview mit BBSR-Direktor Harald Herrmann* [Reversal of trend for the new construction of housing initiated: Interview with Harald Herrmann, Director of BBSR]. Retrieved from www.bbsr.bund.de/BBSR/DE/Home/Topthemen/interview_herrmann_wohnungsbau.html.

Bundesinstitut für Bau-, Stadt- und Raumforschung (BBSR). (2017b). Machbarkeits- und Umsetzungsstudie für eine Klimakomponente im Wohngeld [Feasibility and implementation study for a climate component in housing benefit]. *BBSR-Online-Publikation*, (5). Bonn: BBSR. Retrieved from www.bbsr.bund.de/BBSR/DE/Veroeffentlichungen/BBSROnline/2017/bbsr-online-05-2017-dl.pdf?__blob=publicationFile&v=2.

Bundesinstitut für Bau-, Stadt- und Raumforschung (BBSR). (n.d.). *Variowohnungen* [Vario apartments]. Retrieved from www.forschungsinitiative.de/variowohnungen/modellvorhaben/.

Bundesministerium für Justiz und Verbraucherschutz (BMJV). (2017). *Wirksamkeit der in 2015 eingeführten Regelungen zur sogenannten Mietpreisbremse in Regionen mit angespannten Wohnungsmärkten.* [Effectiveness of the regulation for the so-called rental price brake introduced in 2015 in regions with strained housing markets]. Berlin: BMJV. Retrieved from www.mietpreisbremse.bund.de/WebS/MPB/SharedDocs/Downloads/DE/Studie_Wirksamkeit_MPB.pdf;jsessionid=4992193CFF4C9B98744BD3646BBB9F28.2_cid324?__blob=publicationFile&v=1.

Bundesministerium für Umwelt, Naturschutz, Bau und Reaktorsicherheit (BMUB). (2014). Aktionsprogramm Klimaschutz 2020 [Climate action programme 2020]. Berlin: BMUB. Retrieved from www.bmub.bund.de/fileadmin/Daten_BMU/Download_PDF/Aktionsprogramm_Klimaschutz/aktionsprogramm_klimaschutz_2020_broschuere_bf.pdf.

Bundesministerium für Umwelt, Naturschutz, Bau und Reaktorsicherheit (BMUB). (2015a). *Bericht der Baukostensenkungskommission im Rahmen des Bündnisses für bezahlbares Wohnen und Bauen: Endbericht November 2015* [Report of the commission of the reduction of construction costs within the framework of the alliance for affordable housing and construction]. Berlin: BMUB. Retrieved from www.bmub.bund.de/fileadmin/Daten_BMU/Download_PDF/Wohnungswirtschaft/buendnis_baukostensenkungskommission_bf.pdf.

Bundesministerium für Umwelt, Naturschutz, Bau und Reaktorsicherheit (BMUB). (2015b). *Wohngeldreform zum 1. Januar 2016* [The reform of housing benefit of 1 January 2016]. Berlin: BMUB. Retrieved from www.bmub.bund.de/fileadmin/Daten_BMU/Pools/Broschueren/wohngeld_broschuere_bf.pdf.

Bundesministerium für Umwelt, Naturschutz, Bau und Reaktorsicherheit (BMUB). (2015c). Bau und Reaktorsicherheit, *Barbara Hendricks startet neues Förderprogramm für Studentenwohnungen* [Barbara Hendricks launches new subsidy programme for student housing]. Retrieved from www.bmub.bund.de/presse/pressemitteilungen/pm/artikel/barbara-hendricks-startet-neues-foerderprogramm-fuer-studentenwohnungen/.

Bundesministerium für Umwelt, Naturschutz, Bau und Reaktorsicherheit (BMUB). (2015d). *Abschlussbericht der Arbeitsgruppe 'Aktive Liegenschaftspolitik' im Bündnis für bezahlbares Wohnen und Bauen* [Final report of the working group 'active real estate policy' within the alliance for affordable housing and construction]. Berlin: BMUB.

Bundesministerium für Umwelt, Naturschutz, Bau und Reaktorsicherheit (BMUB). (2016). *Mehr Wohn- und Lebensqualität durch weniger Barrieren* [More housing and living quality through fewer barriers]. Retrieved from www.bmub.bund.de/themen/stadt-wohnen/wohnraumfoerderung/altersgerecht-wohnen/wohn-und-lebensqualitaet-verbessern/.

Bundesministerium für Umwelt, Naturschutz, Bau und Reaktorsicherheit (BMUB). (2017). *Wohnungs- und Immobilienmarkt* [Housing and real estate market]. Retrieved from www.bmub.bund.de/themen/stadt-wohnen/wohnungswirtschaft/wohnungs-und-immobilienmarkt/.

Bundesministerium für Umwelt, Naturschutz, Bau und Reaktorsicherheit (BMUB). (n.d.). *Variowohnungen: Die Ziele* [Vario apartments: The objectives]. Retrieved from www.forschungsinitiative.de/variowohnungen/die-ziele/.

Bodelschwingh, A., Dettmann, M., & Schlichting, H. (2016). *Wiedervermietungsmieten und Mietpreisbremse in Berlin* [Rents of subsequently renewed rental contracts and rental control in Berlin]. Berlin: RegioKontext. Retrieved from www.berliner-mieterverein.de/uploads/2016/05/pm1616-Anl1-RegioKontext-Kurzanalyse-Mietpreisbremse.pdf.

Burkert, J., & Fischer, B. (2016). Sozial, nachhaltig, bezahlbar: Modellvorhaben zum Bau von Variowohnungen [Social, sustainable, affordable: Pilot projects for the construction of vario apartments]. *Informationen aus der Forschung des BBSR*, (6), 9. Bonn: BBSR. Retrieved from www.bbsr.bund.de/BBSR/DE/Veroeffentlichungen/BBSRInfo/2016/bbsr-info-6-2016-dl.pdf?__blob=publicationFile&v=2.

Deutsche Bundesregierung. (2013). *Deutschlands Zukunft gestalten: Koalitionsvertrag zwischen CDU, CSU und SPD. 18. Legislaturperiode* [Shaping the future of Germany: Coalition agreement between CDU, CSU and SPD. 18. Legislative Period].

Retrieved from www.bundesregierung.de/Content/DE/_Anlagen/2013/2013-12-17-koalitionsvertrag.pdf?__blob=publicationFile&v=2.

Forschung und Beratung für Wohnen, Immobilien und Umwelt GmbH (F+B). (2017). *F+B-Wohn-Index Deutschland Q4/2016: Eigentumswohnungen treiben F+B-Wohn-Index um +1,2% – Mietwachstum schwächt sich nur leicht ab – Resultat wohnungspolitischer Eingriffe?* [F+B housing index Germany Q4/2016: Owner-occupied dwellings drive F+B housing index up by +1,2% – rental growth slows only slightly – result of housing policy intervention?]. Hamburg: F+B Forschung und Beratung für Wohnen, Immobilien und Umwelt GmbH. Retrieved from www.f-und-b.de/files/fb/content/Dokumente/Publikationen/F+B-Wohn-Index_2016Q4.pdf.

Held, T., & Waltersbacher, M. (2015). Wohnungsmarktprognose 2030 [Housing market forecast 2030]. *BBSR-Analysen KOMPAKT*, (7). Bonn: BBSR. Retrieved from www.bbsr.bund.de/BBSR/DE/Veroeffentlichungen/AnalysenKompakt/2015/DL_07_2015.pdf?__blob=publicationFile&v=5.

KfW. (n.d.). *Jetzt modernisieren und heute schon an morgen denken* [Modernise now and think already today about tomorrow]. Retrieved from www.kfw.de/inlandsfoerderung/Privatpersonen/Bestandsimmobilien/Barrierereduzierung/.

Kholodilin, K., Mense, A., & Michelsen, C. (2016). Die Mietpreisbremse wirkt bisher nicht [Rent control not effective to date]. *DIW Wochenbericht*, (22), 491–499. Retrieved from www.diw.de/documents/publikationen/73/diw_01.c.535234.de/16-22.pdf.

Kholodilin, K., Mense, A., & Michelsen, C. (2018). Mietpreisbremse ist besser als ihr Ruf, aber nicht die Lösung des Wohnungsmarktproblems [Rent control is better than its reputation but it is not the solution of the problem of the housing market]. *DIW Wochenbericht*, 7, 107–117. Retrieved from www.diw.de/documents/publikationen/73/diw_01.c.578092.de/18-7-1.pdf.

Körner-Blätgen, N., & Sturm, G. (2016). Wandel demografischer Strukturen in deutschen Großstädten [Change of demographic structures in German cities]. *BBSR-Analysen KOMPAKT*, (4). Bonn: BBSR. Retrieved from www.bbsr.bund.de/BBSR/DE/Veroeffentlichungen/AnalysenKompakt/2016/ak-04-2016-dl.pdf?__blob=publicationFile&v=2.

Landeshauptstadt Stuttgart. (n.d.). *SIM: Das Stuttgarter Innenentwicklungsmodell* [The inner development model of Stuttgart]. Retrieved from www.stuttgart.de/SIM.

muenchen.de. (n.d.). *Sozialgerechte Bodennutzung (SoBoN)* [Socially just land use]. Retrieved from www.muenchen.de/rathaus/Stadtverwaltung/Kommunalreferat/immobilien/sobon.html.

Müller, M. (2017). Gespaltene Mietwohnungsmärkte erfordern eine regional differenzierte Wohnungspolitik [Divided housing markets require a regionally differentiated housing policy]. *KfW Research*, (158).

Neitzel, M., & Walberg, D. (2016). *Instrumentenkasten für wichtige Handlungsfelder der Wohnungsbaupolitik* [Toolbox for important fields of action of housing policy]. Bochum: InWIS – Institut für Wohnungswesen, Immobilienwirtschaft, Stadt- und Regionalentwicklung & Arbeitsgemeinschaft für zeitgemäßes Bauen e.V. (ARGE//eV).

Neitzel, M., Klöppel, K., & Dylewski, C. (2014). *Wirkungsanalyse der Mietrechtsänderungen – Teil 1: Mietpreisbremse* [Impact analysis of changes in tenancy law – part 1: Rent control]. Bochum: InWIS. Retrieved from http://ivd.net/wp-content/uploads/2016/04/InWIS-BID-Wirkungsanalyse_Mietrechtsaenderungen.pdf.

NRW.BANK. (2016a). *NRW.BANK.Flüchtlingsunterkünfte* [NRW.Bank accommodation for refugees]. Retrieved from www.nrwbank.de/de/foerderlotse-produkte/NRWBANK-Fluechtlingsunterkuenfte/15731/nrwbankproduktdetail.html?backToResults=false.

NRW.BANK. (2016b). *Förderung von Wohnraum für Flüchtlinge* [Subsidies for housing for refugees]. Retrieved from www.nrwbank.de/de/foerderlotse-produkte/Foerderung-von-Wohnraum-fuer-Fluechtlinge/15761/produktdetail.html?backToResults=false.

Prognos. (2014). *Evaluation des KfW-Programms Altersgerecht Umbauen: Endbericht* [Evaluation of the KfW programme senior-friendly conversion]. Basel: Author. Retrieved from www.kfw.de/PDF/Download-Center/Konzernthemen/Research/PDF-Dokumente-alle-Evaluationen/Prognos_Evaluation-KfW-Programm-Altersgerecht-Umbauen.pdf.

Stadt Köln. (2014). *Das Kooperative Baulandmodell Köln: Leitfaden für Projektentwickler und Investoren* [The cooperative building land development model of Cologne: Guidelines for project developers and investors]. Köln. Retrieved from www.wohnungsbauforum-koeln.de/fileadmin/Dateien/Daten/Materialien_zum_Download/ab_2015/baulandmodell-broschuere2014.pdf.

Tchouvakhina, M., & Brüggemann, A. (2014). Altersgerechter Wohnraum: Große Versorgungslücke, dringender Investitionsbedarf [Senior-friendly housing: Large gap in supply, urgent need for investments]. *KfW Economic Research Fokus Volkswirtschaft*, (65). Retrieved from www.kfw.de/PDF/Download-Center/Konzernthemen/Research/PDF-Dokumente-Fokus-Volkswirtschaft/Fokus-Nr.-65-Juli-2014.pdf.

Technische Universität Darmstadt, & ISP Eduard Pestel Institut für Systemforschung e.V. (2016). *Deutschland-Studie 2015: Wohnraumpotentiale durch Aufstockungen* [Study for Germany 2015: Potentials for housing through addition of another storey]. Darmstadt, Hannover.

15 Conclusion

Innovations in affordable housing governance and finance – cases compared and contrasted

Gerard van Bortel, Vincent Gruis, Joost Nieuwenhuijzen, and Ben Pluijmers

Introduction

In the introduction of this book, we defined key concepts and generally discussed recent developments towards increased involvement of community and market actors in the provision and management of affordable housing. This provided the context and conceptual groundwork for our international collaborative research project, in which various shapes of increased involvement of communities and market actors in the governance and finance of affordable housing have been explored.

The chapters in this book presented various innovative models for the provision of affordable housing across Europe and incorporated international perspectives from Australia and the USA. In this concluding chapter, we compare and contrast these developments and discuss their implications for policy, practice and research on the basis of the research questions of this book (see Figure 15.1).

First, we focus on inquiries concerning the governance arrangements with regards to the division of rights and responsibilities that fit within existing institutional frameworks. Next, we use the hybrid 'state, market, community, and third-sector' framework (Chapter 1) to classify the various governance mechanisms at play within each of the numerous innovations presented in this book. Then, we summarize the benefits, drawbacks, and potential for growth of hybrid governance and finance arrangements. We conclude this chapter with some general recommendations for policy, practice, and research.

Please note that throughout this book, we have used a broad and generous definition of what constitutes an 'innovation'. Consequently, approaches labelled as innovations may be standard practice in some countries, while completely novel in others. The Low Income Housing Tax Credits (LIHTCs) in the USA, for example, have been around for over 30 years but could constitute an innovation for other countries when attracting private sector funding. Housing cooperatives are another example. These often resident-led organisations are well-known phenomena in the housing systems of Austria and Sweden (Chapters 3 and 6 respectively), but relatively new in Spain (Chapter 2).

- How are the rights and responsibilities divided between the actors in these hybrid shapes of housing provision?
- How do these new arrangements fit into existing institutional frameworks? Are they stimulated, enabled or hampered by current legislative and administrative arrangements?
- Which of these hybrid arrangements is more likely to grow and which will remain a marginal phenomenon?
- What impact can be expected on the currently dominant providers of affordable housing? Will they lose a significant part of their market share? (How) can or should they adapt to these trends to remain future proof and keep, or increase, their added value to and associated legitimacy in society?
- What can be expected from the long-term effects of these new arrangements? Will they prove to be sustainable in terms of availability, quality, and affordability? What is the impact of increased private finance on long-term performance according to these universal criteria of social housing?

Figure 15.1 Research questions.

Governance – roles of actors

In Chapter 1, we stated that emerging affordable housing partnerships and finance arrangements lead to questions about the division of rights and responsibilities between actors and how these new forms of governance fit within the existing institutional contexts. In this section, we will discuss this by indicating key roles of residents, the state, third sector actors, and market or private sector actors.

The role of residents and communities

One of the trends underpinning this book is the notion of increased involvement of residents and local communities in affordable housing provisions. This trend is clearly visible in several contributions to this book. However, this development is far from homogeneous. Some chapters provide strong examples of resident-led initiatives, such as the *Baugruppen* and *Mietshäuser Syndikat* (Tenant Syndicate) in Austria (Chapter 3, by Lang and Gruber) and the emerging senior and intergenerational housing cooperatives in Spain (Chapter 2, by Etxezarreta, Merino, Cano, Dol, and Hoekstra). Other innovations genuinely involve residents in housing management issues but are also more institution-led, for example, the new social and affordable rental housing solutions in Italy (Chapter 3, by Ferri, Pogliana, and Rizzica) and the involvement of residents in the improvement of housing services by a London-based housing association

(Chapter 5, by Manzi and Glover-Short). In many other chapters, residents have a far more passive role and are predominantly approached as housing *consumers* and not as *co-producers* of housing solutions.

Especially noteworthy, in this context, is Adamson's comparative analysis of resident co-production (Chapter 8) in the Australian and English social housing sectors. This contribution highlights how important it is to understand the different target groups for affordable housing when looking at resident participation. When comparing social housing residents in the UK and Australia, Adamson concluded how the social capital of residents impacts the role they can play in the co-production of affordable housing. He identified two distinctive models of housing co-production: *communal housing service co-production* that can be found in the less residualised English social housing sector, and *individual tenancy co-production*, to be found in the rather marginalised Australian social housing sector with tenants that have limited social capital. The first form of co-production entails the representation of tenants with adequate social capital in the governance and management of social landlords, ranging from board memberships to scrutiny panels and mystery shopper roles. Tenants are actively involved in the design, delivery, and improvement of housing services (Chapter 5, by Manzi and Glover-Short). In contrast, the latter form of co-production focuses on the empowerment of residents in order to increase social inclusion and support tenants in their ability to meet basic tenancy obligations. According to Adamson, these models are not contradictory but can be highly complementary, if combined.

The complementary forms of housing co-production identified by Adamson can also be found in the contribution by Bratt, Rosenthal, and Wiener (Chapter 7) on non-profit social landlords in the USA. Non-profit housing providers not only use housing as a platform for the social progress of residents by providing remedial services to empower their residents and strengthen their ability to fulfil tenancy obligations (see Adamson's 'tenancy co-production'), but also invite resident feedback to identify investment needs and determine amenities and services that add the most value for residents (see Adamson's 'housing service co-production'). Some social housing providers in the USA see these services as part of a larger community-building and engagement strategy. Providing these services is a financial and organisational challenge for many housing organisations. However, understanding the holistic importance of addressing the needs and activating the capabilities of residents is a developing focus in many housing sectors, see for example the various forms of collaborative housing and co-production presented in this book.

A more specific example of an approach to activate and develop the capabilities of residents can be found in the participatory monumental mural design projects aimed at decorating the side-facades of apartment buildings in a meaningful way (Chapter 9, by Toutain Rosec and Schaefer). Residents are involved in the co-production of a shared heritage and history of their neighbourhood through the creation of mural designs. This mitigates the impact of growing urban uniformity and the loss of identity and heritage of places and people.

Residents are involved from the start in the development of a shared community narrative that the murals aim to convey.

Also in the emerging Italian social and affordable housing sector (Chapter 4) resident participation is seen as beneficial in its own right; it fosters a sense of belonging and social cohesion. Complementary, strong resident involvement is also regarded as an instrument to strengthen the affordable housing business case by reducing resident-related risks, such as rent arrears, high maintenance, vandalism, and turnover costs. The affordable housing projects entail a combination of bottom-up, resident involvement in the design and delivery of housing management services, as found in co-housing initiatives, and a more top-down oriented approach for asset development and housing management strategies that can be found in the established sector of Italian housing co-operatives.

The chapter by Manzi and Glover-Short (Chapter 5) demonstrates how changes in the governance and management in a London housing association, designed to introduce wide-scale resident participation, resulted in service efficiencies, performance improvements, and changes to working practices. The housing association strongly believed that residents should be at the heart of organisational decision making to ensure a robust local profile and to improve performance. This was a key principle informing the newly implemented governance structure. Arguably, the most innovative feature of this structure was to establish multiple linkages between the organisation and the resident groups and panels to ensure a horizontal and vertical flow of information. Residents were involved in a variety of panels and forums looking at the needs of specific groups and quality of housing services, such as repairs and maintenance and the performance of contractors. Residents even served on interview panels when selecting new staff and could influence change and suggest improvements to service delivery. At the same time, the authors report, housing association staff were keen to stress that whilst they are resident influenced, they are not entirely resident-led, 'We are not a housing cooperative' as one respondent commented.

The role of the state

In this concluding chapter we use 'state' as an umbrella term to refer to government entities on various hierarchical (local, regional, and national) levels. Exploring the role of the state was not the prime focus of this book. This book sought to investigate the role of community and market actors in driving innovations in affordable housing governance and finance. However, one of the most prominent conclusions emanating from the contributions to this book is the strong role of the state in shaping favourable conditions to attract private sector funding for affordable housing and support resident involvement.

Government support served as an important enabler for many of the affordable housing innovations presented in this publication. For example, support in the form of subsidies, cheap loans, and cheap land; and government regulation, such as rent regulation, resident participation requirements, spatial planning rules, and housing construction tenders. Several chapters demonstrate how governments use land allocation policies to foster affordable and adequate housing. For example, the public housing-development competitions organised in Vienna (Chapter 10) and the comparable 'concept procurement' approach used in several German cities to allocate land according to the quality of the housing development concept (Chapter 14).

Government interventions shape market conditions for affordable housing. In the Netherlands (Chapter 13), rent regulation was revised to accommodate an Energy Performance Fee (EPF) to be paid by tenants complementary to their regular rent. This EPF enables the creation of financially viable business cases for deep energy efficient retrofit investments. Through the EPF, the costs saved by residents on their utility bills are used as a source of income for landlords to compensate for the energy retrofit. In Germany, the 'Mietpreisbremse' (rent price brakes) is an attempt by the federal and regional governments to reconcile social and market logics and to mitigate rent increases in high-demand housing markets, preferably without frustrating private sector investments (Chapter 14).

Blessing's contribution on housing finance in the USA (Chapter 11) highlights the important role of government mechanisms to provide the, as phrased by the author, 'carrots and sticks' to incentivise private sector investments in affordable housing; the 'carrots' being the tax-deductions provided by LIHTCs and the 'sticks' the requirements of the Community Reinvestment Act (CRA) to prevent the exclusion of areas from access to bank loans and mortgages, a process that is called 'red-lining'.

In Chapter 4, Ferri, Pogliani and Rizzica discuss how the state can play a crucial role in increasing the involvement of residents, as well as private actors, in shaping the Integrated System of Housing Funds (*Sistema Integrato dei Fondi* [SIF]). This was introduced by the Italian government in 2008 to support social housing, and resulted in a new form of affordable rental housing tenure in Italy. While low-income housing in Italy was traditionally provided by public actors and paid for through public funds, the SIF initiative aimed at boosting social housing provided by partnerships that included a mix of not-for-profit, private, community, and government actors. Ferri, Pogliani and Rizzica specifically investigate the advisory role of the *Fondazione Housing Sociale* (FHS) – a private, non-profit entity that promotes and carries out social and collaborative housing projects and supports the creation of partnerships to deliver this innovative type of housing. The Italian Integrated System of Housing Funds has created a new source for affordable housing finance. It combines investment mechanisms developed and tested in the commercial real-estate sector, complemented by innovative collaborative forms of housing management.

The role of the private sector

Private sector actors are important and sought-after partners for their ability to leverage private sector funding into the affordable housing sector. However, private sector funding comes at a price, and usually direct or indirect financial incentives are needed. Private sector funding is rarely sufficient to fully cover the necessary investments in affordable housing. Hybrid financing arrangements are developed to combine private sector finance with government loans, government guaranties, cheap government-owned land, and subsidies (see for example Chapter 4 on the Italian System of Integrated Housing Investment Funds, and Chapter 10 on the Vienna '*Wohnbauinitiative*' [WBI]).

The incentives to attract private sector funding are often time limited, so are the social requirements expected from private actors, for example to charge below market rents and allocated housing to specific target groups. Affordable housing projects involving paid private sector funding often have a duration ranging from 10 to 35 years. After this period, affordable housing can be transformed to full-market rental or ownership housing. Sometimes the social obligations, in return for government support, only apply to a selection of newly constructed dwellings (Chapter 10).

Private sector involvement in affordable housing provision can create a new, local dynamic, as is demonstrated by Westerdahl's contribution (Chapter 6). The actions of the small and agile private actor explored in this chapter show how, in this context, this actor was able to provide affordable housing solutions quicker than the established cooperative and municipal housing providers, reducing costs through industrialisation and standardisation.

Morrison (Chapter 12) explored the potential of cross-sector joint ventures. The chapter focuses predominantly on the collaboration between local authorities and housing associations in England, but the author clearly identified the potential for a large number of innovative options to further develop joint ventures. These include multiple stakeholder participation, introducing private equity in these joint ventures, with clearly defined return and risk boundaries for the actors involved.

Hybrid financing arrangements sometimes adapt and use investment instruments used in the commercial real-estate sector, opening up new financing sources such as institutional investors and private equity. These arrangements can be less costly for the government budget than other schemes, and can contribute to social mix and inclusion. However, without proper incentives or coercive mechanisms private sector actors can lose interest in affordable housing.

A potential problem with affordable housing fully financed by the private sector is that governments (especially local authorities) can lose control over housing provision. The democratic control of housing policies is diminishing in a situation where affordable housing can only be accomplished through negotiations with private sector actors (see Chapter 7 on affordable private sector housing in Malmö, Sweden). Hybrid financing agreements (such as the Vienna WBI) can be a good alternative to completely market-financed housing construction. WBI provides the government with influence on the quality of the affordable housing produced, and a certain influence on the social character of the subsidised dwellings, albeit only for a limited period.

The role of third sector organisations

Public and social housing organisations have traditionally played a prominent role in many social housing systems. They still do. With the emergence of new community and market actors, not-for-profit housing providers often take on an important new role as intermediary organisations establishing and sustaining networks of very diverse actors. For example, by supporting new collaborative housing initiatives (Chapter 3 by Gruber and Lang). Third sector organisations, such as English housing associations (Chapter 12, by Morrison), Austrian limited-profit organisations (see Chapter 10, by Mundt and Amann), Community Development Corporations in the USA (see Chapter 7), and the Italian *Fondazione Housing Sociale* (Chapter 4 by Ferri, Pogliani and Rizzica) play an important role in creatively combining the various funding resources and reconciling the various institutional (state, market, community, civil society) goals and values of the actors involved.

Bratt, Rosenthal, and Wiener analyse (in Chapter 7) the challenging work environment of non-profit housing providers in the USA, characterised by scarce government resources and highly competitive housing markets. They demonstrate how the combination of social and economic perspectives in a social landlord organisation is mutually reinforcing. This harsh, housing market has increased the need for robustness and professionalism within these organisations in a way that can generate interesting lessons for social housing providers in Europe that are also facing increasingly challenging working conditions and new roles in partnerships with community, public, and private sector actors. The use of complex and hybrid financial models demands high levels of management sophistication, continuous professionalisation and training, a high understanding of housing policies at various levels, and proficiency in housing production and management. Dwindling financial resources and the need for more business efficiency increased the importance of professional asset management and cross-portfolio perspectives to identify and use asset-based equity to attract new investments. Reduced federal resources in the USA have resulted in non-profit development of new financial models and their pursuit of cooperative strategies able to work across organisational boundaries. Consequently, the gradual development of real estate and networking prowess in the US non-profit housing sector has been a subtle but concrete innovation, and has advanced financial management to levels comparable to for-profit, real-estate firms.

Hybridity – classification of partnerships

Hybridity, in the context of this study, refers to market, state, community, and/or third sector actors cooperating in different, innovative settings to provide and manage social housing, which is reflected in more hybrid governance and finance arrangements. The hybridity presented in the chapters can be grouped into two broad categories: hybridity that emerges in the collaboration between organisations (*inter-organisational* hybridity) and hybridity within one organisation (*intra-organisational* hybridity). Inter-organisational hybridity describes organisations with different logics and drivers collaborating, while intra-organisational hybridity describes when these logics and drivers are present within one organisation (see Chapter 1 for a more in-depth discussion on hybridity). The chapters in this book demonstrate that both forms of hybridity are increasing as a result of co-production and new affordable housing finance models.

The provision of affordable housing services in the London housing association discussed in Chapter 5 has developed into more of a hybrid model as a result of co-production. Professionals share their decision-making power much more explicitly with their customers. Manzi and Glover-Short report significant benefits in terms of performance. Resident satisfaction with overall landlord services, tackling anti-social behaviour, managing repairs, and dealing with complaints increased significantly. The role of residents in scrutinising the process was seen as a key safeguard. Although it had no direct consequences for the financing of the housing, it did have financial benefits, in addition to a significant increase in other performance areas as well.

Inter-organisational hybridity is visible in the collaboration between local authorities and private sector actors, for example the new and agile private sector actor explored by Westerdahl (Chapter 6) and the WBI in Vienna discussed by Mundt and Amann (Chapter 10). A salient example of intra-organisational hybridity can be found in Westerdahl's chapter in which he mentions the legal obligation of Sweden municipal housing companies to strive for social purpose as well as to act business-like (Chapter 6) and charge market rents.

A combination of intra- and inter-organisational hybridity is strongly present in Chapter 7 by Bratt, Rosenthal, and Wiener. Non-profit providers in the USA combine social and economic perspectives in their organisation. The non-profit affordable housing sector as a whole also demonstrates a high level of inter-sectorial collaboration in sophisticated and hybrid networks, including non-profit and for-profit developers, government actors, and national non-profit intermediary organisations.

The increasing involvement of community and market actors not only leads to increasing hybridity in existing organisations and collaborative networks, but also results in the creation of new hybrid entities. In Chapter 12 for example, Morrison explores a new form of hybrid organisational structures, special purpose vehicles in affordable housing, notably, the Limited Liability Partnerships (LLPs) between some local authorities and housing associations. These LLPs design, build, and manage the affordable housing and retain outright ownership, and innovatively pool resources and share the costs, risks, and financial rewards.

The collaborative housing initiatives in Austria and Italy, discussed in Chapters 3 and 4 respectively, reflect the development discussed in international literature (Chapter 2) that traditional, social housing providers still play an important role in supporting collaborative housing initiatives, resulting in hybrid cross-sector partnerships. Contrastingly, this hybridity was remarkably absent in the resident-led housing cooperatives in Spain (Chapter 2). These cooperatives emerged in response to government retrenchment from affordable housing provision, but did so with no support from established housing providers; primarily because in Spain, social housing is weakly developed.

Thus, as we can see from the many cases described in this book, innovations for the development, management, or finance of affordable housing rarely emerge from one actor or societal sector alone, but often result from collaborative cross-sector partnerships. In the introduction of this book, we presented the state, market, community, and third-sector framework (Figure 15.2) in order to classify state, market, community, and third sector organisations. Arguably, instead of classifying individual organisations, a more valuable application of this framework could be to analyse the hybridity of the innovations presented in this book.

Tables 15.1, 15.2, and 15.3 present a more detailed assessment of state, market, community, and third sector involvement in each of the initiatives presented in this book. Please note that this is an assessment made by the editors of this book. It may differ from the perspectives of the chapters' authors.

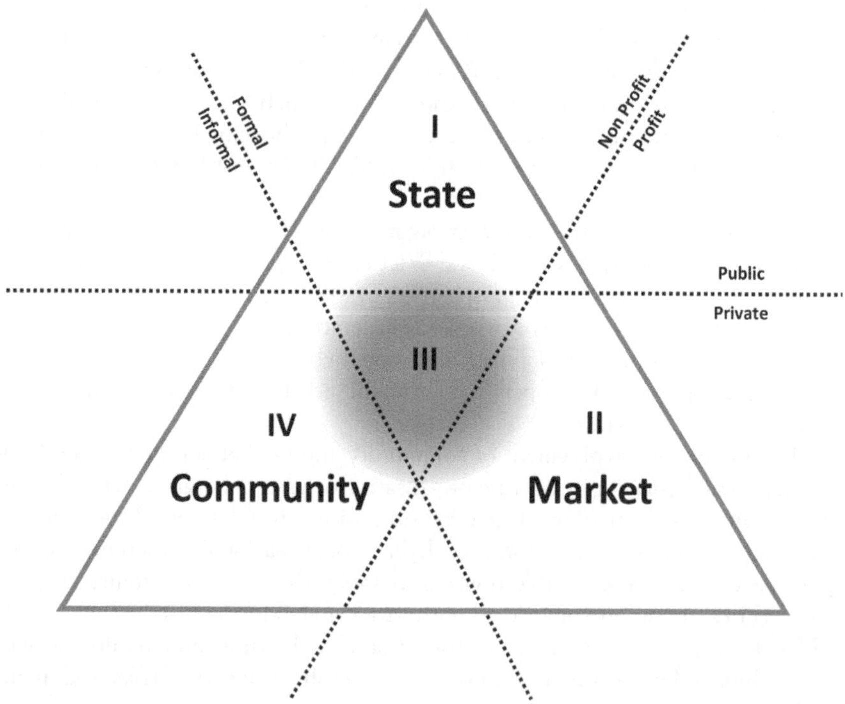

Figure 15.2 Classification of hybrid partnerships in affordable housing.

Source: Brandsen et al. (2005), based on Zijderveld (1999) and Pestoff (1992). Adapted by Van Bortel (2016, p. 50).

Legend: role of sectors in innovations

Very weak	Not involved
Weak	Advice / Mortgage
Moderate	Support / Facilitating / Consultation / Financial guarantee
Strong	Regulation / Participation
Very strong	Investments / Subsidies

Table 15.1 Compare and contrast innovations: collaborative housing

Chapter	*Country*	*Innovation*	*Keyword*	*Sector involvement*			
				I	*II*	*III*	*IV*
				*State**	*Market*	*Third sector*	*Community***
2	Spain	Co-housing cooperative Spain (senior housing)	Potential for combination cooperative housing and care				
		Co-housing cooperative Spain (intergenerational housing)	Difficult to get a mortgage				
3	Austria	Collaborative housing models in Vienna, Participatory project (Model A)	Third-sector-led				
		Collaborative housing models in Vienna, Baugruppen (Model B)	Resident-led with third-sector support				
		Collaborative housing models in Vienna, the Autonomous Baugruppe: '*Wohnheim*' (Model C)	Resident-led				
4	Italy	Social and affordable housing through	Balance between co-housing and cooperative housing				

Notes
* State involvement can entail local, regional and national government entities.
** Community involvement can also include individual and organized residents.

Table 15.2 Compare and contrast innovations: co-production

Chapter	*Country*	*Innovation*	*Keywords*	*Sector involvement*			
				I	*II*	*III*	*IV*
				*State**	*Market*	*Third sector*	*Community***
5	United Kingdom	Resident participation within the housing association sector	Improvement of housing management services				
6	Sweden	Agile private sector delivery of affordable rental housing	Active new private actor, in a context of passive established public sector actors				
7	USA	Organisational adaptations of nonprofit housing organisations in the US	Balancing social and economic perspectives				
8	Australia	Co-production in Australia	Housing service co-production				
	United Kingdom	Co-production in the UK	Tenancy co-production				
9	France	Monumental mural design	Externally facilitated resident participation in regeneration				

Notes
* State involvement can entail local, regional, and national government entities.
** Community involvement can also include individual and organised residents.

Table 15.3 Compare and contrast innovations: housing finance models

Chapter	*Country*	*Innovation*	*Keyword*	*Sector involvement*			
				I	*II*	*III*	*IV*
				*State**	*Market*	*Third sector*	*Community***
10	USA	Low Income Housing Tax Credits (LIHTCs)	'Carrots and sticks' to involve private sector actors in affordable housing provision				
		Community Reinvestment Act (CRA)					
11	United Kingdom	Innovative joint venture between local authority and housing association	Focus on housing finance				
12	Austria	Vienna housing construction initiative '*Wiener Wohnbauinitiative*'	New financing vehicle for affordable housing				
13	The Netherlands	Energy Performance Fee to cover investments in the energy efficiency of affordable housing	Solving the split-incentive dilemma in energy investments				
14	Germany	Rent price brake/ '*Mietpreisbremse*'	Moderate rent increases in high demand areas				
		Housing benefits; climate component	Stimulate sustainable housing refurbishment				
		Subsidy programmes for specific target groups	Elderly, students, and refugees				
		Concept procurement	Land allocation based on development concept quality				

Notes
* State involvement can entail local, regional, and national government entities.
** Community involvement can also include individual and organised residents.

Discussion: benefits, drawbacks, and potential

Benefits

In this book, we have explored recent developments of increased involvement of community and market actors in affordable housing, leading to an increasing hybridity in housing provision. The hybrid forms discussed in this book can have several benefits. They are often less dependent on costly state financial support, which is, in a way, also logical if they are aimed at the middle-income households and not at the core, traditional, target low-income group of social housing. There are other benefits as well, including the spread of financial risks, tenant empowerment, and community development. Tenant co-production and collaborative housing initiatives result in housing and housing services that are better aligned with the needs of residents. New financial models increase the viability of business cases, enabling investments in affordable housing and facilitating ambitious, energy efficient retrofit investments.

Hybridity is sometimes actively stimulated by local government schemes to provide cheap loans and land to consortia of private and third-sector actors (Chapter 12, Vienna). In the case of the London housing association, far-reaching involvement of tenants has created a more hybrid, corporate governance and culture (Chapter 5). In Italy, resident involvement in housing development and management is used to increase social cohesion and strengthen the business cases of affordable housing projects using investment fund frameworks originally developed in the commercial real estate sector.

Drawbacks

There are also some drawbacks attached to private sector finance explored in the contributions to this book. The chapter contributions indicate how private sector involvement in affordable housing comes at a price, such as the time-limited nature of many affordable housing solutions financed by private sector funding. The capacity to accommodate vulnerable, low-income households is limited, as this could create unfeasible business cases. In addition, the partnerships needed to develop the affordable housing projects are complex and involve residents, as well as many government, market, and not-for-profit actors.

Several innovations described in this book are highly dependent on personal initiative, for example, the entrepreneurial spirit of individuals, the drive of residents to collaboratively develop solutions for their housing needs, or the leadership of a social landlord CEO. This invites the questions: to what extent can the momentum created by inspired individuals and groups be sustained longer term, is it transferable to other contexts, and does it provide opportunities for growth? It seems difficult to secure the availability and affordability of housing, as well as maintain increased, active involvement of community actors, tenants, and market actors in the long term.

The contributions to this book do not indicate a significant change in the market share of established affordable housing providers. There are indications however that these providers need to increase their robustness, agility, business efficiency and effectiveness in order to survive in a harsher environment with highly competitive housing markets and reduced government support.

Potential

Several chapters indicated how social and economic principles in housing development and housing management can be mutually reinforcing and beneficial to the survival and growth of affordable housing providers. Resident involvement in the co-production of housing and housing services can mitigate risks in several ways. Affordable housing projects aim to reduce social risks that could damage the business case. Examples include rent arrears, cost associated with high turnover rates, and anti-social behaviour.

Collaborative housing projects contribute to diversification and innovation in social housing. These projects are (still) limited in size but can be considered as test-beds for social innovations in housing with elements to be eventually mainstreamed. Local government can play a crucial role as external enabler of collaborative housing (Chapter 10). Many housing initiatives can only exist because there is a political will to support them. However, evidence suggests that apart from political support, finance is a crucial point here.

It is clear from the chapters in this book that innovations often include the growth of private sector investments in affordable housing. The hybrid financial arrangements thus created combine government subsidies, capital from institutional investors, local authority building plots, and loans from government entities on a national, regional, or local level. These initiatives have the potential for growth but also have a built-in potential for reduction due to the time-limited nature of many government support arrangements.

Private sector involvement in affordable housing usually needs public sector contributions in the form of subsidies, cheap loans, or cheap land. As long as these public sector advantages are available, private sector involvement will continue. But for how long? As long as this question is not answered convincingly, there is still a strong role for the traditional, not-for-profit, and limited-profit social landlords that can do without the 'carrots' and the 'sticks', but are intrinsically motivated to deliver affordable housing and can act as mediators and partners for community and private sector actors.

Conclusion

General remarks

This book provides broad, nuanced, and varied perspectives on innovations in affordable housing governance and finance in nine countries. In these diverse affordable housing landscapes, there are no sweeping, simple, unambiguous solutions or overarching trends. It is much more a matter of carefully adopting certain elements and experiences that are applicable in other contexts. Arguably, one of the main conclusions is the continued important, but shifting, role of the state. Governments are retreating from direct housing provision, but are still important enablers in providing affordable housing support. They have a crucial role in shaping the preconditions for successful community and private sector involvement in affordable housing.

Housing for low-income households is still a domain that needs sustained government support. It should be noted that many initiatives in this book are aimed at households whose income exceed levels that makes them eligible for tradition public and affordable housing, yet who are still unable to afford market prices.

Innovations are context specific. Collaborative housing in Spain, for example, can be regarded as a much more radical social innovation compared to similar initiatives in Vienna. The Spanish initiatives emerged in a very market-driven context, where affordable housing support has been substantially dismantled and support from established housing providers or local authorities was absent. In Vienna support for collaborative housing was stronger and also the local welfare systems delivered much more support in comparison to the Spanish situation where cooperatives needed to solve more fundamental social problems of residents. Well-organised community groups can be crucial to mobilise governmental institutions.

Implications for practice

Established housing actors can enable or impede innovations. The collaborative housing initiatives presented in this book appear to be (still) limited in their ability to reconfigure the pronounced top-down governance in social housing. Established social housing providers and local authorities are still dominant actors in most countries (Chapters 2, 3, and 4).

Resident participation is sound business practice. One of the conclusions emanating from this book is the organisational benefits of resident participation. It nuances the perspective on resident participation as an instrument solely for local participative democracy, but highlights the value of resident participation as part of a permanent feedback loop from residents to landlords. This feedback offers opportunities to better meet residents' needs, improving relationships between residents and staff, and reducing the need to employ expensive external consultants (Chapter 5). Cohesive and mixed communities can reduce business risks (Chapter 4). Combining *service* and *tenancy* co-production has the potential to create a comprehensive resident involvement model (Chapter 8). Social and economic perspectives in housing management are mutually reinforcing.

Organisational robustness and strategic collaboration is needed. Some social housing providers operate in very challenging environments. Dwindling government support and competitive housing markets highlight the need for organisational adaptations and strategic collaboration for business survival (Chapter 7).

This requires high levels of professionalism in strategic asset management, tactical and operational housing management, and financial and network/stakeholder management. Resource scarcity can be a powerful incentive for inter-organisational collaboration and increasing the financial, legal, and asset management expertise in housing providers.

Implications for policy

Whilst this book focused on the impact of increasing involvement of community and market actors in affordable housing, we should not forget the important role of governments in shaping a framework for affordable housing to be sustained and to flourish. Innovations in affordable housing need government support. Affordable housing innovations should be integrated in national and local housing and urban planning policies. Governments, on various hierarchical levels, can create favourable conditions for the creation of affordable housing projects. For example, by modifying legislation and regulations, revising urban planning instruments, acting as initiators, network managers, housing market regulators, improving urban infrastructure, and devising strategies to provide land. Land allocation models based on competitive tenders (see Chapter 10 on Vienna, and Chapter 14 on Germany) can be applied in other countries where the local governments have a strong mandate to develop urban and housing policies.

Innovations are interconnected and often serendipitous. In Italy, for example, the new social and affordable housing tenure (Chapter 4) is underpinned by no less than three interconnected innovations: the ethical real estate fund, public–private partnerships, and the collaborative governance model. The synergy between the CRA and LIHTCs is unique to the US, and also largely incidental (Chapter 11). Yet, it could inspire policy makers to activate similar mechanisms in other settings. US experience highlights the power of regulatory frameworks in achieving investment flows into affordable housing. Both federal policy and legal structures have been credited for creating a cross-sectoral 'organisational field' that helps connect local opportunities for investment in affordable rental housing with investors' organisational goals. Mechanisms of public disclosure, voluntary local monitoring, regulatory power, and competition between investors, have strengthened the impact of the CRA as a significant game-changer. This serendipitous impact can provide inspiration for Europe on how private investment can be harnessed to fund sustainable urban development and affordable housing, and to better inform – and empower – citizens and third sector actors to participate in financial systems.

Mechanisms, such as the CRA, very likely require policy interventions on a national level. However, local authorities can also develop approaches to increase the supply of affordable housing (Chapter 11). Sometimes these approaches include setting up financial, procedural, and regulatory frameworks for affordable housing. But also, directly constructing new affordable housing in joint ventures together with third-sector and private sector actors is an option

(Chapters 10 and 12). It takes strong national government backing for local authorities to take back the lead in affordable housing provision. Policy makers need to devise plans to capture and use the current and future value of land for affordable housing.

Implications for research

Many innovations presented in this book are recent, and their impact on the availability of affordable housing is (still) limited or gradually emerging. Other innovations have been successful for a significant period, but more in-depth research and experimentation is needed to explore the transferability of these practices to other contexts. This provides opportunities for experimentation and intensive collective learning experiences.

Additional research needs to assess the long-term impact and increase our understanding of the critical success factors of the hybrid partnerships underpinning these innovations. What are the enablers and barriers? Which incentives and coercive mechanisms are successful in securing the long-term involvement of private sector actors?

There is a need for further (international) comparative studies to identify how resident involvement can contribute to better quality services, better value for money, long-term financial savings, and reduction of risks, and how participatory approaches can be applied to the wider organisational field of affordable housing. Further collaborative research is needed to explore the transferability potential and to assess the costs and benefits of these new types of housing delivery models in more depth.

References

Brandsen, T., Van den Donk, W., & Putters, K. (2005). Griffins or chameleons? Hybridity as a permanent and inevitable characteristic of the third sector. *International Journal of Public Administration*, 28(9/10), 749–765.

Pestoff, V. (1992). Third sector and co-operative services: An alternative to privatisation. *Journal of Consumer Policy*, 15, 21–45.

Van Bortel, G. (2016). *Networks and fault lines: A network perspective on the role of housing associations in neighbourhood renewal*. PhD thesis. Delft: AB+E Press.

Zijderveld, A. C. (1999). *The waning of the welfare state: The end of comprehensive state succor*. New Brunswick, NJ: Transaction Publishers.

Index

Page numbers in **bold** denote tables, those in *italics* denote figures.